3D COMPUTER GRAPHICS

SECOND EDITION

ALAN WATT

COMPUTER GRAPHICS TITLES FROM ADDISON-WESLEY

SIGGRAPH Conference Proceedings '89 (1989)   *ACM SIGGRAPH*

SIGGRAPH Conference Proceedings '91 (1991)   *ACM SIGGRAPH*

SIGGRAPH Conference Proceedings '92 (1992)   *ACM SIGGRAPH*

Interactive Computer Graphics: Functional, Procedural and Device-Level methods (1989)   *P Burger and D Gillies*

Computer Graphics (1990)   *E Angel*

Computer Graphics: Principles and Practice, 2nd Edn (1990)   *J Foley, A van Dam, S Feiner and J Hughes*

The Renderman Companion: A Programmer's Guide to Realistic Computer Graphics (1990)   *S Upstill*

A Practical Introduction to PHIGS and PHIGS PLUS (1991)   *T Howard, T Hewitt, R Hubbold and K Wrywas*

Graphics Programming with PHIGS and PHIGS PLUS (1993)   *J Kasper and D Arns*

3D Computer Animation (1993)   *J Vince*

Advanced Animation and Rendering Techniques: Theory and Practice (1993) *D Winkler and S Goldberg*

Introduction to Computer Graphics (1994)   *J Foley, A van Dam, S Feiner, J Hughes and R Phillips*

The Mathematica Graphics Guidebook (1994)   *C Smith and N Blachman*

Video Technology for Computer Graphics (1995)   *D Winkler and S Goldberg*

3D COMPUTER GRAPHICS

SECOND EDITION

ALAN WATT

Instituto de Matemática Pura e Aplicada
Rio de Janeiro, Brasil

and

University of Sheffield, England

ADDISON-WESLEY

Harlow, England • Reading, Massachusetts • Menlo Park, California
New York • Don Mills, Ontario • Amsterdam • Bonn • Sydney • Singapore
Tokyo • Madrid • San Juan • Milan • Mexico City • Seoul • Taipei

© 1993 Addison-Wesley Publishing Ltd.
© 1993 Addison-Wesley Publishing Company Inc.

Addison-Wesley Longman Limited
Edinburgh Gate
Harlow
Essex, CM20 2JE
England

The programs in this book have been included for their instructional value. They have been tested with care but are not guaranteed for any particular purpose. The publisher does not offer any warranties of representations, nor does it accept any liabilities with respect to the programs.

Many of the designations used by manufacturers and sellers to distinguish their products are claimed as trademarks. Addison-Wesley has made every attempt to supply trademark information about manufacturers and their products mentioned in this book. A list of the trademark designations and their owners appears on p.xvi

Cover designed by Pencil Box Ltd, Marlow, Buckinghamshire and printed by The Riverside Printing Co. (Reading) Ltd.
Typeset by Keytec Typesetting Ltd.
Printed in Great Britain by Biddles Ltd, Guildford and King's Lynn.

First edition published 1989. Reprinted 1990 (twice) and 1991.
Second edition printed 1993. Reprinted 1994, 1995, 1996, 1997 and 1998.

ISBN 0-201-63186-5

British Library Cataloging in Publication Data
A catalogue record for this book is available from the British Library.

Library of Congress Cataloging in Publication Data applied for.
Catalog card number 93-192437

To Dionéa

Preface

This text is an extensively revised edition of *Fundamentals of Three-Dimensional Computer Graphics* published in 1989. The additions and revisions have come out of the author's experience in using that text for courses over the past three years.

It is a comprehensive introduction to the techniques needed to produce shaded images of three-dimensional solids on a computer graphics monitor. The aim of the book is to give a theoretical understanding of these techniques together with the programming expertise required to implement them.

Three-dimensional computer graphics now embraces a larger number of application areas, from the fantasy world of film and television to more practical areas such as CAD of mechanical engineering parts. In this sense three-dimensional graphics is possibly the most important aspect of computer graphics. While certain aspects are locked into particular areas – parametric surface techniques are used almost exclusively in engineering CAD – users as diverse as architects, molecular scientists and television animators use three-dimensional modelling and rendering techniques.

Many of the methods used in three-dimensional graphics are less than 10 years old and, while many excellent textbooks exist, these have mainly been general texts that have dealt with most of the mainstream topic areas in computer graphics. A good deal of the information needed in three-dimensional graphics is to be found only in research papers. This is particularly true of the techniques that have emerged in the last decade; for example, ray tracing and new reflection models. Implementing computer graphics methods from research papers is sometimes a difficult and tedious business. Details that are important to the implementer are quite rightly omitted from such publications, and would-be image synthesizers sometimes find themselves spending an inordinate time rediscovering the important practical tricks that are necessary to produce a rendered image.

Because computer graphics has spawned a larger number of different methods, as the applications have grown and diversified, it is now almost impossible to write a comprehensive but standard-length text on the subject. These observations point to the need for more specialist texts that concentrate on important and unifying topics in the subject. This is such a text. Its aim is to deal with one of the mainstream areas of computer graphics and also to provide a level of detail important to implementers. In this respect, nearly all of the technique illustrations have been produced by the author using programs described in the text. Pascal procedures, implementing the crucial parts of methods at their final level of detail, are included. The inclusion of procedures also goes some way to solving the problem of algorithm and method description.

Pascal is chosen for two reasons:

- Although it is not the lingua franca that its adherents often claim, it is at least as good as a pseudocode, and, with the exception of data structures, its translation into other high level languages is straightforward. (A language that has recently become fashionable in computer graphics is C. Although appreciating the practical advantages of C, it is not clear to your author that C offers any significant advantages, as a vehicle for describing algorithms, over Pascal.)
- It enables effective data structures to be implemented. The shading and representation of three-dimensional solids are inseparable topics and a text that deals with rendering should also deal, at some length, with three-dimensional data structures.

Currently the most popular hardware arrangement used in high quality rendering applications is a host processor that performs high level programming, driving a graphics terminal that is little more than a screen memory. The host is either in the same box, in which case the term graphics workstation is used, or it is in a separate enclosure and the graphics facility is called a terminal. (By 'high quality' we mean 24-bit screen memories; the most popular arrangement for 8-bit screen memories is the ubiquitous PC, enhanced with some extra hardware.)

For rendering shaded three-dimensional objects the programmer requires just one utility:

$dev\_Write\_Pixel(x,y,R,G,B)$

which transfers a three component colour into location (x,y) in the screen memory. This is an advantageous situation for authors of computer graphics textbooks because it means that programming illustrations can be almost completely device independent. Indeed, the programs given in this book will run on any host that accepts standard Pascal and will drive, with trivial alterations, any general-purpose graphics terminal.

The processing division between the host and graphics terminal processors is changing rapidly. Terminal utility packages are beginning to offer, for example, interpolative polygon shading and Z-buffer hidden surface removal. The trend is towards integrated workstations and away from the host terminal metaphor. This move is reflected in proposed extensions to the graphics standard PHIGS. PHIGS+ is intended to reflect this trend and includes lighting and shading as well as new three-dimensional primitives.

Efficiency in computer graphics is an important topic. Studios producing three-dimensional animated sequences always have a fixed generation time limit per frame that is imposed by the length of the sequence, the hardware available and the rendering technique used (not to mention the budget). In this text the program procedures are written to illustrate techniques and although efficiency considerations are touched on from time to time, it is difficult to combine such factors with sound theoretical explanations. Efficiency in graphics programming is extremely context dependent and involves such factors as rendering at the lowest appropriate spatial resolution, varying the rendering resolution as a function of the size of the object, using the least expensive reflection model that is appropriate, writing critical code in assembly language and increasing the workload of the graphics terminal processor by loading heavily used routines into it. Although it has been tried, in the text, to avoid gross abuse of processing time, efficiency is generally sacrificed for programming transparency. Efficiency in Phong shading is treated as a topic in its own right.

A significant proportion of the text is devoted to reflection or shading models. The current thrust of research in this area is towards greater and greater realism. Reflection models are continually being refined. The oft-stated goal of such efforts is to produce images that are indistinguishable from images obtained from, say, a television camera. The price that is always paid for more accurate reflection models is, of course, significant increases in computation time. This may not be such a vital consideration in the future, with the continuing decrease in the cost of processing units, but the relentless pursuit of reality in computer graphics does seem to be, in one sense, aimless.

The explosive demand for processor power in computer graphics is also driven by the related factor of increased resolution. Not only do algorithms increase their complexity, but at the same time the spatial resolution of graphics terminals increases, resulting in resource requirements that tend to obey a growth law with an index somewhere between 2 and 3.

One of the major application areas of computer graphics is in the entertainment and advertising industry. Here accurate reality is not necessarily a desirable goal. The appeal of computer graphics in a television commercial or title sequence is the super-reality or computer signature of the images. Images are striking partly because they are recognizably computer generated. To 'reduce' this effect by increasing their authenticity is to reduce their appeal and utility. After all, it is much easier to digitize real scenes using a television camera. In this respect a recent trend is to mix video and computer graphics images.

The treatment in this text of reflection models is restricted to the commonly used methods, although the more advanced and recent methods are not totally ignored. Reflection models are introduced in a sequence that reflects both their historical emergence and their complexity.

One of the main aims of this book is to provide implementation details and this means selecting a particular method to implement each part of the rendering process, rather than cataloguing processes and briefly describing each. Hidden surface removal, for example, is a good illustration of a stage in rendering where a choice of algorithms is possible. Where there is such a choice the selection of technique has been motivated by its popularity, acceptance and ease of implementation. In most cases these aims do not conflict with programming efficiency.

Nearly all the screen images in the text have been produced using the basic software described in the text. Some of the images are based on simple and effective ideas or illustrations produced by other computer graphics workers. In such cases accreditation is given to the producer of the original image.

The chapter structure enables the book to be read in any order. Most chapters are self contained.

Finally, although the book aims at being a 'how to do it' manual rather than a 'how it has been done' book, there are certain topics which, because of their nature, resist this approach. In particular, the chapter on three-dimensional animation is a description of the major approaches to this topic.

Programs, teaching and learning

The code in this book is in one of three forms: Pascal pseudocode for the algorithms where this seems appropriate, Pascal procedures for all other algorithms and a complete rendering system in Appendix B and Appendix C. This consists of a wireframe program complete with a view point interface and a comprehensive data structure. Appendix C contains the additional procedures required for a Z-buffer based rendering system with Gouraud shading. The data for the Utah teapot is reproduced in Appendix D.

Appendices A, B and C are intended to be an integral part of the book that can be used for more detailed further study. In particular, Appendix A is an example of the use of three-dimensional linear transformations. Appendix B is a study of data structures, wireframe drawing and general viewing systems. Appendix C extends the second appendix with rendering techniques described in Chapter 5.

The software is designed to be a learning aid to the techniques in the text and, with the single exception of ray tracing, all techniques can be grafted onto the supplied rendering system.

If the text is used for teaching or self-study, the student can be supplied with the rendering software to gain basic view point experience, and the techniques covered in each chapter used as exercises. All the procedures have been integrated into the basic rendering system and in most cases no modifications are required to the data structure. Except where otherwise stated all the colour pictures were produced by this software.

A disk containing the code in Appendices B, C and D is available at a nominal charge. Contact the author at the Department of Computer Science, University of Sheffield S10 2TN.

Projects, notes and suggestions

The projects are meant to be an integral part of the text and can be usefully read, even if you do not implement them. Many important points are examined that expand on topics in the chapters. Implementation points that are too detailed to be covered in the chapters are dealt with in the context of a project. Some useful background information is also given – Gauss–Seidel in the context of radiosity and Fourier theory for anti-aliasing.

Each project is classified with a heading. Projects marked (*) are fairly lengthy, contain some scope for original work and could be used as a major course assignment.

Have fun.

Acknowledgements

It would have been difficult to have produced this book without the prodigious contributions made by my research students: Keith Harrison, Dave Mitchell and Steve Maddock. They wrote the code, produced the line plotter illustrations and generated all the original colour plates. I am indebted to them for many useful suggestions and criticisms and for the donation of their time. Dave made extensive contributions to Chapter 5 and he and Keith developed the H-test. Steve assisted with Chapter 6. My colleague, Jim McGregor, wrote a recursive ray tracer as an example of recursion for undergraduates and contributed to Chapter 8. Sometime undergraduates – Andy Price and Nigel Rasberry developed the ASL animation project. Bill Sproson (formerly of the BBC, and author of the text *Colour Science in Television and Display Systems*) checked Chapter 14.

But I should mention my collaborators at Addison-Wesley. Sarah Mallen has been a source of encouragement in a world of slipped deadlines; the production staff, Lynne Balfe and Sheila Chatten coped with the usual tiresome preproduction problems and endless alterations with great efficiency and cheerfulness.

Alan Watt
Instituto de Matemática Pura e Aplicada
Rio de Janeiro, Brasil
May 1993

Contents

1 | Three-dimensional Geometry in Computer Graphics

1.1 Manipulating three-dimensional structures

Transformations are important tools in generating three-dimensional scenes. They are used to move objects around in an environment, and also to construct a two-dimensional view of the environment for a display surface. This chapter deals with basic three-dimensional transformations, and introduces some useful shape-changing transformations and basic three-dimensional geometry that we will be using throughout the text.

In computer graphics the most popular method for representing an object is the polygon mesh model. This representation is fully described in Chapter 2. All we need to know at this stage is that somehow we can represent an object as a list of points in three-dimensional space. We do this by representing the surface of an object as a set of connected planar polygons where each polygon is a list of points. This form of representation is either exact or an approximation depending on the nature of the object. A cube, for example, can be represented exactly by six squares. A cylinder, on the other hand, can only be approximated by polygons; say six rectangles for the curved surface and two hexagons for the end faces. The number of polygons used in the approximation determines how accurately the object is represented and this has repercussions in modelling cost, storage and rendering cost and quality. The popularity of the polygon mesh modelling technique in computer graphics is undoubtedly due to its inherent simplicity and the development of inexpensive shading algorithms that work with such models.

A polygon mesh model consists of a structure of vertices, each vertex being a three-dimensional point in so-called **world coordinate space**. Later we will be concerned with how vertices are connected to form polygons and how polygons are structured into complete objects. But to start with, we shall consider objects just as a set of three-dimensional vertices and look at how these are transformed in three-dimensional space using linear transformations.

1.2   Affine transformations

Three-dimensional affine transformations are the transformations that effect rotation, scaling, shear and translation. An affine transformation can be represented by a matrix and a set of affine transformations can be combined into a single overall affine transformation. Technically we say that an affine transformation is made up of any combination of linear transformations (rotation, scaling and shear) followed by translation (technically, translation is not a linear transformation).

Objects are defined in a world coordinate system which is conventionally a right-handed system. Right-handed and left-handed three-dimensional coordinate systems are shown in Figure 1.1. Right-handed systems are the standard mathematical convention although left-handed systems have been, and still are, used in the special context of viewing systems in computer graphics. We deal with this point in Section 3.1.1. The difference between the two systems is the sense of the z axis as shown in Figure 1.1. Rotating your fingers around the z axis, from the positive x axis to the positive y axis, gives a different z direction for your thumb depending on which system is used.

It is sometimes convenient to define objects in their own **local coordinate system**. There are three reasons for this. When a three-dimensional object is modelled, it is useful to build up the vertices with respect to some reference point in the object. In fact a complex object may have a number of local coordinate systems, one for each subpart. It may be that the same object is to appear many times in a scene and a definition with a local origin is the only sensible way to set this up. Instancing an object by applying a mix of translations, rotation and scaling transformations can then be seen as transforming the local coordinate system of each object to the world coordinate system. Finally, when an object is to be rotated, it is easier if the rotation is defined with respect to a local reference point such as an axis of symmetry. (This philosophy is adopted, for example, in the graphics standard PHIGS, where the programmer defines structures in the modelling coordinate system. 'Modelling transformations' define the mapping from this coordinate space to world coordinate space.)

A set of vertices or three-dimensional points belonging to an object can be transformed into another set of points by a **linear transformation**.

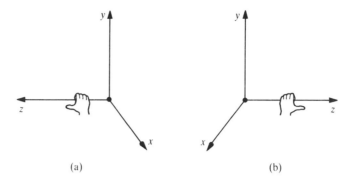

Figure 1.1
(a) Right-handed and
(b) left-handed
coordinate systems.

(a)   (b)

Both sets of points remain in the same coordinate system. Matrix notation is used in computer graphics to describe the transformations and the de facto convention in computer graphics is to have the the point or vector as a row matrix, followed by the transformation matrix T.

Using matrix notation, a point V is transformed under translation, scaling and rotation as:

$$V' = V + D$$
$$V' = VS$$
$$V' = VR$$

where D is a translation vector and S and R are scaling and rotation matrices.

These three operations are the most commonly used transformations in computer graphics and to enable them to be treated in the same way and combined, we use **homogeneous coordinates**. Effectively, we increase the dimensionality of the space to make translation a linear transformation. In practice, this provides us with a unified system for the specification of transformations. In a homogeneous system a vertex

$$V(x, y, z)$$

is represented as

$$V(X, Y, Z, w)$$

for any scale factor $w \neq 0$. The three-dimensional cartesian coordinate representation is then:

$$x = X/w$$
$$y = Y/w$$
$$z = Z/w$$

In computer graphics w is always taken to be 1 and the matrix representation[†] of a point is

$$[x \quad y \quad z \quad 1]$$

Translation can now be treated as matrix multiplication, like the other two transformations, and becomes

$$V' = VT$$

$$[x' \quad y' \quad z' \quad 1] = [x \quad y \quad z \quad 1] \begin{bmatrix} 1 & 0 & 0 & 0 \\ 0 & 1 & 0 & 0 \\ 0 & 0 & 1 & 0 \\ T_x & T_y & T_z & 1 \end{bmatrix}$$

$$= [x \quad y \quad z \quad 1] \, T$$

This specification implies that the object is translated in three dimensions by applying a displacement T_x, T_y and T_z to each vertex that defines the object. The matrix notation is a convenient alternative to writing the transformation as a set of three equations:

$$x' = x + T_x$$
$$y' = y + T_y$$
$$z' = z + T_z$$

The set of transformations is completed by scaling and rotation. First, scaling:

$$V' = VS$$

$$S = \begin{bmatrix} S_x & 0 & 0 & 0 \\ 0 & S_y & 0 & 0 \\ 0 & 0 & S_z & 0 \\ 0 & 0 & 0 & 1 \end{bmatrix}$$

Here S_x, S_y and S_z are scaling factors. For uniform scaling, $S_x = S_y = S_z$; otherwise differential scaling occurs along these axes for which the scaling factor is non-unity. Again the process can be expressed less succinctly by a set of three equations:

$$x' = xS_x$$
$$y' = yS_y$$
$$z' = zS_z$$

applied to every vertex in the object.

---

† This text adopts the convention of using row vectors to represent three-dimensional points. This was, until fairly recently, the de facto standard in computer graphics. The de jure standard, adopted by PHIGS and, for example, Foley *et al.* (1989) is to use column vectors; this is of course the convention used by mathematicians. We have decided to stick with the traditional computer graphics convention for the eminently sensible reason that when transformation matrices are concatenated the left to right order in which they appear in the concatenation product is the order in which the corresponding transformations are applied.

To rotate an object in three-dimensional space we need to specify an axis of rotation. This can have any spatial orientation in three-dimensional space, but it is easiest to consider rotations that are parallel to one of the coordinate axes. The transformation matrices for counterclockwise rotation about the X, Y and Z axes respectively are:

$$R_x = \begin{bmatrix} 1 & 0 & 0 & 0 \\ 0 & \cos\theta & \sin\theta & 0 \\ 0 & -\sin\theta & \cos\theta & 0 \\ 0 & 0 & 0 & 1 \end{bmatrix}$$

$$R_y = \begin{bmatrix} \cos\theta & 0 & -\sin\theta & 0 \\ 0 & 1 & 0 & 0 \\ \sin\theta & 0 & \cos\theta & 0 \\ 0 & 0 & 0 & 1 \end{bmatrix}$$

$$R_z = \begin{bmatrix} \cos\theta & \sin\theta & 0 & 0 \\ -\sin\theta & \cos\theta & 0 & 0 \\ 0 & 0 & 1 & 0 \\ 0 & 0 & 0 & 1 \end{bmatrix}$$

The Z axis matrix specification is equivalent to the following set of three equations:

$$x' = x \cos\theta - y \sin\theta$$
$$y' = x \sin\theta + y \cos\theta$$
$$z' = z$$

Figure 1.2 shows examples of these transformations operating on a cube with one of its vertices at the origin.

The inverse of these transformations is often required. T^{-1} is obtained by negating T_x, T_y and T_z. Replacing S_x, S_y and S_z by their reciprocals gives S^{-1}, and negating the angle of rotation gives R^{-1}.

Any set of rotations, scalings and translations can be multiplied or concatenated together to give a **net transformation matrix**. For example if:

$$[x' \quad y' \quad z' \quad 1] = [x \quad y \quad z \quad 1]\, M_1$$

and

$$[x'' \quad y'' \quad z'' \quad 1] = [x' \quad y' \quad z' \quad 1]\, M_2$$

then the transformation matrices can be concatenated:

$$M_3 = M_1 M_2$$

and

$$[x'' \quad y'' \quad z'' \quad 1] = [x \quad y \quad z \quad 1]\, M_3$$

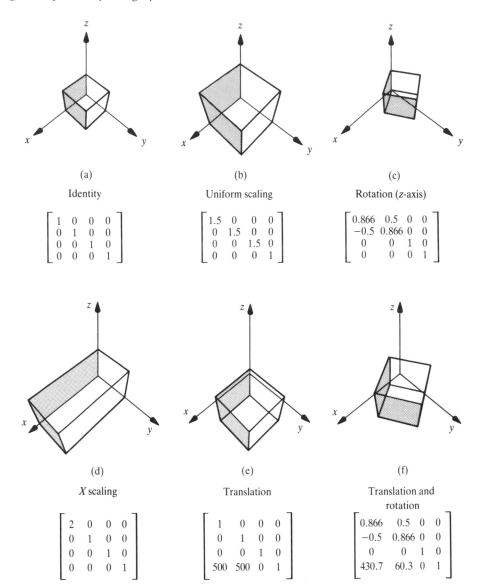

(a)
Identity

$$\begin{bmatrix} 1 & 0 & 0 & 0 \\ 0 & 1 & 0 & 0 \\ 0 & 0 & 1 & 0 \\ 0 & 0 & 0 & 1 \end{bmatrix}$$

(b)
Uniform scaling

$$\begin{bmatrix} 1.5 & 0 & 0 & 0 \\ 0 & 1.5 & 0 & 0 \\ 0 & 0 & 1.5 & 0 \\ 0 & 0 & 0 & 1 \end{bmatrix}$$

(c)
Rotation (z-axis)

$$\begin{bmatrix} 0.866 & 0.5 & 0 & 0 \\ -0.5 & 0.866 & 0 & 0 \\ 0 & 0 & 1 & 0 \\ 0 & 0 & 0 & 1 \end{bmatrix}$$

(d)
X scaling

$$\begin{bmatrix} 2 & 0 & 0 & 0 \\ 0 & 1 & 0 & 0 \\ 0 & 0 & 1 & 0 \\ 0 & 0 & 0 & 1 \end{bmatrix}$$

(e)
Translation

$$\begin{bmatrix} 1 & 0 & 0 & 0 \\ 0 & 1 & 0 & 0 \\ 0 & 0 & 1 & 0 \\ 500 & 500 & 0 & 1 \end{bmatrix}$$

(f)
Translation and
rotation

$$\begin{bmatrix} 0.866 & 0.5 & 0 & 0 \\ -0.5 & 0.866 & 0 & 0 \\ 0 & 0 & 1 & 0 \\ 430.7 & 60.3 & 0 & 1 \end{bmatrix}$$

Figure 1.2
Examples of affine
transformations on a
cube located with one
edge along the z axis.

Athough translations are commutative, rotations are not and

$$R_1 R_2 \neq R_2 R_1$$

A general transformation matrix will be of the form:

$$\begin{bmatrix} a_{11} & a_{12} & a_{13} & 0 \\ a_{21} & a_{22} & a_{23} & 0 \\ a_{31} & a_{32} & a_{33} & 0 \\ t_x & t_y & t_z & 1 \end{bmatrix}$$

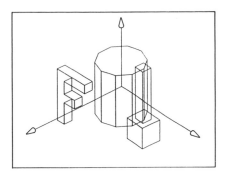

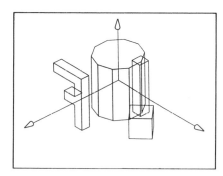

Figure 1.3
Two scenes built up using instances of the same objects (see text for details of transformations).

The 3×3 upper left submatrix A is the net rotation and scaling while (t_x, t_y, t_z) gives the net translation.

A typical use of transformation matrices in computer graphics is to build up a scene that consists of instances of predefined objects. An example of two scenes, built up from instances of the same objects, is given in Figure 1.3. The precise effect of the transformations is unimportant; the two scenes should be compared so that a general feel for the effect of the transformations is obtained.

Three objects are subject to transformations, from positions centred on the origin, as follows:

(1) First cube:
     Scale   (0.4, 0.4, 0.4)   (S_x, S_y, S_z)
     Rotation   (0, 0, 0)   (counterclockwise in degrees about X, Y and Z axis)

Translation $(0.5, 1.7, -0.6)$ (T_x, T_y, T_z)

Composite matrix

$$
\begin{bmatrix}
0.4 & 0.0 & 0.0 & 0.0 \\
0.0 & 0.4 & 0.0 & 0.0 \\
0.0 & 0.0 & 0.4 & 0.0 \\
0.5 & 1.7 & -0.6 & 1.0
\end{bmatrix}
$$

(2) F:
  Scale $(1, 1, 1)$
  Rotation $(0, 0, 0)$
  Translation $(1.7, -0.4, 0)$

Composite matrix

$$
\begin{bmatrix}
1.0 & 0.0 & 0.0 & 0.0 \\
0.0 & 1.0 & 0.0 & 0.0 \\
0.0 & 0.0 & 1.0 & 0.0 \\
1.7 & -0.4 & 0.0 & 1.0
\end{bmatrix}
$$

(3) Second cube:
  Scale $(0.2, 0.2, 1)$
  Rotation $(0, 0, 0)$
  Translation $(0.5, 1.7, 0.8)$

Composite matrix

$$
\begin{bmatrix}
0.2 & 0.0 & 0.0 & 0.0 \\
0.0 & 0.2 & 0.0 & 0.0 \\
0.0 & 0.0 & 1.0 & 0.0 \\
0.5 & 1.7 & 0.8 & 1.0
\end{bmatrix}
$$

(4) Cylinder:
  Scale $(0.9, 0.9, 1)$
  Rotation $(0, 0, 0)$
  Translation $(0, 0, 0)$

Composite matrix

$$
\begin{bmatrix}
0.9 & 0.0 & 0.0 & 0.0 \\
0.0 & 0.9 & 0.0 & 0.0 \\
0.0 & 0.0 & 1.0 & 0.0 \\
0.0 & 0.0 & 0.0 & 1.0
\end{bmatrix}
$$

For comparison, the second scene data (this time without the composite matrix) is given:

(1) First cube:
  Scale $(0.4, 0.4, 0.4)$

	Rotation	$(0, 0, 45)$
	Translation	$(0.5, 1.7, -0.6)$

(2) F:

Scale $\qquad$ $(1, 1, 1)$

Rotation $\qquad$ $(0, 0, 180)$

Translation $\qquad$ $(1.7, -0.4, 0)$

(3) Second cube:

Scale $\qquad$ $(0.2, 0.2, 1)$

Rotation $\qquad$ $(0, 0, 0)$

Translation $\qquad$ $(0.5, 1.7, 0.8)$

(4) Cylinder:

Scale $\qquad$ $(0.9, 0.9, 1)$

Rotation $\qquad$ $(0, 0, 0)$

Translation $\qquad$ $(0, 0, 0)$

The ability to concatenate transformations to form a net transformation matrix is useful, because it gives a single matrix specification for *any* linear transformation. For example, consider rotating a body about a line parallel to the Z axis which passes through the point $(T_x, T_y, 0)$ and also passes through one of the vertices of the object. Here we are implying that the object is not at the origin and we wish to apply rotation about a reference point in the object. We cannot simply apply a rotation matrix, because this is defined with respect to the origin and an object not positioned at the origin would rotate *and* translate – not usually the desired effect. Instead we have to derive a net transformation matrix as follows:

(1) translate the object to the origin,

(2) apply the desired rotation, and

(3) translate the object back to its original position.

The net transformation matrix is:

$$
T_1 R T_2 =
\begin{bmatrix}
1 & 0 & 0 & 0 \\
0 & 1 & 0 & 0 \\
0 & 0 & 1 & 0 \\
-T_x & -T_y & 0 & 1
\end{bmatrix}
\begin{bmatrix}
\cos\theta & \sin\theta & 0 & 0 \\
-\sin\theta & \cos\theta & 0 & 0 \\
0 & 0 & 1 & 0 \\
0 & 0 & 0 & 1
\end{bmatrix}
\begin{bmatrix}
1 & 0 & 0 & 0 \\
0 & 1 & 0 & 0 \\
0 & 0 & 1 & 0 \\
T_x & T_y & 0 & 1
\end{bmatrix}
$$

$$
=
\begin{bmatrix}
\cos\theta & \sin\theta & 0 & 0 \\
-\sin\theta & \cos\theta & 0 & 0 \\
0 & 0 & 1 & 0 \\
(-T_x\cos\theta + T_y\sin\theta + T_x) & (-T_x\sin\theta - T_y\cos\theta + T_y) & 0 & 1
\end{bmatrix}
$$

This process is shown in Figure 1.4 where θ is 30°.

Figure 1.4
The stages in building up the rotation of an object about one of its own vertices. The rotation is about an axis parallel to the Z axis at point $(T_x, T_y, 0)$. A two-dimensional projection (with the Z axis coming out of the paper) is shown for clarity. (a) Original object at $(T_x, T_y, 0)$. (b) Translate to the origin. (c) Rotate about the origin. (d) Translate to $P(T_x, T_y, 0)$.

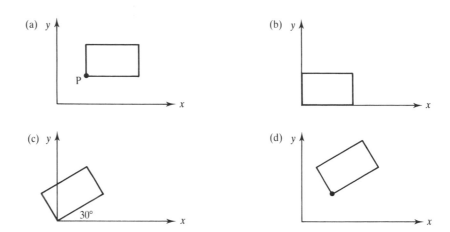

1.3 Transformations for changing coordinate systems

Up to now we have discussed transformations that operate on points expressed relative to one particular coordinate system. In many contexts in computer graphics we need to derive transformations that take points from one coordinate system into another. One of these contexts has already been mentioned – the use of coordinate systems that are local or particular to objects.

Consider two coordinate systems with axes parallel, that is, the systems only differ by a translation. If we wish to transform points currently expressed in system 1 into system 2 then we use the *inverse* of the transformation that takes the origin of system 1 to that of system 2. That is, a point $(x, y, z, 1)$ in system 1 transforms to a point $(x', y', z', 1)$ by:

$$[x', y', z', 1] = [x, y, z, 1] \begin{bmatrix} 1 & 0 & 0 & 0 \\ 0 & 1 & 0 & 0 \\ 0 & 0 & 1 & 0 \\ -T_x & -T_y & -T_z & 1 \end{bmatrix}$$

$$= T_{12}$$

$$= (T_{21})^{-1}$$

which is the transformation that translates the origin of system 1 to that of system 2 (where the point is still expressed relative to system 1). Another way of putting it is to say that the transformation generally required is the inverse of the transformation that takes the old axes to the new axes within the current coordinate system.

This is an important result because we generally find transformations between coordinate systems by considering transformations that operate on origins and axes. In the case of viewing systems, a change in coordinate systems involves both translation and rotation, and we find the required transformation in this way by considering a combination of rotations and translations.

1.4   Structure-deforming transformations

The above linear transformations either move an object (rotation and translation) or scale the object. Uniform scaling preserves shape. Using different values of S_x, S_y and S_z the object is stretched or squeezed along particular coordinate axes. In this section a set of transformations that deform the object is introduced. These are fully described by Barr (1984) where they are termed 'global deformations'. The particular deformations detailed in this paper are tapering, twisting and bending.

Barr uses a formula definition for the transformations:

$$X = F_x(x)$$
$$Y = F_y(y)$$
$$Z = F_z(z)$$

where (x, y, z) is a vertex in an undeformed solid and (X, Y, Z) is the deformed vertex. Using this notation the scaling transformation above is:

$$X = S_x(x)$$
$$Y = S_y(y)$$
$$Z = S_z(z)$$

Tapering is easily developed from scaling. We choose a tapering axis and differentially scale the other two components, setting up a tapering function along this axis. Thus to taper an object along its Z axis:

$$X = rx$$
$$Y = ry$$
$$Z = z$$

where:

$$r = f(z)$$

a linear or non-linear tapering profile or function. Thus the transformation becomes a function of r. That is, we change the transformation depending on where in the space it is applied. In effect, we are scaling a scaling transformation.

Global axial twisting can be developed as a differential rotation, just as tapering is a differential scaling. To twist an object about its z axis we apply:

$$X = x \cos \theta - y \sin \theta$$
$$Y = x \sin \theta + y \cos \theta$$
$$Z = z$$

where:

$$\theta = f(z)$$

and $f'(z)$ specifies the rate of twist per unit length along the Z axis.

A global linear bend along an axis is a composite transformation comprising a bent region and a region outside the bent region where the deformation is a rotation and a translation.

Barr defines a bend region along the Y axis as:

$$y_{min} \leq y \leq y_{max}$$

the radius of curvature of the bend is $1/k$ and the centre of the bend is at $y = y_0$. The bending angle is:

$$\theta = k(y' - y_0)$$

where:

$$y' = \begin{cases} y_{min} & y \leq y_{min} \\ y & y_{min} < y < y_{max} \\ y_{max} & y \geq y_{max} \end{cases}$$

The deforming transformation is given by:

$$X = x$$

$$Y = \begin{cases} -\sin \theta(z - 1/k) + y_0 & y_{min} \leq y \leq y_{max} \\ -\sin \theta(z - 1/k) + y_0 + \cos \theta(y - y_{min}) & y < y_{min} \\ -\sin \theta(z - 1/k) + y_0 + \cos \theta(y - y_{max}) & y > y_{max} \end{cases}$$

$$Z = \begin{cases} \cos \theta(z - 1/k) + 1/k & y_{min} \leq y \leq y_{max} \\ \cos \theta(z - 1/k) + 1/k + \sin \theta(y - y_{min}) & y < y_{min} \\ \cos \theta(z - 1/k) + 1/k + \sin \theta(y - y_{max}) & y > y_{max} \end{cases}$$

Figure 1.5 shows an example of each of these transformations. The deformation on the cube is an intuitive reflection of the effects and the same transformations are applied to the Utah teapot. Plate 1 shows a rendered version of a polygon mesh object (a corrugated cylinder) that has been twisted and tapered.

Non-constrained, non-linear deformations cannot be applied to polygon meshes in general. One problem is the connectivity constraints between vertices. For example, we cannot twist a cube, represented as six surfaces

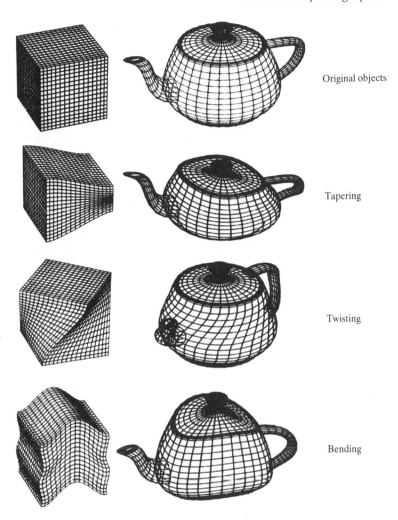

Original objects

Tapering

Twisting

Bending

Figure 1.5
Structure-deforming
transformations.

without limit, and retain a structure suitable for rendering. Another problem is that deformations where vertices move apart have the effect of reducing the polygonal resolution of the original model, giving rise to a degradation in silhouette edge aliasing (dealt with in detail later). Thus the polygonal resolution of the object model constrains the nature of the deformation and this can only be overcome by subdivision of the original mesh as a function of the 'severity' of the deformation.

1.5   Vectors in computer graphics

Vectors are used in a variety of contexts in computer graphics. This section covers the basic operations that are subsequently used throughout the text.

A **vector** is an entity that possesses magnitude and direction. A three-dimensional vector is a triple:

$$V = (v_1, v_2, v_3)$$

where each component v_i is a scalar.

In computer graphics we are also interested in an entity called a **ray** (mathematically known as a **directed line segment**), that possesses position, magnitude and direction. If we imagine a ray to be a physical line in three-space, then its position is the position of the tail of the line, its magnitude the length of the line between its head and tail, and its direction the direction of the line. A ray can be specified by two points or by a single point, and a vector. If the end points of the ray are (x_1, y_1, z_1) and (x_2, y_2, z_2) respectively, then the vector is given by:

$$V = (x_2 - x_1, y_2 - y_1, z_2 - z_1)$$

1.5.1   Addition of vectors

Addition of two vectors V and W, for example, may be defined as:

$$\begin{aligned}X &= V + W \\ &= (x_1, x_2, x_3) \\ &= (v_1 + w_1, v_2 + w_2, v_3 + w_3)\end{aligned}$$

Geometrically, this is interpreted as follows. The 'tail' of W is placed at the 'head' of V and X is the vector formed by joining the tail of V to the head of W. This is shown in Figure 1.6 for a pair of two-dimensional vectors together with an alternative, but equivalent, interpretation.

Figure 1.6
Two geometric interpretations of the sum of two vectors.

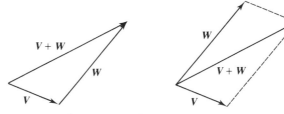

1.5.2   Length of vectors

The magnitude or length of a vector is defined as:

$$|V| = (v_1{}^2 + v_2{}^2 + v_3{}^2)^{1/2}$$

and we interpret this geometrically as the distance from its tail to its head.

We **normalize** a vector to produce a unit vector, which is a vector of length equal to one. The normalized version of V is:

$$U = \frac{V}{|V|}$$

which is a vector of unit length having the same direction as V. We can now refer to U as a direction. Note that we can write:

$$V = |V|U$$

which is saying that any vector is given by its magnitude times its direction.

1.5.3   Normal vectors and cross products

In computer graphics considerable processing is carried out using vectors that are **normal** to a surface. For example, in a polygon mesh model (Chapter 2) a normal vector is used to represent the orientation of a surface when comparing this with the direction of the light. Such a comparison is used in reflection models to compute the intensity of the light reflected from the surface. The smaller the angle between the light vector and the vector that is normal to the surface, the higher is the intensity of the light reflected from the surface (Chapter 4).

A normal vector to a polygon is calculated from three (non-collinear) vertices of the polygon. Three vertices define two vectors V_1 and V_2 (Figure 1.7) and the normal to the polygon is found by taking the **cross product** of these:

$$N_p = V_1 \times V_2$$

The cross product of two vectors V and W is defined as:

$$X = V \times W$$
$$= (v_2 w_3 - v_3 w_2)\mathbf{i} + (v_3 w_1 - v_1 w_3)\mathbf{j} + (v_1 w_2 - v_2 w_1)\mathbf{k}$$

where $\mathbf{i}$, $\mathbf{j}$ and $\mathbf{k}$ are standard unit vectors:

$$\mathbf{i} = (1, 0, 0)$$
$$\mathbf{j} = (0, 1, 0)$$
$$\mathbf{k} = (0, 0, 1)$$

that is, vectors orientated along the coordinate axes that define the space in which the vectors are embedded.

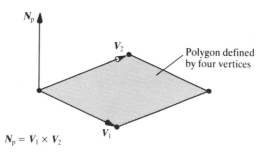

Figure 1.7
Calculating the normal vector to a polygon.

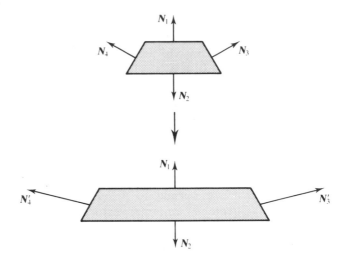

Figure 1.8
The effect of
differential scaling on
surface normals:
$S_x = 2$, $S_y = 1$ and
$S_z = 1$.

Geometrically, a cross product, as we have implied, is a vector whose orientation is normal to the plane containing the two vectors forming the cross product. When determining the surface normal of a polygon, the cross product must point outwards with respect to the object. In a right-handed coordinate system the sense of the cross product vector is given by the right-hand rule. If the first two fingers of your right hand point in the directions of V and W then the direction of X is given by your thumb.

A problem arises when transformations are applied to surface normals in polygon mesh models. At the beginning of this chapter we discussed affine transformations that operate on the vertices of polygonally defined objects. In a polygon mesh object it makes sense to calculate all the required normals once only and to store these as part of the object database. The sense of this procedure becomes apparent if you consider that complex objects can be represented by tens or even hundreds of thousands of polygons. The normals are then subject to the same modelling transformations (translation, rotation, scaling and so on) as the polygon vertices. This is preferable to recalculating the normals every time the vertices are transformed. However, consider Figure 1.8 that shows a two-dimensional object subject to an affine, but anisotropic, transformation. The only anisotropic affine transformation that tends to concern us in computer graphics is differential scaling. Figure 1.8 shows a scaling transformation where:

$$S_x = n$$
$$S_y = 1$$
$$S_z = 1$$

It can be seen intuitively from the diagram that if the same scaling is applied to the surface normal components, we end up with vectors that are, in general, no longer surface normals. It can be shown (Glassner, 1990) that the required transformation which preserves the orientation of the vectors is:

$$S_x' = 1/S_x$$
$$S_y' = 1/S_y$$
$$S_z' = 1/S_z$$

so that a transformed surface normal N' is given by:

$$(N_x', N_y', {}'N_z') = \left(\frac{N_x}{S_x}, \frac{N_y}{S_y}, \frac{N_z}{S_z} \right)$$

This consideration equally applies to vertex normals (Chapter 5) which are also calculated once only and stored in the object database.

If the surface is a bicubic parametric surface (Chapter 6), then the orientation of the normal vector varies continuously over the surface. We compute the normal at any point (u, v) on the surface again by using a cross product. This is done by first calculating tangent vectors in the two parametric directions. (The procedure is outlined here for the sake of completeness; full details are given in Chapter 6). For a surface defined as $Q(u, v)$ we find:

$$\frac{\delta}{\delta u} Q(u, v) \quad \text{and} \quad \frac{\delta}{\delta v} Q(u, v)$$

We then define:

$$N_s = \frac{\delta Q}{\delta u} \times \frac{\delta Q}{\delta v}$$

1.5.4   Normal vectors and dot products

The most common use of a **dot product** in computer graphics is to provide a measure of the angle between two vectors, where one of the vectors is a normal vector to a surface or group of surfaces. Common applications are shading (the angle between a light direction vector and a surface normal) and visibility testing (the angle between a viewing vector and a surface normal).

The dot product of vectors V and W is defined as:

$$X = V \cdot W$$
$$= v_1 w_1 + v_2 w_2 + v_3 w_3$$

Figure 1.9 shows two vectors. Using the cosine rule we have:

$$|V - W|^2 = |V|^2 + |W|^2 - 2|V||W| \cos \theta$$

Figure 1.9
The dot product of the
two vectors is related
to the cosine of the
angle between them:
$$\cos \theta = \frac{V \cdot W}{|V||W|}.$$

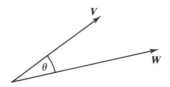

where θ is the angle between the vectors. Also it can be shown that:

$$|V - W|^2 = V^2 - 2VW + |W|^2$$

thus:

$$V \cdot W = |V||W| \cos \theta$$

giving:

$$\cos \theta = \frac{V \cdot W}{|V||W|}$$

or, the angle between two vectors is the dot product of their normalized versions.

We can use the dot product to project a vector onto another vector. Consider a unit vector V. If we project any vector W onto V (Figure 1.10) and call the result X, then we have:

$$|X| = |W| \cos \theta$$
$$= |W| \frac{V \cdot W}{|V||W|}$$
$$= V \cdot W \tag{1.1}$$

because V is a unit vector. Thus the dot product of V and W is the length of the projection of W onto V.

A property of the dot product used in computer graphics is its *sign*. Because of its relationship to $\cos \theta$ the dot product of V and W (where V and W are of any length) has the following sign:

$$V \cdot W > 0 \qquad \text{if } \theta < 90°$$
$$V \cdot W = 0 \qquad \text{if } \theta = 90°$$
$$V \cdot W < 0 \qquad \text{if } \theta > 90°$$

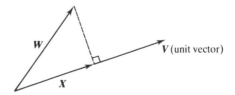

Figure 1.10
$|X| = V \cdot W$ is the
length of the projection
of W onto V.

1.5.5 Vectors associated with the normal vector

There are three important vectors that are associated with the surface normal. They are the **light direction vector**, L, the **reflecting vector** or **mirror vector**, R, and the **viewing vector**, V. The light direction vector L is a vector whose direction is given by the line from the tail of the surface normal to the light source, which in simple shading contexts is defined as a single point. This vector is shown in Figure 1.11(a). The reflection vector R is given by the direction of the light reflected from the surface due to light incoming along direction L. Sometimes called the 'mirror direction', geometric optics tells us that the outgoing angle equals the incoming angle as shown in Figure 1.11(b).

Consider the construction shown in Figure 1.12. This shows:

$$R = R_1 + R_2$$
$$R_1 = -L + R_2$$

thus:

$$R = 2R_2 - L$$

From Equation 1.1:

$$R_2 = (N \cdot L)N$$

and

$$R = 2(N \cdot L)N - L \qquad (1.2)$$

Figure 1.11(c) shows a view vector V. Note that this vector has any arbitrary orientation; we are normally interested in that component of light incoming in direction L that is reflected along V. This will depend in general on both the angles ϕ_v and θ_v. We also note that the intensity of outgoing light depends on the incoming angles ϕ_i and θ_i, and this is usually described as a bidirectional dependence, because two angles, (ϕ_v, θ_v) and (ϕ_i, θ_i) in three-dimensional space, are involved.

Projects, notes and suggestions ————————————

1.1 Wireframe scenes

Implement a program (see Appendix B) that enables a user to set up a scene that consists of a number of objects which are viewed (using viewing system I, Chapter 3) in wireframe mode.

1.2 Animating a wireframe scene

Enhance the program in Project 1.1 to include an animation facility that displays a scene, increments the transformation matrix elements and displays a new scene and so on.

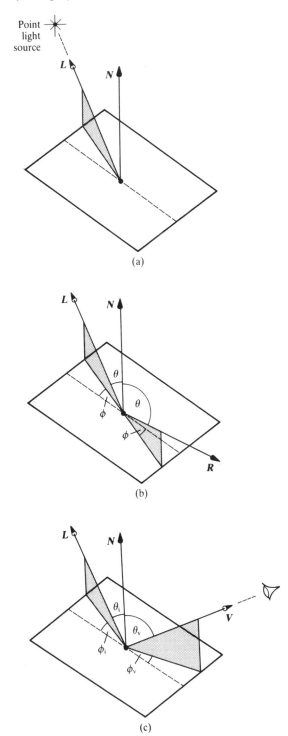

Figure 1.11
Vectors associated with
the normal vector.
(a) *L*, the light
direction vector. (b) *R*,
the reflection vector.
(c) *V*, the view vector,
is a vector of any
orientation.

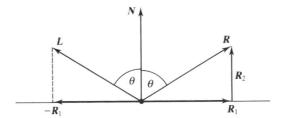

Figure 1.12
Construction for the
reflection vector **R**.

This is the basis technique used by 'tumbling logo' programs seen in TV title sequences. Now provide an animation facility for the 'virtual camera' by causing the viewing system parameters also to be animated.

1.3   Interacting with a wireframe object (*)

Write a simple modelling program that enables a user to select a vertex of a wireframe model displayed on the screen and to pull the vertex around in three-dimensional space to alter the shape of the object.

The project highlights a number of problems with this type of interaction. First you will possibly only have access to a two-dimensional locator device, and this has to be used both as a three-dimensional pick to select a vertex and as a three-dimensional locator to move the vertex around.

Vertex selection can be reduced to a two-dimensional problem if the vertices do not overlap in screen space. Maintaining a list of (x_s, y_s) positions of each vertex in the object, for a particular view, together with a spatial tolerance will enable a vertex to be selected in two-dimensional screen space.

To move the vertex around, the two-dimensional locator needs to be used in three-dimensional space. An obvious approach is to use, say, a mouse in two operational modes; one the normal coupled x,y mode, which will allow movement in an x_w, y_w plane, the other mode simulating a potentiometer and allowing movement up and down the z_w axis. (Extending the use of a mouse to accommodate three-dimensional graphics is a relatively unexplored topic. Three-dimensional locator devices exist but they are uncommon.)

Moving the vertex around means redrawing, say in a different colour, those edges that join at the vertex. If your workstation is powerful enough then you can implement this animated feedback loop by redrawing the entire object. Otherwise two-dimensional line-drawing utilities need to be animated in an 'erase–draw' sequence, under control of an exclusive-or Raster_op so that moving lines to not erase stationary lines.

The vertex dragging needs to be operated in two modes, move and fix. See Foley *et al.* (1989) for full details on two-dimensional interactive techniques.

1.4   Animated sequences and Barr's transformations

Generate an animated sequence showing a wireframe model of, say, a rectangular solid deforming. Do this by controlling a single parameter in one of Barr's transformations. Investigate the possibility of controlling two parameters, say bending and twisting, simultaneously.

2 | Representation of Objects

2.1 Representation and modelling of geometric objects

A number of representational forms for three-dimensional objects have been developed in computer graphics. Some of these arise out of applications and the data structure is determined wholly by the modelling strategy. For example, in solid modelling, a method known as CSG is both a representational form and a method that facilitates a form of graphical interaction that enables engineering parts to be built up. Some forms are determined by the rendering algorithms. Implicitly defined spheres abound in ray-traced images because these are the easiest objects to ray trace. A coarse 'patch' representation is required by the radiosity method because a solution in reasonable time is only possible if the environment is represented by patches or elements that are large.

The factors that the representation tends to determine are:

- the data structure, the form of the processing algorithms and the design of fixed program hardware;
- the cost of processing an object through a three-dimensional pipeline;
- the final appearance of an object – some forms are more approximate than others;
- the ease or otherwise of editing the shape of the object.

We shall look at four representational forms arranged approximately in order of importance and frequency of use. These are:

(1) *Polygonal* Objects are approximated by a net of planar polygonal facets.

(2) *Bicubic parametric patches* Objects are represented exactly by nets of

elements called **patches**. These are polynomials in two parametric variables and are usually cubic.

(3) *Constructive solid geometry (CSG)*   Used in solid modelling – an object is represented exactly by a collection of 'elementary' objects such as spheres, cylinders and boxes.

(4) *Space subdivision techniques*   Embedding an object in a space where points in the space are labelled according to object occupancy.

In the above summary, 1 and 4 are schemes that approximate (to a controllable extent) the form of the object that they represent. On the other hand, schemes 2 and 3 are exact representations. Another categorization that is important is whether the representation is of the surface or boundary of the object, or whether the entire volume of the object is represented. Schemes 1 and 2 are boundary representations and 3 and 4 are volume representations. Note that the most commonly used form – the polygonal representation – is an approximate boundary scheme.

Occasionally in texts implicit functions are mentioned as an object representation form. An implicit function is, for example:

$$x^2 + y^2 + z^2 = r^2$$

which is the implicit definition for a sphere. These are of limited usefulness in computer graphics because there is a limited number of objects that can be represented in this way, and because it is an inconvenient form as far as rendering is concerned. For these reasons we will not pursue it further in this text.

2.2   Polygonal representation

This is the classic representational form in three-dimensional graphics. An object is represented by a mesh of polygonal facets. In the general case, an object possesses curved surfaces and the facets are an approximation to such a surface (Figure 2.1). A **polygon mesh** representation is formally called a **boundary representation** or **B rep** because it is a geometric and topological description of the boundary or surface of the object.

Polygonal representations are ubiquitous in computer graphics. There are two reasons for this. Modelling or creating polygonal objects is straightforward; however there are certain practical difficulties. The accuracy of the model, or the difference between the faceted representation and the curved surface of the object, is usually arbitrary. As far as final image quality is concerned, the size of individual polygons should ideally depend on local spatial curvature. Where the curvature changes rapidly, more polygons are required per unit area of the surface. These factors tend to be related to the

Figure 2.1
Approximating a
curved surface using
polygonal facets.

method used for creating the polygons. If, for example, a mesh is being built
from an existing object, by using a three-dimensional digitizer to determine
the spatial coordinates of polygon vertices, the operator will decide on the
basis of experience how large each polygon should be. Sometimes polygons
are extracted algorithmically (as in, for example, the creation of an object as
a solid of revolution or in a bicubic patch subdivision algorithm) and a more
rigorous approach to the rate of polygons per unit area of the surface is
possible.

One of the most significant developments in three-dimensional
graphics was the emergence of **shading algorithms** that deal efficiently with
polygonal objects, and at the same time, through an interpolation scheme,
diminish the visual effect of piecewise linearities in the representation. This
factor, together with recent developments in fixed program rendering hardware, has secured the entrenchment of the polygon mesh structure. In fact,
a polygon mesh structure is used not only as a modelling data structure, but
as an intermediate form for many other data structures. We have already
mentioned bicubic patches. Here the source data structure is converted into
polygons as an overall rendering strategy that results in a lower coding
complexity than that required to render directly from the patch description.
The same approach is often taken with CSG structures.

In the simplest case, a polygon mesh is a structure that consists of
polygons represented by a list of (x, y, z) coordinates that are the polygon
vertices (edges are either represented explicitly or implicitly as we shall see
in a moment). Thus the information we store to describe an object is finally
a list of points or vertices. We may also store, as part of the object representation, other geometric information that is used in subsequent processing.
These are usually polygon normals and vertex normals (see Section 5.3.1).
Calculated once only, it is convenient to store these in the object data
structure and have them undergo any linear transformations that are applied
to the object.

It is also convenient to order polygons into a simple hierarchical structure (Figure 2.2). Polygons are grouped into surfaces and surfaces are
grouped into objects. For example, a cylinder possesses three surfaces: a
planar top and bottom surface together with a curved surface. The reason
for this grouping is that we must distinguish between those edges that are
part of the approximation – edges between adjacent rectangles in the curved

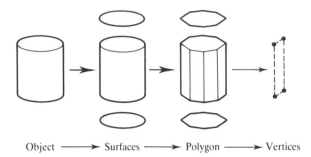

Figure 2.2
Object as a hierarchy.

surface of the cylinder, for example – and edges that exist in reality. The way in which these are subsequently treated by the rendering process is different.

The important feature of this representation is that polygons are independent entities and can be treated as such by the renderer. This has implications in the renderer design; the most popular rendering strategy is to treat polygons independently, processing them into the frame memory using a Z-buffer hidden surface removal algorithm in conjunction with interpolative shading.

It is sometimes said that the main deficiency of this representation is that the topological relationship between polygons is 'buried'. For example, it is not easy to ascertain which polygons share a vertex. This information is required by shading algorithms. The importance of this point depends on the eventual use of the model. For most standard rendering contexts (that is, non-CAD applications) the model is fixed at the creation stage and is only thereafter subject to linear transformations. Topological relationships required to calculate the aforementioned vertex normals are not required after the creation phase, and the incorporation of derived geometric attributes in the model database is all that is required.

An alternative approach to representing a polygonal object is to store the shared edges explicitly (that is, the shared edges, not the real edges). This scheme is shown in Figure 2.3 where the topmost level of the surface

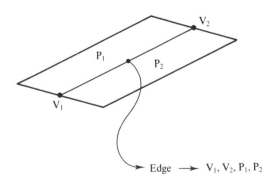

Figure 2.3
Explicit representation
of shared edges.

hierarchy is a set of edges. Each edge is a list of four indices – two vertices and two polygons that share the edge.

The motivation for an edge-based approach is effiency in the rendering processes. When polygons are rendered there are processing overheads associated with each edge – specifically, clipping polygons to a view volume and finding the set of pixels through which an edge passes. If polygons are treated separately, shared edges are processed twice, adding to the overall costs. These can become significant as the complexity of an object grows in terms of the number of polygons representing it is concerned.

2.2.1   Modelling polygonal objects

Although a polygon mesh is the most common representational form in computer graphics, **modelling**, although straightforward, is somewhat tedious. The popularity of this representation derives from: the ease of modelling, the emergence of rendering strategies (both hardware and software) to process polygonal objects, and the important fact that there is no restriction whatever on the shape or complexity of the object being modelled.

Modelling strategies are mainly brute force. Interactive development of a model is possible by 'pulling' vertices around with a three-dimensional locator device but important factors, transparent to the user, need to be embedded in such a system. The main requirement is to ensure an 'adequate' approximation to the object being developed. If the user makes a change in the spatial curvature of the object approximated by the current polygon mesh (by moving one or a number of vertices) then new facets may need to be generated to maintain the adequacy of the approximation. Consider, for example, starting with a rectangular solid and twisting it by rotating opposite faces in opposite directions. As the twist is increased, the rate of change of curvature over the deformed faces will increase.

Three common examples of polygon modelling strategies are:

(1) Using a three-dimensional digitizer or adopting a similar manual strategy.
(2) Using an automatic device such as a laser ranger.
(3) Generating an object from a mathematical description.
(4) Generating an object by sweeping.

The first two modelling methods convert real objects into polygon meshes, the next two generate models from definitions.

Manual modelling of polygonal objects
The easiest way to model a real object is by manually using a **three-dimensional digitizer**. The operator uses experience and judgement to emplace points on an object which are to be polygon vertices. The three-dimensional coordinates of these vertices are then input into the system via a

Figure 2.4
A skimming algorithm joins points on consecutive contours to make a three-dimensional polygonal object from the contours.

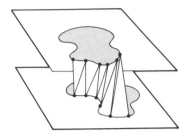

straightforward. A common strategy for ensuring an adequate representation is to draw a net over the surface of the object. Where curved net lines intersect defines the position of the polygon vertices.

Automatic generation of polygonal objects

A device that is capable of creating very accurate or high resolution polygon mesh objects from real objects is a **laser ranger**. The object is placed on a rotating table in the path of the beam. The table also moves up and down vertically. The laser ranger returns a set of contours – the intersection of the object and a set of closely spaced parallel planes – by measuring the distance to the object surface. A 'skinning' algorithm, operating on pairs of contours (Figure 2.4) converts the boundary data into a very large number of polygons. Figure 2.5 shows a rendered version of a statue head polygonized in this way. There are approximately 400 000 polygons in the representation.

Mathematical modelling of polygon objects

Generating an object from a mathematical description is most easily carried out by sweeping a cross-section. Project 2.1 describes a simple example. The polygonal resolution is easily controlled by the generating algorithm, but shape-dependent resolution problems can still occur. In the case of a toroid generated by sweeping a circular cross-section around a circular path, polygons will be larger on the outside face of the toroid compared with those on the inside face.

Figure 2.5
A rendered version of a complex polygonal object that was modelled automatically. There are approximately 400 000 polygons in the model.

Generating polygon objects by sweeping

The previous idea can be generalized to some extent by two extensions. First, we can sweep a cross-section along any curve. The curve along which the cross-section is swept can be any arbitrary curve, say one generated interactively by the user applying techniques described in Chapter 6. Second, the cross-section can be allowed to vary in shape as it is swept. These generalizations enable the production of objects called **ducted solids** or **generalized cylinders**.

Consider a parametrically defined cubic along which the cross-section is swept. This can be defined (see Chapter 6) as:

$$Q(u) = au^3 + bu^2 + cu + d$$

Now if we consider the simple case of moving a constant cross-section without twisting it along the curve, we need to define intervals along the curve at which the cross-section is to be placed, and joined vertex to vertex with the previous emplacement, with straight lines.

Two problems present themselves. First, what are the intervals at which the points occur along the curve? Second, we need a reference coordinate system, known as a **frame**, in which to orientate the cross-section.

Consider the first problem. Dividing u into equal intervals will not necessarily give the best results. In particular, the points will not appear at equal intervals along the curve. A procedure, known as **arclength parametrization**, divides the curve into equal intervals, but this procedure is not straightforward (it is described in detail by Watt and Watt (1992)). Arclength parametrization may also be inappropriate. What is really required is a scheme that divides the curve into intervals that depend on the curvature of the curve. When the curvature is high the rate of polygon generation needs to be increased so that more polygons occur when the curvature twists rapidly. The most direct way to do this is to use the curve subdivision algorithm (Section 6.6) and subdivide the curve until a linearity test is positive.

The second problem is somewhat easier to deal with. Having defined a set of sample points we need to define a reference frame or coordinate system at each. This is done by deriving three mutually orthogonal vectors that form the coordinate axes. There are many possibilities.

A common one is the **Frenet frame**. The Frenet frame is defined by the origin or sample point, P, and three vectors T, N and B (Figure 2.6). T is the unit length tangent vector:

$$T = \frac{V}{|V|}$$

where V is the derivative of the curve:

$$V = 3au^2 + 2bu + c$$

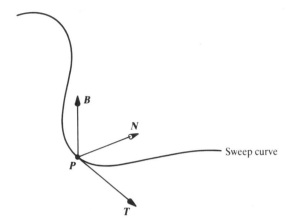

Figure 2.6
The Frenet frame at
sample point *P* on a
sweep curve.

The principal normal *N* is given by:

$$N = \frac{K}{|K|}$$

where:

$$K = V \times A \times \frac{V}{|V|^4}$$

and *A* is the second derivative of the curve:

$$A = 6au + 2b$$

Finally, *B* is given by

$$B = T \times N$$

Figure 2.7 shows examples of two objects modelled using this technique. In Figure 2.7(a) a circle of varying radius is swept along a straight line. The variation in the radius is set up by interactively defining a profile curve. Figure 2.7(b) shows the object produced by sweeping the varying radius circle along an axis that is itself a curve. This cross-sectional design philosophy is extended in Chapter 6.

2.3   Bicubic parametric patch nets

Intuitively, the step from polygon meshes to patch meshes is straightforward. If we consider a mesh of four-sided polygons approximating a curved surface, then a parametric **patch mesh** can be considered to be a set of curvilinear polygons which actually lie in the surface. Patches are treated comprehensively in Chapter 6; here we examine them in comparison with other representational forms.

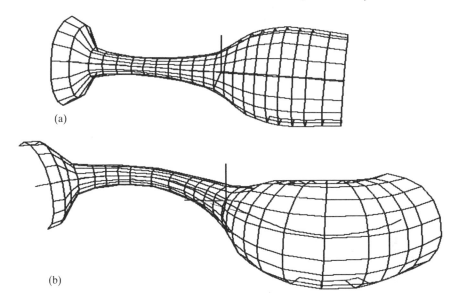

(a)

(b)

Figure 2.7
(a) A polygonal object modelled by sweeping a varying circle along a straight line. (b) A polygonal object modelled by sweeping a varying circle along a (cubic) curve.

First, we note that a patch is a curved surface and that every point in the patch is defined. The definition $Q(u,v)$ is in terms of two parameters, u,v, where $0 \leqslant u$, $v \leqslant 1$, and the function Q is a cubic polynomial. The precise values of the coefficients in the cubic determine $Q(u,v)$. A special and convenient way of defining these is to use 16 three-dimensional points known as **control points**. Four of these points are the corner points of the patch. Such a definition is used by a predefined polynomial form known as a **basis function**. The 16 control points are plugged into this definition and a unique $Q(u,v)$ is obtained. The shape of the patch is determined entirely from the position of the control points. An example of a single (Bézier) patch and the relationship between the patch shape and the control points is shown in Figure 2.8.

For most applications, object modelling or building a data structure representation of a three-dimensional object is more difficult when bicubic patches are used. (Quite complex real objects are easily polygonized by using a three-dimensional digitizer and operating software.) Sixteen control points have to be specified for each patch and there is another more signifi-cant practical problem. To maintain the 'integrity' of the representation, continuity constraints need to be maintained across all boundaries. A patch cannot be set up without regard to its neighbours. Because of this, patch descriptions tend to be generated semi-automatically using, for example, a sweeping strategy for modelling (see Section 2.3.1).

Set against these disadvantages, there are a number of advantages that give surface patches their use in CAD. The representation is 'fluid' and by using software to adjust the position of the control points, the shape of an object can be adjusted. However, this is not as easy as it sounds, again

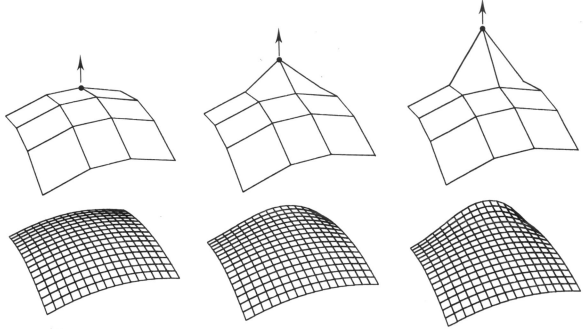

Figure 2.8
The relationship
between the position of
control points and the
shape of a patch.

because of the necessity to maintain the continuity conditions between patches.

Another advantage of bicubic patch representation is that because it is an exact analytical form, mass properties such as volume, surface area and moments of inertia can be extracted from the description. This property is fully exploited in CAD systems.

Finally, it should be mentioned that object representations at high three-dimensional resolution can demand large memory volumes. This means both high memory cost and database transfer time penalties. When rendering complex multi-object scenes, database accesses can become significant. A bicubic parametric patch object database, an exact representation, is on the other hand extremely economical.

The **Utah teapot** will suffice as an example here. A wireframe of lines of constant u and v is shown in Figure 2.9. The object is made up of 32 Bézier patches given in Appendix D. A single patch is shown as a heavy line. (Also shown in this figure is a composite control point polyhedron.) This representation consists of:

32 patches × 16 control points/patch

This is reduced (because most patches share 12 control points with neighbouring patches) to 306 vertices in this case

= 306 × 3 real numbers

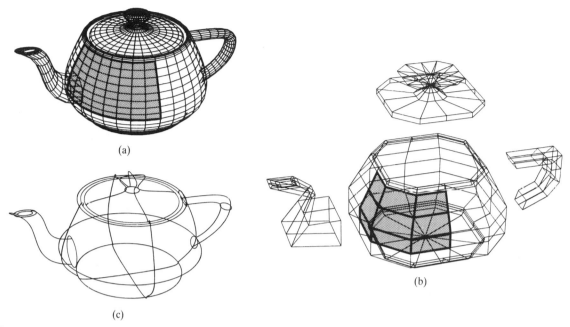

(a)

(b)

(c)

Figure 2.9
The Utah teapot. (a)
Lines of constant u and
v. The teapot is made
up of 32 Bézier
patches. A single patch
is shown shaded. (b) A
wireframe of the
control points. The
shaded region shows
the control polyhedron
for the shaded patch.
(c) A wireframe of the
patch edges.

On the other hand, a 'reasonable' polygon mesh representation would be:

Approximately 2048 × four-sided polygons
= 2048 × 3 real numbers

Thus the polygon mesh model, an *inaccurate* representation, uses almost seven times as much memory.

A related advantage here concerns rendering distant objects that project onto a small screen area. Using a fixed resolution polygon mesh model means paying the same database transfer penalty irrespective of the number of pixels occupying the final projection. A subdivision scheme of parametric patches (Chapter 6) would be more economical in this respect (although invoking higher scan conversion time penalties). In such a scheme, the original patches are converted into a polygon mesh representation by subdivision. This subdivision can stop at any level. In particular, subdivision can be terminated when a patch subdivision product is contained within a pixel area. This contrasts with a polygon mesh object where a complex object viewed from a distance may have the effect of a number of polygons all projecting onto the same pixel.

2.3.1   Modelling objects with patch nets

There are two practical modelling strategies that can be used to create parametric patch models. Both of these methods require some detailed knowledge of the underlying theory of bicubic parametric patch

Figure 2.10
A schematic
representation of
surface fitting. (a) A set
of points in
three-space. (b) Fitting
curves through the
points in two
parametric directions.
(c) The grid of curves
from the boundaries of
patches.

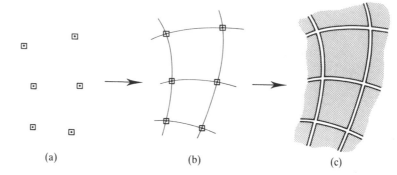

(a)   (b)   (c)

representation; a discussion of these is postponed until Chapter 6. At this
stage, for the sake of completeness, both methods are simply outlined; this
will suffice as an introduction for the more detailed information given in
Chapter 6.

The first method, called **surface fitting**, is basically a particular
method of doing surface interpolation. A set of points is made available
which lie in the surface of the object to be represented and a patch description is produced from these points. Analogous to fitting a line through a
number of points in a plane, we fit a surface through a number of points in
three-space. Thus the method is suitable for modelling objects from some
abstraction or fitting a surface to points obtained by digitizing a real object.
The difference, of course, between this technique and obtaining a polygon
mesh representation, is that a continuous surface is obtained from the digitized points. Note, however, that in the case of a real object, the patch
surface will not match exactly the surface from which the points were digitized. The exactness of the representation depends on the number of points
through which the surface is fitted or the spatial extent of the patches within
the net.

The principle of the process is shown in Figure 2.10. We start with a
set of points in three-space. The next step fits a curve through the points in
two parametric directions, u and v. This curve network is partitioned into
sets of curvilinear quadrilaterals. (In fact these form the edges of the individual patches.) From each quadrilateral the control points for an individual
patch are obtained. The curve network is 'filled in' with surface patches.
Figure 2.11 shows a curve network obtained from a set of points digitized
from a real object together with the rendered version of the patch description.

The second method in parametric patch modelling is cross-sectional
sweeping. A schematic representation is given in Figure 2.12. A more
detailed description is given in Section 6.9.2. Just as in polygon mesh modelling we define an axis or sweep curve. This will be a cubic curve. A cross-
section is also defined, either from a single cubic curve, as shown in the
figure, or as a set of cubic curve segments. The cross-section curve (or
curves) is placed at appropriate intervals using the same techniques

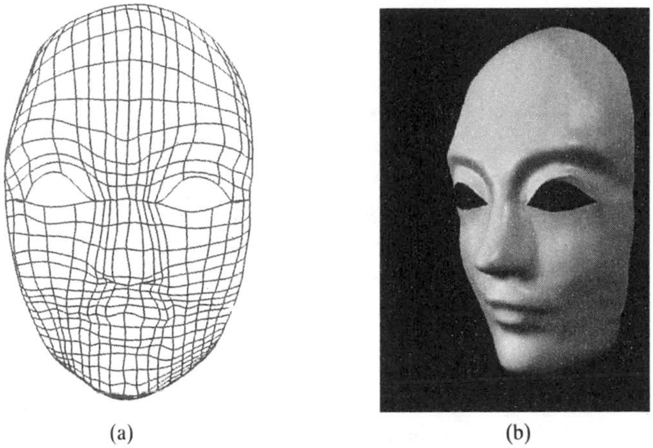

Figure 2.11
(a) A curve network obtained by interpolation through digitized points. (b) A rendered verson of the patch model obtained from (a).

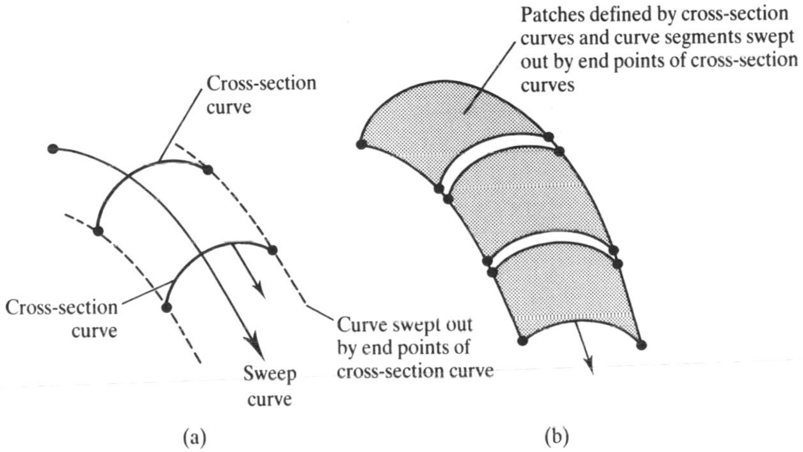

(a) (b)

Figure 2.12
Generating bicubic parametric patches by sweeping a cross-section curve along a sweep curve.

Cross-section curve

Patches defined by cross-section curves and curve segments swept out by end points of cross-section curves

Cross-section curve

Curve swept out by end points of cross-section curve

Sweep curve

(a) (b)

described in Section 2.2.1. Refer to Figure 2.12(a). This shows two cross-section curves placed at two consecutive sample points along the sweep curve. Another pair of cubic curves are swept out by the two end points of the cross-section segment. These four curves form the boundary of a patch and a patch description is then obtained. Placing another cross-section at the next sample point on the sweep curve will enable another patch to be defined and so on. Eventually a generalized cylinder is obtained.

2.4 Constructive solid geometry

The motivation for this type of representation is to facilitate an interactive mode for solid modelling. The idea is that objects are usually parts that will eventually be manufactured by casting, machining or extruding, and they can be built up by combining simple elementary objects called **geometric primitives**. These primitives are, for example, spheres, cones, cylinders or rectangular solids, and they are combined using **boolean set operators** and **linear transformations**. An object is stored as a tree. The leaves contain simple primitives and the nodes store operators or linear transformations. Because the representation defines not only the shape of the object but also its modelling history, simple shape editing is possible. For example, increasing the diameter of a hole through a rectangular solid means a trivial alteration – the radius of the cylinder primitive is increased. This contrasts with the polygon mesh B rep where the same operation is distinctly non-trivial. Even although the constituent polygons of the cylindrical surface are easily accessible in a hierarchical scheme, to generate a new set of polygons means reactivating whatever modelling procedure was used to create the original polygons. Also, account has to be taken of the fact that to maintain the same accuracy more polygons will have to be used.

Boolean set operators are used both as a representational form and as a user interface technique. A user specifies primitive solids and combines these using the boolean set operators. The representation of the object is a reflection or recording of the user interaction operations. Thus we can say that the modelling and representation are not separate (as they are in the other forms described in this chapter). The modelling activity *becomes* the representation. An example will demonstrate the idea.

Figure 2.13 shows the boolean operations possible between solids. Figure 2.13(a) shows the union of two solids. If we consider the objects as 'clouds' of points, the union operation encloses all points lying within the original two bodies. The second example (Figure 2.13b) shows the effect of a difference or subtraction operator. A subtraction operator removes all those points in the first body that are contained within the second. In this case, a cylinder is defined and subtracted from the object produced in Figure 2.13(a). Finally, an example is shown of an intersect operation (Figure 2.13c). Here a solid is defined that is made from the union of a cylinder and a rectangular solid (the same primitives as in Figure 2.13a). This solid then intersects with the object produced in Figure 2.13(b). An intersect operation produces a set of points that are contained by *both* the bodies.

Figure 2.14 shows a constructive solid geometry (CSG) representation that reflects the construction of a simple object. Three original solids appear at the leaves of the tree: two boxes and a cylinder. The boxes are combined using a union operation and a hole is 'drilled' in one of the boxes by defining a cylinder and subtracting it from the two-box assembly.

The power of boolean operations is further demonstrated in the following examples. In the first example (Figure 2.15a), two parts developed separately are combined to make the desired configuration by using the union operator followed by a difference operator. The second example (Figure 2.15b) shows a complex object constructed only from the union of cylinders, which is then used to produce, by subtraction, a complex housing.

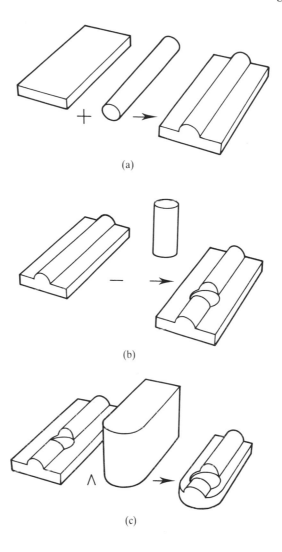

(a)

(b)

Figure 2.13
Boolean operations
between solids in CSG
modelling: (a) union,
(b) subtraction and (c)
intersect.

(c)

Although there are substantial advantages in CSG representation, it does suffer from drawbacks. A practical problem is the computation time required to produce a rendered image of the model. A more serious drawback is that the method imposes limitations on the operations available to create and modify a solid. Boolean operations are global – they affect the whole solid. Local operations, say a detailed modification on one face of a complex object, cannot be easily implemented by using set operations. This fact has led to many solid modellers using B rep as the underlying representation. Incidentally, there is no reason why boolean operations cannot be incorporated in B rep systems. For example, DESIGNBASE (Chiyokura,

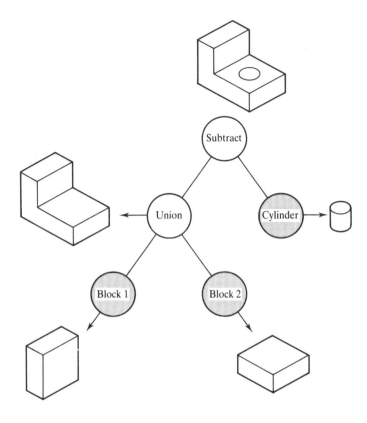

Figure 2.14
A CSG tree reflecting
the construction of a
simple object made
from three primitives.

1988) incorporates boolean operations but uses a B rep to represent the object.

The trade-off between these two representations has resulted in a debate that has lasted for 15 years (see Chiyokura (1988) for a good discussion of the relative merits of each system).

2.5 Space subdivision techniques

Space subdivision techniques are methods that consider the whole of object space and label each point in the space according to object occupancy. Thus in a brute-force scheme we might divide up all of world space into regular or cubic voxels and label each voxel. Clearly, this is very costly in terms of memory consumption, and a number of schemes are available that impose a structural organization on the basic voxel labelling scheme.

In three-dimensional computer graphics such data representations are used most often as secondary or auxiliary data structures. For example, rendering objects that are represented by a CSG tree is not straightforward. One strategy is to convert the CSG tree into an intermediate data structure

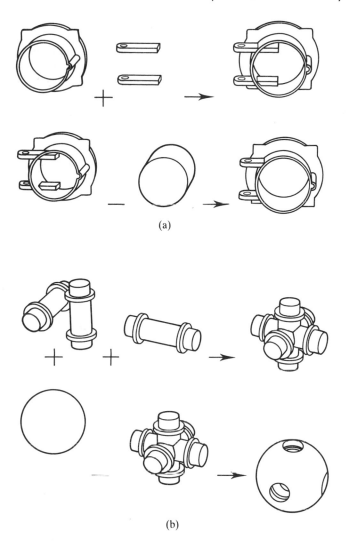

(a)

(b)

Figure 2.15
Examples of
geometrically complex
objects produced from
simple objects and
boolean operations.

of a spatial subdivision type and render from this. This strategy is discussed in more detail in Section 2.6.3.

Another example is the use of spatial subdivision in ray tracing. Here, instead of asking the question: 'does this ray intersect with any objects in the scene?' which implies a very expensive intersection test to be carried out on each object, we pose the question: 'what objects are encountered as we track a ray through voxel space?' This requires no exhaustive search through the primary data structure for possible intersections and is a much more practical strategy. The use of space subdivision in ray tracing is discussed in Chapter 8. We will now look at a few examples, starting with the most frequently encountered – **octrees**.

2.5.1   Octrees

An octree is an established hierarchical data structure that specifies the occupancy of cubic regions of object space. The cubic regions are often called **voxels**. It has been used extensively in image processing and computer graphics (see, for example, Doctor and Torborg (1981), Jacklins and Tanimoto (1980), Meagher (1982) and Yamaguchi *et al.* (1984)).

An octree is a data structure that describes how the objects in a scene are distributed throughout the three-dimensional space occupied by the scene. The ideas involved in an octree representation can be more easily demonstrated by using a **quadtree** to represent the occupancy of a two-dimensional region. Figure 2.16 shows a two-dimensional region containing some simple objects together with a quadtree representation of the region

Figure 2.16
Quadtree representation of a two-dimensional scene at the pixel level. A similar method is used to represent a three-dimensional scene by an octree.

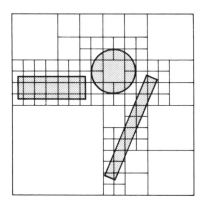

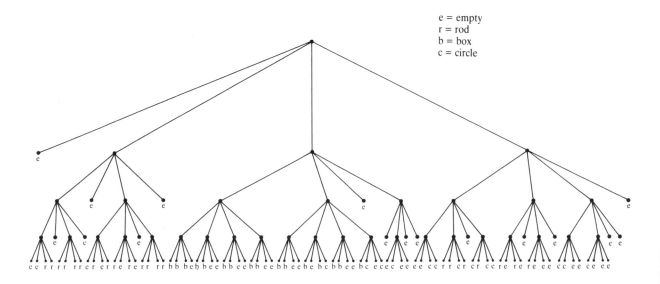

e = empty
r = rod
b = box
c = circle

Figure 2.17
Ordering scheme for
child nodes in quadtree
illustrations.

and the objects. The tree is created by starting with a square region representing the whole of the occupied space. This region is represented by the node at the top of the tree. (In the three-dimensional case, the region would be a cube.) Because the region is occupied by objects, it is subdivided into four subregions, represented by the four child nodes in the tree. Figure 2.17 indicates the ordering scheme used for the child nodes. (In the three-dimensional case, a region would be subdivided into eight subregions, and the node representing the region would have eight children – hence the term octree.) Any subregion that is occupied by objects is further subdivided until the size of the subregion corresponds to the maximum resolution required of the representation scheme.

Thus, there are two types of terminal node in the tree. Some terminal nodes correspond to subregions that are unoccupied by objects, while others correspond to cells of minimum size that are occupied by part of an object. Note that, in the two-dimensional case, objects have been represented by their boundaries and the interior of an object counts as unoccupied space. In the three-dimensional case, objects are represented by their surfaces and we would only subdivide regions that contain parts of the surface.

There are actually two ways in which the octree decomposition of a scene can be used to represent the scene. First, an octree as described above can be used in itself as a complete representation of the objects in the scene. The set of cells occupied by an object constitute the representation of the object. However, for a complex scene, high-resolution work would require the decomposition of occupied space into an extremely large number of cells and this technique requires enormous amounts of data storage. A common alternative is to use a standard data structure representation of the objects and to use the octree as a representation of the distribution of the objects in the scene. In this case, a terminal node of a tree representing an occupied region would be represented by a pointer to the data structure for any object intersecting that region. Figure 2.18 illustrates this possibility in the two-dimensional case. Here the region subdivision has stopped as soon as a region is encountered that intersects only one object. A region represented by a terminal node is not necessarily completely occupied by the object associated with that region. The shape of the object within the region would be described by its data structure representation. In the case of a surface model representation of a scene, the 'objects' would be polygons or patches.

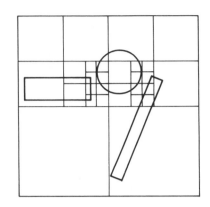

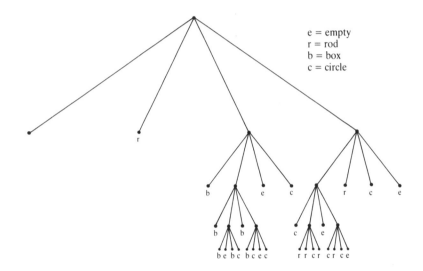

Figure 2.18
Quadtree
representation of a
two-dimensional scene
down to the level of
cells containing at most
a single object.
Terminal nodes for
cells containing objects
are represented by a
pointer to a data
structure
representation of the
object.

In general, an occupied region represented by a terminal node could intersect with several polygons and would be represented by a list of pointers into the object data structures.

2.5.2   BSP trees

The auxiliary structure used to represent the subdivision is essentially an octree, but the precise data structure representation used to index the octree differs from those described previously. It is termed a **binary space partitioning tree**, or **BSP tree**.

Figure 2.19 demonstrates the idea in two dimensions. It contains a one-level subdivision of a square region together with the one-level quadtree representation and the corresponding BSP tree. A simple extension to three dimensions enables an octree to be coded as a BSP tree. Each non-terminal node in the BSP tree represents a single partitioning plane that divides occupied space into two. A terminal node represents a region that is not further subdivided and would contain pointers to data structure representations of the objects intersecting that region (again typically one or two).

A BSP tree would be used in ray tracing (see Chapter 8) in just the same way as in the basic octree technique described earlier. To track a ray into a new region, a point (x, y, z) in that region is generated. The node in the tree corresponding to this point is found by checking the point (x, y, z) against the plane equation at each node and following the appropriate branch at each node. The ray is then checked for intersection with any objects in the region represented by the terminal node of the BSP tree that is found by this search.

Figure 2.19
Quadtree and BSP tree representations of a one-level subdivision of a two-dimensional region.

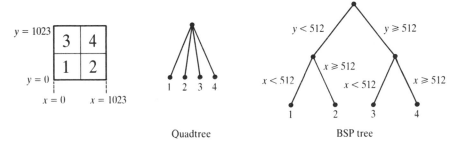

Quadtree   BSP tree

Adaptive subdivision with a BSP tree
When a BSP tree is used to represent a subdivision of space into cubic cells, it shows no significant advantage over a direct data structure encoding of the octree. However, nothing said above requires that the subdivision should be into cubic cells. In fact, the idea of a BSP tree was originally introduced by Fuchs (1980), where the planes used to subdivide space could be at any orientation. In Fuchs (1980), the BSP structure was used as an aid to sorting the planes in a scene into a back-to-front ordering consistent with a given view point. The planes used to subdivide space were the planes defined by the polygons constituting the scene. These planes could lie at any orientation.

In ray tracing, it is convenient if the partitioning planes lie at right angles to the axes as this simplifies the test to see on which side of a plane a point lies. However, a scheme where the position of the partitioning planes depends on the distribution of the objects within occupied space has certain advantages.

Objects will often be unevenly distributed throughout occupied space. This is particularly the case when the 'objects' are actually patches used to approximate the surfaces of real objects. A single real object will be

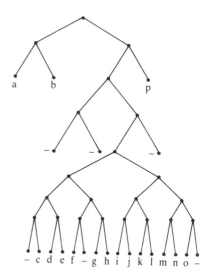

Figure 2.20
Straightforward
subdivision of a
two-dimensional scene
containing 'objects'
a–p unevenly
distributed throughout
the scene. The search
path length in the tree
for most objects is 8.

represented by a large cluster of patches in space and there will be relatively
large regions of empty space between objects.

We can easily illustrate the idea of adaptive partitioning in two dimensions and give some idea of why it is advantageous. Figures 2.20 and 2.21
show two alternative partitions of a region containing 16 objects labelled 'a'
to 'p'. These objects are rather unevenly distributed throughout this region.
In Figure 2.20, a straightforward quadtree subdivision has been used and
this has been represented by a BSP tree. The maximum depth of this tree is
eight, and this would be the maximum length of search required to identify
the region in which a given point lies.

In Figure 2.21, adaptive partitioning has been used. At each step, a
partitioning line has been chosen that divides the current region in such a
way that the region contains equal numbers of objects on either side of the
line. This results in a more balanced BSP tree in which the maximum search
length is four.

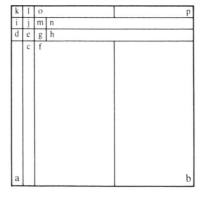

Figure 2.21
Adaptive BSP
subdivision of a
two-dimensional scene
with unevenly
distributed objects. The
maximum search path
length in the BSP tree
is reduced to 4.

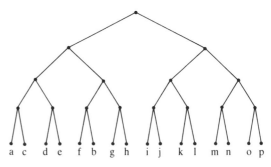

2.6   Rendering strategies

This section briefly overviews the main or common rendering strategies that are used in conjunction with the object representation modes described above. The idea is to give you an overall view of the rendering process; the detailed operations that are carried out in each stage of the process are covered in later chapters. Bringing overviews of the different strategies together at this stage gives you a chance to consider the rendering implications of the different representational forms from a comparative point of view.

Rendering is a jargon word that has come to mean 'the collection of operations necessary to project a view of an object or a scene onto a view surface'. The object is lit and its interaction with a light source is calculated to produce a shaded version of the scene. The major rendering strategies are determined by the object representation and the algorithm options available for the internal processes. At this stage we will look at how the object representation influences things.

2.6.1   Rendering polygonal objects

As we have already discussed, polygonal objects are by far the most common representational form in computer graphics, and fixed program hardware is now available on many graphics workstations which renders an object or objects from a polygonal database.

The input to a polygonal renderer is a list of polygons and the output is a colour for each pixel on the screen. The major advantage of polygonal renderers is that algorithms have evolved that treat polygons as single entities or units. This makes for very fast and simple processing. However, we should note that these advantages are eroded as objects become more and more complex. Contexts, where objects are described by hundreds of thousands of polygons, are not uncommon. An example was shown in Figure 2.5.

The best way to break down the overall rendering process is to consider an object description through a number of **coordinate spaces**. In each space, operations are carried out. The different coordinate spaces facilitate certain processes and specifications (Figure 2.22).

An object is usually stored in a database using vertex coordinates that are expressed in a **local** or **modelling coordinate system**. An origin may be a convenient point located in the object itself, for example the corner of a cube.

To build up a scene, objects specified in a modelling coordinate system (Figure 2.23a) may have three-dimensional transformations applied to them. This embeds the object in **world coordinate space**, a space common to all objects in a scene (Figure 2.23b). In this space we also establish the

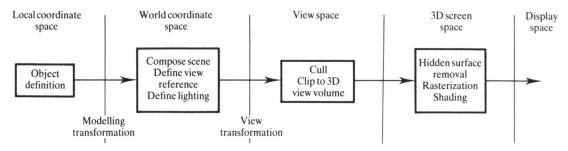

Figure 2.22
A 3D rendering
pipeline.

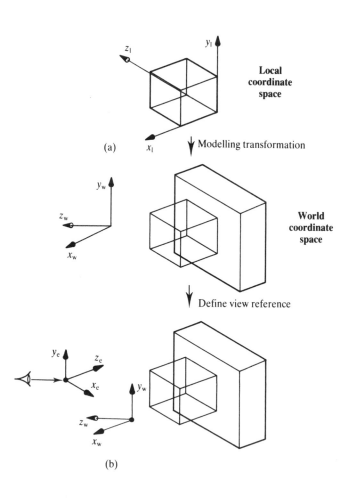

Figure 2.23
A simple example
processed by the
rendering pipeline.

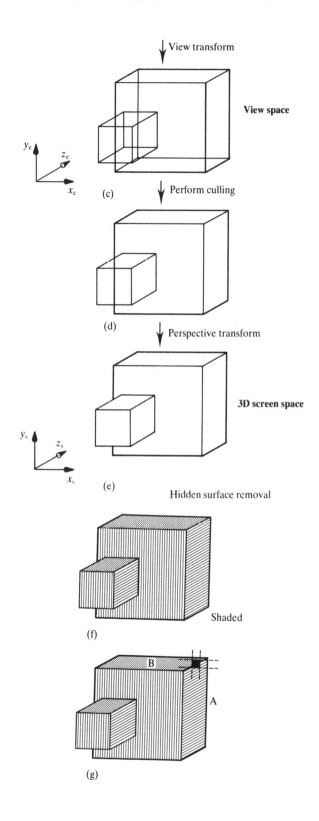

Figure 2.23 cont.

position of the light source, or sources, that illuminate the scene. In world coordinate space a **view reference** is set up. This is the view coordinate system origin. (This may be the actual point from which the object is viewed – the **view point**. Such details are left to Chapter 3, which gives a complete description of viewing systems.)

The object is transformed into **view** or **eye coordinate space** (Figure 2.23c) and it is in this space that the various specifications concerning the view are made. We need to establish, for example, a viewing direction, how far away from the scene a viewer is, what kind of projection onto the view plane is required, and so on. Sometimes the notion of a synthetic camera is employed. This gives the useful analogy of the external and internal attributes of the camera. The position of the camera and the direction in which it is pointing are external attributes. The nature of the picture formed on the film depends on internal attributes, such as lens type, which are analogous to options that can be specified in a comprehensive viewing system.

In eye space an operation is performed known as **culling** (Figure 2.23d). This removes entire polygons that cannot possibly be visible from the view point. The difference between culling and **hidden surface removal** can be seen by comparing Figure 2.23(d) with Figure 2.23(e). The front-facing polygon of the larger object is partially hidden by the smaller cube. Culling removes three faces from each cube, but all of the front face of the larger solid is deemed to be visible. A general hidden surface removal algorithm solves this problem as it deals with visibility at a subpolygon level. The culling operation only considers polygons in their entirety for each object and it cannot resolve the overlapping object problem. Culling is described in detail in Section 5.2.

The final two operations that are carried out on the polygons are **shading** and **rasterization** (Figures 2.23f and g). For a common type of rendering, described in Chapter 5, these operations are carried out in three-dimensional screen space. Shading compares the orientation of each polygon with the light source direction and assigns a shade to the interior of the polygon. Rasterization works out which value to allot to each pixel in the projection. As can be seen from Figure 2.23(g) this is a non-trivial process. It involves a conversion from the precise geometric specification of the polygon to a spatial approximation. A simple renderer may allot the shade of face A to the pixel shown. A more elaborate strategy may discern that the pixel shown is overlapped by two faces and allot a shade intermediate to that allocated to faces A and B to the pixel. Such considerations are the province of **anti-aliasing** algorithms.

In the process described above, the first four operations are common to any renderer and involve transformations. The final operations may vary among renderers, depending on the algorithms selected to perform hidden surface removal, shading and rasterization. Also, these processes are usually non-separable and non-consecutive. For the most common renderer design they are all carried out simultaneously in the innermost pixel loop of the process.

Finally, a process not shown in Figure 2.23(e) is clipping to a three-dimensional **view volume**. A computer graphics system differs from a real camera in one important respect – a three-dimensional view volume can be specified. A volume region in view space can be set up and any object information outside this space removed. Thus, for example, we could remove all objects or part objects within a certain distance of the camera. The implied three-dimensional clipping operation is carried out in eye space.

A point not discussed so far is the order in which polygons are fetched from the database. We have implied that the pipeline treats polygons as single entities and if one polygon at a time is passed down the pipeline, then this constrains the selection of the hidden surface removal algorithm. A particular 'flow' organization that is recommended and discussed in Chapter 5 is a 'by polygon Z-buffer' approach. This method implies that individual polygons can be fetched from the database in any order, processed as an independent unit and their shaded version stored in the screen memory which is continually updated as more polygons pass through the pipeline. In the time that it takes to pass all the polygons through the renderer, the image on the screen may change many times as polygons nearer to the viewer obscure those already on the screen that are farther away.

2.6.2 Rendering a parametric patch net

The best approach to rendering bicubic parametric patches is to preprocess the representation and convert the patches into planar polygons. This results in low code complexity (although there are certain problems which are discussed in Section 6.6).

On the face of it this is something of a contradiction; why, having modelled an object using the higher accuracy of patch representation, do we resort to approximating it with polygons? There are two justifications. First, it may be that the original patch representation is necessary because, for example, an interactive modelling environment is required. Second, as far as accuracy is concerned, the patch representation is converted into polygons via a subdivision or splitting process and we have complete control over the extent of the subdivision and the final size of the polygons. We can even make the polygon size depend on the local curvature of the patch – an ideal that we referred to when discussing polygon mesh representation. Another advantage of the method is that it acts as as unification with polygon mesh rendering. As was implied earlier, rendering software and fixed program hardware for polygonal models is readily available.

Note that, in general, there will far more polygons in the converted model than there are patches in the parametric model.

Again, we will simply overview the process deferring consideration of detail until Chapter 6. The preprocess that allows us to convert a patch net

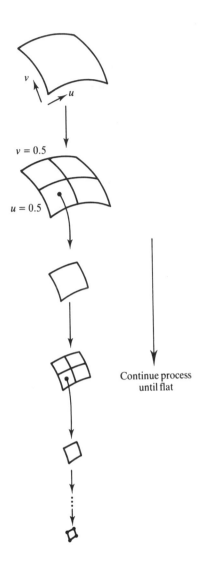

Figure 2.24
A representation of the
patch splitting process.

into a set of polygons contains just two stages. The first is basis conversion. If the patch basis is not Bézier, then we convert the patch representation to this form. This just involves matrix multiplication. This step considerably simplifies the second stage – patch splitting itself. Figure 2.24 gives an idea of the process. A patch is simply subdivided until a flatness criterion is satisfied. Subdivision is carried out by 'drawing' isoparametric curves at each level ($u = 0.5$, $v = 0.5$) which define four patches within the original. The flatness criterion is a simple geometric test that looks at the distance between a plane through the corner points of the patch and the patch surface.

2.6.3   Rendering a CSG description

Rendering strategies for CSG models are disparate. The distinguishing feature of CSG representation is that it is not a boundary representation. In the other two forms the surface represented is the boundary of the object dividing three-space into two regions – internal and external to the object. In CSG representation, the object database is a tree that relates a set of primitive objects to each other via boolean operations. You will recall that this representation regime facilitates powerful interactivity. The price that we pay for this is an expensive and complex rendering strategy.

The main problem involved in rendering CSG objects is how to derive a boundary representation from the CSG database. Three techniques have evolved:

(1) CSG ray tracing,

(2) conversion to a voxel representation followed by volume rendering (Chapter 9), and

(3) using a version of the Z-buffer algorithm (Chapter 5).

Here we will briefly look at the first of these approaches. This is a fairly straightforward adaption of the standard ray tracing techniques described in Chapter 8.

The evaluation of an object from a CSG description can be achieved by reducing the problem to one dimension. To do this we cast a ray from each pixel in the view plane. In the simplest (parallel projection) case we explore the space of the object with a set of parallel rays. The process divides into two stages. First, consider a single ray. Every primitive instance is compared against this ray to see if it intersects the primitive. This means solving a line quadric intersection test, as described in Chapter 8. Any intersections are sorted in Z depth. We have a ray/primitive classification for each ray (Figure 2.25) and can now look at any boolean combinations between the first two primitives encountered along the ray. From Figure 2.26 it is easily seen that evaluating the boolean operations between primitives along a ray is straightforward. A shading value can then be allocated to the pixel by a simple reflection model applied at the first intersection along the ray. Note from Figure 2.26 that this point varies according to the boolean operations between the primitives.

Ray tracing in this way is the 'classical' method of rendering the CSG model. It is, however, extremely expensive, as we shall discover in Chapter 8. Finally, note that the method integrates into a single model:

(1) evaluation of a boundary representation from a CSG description,

(2) hidden surface removal – only intersections with the two primitives nearest to the viewer are considered,

(3) shading.

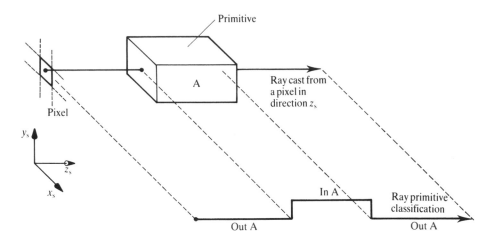

Figure 2.25
Deriving a
ray/primitive
classification.

Note that all operations take place in screen space and we would map directly from the space of the CSG description into screen space. We bypass the complexities of view space if we use a parallel projection as described earlier.

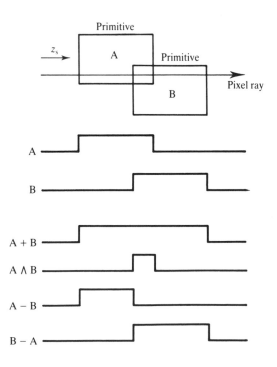

Figure 2.26
Evaluating boolean
operations along a ray.

Projects, notes and suggestions ━━━━━━━━━

2.1 Volume sweeping

Volume sweeping is a common technique in CAD for generating ducted solids. For example, a toroid can be generated by sweeping a circle around the circumference of another circle.

Generate a wireframe model of, say, a toroid, in this manner. A polygon mesh representation can be obtained, for the purposes of a wireframe, by sweeping a cross-sectional polygon with, say, n vertices around a circle and generating $n - 1$ polygons (on the fly) as the cross-section is moved from one incremental position to the other.

A parametric representation for the purpose of vertex generation is:

$$x = (R + r \cos \phi) \cos \theta$$
$$y = (R + r \cos \phi) \sin \theta$$
$$z = r \sin \phi$$

This scheme is shown in Figure 2.27 and will result in the standard program structure for this method of a nested loop.

Note that, in general, there are potential problems with this technique that you may have to consider. For example, with the toroid, the size of the polygons on the inside is less than those on the outside and this discrepancy is a function of both the generating radius and the radius of the cross-section. Such discrepancies can cause visible shading defects.

Investigate variations on the toroid: for example, modulate the generating radius with a sine wave (whose amplitude is small with respect to the radius).

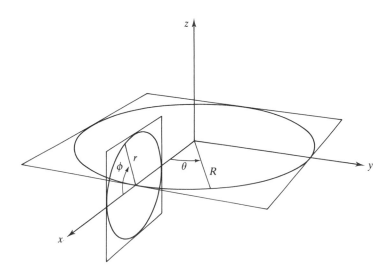

Figure 2.27
Parametric scheme for generating a wireframe toroid.

2.2   Volume sweeping and modelling

Using suitable two-dimensional interactive techniques (see, for example, rubber-banding in Foley *et al.* (1989)) design a system that enables any two-dimensional piecewise linear shape to be developed.

Input this shape as a cross-section to a module that derives a three-dimensional polygon mesh model by rotating the cross-section around a selected circumference.

2.3   Ducting (extruding and rotating)

Use circular cross-sections to generate a polygon mesh model of a fibre optics cable as shown in Figure 2.28. This particular model is not well visualized by a wireframe. Short of rendering, how can the wireframe display be improved?

Figure 2.28
General ducting, creating a fibre optics cable by translating or extruding the cross-section and rotating.

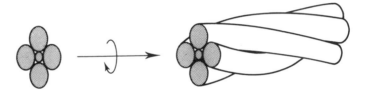

2.4   Quadric surfaces

Using a similar technique to Project 2.1 build up a library of polygon mesh objects from quadric surfaces such as those shown in Figure 2.29 whose definitions are:

- Ellipsoid

$$x^2/a^2 + y^2/b^2 + z^2/c^2 - 1 = 0$$

where a, b and c are the semi-axes of the ellipse. $(0,0,0)$ is the centre of the ellipsoid and the solid can be generated by revolving:

$$x^2/a^2 + z^2/c^2 - 1 = 0 \qquad y = 0$$

contained in the $x-z$ plane about the z axis.

- Hyperboloid:

$$x^2/a^2 + y^2/b^2 - z^2/c^2 - 1 = 0$$

and

$$x^2/a^2 + y^2/b^2 - z^2/c^2 + 1 = 0$$

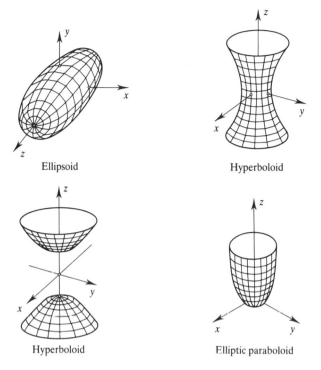

Figure 2.29
Quadric surfaces.

(0,0,0) is the centre of the object and the hyperboloid is obtained by revolving:

$$x^2/a^2 - z^2/c^2 \pm 1 = 0 \qquad y = 0$$

about the z axis.

- Elliptic paraboloid:

$$x^2/a^2 + y^2/b^2 = z$$

rotate:

$$x^2/a^2 - z = 0 \qquad y = 0$$

about the z axis.

3 | Viewing Systems

3.1 Introduction

Although various three-dimensional display devices exist, most computer graphics view surfaces are two-dimensional. Thus a three-dimensional pipeline – the jargon term used to describe the various processes in converting from three-dimensional world coordinate space to a two-dimensional representation – must contain a projective transformation and a viewing transformation, the minimum requirements to convert a three-dimensional scene to a two-dimensional projection.

A comprehensive study of viewing systems is necessary for a number of reasons. Even although you may be in the fortunate position of not having to implement a viewing system, the use of any system requires a firm understanding of the way in which the various parameters determine the nature of the projection on the screen.

For reasons that will become clear, it is easiest to consider the entire transformation of the set of vertices, representing an object, onto a two-dimensional view surface in two parts. We can consider a transformation, T_{view} from a world coordinate system to a viewing coordinate system (x_v, y_v, z_v). Here vertices are expressed in a left-handed coordinate system with the origin sometimes known as the **view point** or **view reference point**. In this text we mostly consider this point to be the position of a viewer's eye or the position at which a virtual camera is placed. The second transformation, T_{pers} or T_{ort} projects three-dimensional points in **view space** onto the two-dimensional **view plane**. Separating the transformations in this way means that we can isolate the geometry of the projections from the fact that, in general, the projection plane can have any position and orientation in world coordinate space.

A minimum viewing system is thus a set of parameters that enables a series of transformations to be set up which have the effect of mapping points in world coordinate space onto the view surface. Such a system allows a user to specify a projective transformation and it enables the view plane to be positioned anywhere in world coordinate space.

A full viewing system will also determine a **view volume**, that subset of world coordinate space which is to be included in the transformation process. This definition enables a user to select particular regions of interest within the world coordinate system. A requirement connected with this is the definition of a window in the view plane – a **view plane window**.

To explain how viewing systems work we have adopted the approach of developing a more and more elaborate system, starting with a simple system and gradually adding more and more facilities. Five systems are described: an extremely simple but limited four-parameter system; three versions of a practical system (differing in their interface requirements and whether a view volume is incorporated or not); and a completely general system based on the GKS and PHIGS model. Working through the evolution of a more and more complex viewing system will also help in understanding the extra factors involved in general viewing systems.

For the first three systems, we describe the transformation T_{view} that transforms points from world coordinate space to view space. The first simple system is heavily constrained – the viewing direction is always towards the world coordinate origin. The second and third systems are less constrained, allowing the viewer to look in any direction. Section 3.5 describes the projective transformation, T_{pers}, from view space onto the view plane. This transformation is common to the first three systems. A complete transformation is formed by selecting one of the three T_{view} transformations and concatenating with the common T_{pers}. Viewing system IV introduces the idea of a view volume and a view plane window, but for ease of implementation does not incorporate the full generality of the standards system. Viewing system V describes a full standard system.

3.1.1   A note, a warning, a tale of woe

Right-handed coordinate systems are a standard mathematical convention. The following sections attempt to describe how viewing systems work through a hierarchy of five systems that increase in complexity. In three-dimensional computer graphics the world coordinate system is conventionally a right-handed system. When considering viewing systems it is pedagogically advantageous to consider the view space (or eye space) and the three-dimensional screen space as left-handed coordinate systems. This is because in view space larger z values are farther from the viewer, and in three-dimensional screen space increasing z values 'go into' the screen – another natural interpretation. However, this eminently sensible tradition was abandoned by PHIGS (viewing system V, Section 3.9) in favour of making *all* coordinate systems right handed. Your author stubbornly persists in the view that this uniformity confers no advantages, but PHIGS is an international standard and this we must recognize. This text thus adopts left-handed systems for the view and screen space in viewing systems I–IV, but conforms to PHIGS for viewing system V. The geometrically trivial difference that this makes should diminish the potential for confusion and we retain the intuitive advantages of left-handed systems for viewing systems I–IV.

3.2 Viewing system I

A summary of the features of this viewing system is as follows:

(1) Interface requirements are:
    (a) one three-dimensional point (specified by two angles and a distance) and
    (b) one view plane distance.

(2) Viewing direction is constrained.

(3) View plane orientation is constrained.

(4) No view volume is specified.

(5) No view plane window is specified.

(6) Centre of projection is the view point and a perspective projection is used.

In this system a user specifies a view point or eye point (three parameters or a vector) and a view plane distance (one parameter). A viewing direction or view plane normal is established by the line from the view point to the world coordinate origin. This constraint is fine for single object scenes, where the object is disposed about the world coordinate origin, but is an unworkable constraint in the case of multi-object scenes. It is simple to implement and understand and is a useful system in which to gain experience of the interaction of parameters in a viewing system.

A view coordinate system (x_v, y_v, z_v) is established at the view point. z_v is coincident with the viewing direction and the direction of y_v can be set, for example by embedding it in the plane containing z_v and z_w. A perspective projection is used with the centre of projection at the view point and the fourth parameter is the distance d from the view point to the view plane (this is used when the scene is projected onto the view plane as described in Section 3.5). A screen coordinate system is established in the view plane by making y_s parallel to y_v (see Section 3.5). This set-up is shown in Figure 3.1. An easy and intuitive user interface is possible if a spherical coordinate system is used to specify the view point position. Consider the line from the view point to the world coordinate origin. μ is the distance from the world

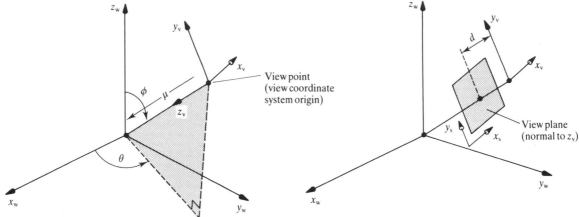

Figure 3.1
Viewing system I: a simple (four-parameter) viewing system. A view coordinate system is established at the view point. y_v is parallel to y_s and z_v points towards the world coordinate origin. The world coordinate system is right handed, the view coordinate system left handed.

coordinate origin to the view point along this line, θ is the angle that the plane containing the line and the perpendicular to the viewing system origin makes with the x_w axis and ϕ is the angle the line makes with the z_w axis.

To transform points from one system to another we need a combination of translations and rotations. For example, to change the origin of a coordinate system from $(0,0,0,1)$ to $(t_x,t_y,t_z,1)$ we require the transformation:

$$\begin{bmatrix} 1 & 0 & 0 & 0 \\ 0 & 1 & 0 & 0 \\ 0 & 0 & 1 & 0 \\ -t_x & -t_y & -t_z & 1 \end{bmatrix}$$

and we note that this is the inverse of the transformation that would take a point from $(0,0,0,1)$ to $(t_x,t_y,t_z,1)$. Similarly, the transformation matrix for clockwise rotation of a coordinate system is the same as that for counter-clockwise rotation of a point relative to the coordinate system.

The following transformation transforms the world coordinate points to view coordinate points:

$$[x_v \; y_v \; z_v \; 1] = [x_w \; y_w \; z_w \; 1] \begin{bmatrix} -\sin\theta & -\cos\theta\cos\phi & -\cos\theta\sin\phi & 0 \\ \cos\theta & -\sin\theta\cos\phi & -\sin\theta\sin\phi & 0 \\ 0 & \sin\theta & -\cos\phi & 0 \\ 0 & 0 & \mu & 1 \end{bmatrix}$$

$$= [x_w \; y_w \; z_w \; 1] \, T_{\text{view}}$$

This matrix is derived in four steps:

(1) The translation that takes the world coordinate origin to the view point.
(2) Rotate through $(90° - \theta)$ in a clockwise direction about the new z axis.

(3) Rotate through $(180° - \phi)$ about the new z axis, making the new z axis point towards the world coordinate origin.

(4) Transform to a left-handed system.

A full derivation of this transformation is given in Appendix A.

3.3   Viewing system II

A summary of the features of this viewing system is:

(1) Interface requirements are:
   (a) two three-dimensional points,
   (b) one twist angle, and
   (c) one view plane distance.
(2) No view volume is specified.
(3) No view plane window is specified.
(4) Centre of projection is the view point and a perspective projection is used.

The problem with three-dimensional viewing systems is that as the system becomes more and more general, to include for example, view volumes, view plane window and oblique projections, the number of parameters required to specify a view grows, and makes a user interface consequently more difficult. Two compromise systems, that do not allow full generality, but which overcome the limitation of the first system and allow a reasonably easy interface are now described.

The second system is best introduced by considering a synthetic camera (Figure 3.2). In this viewing system we can point the camera in any direction; the view plane normal or viewing direction is no longer constrained to point at the origin of the world coordinate system. Also, the camera can be rotated about the view plane normal by specifying a twist angle. These are the normal degrees of freedom that a real photographer would use to position a real camera.

We establish a camera position C, which is the view reference point or origin of the view coordinate system and the centre of projection. A view plane, normal to the z_v axis, is specified at a distance d from this origin as before. The direction in which the camera is pointing is determined by a point of interest or focus point F. These two points, C and F, define the z_v axis of the viewing coordinate system, and a twist angle establishes the rotation of the camera about this axis and the direction of the y_s axis in the view plane. C is input as a point (e, f, g). F is also input as a point and a unit vector (with components (a, b, c)) is derived by subtracting C from F and normalizing the resulting vector. The system thus requires a user to specify

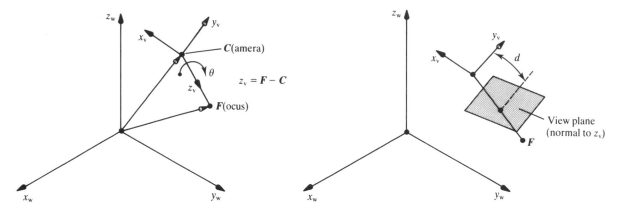

Figure 3.2
Viewing system II: using a camera point C, a focus point F and a twist angle θ that rotates a virtual camera about its viewing direction $F - C$. The world coordinate system is right handed, the view coordinate system is left handed.

two three-dimensional points C and F, a twist angle and a view plane distance d.

The notion of a camera is especially useful in three-dimensional animation where the path of one (or a number) of cameras may be choreographed as part of a sequence.

The viewing transformation can be derived from the following steps. First, if the camera is positioned at the world coordinate origin, pointing in a direction defined by the point of interest F, then it can be shown that:

$$V = \begin{bmatrix} \dfrac{b}{(1-c^2)^{1/2}} & \dfrac{-a}{(1-c^2)^{1/2}} & a & 0 \\ \dfrac{-ac}{(1-c^2)^{1/2}} & \dfrac{-bc}{(1-c^2)^{1/2}} & b & 0 \\ 0 & (1-c^2)^{1/2} & c & 0 \\ 0 & 0 & 0 & 1 \end{bmatrix}$$

This comes about by expressing the required direction as two rotations using vector notation for the sines and cosines of the two angles.

If we then generalize the camera position, placing it at point (e,f,g), and include rotation through an angle θ about $C-F$ then the three components of the view transformation matrix are:

$$V_1 = \begin{bmatrix} \cos\theta & \sin\theta & 0 & 0 \\ -\sin\theta & \cos\theta & 0 & 0 \\ 0 & 0 & 1 & 0 \\ 0 & 0 & 0 & 1 \end{bmatrix}$$

This component comes about by considering a view system with the camera at the origin pointing along the x axis and rotated through angle θ. To transform world coordinate points into this system we require V_1.

The second component is:

$$V_2 = V \text{ (as above)}$$

The camera is still at the origin but pointing in a direction $F-C$. To transform into this system we now require V_1V_2.

The third component is:

$$V_3 = \begin{bmatrix} 1 & 0 & 0 & 0 \\ 0 & 1 & 0 & 0 \\ 0 & 0 & 1 & 0 \\ -e & -f & -g & 1 \end{bmatrix}$$

Finally, the camera is at point (e,f,g) and we have,

$$T_{\text{view}} = V_1 \, V_2 \, V_3$$

Note that a singularity exists when $c^2 = 1$. This is when the camera is pointing vertically up or vertically down, $(a,b,c) = (0,0,1)$ or $(0,0,-1)$ and should be dealt with by a special case.

This viewing transformation will cope with most situations in computer graphics and it avoids the difficult user interface associated with general viewing systems advocated by the standards GKS and PHIGS.

3.4   Viewing system III

A summary of the features of this viewing system are:

(1) Interface requirements are:
   (a) two vectors and one three-dimensional point, and
   (b) one view plane distance.
(2) No view volume is specified.
(3) No view plane window is specified.
(4) Centre of projection is the view point and a perspective projection is used.

An alternatively specified practical system and one that is closer to the standard philosophy of GKS and PHIGS is to use vectors in the user interface rather than three-dimensional points and an angle. Thus there is no essential difference between viewing systems II and III except in the specification and interface implications. Also, we introduce an extra parameter (a vector) that enables us to establish a right- or left-handed coordinate system for the view space. The system is specified by two vectors and a position (Figure 3.3):

(1) A camera position C. This point is also the centre of projection and is the same as the point C in the previous system.
(2) A viewing direction vector N (the positive z_v axis), a vector normal to the view plane.

(3) An 'up' vector **V** that orients the camera about the view direction and establishes with **N** the orientation of the view plane window within the view plane.

(4) An (optional) vector **U** to denote the direction of increasing x in the eye coordinate system. This establishes a right- or left-handed coordinate system (**UVN**).

This time we consider T_{view} to split into a translation **T** and a change of basis **B**:

$$T_{\text{view}} = TB$$

where:

$$T = \begin{bmatrix} 1 & 0 & 0 & 0 \\ 0 & 1 & 0 & 0 \\ 0 & 0 & 1 & 0 \\ -C_x & -C_y & -C_z & 1 \end{bmatrix}$$

that is, as V_3 in the previous system.

It can be shown (Fiume, 1989) that **B** is given by:

$$B = \begin{bmatrix} U_x & V_x & N_x & 0 \\ U_y & V_y & N_y & 0 \\ U_z & V_z & N_z & 0 \\ 0 & 0 & 0 & 1 \end{bmatrix}$$

The only problem now is specifying a user interface for the system and mapping whatever parameters are used by the interface into **U**, **V** and **N**. A user needs to specify **C**, **N** and **V**. **C** is easy enough as we have already discussed. **N**, the viewing direction or view plane normal, can be entered, say, using two angles in a spherical coordinate system as in the previous system:

θ the azimuth angle

ϕ the colatitude or elevation angle

Figure 3.3
Viewing system III: using a camera point, a viewing direction vector **N**, an up vector **V** and an optional vector **U**. The world coordinate system is right handed, the view coordinate system is left handed.

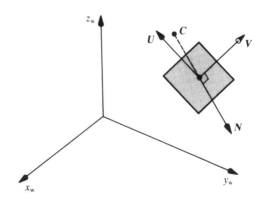

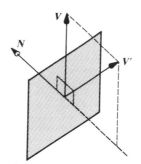

Figure 3.4
Viewing system III.
The up vector *V* can be
calculated from an
'indication' given by
V'.

where:

$$N_x = \sin \phi \cos \theta$$
$$N_y = \sin \phi \sin \theta$$
$$N_z = \cos \phi$$

V is more problematic. For example, a user may require 'up' to be the same sense as 'up' in the world coordinate system. However, this cannot be achieved by setting:

$$V = (0,0,1)$$

because *V* must be perpendicular to *N*. A sensible strategy is to allow a user to specify an approximate orientation for *V*, say *V'* and have the system calculate *V*. Figure 3.4 demonstrates this. *V'* is the user-specified up vector. This is projected onto the view plane:

$$V = V' - (V' . N)N$$

and normalized. *U* can be specified or not depending on the user's requirements. If *U* is unspecified, it is obtained from:

$$U = N \times V$$

resulting in a left-handed coordinate system.

3.5   View plane projection for viewing systems I–III

At this stage we consider the second of the transformations that we require to take us from world coordinate space into screen space. This is the projective transform from view space or eye space that projects the scene information onto the view plane. (A device-dependent transformation would then take us from the view plane into real screen space.)

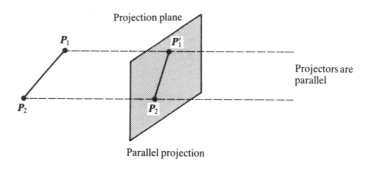

Parallel projection

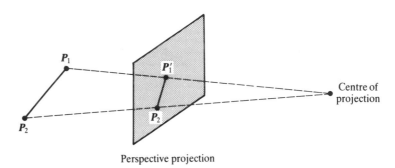

Perspective projection

Figure 3.5
Two points projected
onto a plane using
parallel and
perspective
projections.

Because the viewing surface in computer graphics is deemed to be flat, we consider the class of projections known as **planar geometric projections**. Two basic projections, perspective and parallel, are now described. These projections and the difference in their nature is illustrated in Figure 3.5.

A **perspective projection** is the more popular or common choice in computer graphics because it incorporates foreshortening. In a perspective projection relative dimensions are not preserved, and a distant line is displayed smaller than a nearer line of the same length (Figure 3.6). This effect enables human beings to perceive depth in a two-dimensional photograph or a stylization of three-dimensional reality. A perspective projection is characterized by a point known as the **centre of projection** and the projection of three-dimensional points onto the view plane is the intersection, in the view plane, of the lines from each point to the centre of projection. These lines are called **projectors**.

In viewing systems I–IV we invoke the not impractical constraint that the line from the centre of projection to the centre of the view plane (or, more precisely, the centre of the view plane window) is parallel to the view plane normal. This considerably simplifies the view plane projection mathematics. In viewing system V we consider the implication of removing this constraint.

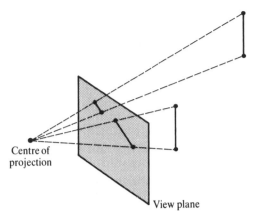

Figure 3.6
In a perspective
projection a distant line
is displayed smaller
than a nearer line of
the same length.

Figure 3.7 shows how a perspective projection is derived. Point P (x_v, y_v, z_v) is a three-dimensional point in the viewing coordinate system. This point is to be projected onto a view plane normal to the z_v axis and positioned at distance d from the origin of this system. Point P' is the projection of this point in the view plane and has two-dimensional coordinates (x_s, y_s) in a view plane coordinate system with the origin at the intersection of the z_v axis and the view plane. In this system we consider the view

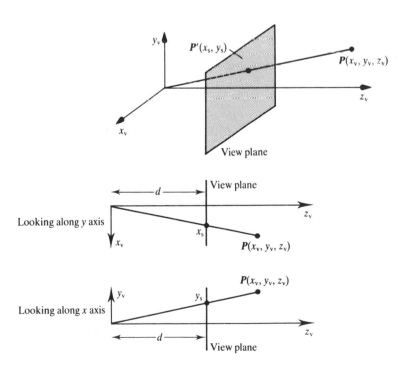

Figure 3.7
Deriving a perspective
transformation.

plane to be the view surface or screen. This point is taken up in the next section.

Similar triangles give:

$$\frac{x_s}{d} = \frac{x_v}{z_v} \qquad \frac{y_s}{d} = \frac{y_v}{z_v}$$

$$x_s = \frac{x_v}{z_v/d} \qquad y_s = \frac{y_v}{z_v/d}$$

To express this non-linear transformation as a 4×4 matrix we can consider it in two parts – a linear part followed by a non-linear part. Using homogeneous coordinates we have:

$$X = x_v$$
$$Y = y_v$$
$$Z = z_v$$
$$w = z_v/d$$

We can now write

$$[X\ Y\ Z\ w] = [x_v\ y_v\ z_v\ 1]\ T_{\text{pers}}$$

where

$$T_{\text{pers}} = \begin{bmatrix} 1 & 0 & 0 & 0 \\ 0 & 1 & 0 & 0 \\ 0 & 0 & 1 & 1/d \\ 0 & 0 & 0 & 0 \end{bmatrix}$$

following this with the perspective divide, we have:

$$x_s = X/w$$
$$y_s = Y/w$$
$$z_s = Z/w$$

In a **parallel projection**, if the view plane is normal to the direction of projection then the projection is orthographic and we have:

$$x_s = x_v \qquad y_s = y_v \qquad z_v = 0$$

Expressed as a matrix:

$$T_{\text{ort}} = \begin{bmatrix} 1 & 0 & 0 & 0 \\ 0 & 1 & 0 & 0 \\ 0 & 0 & 0 & 0 \\ 0 & 0 & 0 & 1 \end{bmatrix}$$

We now look at some simple examples that illustrate how parameters in viewing system III change the projection of a simple object. Figure 3.8 shows five projections. These are:

Figure 3.8
Five examples of
viewing system III. (a)
The reference view. V'
is set to (0,0,1) – the
virtual camera is in the
'up' position. (b) The
same as (a) except that
C has been moved
further away from the
world coordinate
origin. (c) V is given a
non-zero y component
– equivalent to rotating
the virtual camera
about its viewing
direction. (d) As view
(a) but N is changed by
rotating about the z_w
axis (increasing its y
component). (e) As
view (a) except that
both the distance of the
view point from the
origin and d, the view
plane distance, are
reduced to small
integers greatly
exaggerating the
perspective effect.

(a) The reference figure centred at the world coordinate origin. V', the up vector, is set to (0,0,1). That is, the virtual camera is in the 'up' position, where 'up' is deemed to be the direction specified by the z_w axis.

(b) This view is as (a) except that the view point C has been moved further from the world coordinate origin. The same viewing direction has been maintained.

(c) This view is as (a) except that V is given a non-zero y component – equivalent to rotating the camera about the direction it is pointing.

(d) This view is as (a) but N is changed by rotating it about the z_w axis (by increasing its y component).

(e) As (a) except that both the distance of the view point from the origin and d, the view plane distance, are reduced to small integers and become comparable with the extent of the object. This greatly exaggerates the perspective effect.

3.6 Viewing system IV

A summary of the features of this viewing system is:

(1) Interface requirments are:
(a) two vectors and one point, and
(b) one view plane distance (which is also the **near plane distance**) and one **far plane distance**.

(2) A view volume is specified but the view plane is constrained to be coincident with the near plane.

(3) A view window is specified but it is square and symmetrically disposed about the 'centre' of the view plane.

(4) The centre of projection is the view point and a perspective projection is used.

Up to now we have not used the concept of a **view volume** in our simplified viewing systems. This means that in viewing systems I–III all the information in the scene is projected onto the view plane. This has two implications. First, because we are not using a view volume we are relying on a two-dimensional clipping algorithm to eliminate any information in the view plane that falls outside the view plane window. This is fine for wireframe displays, because any line-drawing utilities that we will be using will almost certainly have a clipping utility associated with them. However, for rendered scenes things are not so simple. Second, for the projection to 'make sense' we have to ensure that the view point is *always* outside that volume that encloses the entire scene. It would make no sense, for example, to include in a projection information that was behind the view point.

As far as a general three-dimensional rendering pipeline is concerned, we need to define a view volume. This is a truncated pyramid in view space against which we clip the polygons that make up the scene. To define this view volume we need to specify a near plane, a far plane and a view plane window (Figure 3.9). In this system we make the simplification or constraint that the near plane should be coincident with the view plane. Also to simplify the maths we define a view plane window symmetrically disposed about the view plane centre (the intersection of the line from the view point C in the direction of the viewing direction and the view plane). This is a system that appeared in an early classic textbook on computer graphics (Newman and Sproull, 1981). Incidentally, note from Figure 3.9 that such a (computer graphics) system is significantly different to a real camera system in that

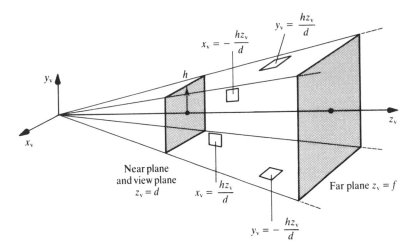

Figure 3.9
Viewing system IV: view frustum formed by six planes and the view volume. This is a left-handed coordinate system.

information immediately in front of the camera can be clipped out. A real camera does not possess (except in the form of optical limitations) a near and a far plane.

The view volume is then specified by six planes:

$$x_v = \pm\frac{hz_v}{d}$$
$$y_v = \pm\frac{hz_v}{d}$$
$$z_v = d$$
$$z_v = f$$

where:

  $2h$ is the view plane window dimension
  d is the view plane distance and the near plane distance
  f is the far plane distance

Plate 2 shows the interaction of an object with a view volume where the object is partially inside and partially outside the view volume.

3.7 View plane projection for viewing system IV

We now require a T_{pers} in terms of these parameters. Also at this stage we define the concept of three-dimensional screen space and a point in such a space as:

$$[x_s, y_s, z_s, 1]$$

where we need to set z_s to a special value (other than z_v). The reason for this is that three-dimensional clipping is best performed in this space for reasons explained in Section 3.8. Also, the most popular option for hidden surface removal, the Z-buffer algorithm (Chapter 5), has to be carried out in this space. (The Z-buffer algorithm can be used for viewing systems I–III with z_s set equal to z_v). The screen space depth considerations are:

(1) z_s needs to be normalized so that precision is maximized.

(2) Lines in view space need to transform into lines in screen space.

(3) Planes in view space need to transform into planes in screen space.

It can be shown (Newman and Sproull, 1981) that these conditions are satisfied provided the transformation of z takes the form:

$$z_s = A + B/z_v$$

where A and B are constants. These constants are determined from the following constraints:

(1) Choosing $B < 0$ so that as z_v increases then so does z_s. This preserves our intuitive notion of depth. If one point is behind another, then it will have a larger z_v value; if $B < 0$ it will also have a larger z_s value.

(2) Normalizing the range of z_s values so that the range $z_v \in [d,f]$ maps into the range $z_v \in [0,1]$.

The full perspective transformation is now given by:

$$x_s = d\frac{x_v}{hz_v}$$

$$y_s = d\frac{y_v}{hz_v}$$

$$z_s = \frac{f(1 - d/z_v)}{f - d}$$

where the additional constant, h, appearing in the transformation for x_s and y_s, ensures that these values fall in the range $[-1,1]$ over the square screen. Adopting a similar manipulation to that in Section 3.5, we have

$$X = \frac{d}{h}x_v$$

$$Y = \frac{d}{h}y_v$$

$$Z = fz_v/(f - d) - df/(f - d)$$

$$w = z_v$$

giving:

$$[X\ Y\ Z\ w] = [x_v\ y_v\ z_v\ 1]\ T_{pers}$$

where:

$$T_{\text{pers}} = \begin{bmatrix} d/h & 0 & 0 & 0 \\ 0 & d/h & 0 & 1 \\ 0 & 0 & f/(f-d) & 1 \\ 0 & 0 & -df/(f-d) & 0 \end{bmatrix} \quad \textbf{(3.1)}$$

This is then followed by the non-linear so-called perspective divide essential

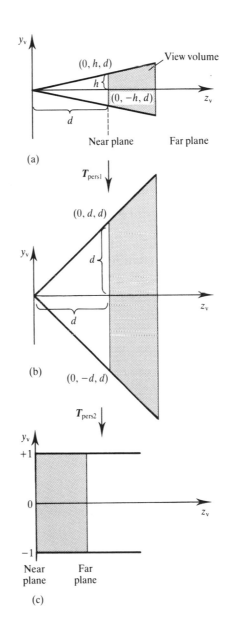

Figure 3.10
Transformation of the view volume into a canonical view volume (a box) using two matrix transformations.

to generating a perspective image. This converts the homogeneous point (X,Y,Z,w) into a three-dimensional point in screen space (x_s, y_s, z_s):

$$x_s = X/w$$
$$y_s = Y/w$$
$$z_s = Z/w$$

It is instructive to convert matrix (3.1) into a product of two matrices:

$$T_{pers} = \begin{bmatrix} d/h & 0 & 0 & 0 \\ 0 & d/h & 0 & 0 \\ 0 & 0 & 1 & 0 \\ 0 & 0 & 0 & 1 \end{bmatrix} \begin{bmatrix} 1 & 0 & 0 & 0 \\ 0 & 1 & 0 & 0 \\ 0 & 0 & f/(f-d) & 1 \\ 0 & 0 & -fd/(f-d) & 0 \end{bmatrix}$$

$$= T_{pers1} T_{pers2}$$

This enables a useful graphical visualization of the process. The first matrix is a scaling (d/h) in x and y. This converts a view volume from a truncated pyramid with sides sloping at an angle determined by h/d into a regular pyramid with sides sloping at 45° (Figure 3.10). For example, point:

$(0,h,d,1)$ transforms to $(0,d,d,1)$

and point:

$(0,-h,d,1)$ transforms to $(0,-d,d,1)$

The second transformation maps the regular pyramid into a box. The near plane maps into the xy plane and the far plane is mapped into $z=1$. For example, point:

$(0,d,d,1)$ transforms to $(0,d,0,d)$

which is equivalent to $(0,1,0,1)$.

3.8   Clipping for viewing system IV

The use of a slightly constrained viewing system provides us with significant benefits when we come to clip objects against the view volume. Clipping involves testing the object against the viewing frustum and this is necessary for the following two reasons:

• A view point or camera position is an arbitrary point initially specified in world space. Clearly we do not wish to deal with objects that do not contribute to the final image, such as objects that are behind the view point, for example.

• The screen space transformation is ill-defined outside the viewing frustum. There is a singularity at $z_v = 0$. Moreover, a mirrored region in homogeneous space, corresponding to negative w, also maps into the viewing frustum.

A given object in relation to the viewing frustum can fall into one of three categories:

(1) The object lies completely outside the viewing frustum in which case it is discarded.

(2) The object lies completely inside the viewing frustum in which case it is transformed into screen space and rendered.

(3) The object intersects the viewing frustum in which case it is clipped against it and then transformed into screen space.

The clipping operation can be performed on the homogeneous coordinates just before the perspective division. Translating the definition of the viewing frustum above into homogeneous coordinates gives us the clipping limits:

$$-w \leq x \leq w$$
$$-w \leq y \leq w$$
$$0 \leq z \leq w$$

The clipping algorithm (Section 5.2) clips all four of the homogeneous coordinates – w is treated no differently to any other of the components.

3.9   Viewing system V (PHIGS)

The final viewing system that we look at is the standard system adopted by GKS and PHIGS.

An unfortunate aspect of the standards viewing systems is that because they afford such generality they are hopelessly cumbersome and difficult to interface with. Even if a subset of parameters is used, the default values for the unused parameters have to be appreciated and understood. Perhaps this is inevitable. The function of a standard, in one sense, is not to reflect common usage but to define a complete set of facilities that a user may require in a general viewing system. That some of these facilities will hardly ever be used is unfortunate.

3.9.1   Overview of viewing system V

We start by overviewing the extensions that PHIGS offers over viewing system IV. These are:

(1) The notion of a view point or eye point that establishes the origin of the view coordinate system and the centre of projection is now discarded. The equivalent of view space in PHIGS is the **view reference coordinate** (VRC) system established by defining a **view reference point** (VRP). A centre of projection is established separately by defining a **projection reference point** (PRP).

(2) Feature 1 means that a line from the centre of projection to the centre of the view plane window need not be parallel to the view plane normal. The implication of this is that oblique projections are possible. This is equivalent, in the virtual camera analogy, to allowing the film plane to tilt with respect to the direction in which the camera is pointing. This effect is used in certain camera designs to correct for perspective distortion in such contexts as photographing a tall building from the ground.

(3) Near and far clipping planes are defined as well as a view plane. In viewing system IV we made the back clipping plane coincident with the view plane.

(4) A view plane window is defined that can have any aspect ratio and can be positioned anywhere in the view plane. In viewing system IV we defined a square window symmetrically disposed about the 'centre' of the view plane.

(5) Multiple view reference coordinate systems can be defined or many views of a scene can be set up.

The main problem with viewing systems I–IV, as far as generality is concerned, is to do with the notion of distance. We have used the idea of a view point distance to reflect the dominant intuitive notion that the further the view point is from the scene, the smaller will be the projection of that scene on the view plane. The problem arises from the fact that in any real system, or in a general computer graphics system, there is no such thing as a view point. We can have a centre of projection and a view plane, and in a camera or eye analogy this is fine. In a camera the view plane or film plane is contained in the camera. The scene projection is determined by both the distance of the camera from the subject and the focal length of the lens. However, in computer graphics we are free to move the view plane at will with respect to the centre of projection and the scene. There is no lens as such. How then do we categorize distance? Do we use the distance of the view plane from the world coordinate origin, the distance of the centre of projection from the world coordinate origin or the distance of the view plane from the centre of projection? The general systems such as PHIGS leave the user to answer that question. It is perhaps this attribute of the PHIGS viewing system that makes it appear cumbersome.

PHIGS categorizes a viewing system into three stages (Figure 3.11). Establishing the position and orientation of the view plane is known as **view orientation**. This requires the user to supply:

- the view reference point (VRP) – a point in world coordinate space;
- the viewing direction or view plane normal (VPN) – a vector in world coordinate space;
- the view up vector (VUV) – a vector in world coordinate space.

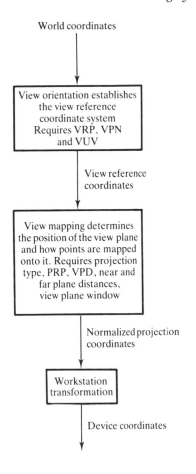

Figure 3.11
Viewing system V:
establishing a viewing
system in PHIGS.

The second stage in the process is known as **view mapping** and determines how points are mapped onto the view plane. This requires:

- the projection type (parallel or perspective);

- the projection reference point (PRP) – a point in VRC space;

- a view plane distance (VPD) – a real in VRC space;

- a back plane and a front plane distance – reals in VRC space;

- view plane window limits – four limits in VRC space;

- projection viewport limits – four limits in normalized projection space (NPC).

This information is used to map information in the VRC or VRCs into **normalized projection coordinates** (NPCs). NPC space is a cube with coordinates in each direction restricted to the range 0–1. The rationale for this space is to allow different VRCs to be set up when more than one view of a scene is required (and mapped subsequently into different view ports on the screen). Each view has its own VRC associated with it, and different views are mapped into NPC space.

The final processing stage is the workstation transformation, that is, the normal device-dependent transformation. These aspects are now described in detail.

3.9.2   The view orientation parameters

In PHIGS we establish a view space coordinate system whose origin is positioned *anywhere* in world coordinate space by the VRP. Together with the VPN and the VUV this defines a right-handed coordinate system with axes *U*, *V* and *N*. *N* is the viewing direction and *UV* defines a plane that is either coincident with or parallel to the view plane. (The VUV has exactly the same function as *V'* in Section 3.4). The cross product of VUV and VPN defines *U* and the cross product of VPN and *U* defines *V*:

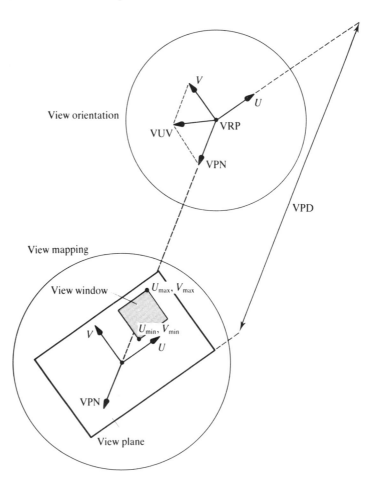

Figure 3.12
PHIGS – view orientation and view mapping parameters. Note that this is a right-handed coordinate system.

$$U = (VUV) \times (VPN)$$
$$V = (VPN) \times U$$

An interface to establish the VPN can easily be set up using the suggestion given in Project 3.1. (Note that the VUV must not be parallel to the VPN.) The geometric relationship between the orientation and mapping parameters is shown in Figure 3.12.

Thus the view orientation stage establishes the position and orientation of the VRC relative to the world coordinate origin. The view plane specification is defined relative to the VRC and so far this philosophy is similar to viewing system IV. (Except that we are now considering a right-handed system and the VRC is simply the view space origin. It does not have the special significance that it is also the centre of projection for a perspective projective projection.)

3.9.3 The view mapping parameters

The view mapping stage defines how the scene, and what part of it, is projected onto the view plane. In the view orientation process the parameters were defined in world coordinate space. In this stage the parameters are defined in view space.

First, the view plane is established. This is a plane of (theoretically) infinite extent, parallel to the *UV* plane and at a distance given by the VPD from the VRP. As in viewing system IV, a view volume is established by defining front and back planes, together with a view window. A view window is any rectangular window in the view plane. It is defined by minimax coordinates in two-dimensional view space, that is, the *UV* coordinates transformed along the VPN into the view plane. These are (u_{min}, v_{min}) and (u_{max}, v_{max}). These relationships are shown for a parallel and a perspective projection in Figure 3.13.

A projection type and PRP complete the picture. The PRP as we stated above need not lie on a line, parallel to the VPN, and through the centre of the view plane window. If it lies off this line an oblique projection will be formed.

Two possible relationships between the PRP and the view plane window are shown in Figure 3.14. These are:

(a) A line from the PRP to the view plane window centre is parallel to the VPN.

(b) Moving the PRP results in an oblique projection. The condition in (a) is no longer true.

The view plane in more detail

The position and orientation of a view plane are defined by the view reference point (VRP), the view plane distance (VPD) and the view plane normal (VPN) (see Figure 3.12). The viewing direction is thus set by the VPN. Compared with the previous system, which used the camera and a

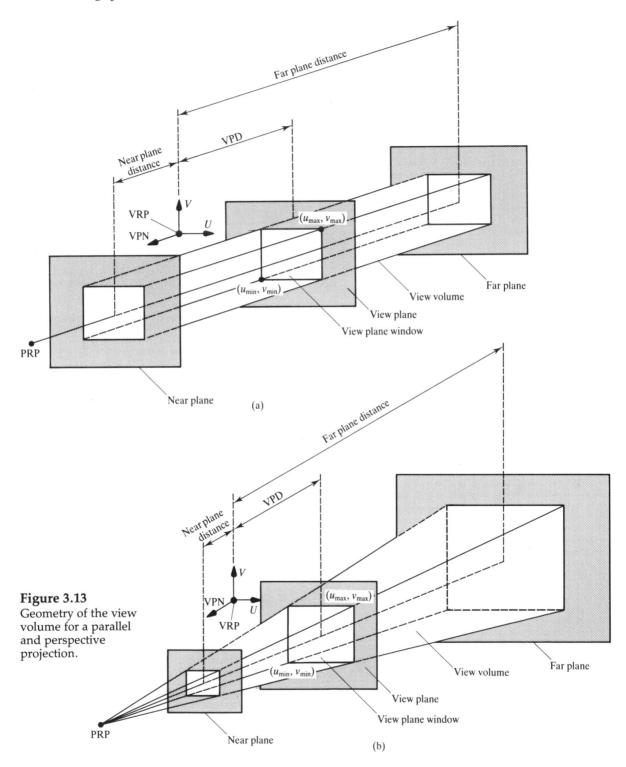

Near plane distance

Far plane distance

VPD

VRP

VPN

(u_{max}, v_{max})

(u_{min}, v_{min})

PRP

Near plane

Far plane

View volume

View plane

View plane window

(a)

Figure 3.13
Geometry of the view volume for a parallel and perspective projection.

Far plane distance

Near plane distance

VPD

VPN

V

U

VRP

(u_{max}, v_{max})

(u_{min}, v_{min})

PRP

Near plane

Far plane

View volume

View plane

View plane window

(b)

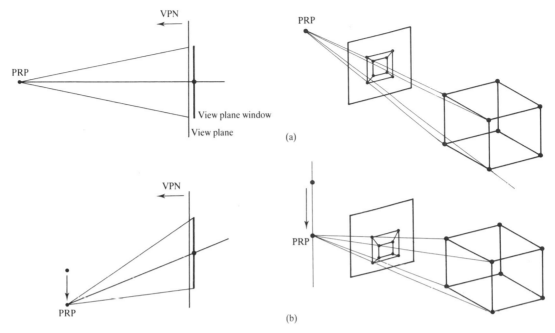

Figure 3.14
(a) 'Standard'
projection and (b)
oblique projection
obtained by moving
the PRP vertically
down in a direction
parallel to the view
plane.

focus point to establish the VPN and a distance d, we now use two vectors –
the VRP and the VPN (plus a distance (VPD) which displaces the VRP
from the view plane). Unlike the previous two systems where the VRP was
also used as a centre of projection, the projection reference point (PRP) has
to be separately specified. The VRP is now just a reference point for a
coordinate system and can be placed anywhere that is convenient. It can, for
example, form the view plane origin, or it can be placed at the world
coordinate origin, or at the centre of the object of interest. Placing it other
than at the view plane origin has the advantage that the VPD has some
meaning as a view distance. If the VRP is located in the view plane the VPD
becomes zero and is redundant as a parameter. Also, to move further or
nearer to an object only the VPD needs changing.

A view plane can be positioned anywhere in world coordinate space.
It can be behind, in front of, or cut through objects (Plate 2). Having
established the position and orientation of a view plane we set up a *uv*
coordinate system in the view plane with the VRP (or its projection with the
view plane) as origin (Figure 3.15). The two-dimensional *uv* coordinate
system and the VPN form a three-dimensional right-handed coordinate system. This enables the 'twist' of the view plane window about the VPN to be
established and a window to be set up (Figure 3.16). This twist is set by the
view up vector (VUV) and the general effect of this vector is to determine
whether the scene is viewed upright, upside down or whatever. The direction of the *v* axis is determined by the projection of the VUV parallel to the
VPN onto the view plane.

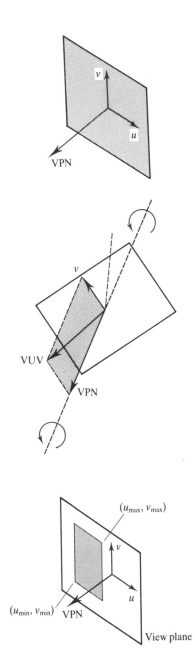

Figure 3.15
A *uv* coordinate system is established in the view plane forming a three-dimensional left-handed (right-handed for GKS-3D and PHIGS) system with the VPN.

Figure 3.16
The VUV establishes the direction of the *v* axis allowing the view plane to 'twist' about the VPN.

Figure 3.17
Establishing a two-dimensional window in the view plane.

With a two-dimensional coordinate system established in the view plane a two-dimensional window can be set (Figure 3.17). This takes care of the mapping from the unconstrained or application-oriented vertex values in world coordinate space to appropriate values in the view plane extent. All other things being equal, this window setting determines the size of the object(s) on the view surface.

3.10　Implementing viewing system V

Having developed transformations for viewing system IV we can deal with viewing system V by extending these. First consider the PRP. In viewing system V this is specified as a point in VRC space, that is, a point relative to the VRC origin. We can deal with the space disparity between the PRP and the VRC by making the PRP the origin. The view plane and clip plane parameters are distances that need to be expressed relative to the centre of projection and this is accomplished by applying the translation (PRP) to them. Our approach is thus to process viewing system V parameters so that it becomes the same as viewing system IV. This gives us the situation shown in Figure 3.18 which should be compared with Figure 3.10(a). Another feature of viewing system V is that we now have a view plane, a near plane and a far plane and the view volume has sides of different slope because we have removed the view plane window constraint of viewing system IV. We note that our view volume is disposed about the $-z$ axis because our view space is now a right-handed system. We adopt the following convention:

Interface values	After transforming the PRP to the VRC origin
VPD	d
Far plane distance	f
Near plane distance	n
u_{max}, u_{min}	x_{max}, x_{min}
v_{max}, v_{min}	y_{max}, y_{min}

(Note that although f and d have a similar interpretation to f and d of viewing system IV they are not the same values. The same symbols have been retained here to save a proliferation in the notation).

T_{pers} now splits into two components and we have:

$$T_{pers} = T_{pers1a}\, T_{pers1b}\, T_{pers2}$$

where T_{pers1b} and T_{pers2} have the same effect as T_{pers1} and T_{pers2} of viewing system IV. These are obtained by modifying T_{pers1} and T_{pers2} to include the view plane window parameters and the separation of the near plane from the view plane.

We first need to shear such that the view volume centre line becomes coincident with the z_v axis. This means adjusting x and y values by an amount proportional to z. It is easily seen that:

$$T_{pers1a} = \begin{bmatrix} 1 & 0 & 0 & 0 \\ 0 & 1 & 0 & 0 \\ \dfrac{x_{max} + x_{min}}{2d} & \dfrac{y_{max} + y_{min}}{2d} & 1 & 0 \\ 0 & 0 & 0 & 1 \end{bmatrix}$$

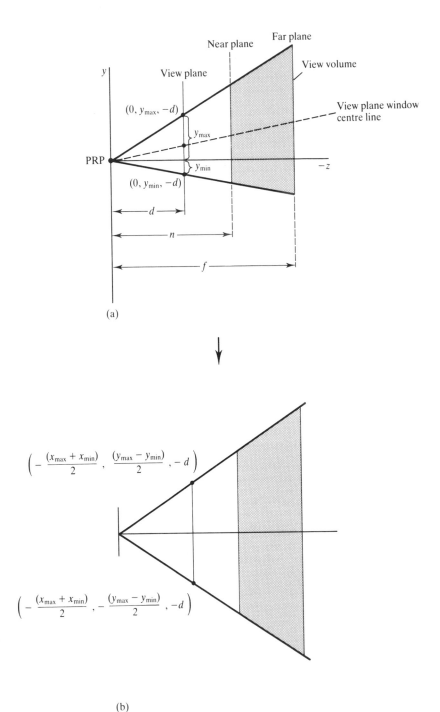

(a)

(b)

Figure 3.18
(a) The situation after making the PRP the origin. (b) After transforming to a symmetrical view volume.

For example, the upper and lower view plane window edges transform as follows:

$(0, y_{max}, -d, 1)$ transforms to

$$\left(-\frac{(x_{max} + x_{min})}{2}, \frac{(y_{max} - y_{min})}{2}, -d, 1\right)$$

and:

$(0, y_{min}, -d, 1)$ transforms to

$$\left(-\frac{(x_{max} + x_{min})}{2}, -\frac{(y_{max} - y_{min})}{2}, -d, 1\right)$$

transforming the original view volume into a symmetrical view volume (Figure 3.18b).

The second transform is:

$$T_{pers1b} = \begin{bmatrix} \dfrac{2d}{x_{max} - x_{min}} & 0 & 0 & 0 \\ 0 & \dfrac{2d}{y_{max} - y_{min}} & 0 & 0 \\ 0 & 0 & 1 & 0 \\ 0 & 0 & 0 & 1 \end{bmatrix}$$

This scaling is identical in effect to T_{pers1} of viewing system IV converting the symmetrical view volume to a 45° view volume. For example, consider the effect of $T_{pers1} = T_{pers1a} \, T_{pers1b}$ on the line through the view plane window centre. This transforms the point:

$$\left(\frac{x_{max} + x_{min}}{2}, \frac{y_{max} + y_{min}}{2}, -d, 1\right) \quad \text{to} \quad (0, 0, -d, 1)$$

making the line from the origin to this point coincident with the $-z$ axis – the required result.

Finally we have:

$$T_{pers2} = \begin{bmatrix} 1 & 0 & 0 & 0 \\ 0 & 1 & 0 & 0 \\ 0 & 0 & f/(f - n) & 1 \\ 0 & 0 & -fn/(f - n) & 0 \end{bmatrix}$$

which maps the regular pyramid into a box.

Projects, notes and suggestions _____

3.1   Viewing system interface

Enhance your basic wireframe program to include a graphical system interface for viewing system I. Do this by designing a view port that maintains a current line-drawing representation of the viewing system parameters; this should be a two-dimensional projection of the viewing system from an appropriate view point (see, for example, Appendix A, Figure A.2).

Figure 3. 19
Proceeding from eye space to screen space. (a) A view of the scene. (b) A view of the viewing system showing the viewing frustum and the view plane. (c) Contents of the view plane window.

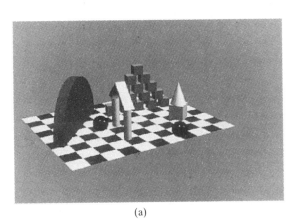

(a)

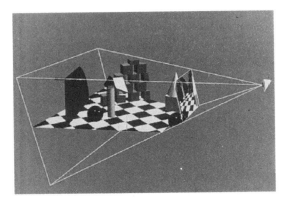 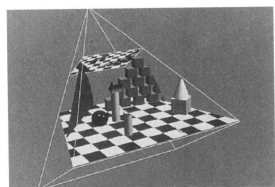

(b)

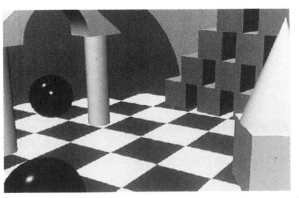 

(c)

We now have two view points: a primary view point used in the main view port for looking at the object, and a view point used for the interaction view port that looks at the primary view point embedded in its spherical coordinate system. This enables a user to move the view point in an intuitive manner from its current position to a new position.

Note that the choice of the view point for the viewing system representation is not arbitrary. If the projection of the viewing system is going to be useful, then a view point should be chosen that is itself a function of the main viewing parameters.

3.2 Computer-assisted learning of viewing systems (*)

People studying viewing systems usually have some difficulty in predicting the effect of the various parameters on the final look of the projected scene. Design a teaching system for viewing systems II–V. One (somewhat elaborate) idea is shown in Figure 3.19. This shows a scene with a wireframe viewing frustum superimposed, together with the appropriate projections.

4 | Reflection and Illumination Models

4.1 Introduction

In this chapter we briefly look at theoretical aspects of reflection and then examine computer graphics reflection models. A reflection model describes the interaction of light with a surface, in terms of the properties of the surface and the nature of the incident light. A **reflection model** is the basic factor in the look of a three-dimensional shaded object. It enables a two-dimensional screen projection of an object to look real – in the sense that a two-dimensional image such as a photograph is an acceptable representation of three-dimensional reality to human visual perception.

Conversely, an **illumination model** defines the nature of the light emanating from a source – the geometry of its intensity distribution and so on. Outside research labs most computer graphics shaders use simple reflection models and extremely simplified illumination models – usually a point source. This works because it works – it produces acceptable results using currently available hardware power and display devices.

The purpose of reflection models in computer graphics is to render three-dimensional objects in two-dimensional screen space such that reality is mimicked to an acceptable level. The phrase 'acceptable level' depends on the context of the application. The higher the degree of reality required, the more complex the reflection model and the greater the processing demands. For example, simple models are used in computer-generated imagery for flight simulators. Even with large multiple processors, the prodigious demands of such systems constrain the accuracy of the reflection models and the geometric representation of the solids. Also, an accurate shading model in a flight simulator may not be as important as texturing a surface. Textures are important depth cues in flight simulators and texture mapping may place as heavy demands on the processor as reflection. On the other hand, a television commercial comprising a short animated sequence may demand, for aesthetic reasons, a much richer reflection model and tens of minutes

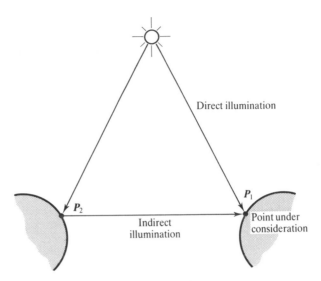

Figure 4.1
Direct and indirect
illumination.

may be spent in generating each frame in the sequence on a single processor. Somewhere between these two extremes is the shading of solid models
in CAD packages. Here a machine part may be designed interactively using
a solid modelling capability. In the design loop a user of such a system may
operate with wireframe models. To visualize the finished object most three-
dimensional CAD systems have a shading option. This will use a basic
reflection model to shade the surfaces of the object. Such a process, running
on a CAD workstation, may take between tens of seconds to a few minutes
to complete.

The reflection models described in this chapter are *local* models. This
means that only the interaction between a point on the surface being shaded
and the light source is considered. No global illumination or illumination
that reaches the point under consideration through an indirect path (reflection from another surface) is considered. The distinction between the two
types of illumination is shown in Figure 4.1.

Generally we can use reflection models on their own, which means
that no object/object or object/environment interaction is evaluated, or we
can embed a local reflection model in a global algorithm framework such as
radiosity (Chapter 10) or ray tracing (Chapter 8). In the simple example
shown in Figure 4.1, a global reflection model might be used to calculate the
indirect illumination impinging on point P_1 from point P_2.

In this chapter we only consider calculating light intensity at a *point*
on a surface. This means that the reflection model is independent of surface
representation. Later, in Chapter 5, we will see that we have to qualify what
we mean by a 'point'; in fact we generally have to calculate the value of the
light intensity for that *area* of the surface that projects onto a pixel on the
screen.

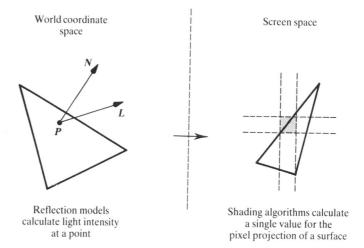

World coordinate
space

Screen space

Figure 4.2
Illustrating the
distinction between
calculating the light
intensity at a point *P* in
world coordinate space
and shading a pixel.

Reflection models
calculate light intensity
at a point

Shading algorithms calculate
a single value for the
pixel projection of a surface

We make the important distinction between reflection models which imitate some aspect of physical light behaviour on a surface and embedding such a model in a scheme that calculates the light intensity in a pixel projection. We will use the term **incremental shading technique** for the latter. Sometimes this distinction is blurred in computer graphics texts. The distinction is demonstrated in Figure 4.2. A reflection model considers the orientation, *N*, of a surface at a point *P*. A light intensity is calculated by comparing *N* with *L*, the light direction vector. To display the surface on the screen we need to calculate single intensity values for the pixels onto which the surface projects.

A reflection model, neither as basic as those used in flight simulation, nor as rich as the current research models in image synthesis, has been in use in computer graphics since the mid-1970s. This is the Phong reflection model described in Section 4.3. Before describing this model we will consider some theoretical factors.

4.2   Theoretical considerations in light reflection

First, an obvious equation:

Light incident at a surface = light reflected + light scattered
+ light absorbed + light transmitted

This is shown diagrammatically in Figure 4.3. Computer graphics attends in most detail to reflected light and also models transmitted light. Note from the diagram that a reflected component can also result from the transmitted component. The intensity and wavelength of light reflected from a surface

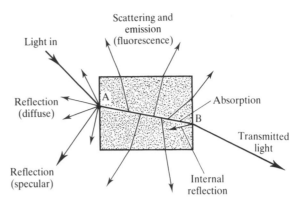

Figure 4.3
Light interactions with
a solid.

depends on the incident wavelength, the angle of incidence, the nature (roughness) of the surface material and its electrical properties (permittivity, permeability and conductivity). The exact interaction is extremely complex. For example, the same surface may be smooth for some wavelengths and rough for others; or for the same wavelength, it may be rough or smooth for different angles of incidence. Also, we have the well-known empirical fact that any surface, regardless of its roughness, will reflect specularly at grazing incidence. A common example of this is sunlight reflected off a black road surface. When the sun is high the road is matte or rough and is black. However, at low angles of incidence a glare is obvious.

The way in which this complex behaviour is parametrized is to use a **bidirectional reflectivity function** (BDRF) and this is now described qualitatively in some detail. This will enable an appreciation of the reflection phenomenon and allow us to assess the limitations of computer graphics models.

Generally we define a BDRF as

$$R_{bd}(\lambda, \phi_i, \theta_i, \phi_v, \theta_v)$$

that relates incoming light in the direction (ϕ_i, θ_i) to outgoing light in the direction (ϕ_v, θ_v) (Figure 4.4). Note the important fact that the BDRF is also a function of wavelength. Theoretically, the BDRF is the ratio of outgoing intensity to incoming energy:

$$R_{bd}(\lambda, \phi_i, \theta_i, \phi_v, \theta_v) = \frac{I_v(\phi_i, \theta_i, \phi_v, \theta_v)}{E_i(\phi_i, \theta_i)}$$

where the relationship between the incoming energy and incoming intensity is given by (Figure 4.5):

$$E_i(\phi_i, \theta_i) = I_i(\phi_i, \theta_i) \cos \theta_i \, d\omega_i$$

This relates the incoming energy to the incoming intensity, the solid angle ω_i in which the energy is contained, and the projected differential area. The solid angle ω of a surface element, as seen from a given point, is defined as

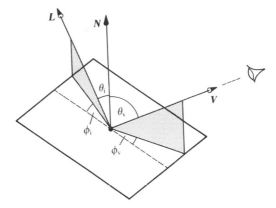

Figure 4.4
A BDRF relates
incoming energy in
direction (ϕ_i, θ_i), to
outgoing intensity in
direction (ϕ_v, θ_v).

the area of the surface element divided by the square of the distance from that point.

He *et al.* (1991) suggest that for computer graphics considerations, the BDRF should be divided into three components: a specular contribution, a directional diffuse contribution and an ideal diffuse contribution. The first two components are due to first-order reflections. The ideal diffuse contribution is due to multiple reflections and subsurface interaction (Figure 4.6).

The specular contribution is mirror-like reflection (Figure 4.7a). If the surface were a perfect mirror then this would be the sole contribution. For a practical surface that exhibits surface roughness, we can still define a specular contribution which is the reflected light intensity in the direction:

$$\phi_v = \phi_i \qquad \theta_v = \theta_i$$

from the mean surface. The relative magnitude of this component depends

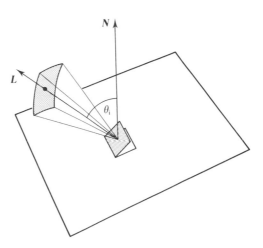

Figure 4.5
Intensity is measured
with respect to
projected area normal
to its direction.

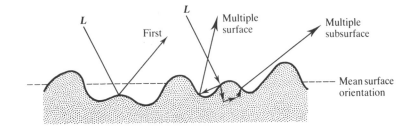

Figure 4.6
Illustrating first
reflections, multiple
surface reflections and
multiple subsurface
reflections.

on the roughness of the surface. The smoother the surface the higher is the
specular contribution. There is also a wavelength dependency.

The directional diffuse contribution (Figure 4.7b) is also dependent on
first-order reflections. When the wavelength of the incoming light becomes
comparable to the size of the surface roughness elements, first reflections
result in diffraction and interference. The reflections spread out in every
direction into a hemisphere centred on the point. However there is usually a
preferred direction. The tendency of this peak is the specular direction for

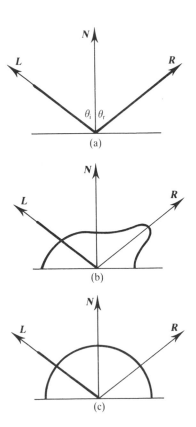

Figure 4.7
The three components
of the BDRF. (a)
Specular reflection
from the mean surface.
(b) Directional diffuse
reflection. (c) Ideal
diffuse reflection.

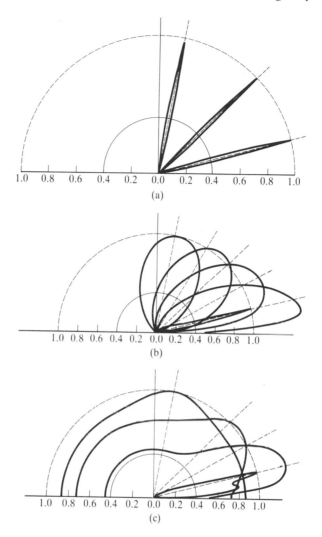

Figure 4.8
Showing the
dependence of BDRFs
on wavelength, angle
of incidence and
material (after He *et al.*,
1991). (a) Roughened
aluminium for $\theta_i = 10°$,
45° and 75°. $\lambda = 2.0$ μm.
(b) Roughened
aluminium for $\theta_i = 10°$,
30°, 45°, 60° and 75°.
$\lambda = 0.5$ μm. (c)
Roughened
magnesium oxide for
$\theta_i = 10°$, 45°, 60° and
75°. $\lambda = 0.5$ μm.

slightly rough surfaces, off-specular direction for intermediate rough surfaces and grazing angle incident light.

Finally, the ideal diffuse contribution reflects uniformly in all directions into the hemisphere (Figure 4.7c). This is due to subsurface scattering interaction. Radiation crossing the first surface is reflected by subsurface scattering centres (for example, paints, ceramics).

Figure 4.8 gives an idea of the differences that BDRFs exhibit as a function of material and wavelength. Parts (a) and (b) show the BDRF for roughened aluminium for $\theta_i = 10°$, 45° and 75° at a wavelength of 2.0 μm. Consider Figure 4.8(a). The behaviour is strongly specular and the surface would look mirror-like. If this BDRF were used in a reflection model that was embedded in a global framework then nearby objects would be reflected in the surface. Figure 4.8(b) is for the same material but the wavelength is reduced to 0.5 μm. The incidence angles are 10°, 30°, 45° and 60°. The surface now exhibits directional diffuse properties. Note that the directional tendency is not along the specular (R) direction and that as the angle of incidence increases specular behaviour starts to emerge. Figure 4.8(c) shows the behaviour of a ceramic surface (roughened magnesium oxide) for $\theta_i = 10°$, 45°, 60° and 75°. Note that this surface changes from almost an ideal diffuse reflector to a directional diffuse then a specular surface as a function of θ_i.

The purpose of dividing the BDRF into three components is to enable an analytical model, based on both physical and wave aspects of optical theory, to be constructed. This gives a definition of BDRF in terms of wavelength, geometry and physical parameters which can then be used in a computer graphics simulation. The first computer graphics model that we describe is completely empirical or phenomenological and it uses a simple formula to imitate aspects of the above behaviour.

4.3   The Phong reflection model

The **Phong reflection model** imitates the above behaviour to a degree that produces a first-order approximation to photorealism. It exhibits no bidirectional dependency whatever, but nevertheless it has found wide acceptance in the computer graphics community and has become the de facto reflection model.

The model is a linear combination of three components – diffuse, specular and ambient. The diffuse component is the ideal diffuse contribution described in the previous section and we evaluate this as:

$$I_d = I_i k_d \cos \theta \qquad 0 \leqslant \theta \leqslant 2\pi$$

where I_i is the intensity of a point light source and θ is the angle between the surface normal at the point being considered and a line from the point to the light source (Figure 4.9). k_d is a wavelength-dependent empirical reflection coefficient described in more detail shortly.

In terms of vector notation, the diffuse contribution can be written as:

$$I_d = I_i k_d (\boldsymbol{L} \cdot \boldsymbol{N})$$

where $\boldsymbol{L}$ is the light direction vector and both $\boldsymbol{L}$ and $\boldsymbol{N}$ are unit vectors. We note that this term is a constant over a planar surface (where θ does not vary). If there is more than one light source then:

$$I_d = k_d \sum_n I_{i,n} (\boldsymbol{L}_n \cdot \boldsymbol{N})$$

where $\boldsymbol{L}_n$ is the direction vector from the nth light source to the point on the surface.

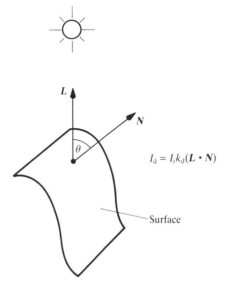

Figure 4.9
The Phong diffuse
coefficient.

$$I_d = I_i k_d (\mathbf{L} \cdot \mathbf{N})$$

Surface

The specular contribution is a function of Ω, the angle between the viewing direction and the mirror direction (Figure 4.10):

$$I_s = I_i k_s \cos^n \Omega$$
$$= I_i k_s (\mathbf{R} \cdot \mathbf{V})^n$$

n is an index that simulates surface roughness. For a perfect mirror n would be infinity and reflected light would be constrained to the mirror direction.

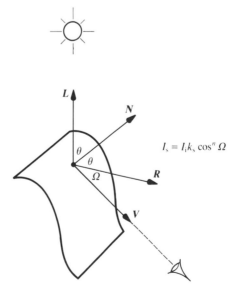

$$I_s = I_i k_s \cos^n \Omega$$

Figure 4.10
The Phong specular
component.

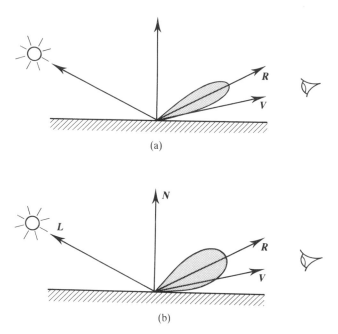

Figure 4.11
(a) Large n simulates a glossy surface; (b) small n simulates a less glossy surface.

For small integer values of n we generate a reflection lobe, where the thickness of the lobe is a function of the surface roughness (Figure 4.11). The effect of the specular reflection term in the model is to produce a so-called **highlight**. This is basically a reflection of the light source spread over an area of the surface to an extent that depends on the value of n. The colour of the specularly reflected light is different to that of the diffuse reflected light. In simple models of specular reflection, the specular component is assumed to be the colour of the light source. If, say, a green surface is illuminated with white light then the diffuse reflection component is green but the highlight is white. Note that because the term depends only on Ω and n there is no bidirectional behaviour. The value of (ϕ_i, θ_i) is immaterial. This is one of the main theoretical defects of the Phong model. k_s is an empirical specular reflection coefficient described in more detail shortly.

Adding the specular and diffuse components together gives a very approximate imitation of the behaviour described in Section 4.2. Consider Figure 4.12. This is a cross-section of the overall reflectivity response as a function of the orientation of the view vector V. The cross-section is in a plane that contains the L vector and the point P and it thus slices through the specular bump. The magnitude of the reflected intensity is the distance from P along the direction V to where V intersects the profile. Figure 4.13 shows a rendered view of this function.

Because there are no global calculations, an ambient component is usually added to the diffuse and specular terms. Such a component illumin- ates surfaces that, because we generally use a point light source, would

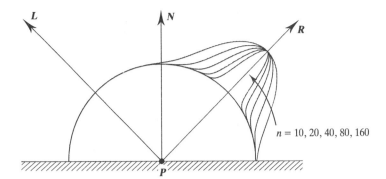

Figure 4.12
The light intensity at point P as a function of the orientation of the viewing vector V.

$n = 10, 20, 40, 80, 160$

otherwise be rendered black. These are surfaces that are visible from the view point but not from the light source. This would give the generally undesirable effect of a scene in darkness only illuminated by something like a flashlight (Plate 3). The ambient component is an approximation to global illumination. In reality such surfaces would be illuminated by indirect illumination, such as multiple reflections from walls. In local reflection models the only thing that we can sensibly do with the complexity of the global component is to ignore it, and the ambient component is normally modelled as a constant. We write:

$$I_g = I_a k_a$$

Adding the diffuse, specular and ambient components together we have:

$$I = I_a k_a + I_i(k_d(L \cdot N) + k_s(R \cdot V)^n) \tag{4.1}$$

Sometimes distance is considered in local reflection models. We can add a term that reduces light intensity as a function of distance of the surface from the light source. This ensures that surfaces of the same orientation, but at different distances from the light source, are not assigned the same intensity. For reasons that are explained later, light sources are considered to be at

Figure 4.13
A rendered version of the function shown as a cross-section in Figure 4.12. The arrow tail is L and the arrow heads are N and R.

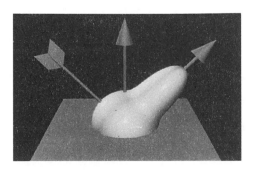

infinity and a measure equal to the distance from the view point to the surface can be used instead. Equation 4.1 becomes:

$$I = I_a k_a + I_i(k_d(\boldsymbol{L}\cdot\boldsymbol{N}) + k_s(\boldsymbol{R}\cdot\boldsymbol{V})^n)/(r + k) \qquad \textbf{(4.2)}$$

4.4   Geometric considerations

The expense of Equation 4.2 can be considerably reduced by making some geometric assumptions and approximations. First, if the light source and the view point are considered to be at infinity then $\boldsymbol{L}$ and $\boldsymbol{V}$ are constant over the domain of the scene. The vector $\boldsymbol{R}$ is expensive to calculate and, although Phong gives an efficient method for calculating $\boldsymbol{R}$, it is better to use a vector $\boldsymbol{H}$. This appears to have been first introduced by Blinn (1977). The specular term then becomes a function of $(\boldsymbol{N}\cdot\boldsymbol{H})$ rather than $(\boldsymbol{R}\cdot\boldsymbol{V})$. $\boldsymbol{H}$ is the unit normal to a hypothetical surface that is oriented in a direction halfway between the light direction vector $\boldsymbol{L}$ and the viewing vector $\boldsymbol{V}$ (Figure 4.14):

$$\boldsymbol{H} = (\boldsymbol{L} + \boldsymbol{V})/2$$

This is the required orientation for a surface to reflect light along the direction $\boldsymbol{V}$. It is easily seen that the angle between $\boldsymbol{R}$ and $\boldsymbol{V}$ is twice the angle between $\boldsymbol{N}$ and $\boldsymbol{H}$ but this can be compensated for, if necessary by adjusting n.

Figure 4.15 shows the difference in the highlight for a single value of n. Using $\boldsymbol{N}\cdot\boldsymbol{H}$ 'spreads' the highlight over a greater area. Equation 4.2 now becomes:

$$I = I_a k_a + I_i(k_d(\boldsymbol{L}\cdot\boldsymbol{N}) + k_s(\boldsymbol{N}\cdot\boldsymbol{H})^n)/(r + k) \qquad \textbf{(4.3)}$$

This now means that the intensity I is solely a function of the surface normal $\boldsymbol{N}$. If $\boldsymbol{L}$ and $\boldsymbol{V}$ are constant vectors then so is $\boldsymbol{H}$. There are two implications of placing the light source at infinity. First, there is no variation of shading over a planar surface (ignoring the effect of the distance denominator

Figure 4.14
$\boldsymbol{H}$ is the normal to a surface orientation that would reflect all the light along $\boldsymbol{V}$.

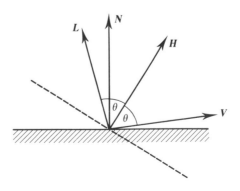

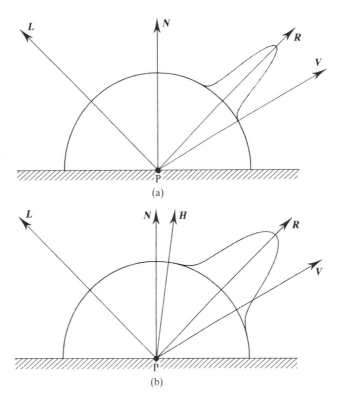

Figure 4.15
The difference between using (a) $R \cdot V$ and (b) $N \cdot H$ for a fixed value of n. Note the difference in the intensity in direction V.

$(r + k)$), because L is now a constant and N does not change over the surface. Second, the shape of the specular highlight changes. In general the variation in $N \cdot H$ over a surface is less if H is a constant than if H is calculated from a varying L.

4.5   Colour

For coloured objects the easiest approach is to model the specular highlights as white (for a white light source) and to control the colour of the objects by appropriate setting of the diffuse reflection coefficients. We use three intensity equations to drive the monitor:

$$I_r = I_a k_{ar} + I_i(k_{dr}(L \cdot N) + k_s(N \cdot H)^n)$$
$$I_g = I_a k_{ag} + I_i(k_{dg}(L \cdot N) + k_s(N \cdot H)^n)$$
$$I_b = I_a k_{ab} + I_i(k_{db}(L \cdot N) + k_s(N \cdot H)^n)$$

Note that the specular term is common to all three equations. Summarizing these three equations as a single expression gives:

$$I(r, g, b) = I_a k_a(r, g, b) + I_i(k_d(r, g, b)(L \cdot N) + k_s(N \cdot H)^n) \quad \textbf{(4.4)}$$

It should be mentioned at this stage that this three-sample approach to colour is a crude approximation and accurate treatment of colour requires far more than three samples. This point is dealt with at some length in Chapter 14.

4.6   Summary of Phong model

The following points summarize the model. Most of the inadequacies or assumptions of the model will be dealt with in the course of the text.

- Light sources are assumed to be point sources. Any intensity distribution of the light source is ignored.
- All geometry except the surface normal is ignored (that is, light source(s) and viewer are located at infinity).
- The diffuse and specular terms are modelled as local components.
- An empirical model is used to simulate the decrease of the specular term around the reflection vector modelling the glossiness of the surface.
- The colour of the specular reflection is assumed to be that of the light source (that is, highlights are rendered white regardless of the material).
- The global term (ambient) is modelled as a constant.

Finally, note that because of its simplicity and the geometric constraints this much-loved reflection model, although it imparts a degree of realism sufficient for many applications, does carry a recognizable computer signature. The overall effect of the lack of interaction between objects in a scene is that they appear plastic-like and floating. Shadows and approximate approaches to global illumination are dealt with in the course of the text and these two additions to the model mediate the floating effect. Also note that the lack of shadows means not only that objects do not cast a shadow on other objects, but also that self-shadowing within an object is omitted. Concavities in an object that are hidden from the light source are erroneously shaded simply on the basis of their surface normal. This effect is often seen in 'tumbling logo' title sequences on TV. In Figure 4.16 a letter 'O' shows that a specular highlight will occur in a region that should be in shadow if a simple local reflection model is used.

4.7   The 20 spheres – an example

This case study is a simple application of the Phong model and shows the effect of varying the proportion of specular to diffuse reflection and n, the specular modelling index, for a simple surface. Plate 4 shows the results of

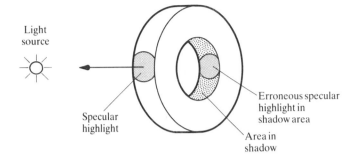

Figure 4.16
Erroneous highlights
are often seen in TV
title sequences.

the program. It is based on an illustration by Roy Hall (Program of Computer Graphics, Cornell University, 1981). Twenty spheres are rendered using different values of k_d, k_s and n for a single intensity equation I_g. The tightness of the specular highlight, achieved by increasing n, varies vertically. Horizontal variation is the ratio of k_d to k_s. At the right-hand side, k_d is unity and k_s is zero. k_d is then reduced to zero and k_s is increased to unity. Also in the plate is a set of intensity profiles for four of the spheres showing, for each sphere, in a plane through the highlight maximum, the contributions from the ambient term (short broken line), the diffuse term (broken line) and the specular term (solid line). For a particular point on the surface of the sphere (or that part of the surface cut by the plane through the highlight centre), the intensity is given by the sum of each profile (that is, the sum of the values from the centre to each profile).

The geometric model for this example is straightforward. We assume that the view point is located along the positive z axis at infinity and that the (x,y) values of the surface can be used directly as screen coordinates. The three-dimensional coordinates of points on the surface of the (visible) hemisphere are calculated and are used to produce the light intensity. This intensity, calculated for a point (x,y,z) on the surface of the hemisphere, is then displayed as pixel (x_s, y_s), where:

$$x_s = x$$
$$y_s = y$$

Incidentally, making up a special geometric or programming model for a particular set of objects to be rendered is a valid and much-used approach. Such are the processing overheads of rendering that a programmer may use context-dependent techniques rather than a general-purpose system. This is particularly so in the case of an animated sequence, where a large number of frames have to be generated using variations of the same model.

The rendering program (Program 4.1) given uses two procedures. *ShadeSphere* initially calculates a point on the surface of the sphere. The surface normal at a point on the surface is simply (x,y,z). This is passed into

Program 4.1   Procedures for shading spheres.

```
procedure ShadeSphere (Kd, Ks: real;
    SpecIndex, Xcentre, Ycentre, radius: integer);
const
    Ilight = 140;
    K = 70.0;
    IaKa = 0.2;
    Hx = 0.325058; Hy = 0.325058; Hz = 0.888074;
    dx = 110.0; dy = 110.0; dz = 110.0;
    Lx = 0.57735; Ly = 0.57735; Lz = 0.57735;
var
    Ig, Irb, x, y, z: integer;
    rsquare, xsquare, ysquare, zsquare, denom, xn, yn, zn, LdotN, NnH,
        dist, distfactor, ambientterm, diffuseterm, specularterm: real;

    procedure CalculateLNandNnH (x, y, z, SpecIndex: integer;
        xn, yn, zn: real; var LdotN, dist, NnH: real);
    var
        NH: real;

    begin
        LdotN := xn*Lx + yn*Ly + zn*Lz;
        if LdotN <= 0.0 then LdotN := 0.0
        else
        begin
            dist := sqrt (sqr (dx − x) + sqr (dy − y) + sqr (dz − z));
            NH := Hx*xn + Hy*yn + Hz*zn;
            NnH := exp (SpecIndex*ln (NH));
        end;
    end; {CalculateLNandNnH}

begin {ShadeSphere}
    rsquare := sqr (radius);
    for y := −radius to radius do
    begin
        ysquare := sqr (y);
        for x := −radius to radius do
        begin
            xsquare := sqr (x);
            if (xsquare + ysquare) <= rsquare then
            begin
                z := round (sqrt (rsquare − xsquare− ysquare));
                zsquare := sqr (z);
                denom := sqrt (xsquare + ysquare + zsquare);
                xn := x/denom; yn := y/denom; zn := z/denom;
                CalculateLNandNnH (x, y, z, SpecIndex, xn, yn, zn, LdotN, dist,
                    NnH);
                ambientterm := IaKa;
```

```
            if LdotN <= 0.0 then
            begin
                Ig := round (255*ambientterm);
                Irb := 0;
            end
            else
            begin
                distfactor := Ilight/(dist + K);
                diffuseterm := distfactor*Kd*LdotN;
                specularterm := distfactor*Ks*NnH;
                Ig := round (255*(ambientterm + diffuseterm + specularterm));
                Irb := round (255*specularterm);
            end;
            WritePixel (Xcentre + x, Ycentre + y, Irb, Ig, Irb);
        end;
      end;
    end;
  end; {ShadeSphere}
```

CalculateLNandNnH. In this procedure the light direction vector, **L**, its distance from the object *d*, and the vectors **V** and **H** are each declared as constants. The first calculation in this procedure is the dot product $\mathbf{L}\cdot\mathbf{N}$. If this is less than zero then the point under consideration is not visible from the light source, as discussed. Alternatively, we can say that the angle between the surface normal **N** and the light direction vector **L** is greater than 90°. (It is instructive to examine the effect of omitting this **if** statement.) Note that if $\mathbf{L}\cdot\mathbf{N}$ is negative then that point on the surface is not visible to the light source and both $\mathbf{L}\cdot\mathbf{N}$ and $\mathbf{N}\cdot\mathbf{H}$ are set to zero.

Finally, note that twiddling the intensity is usually necessary to produce a nice result. The brightest highlight in the illustration is maximum intensity white. Theoretically this is wrong. We are viewing along the positive *z* axis and the highlight intensity should only be the maximum value if we are viewing along the light direction vector, that is:

$$\mathbf{V} = \mathbf{L}$$

If, for example, we were producing an animated sequence and intended to move the view point around the sphere, then the highlight seen from the *z* axis would be dimmer than that seen when viewing along the light direction vector. Another point in this connection is saturation of the highlight. If k_s is adjusted so that the calculated highlight intensity never exceeds the light source intensity or the maximum (RGB) value then for a sphere only one pixel will be rendered at maximum white. It may be desirable to allow the highlight intensity to saturate and render an area of pixels at maximum white. The visual effect of this factor worsens with increasing *n*.

One of the points of this case study is to demonstrate that a straightforward implementation of simple reflection models will not always produce acceptable results. As we have seen, a considerable degree of ad hoc adjustment is necessary.

4.8 Using look-up tables with reflection models

A video **look-up table** (LUT) or colour table is a hardware table interposed between the screen memory and the image display system. Its original *raison d'être* was to 'extend' the colour range of a graphics terminal. For example, with an 8-bit screen memory a pixel on the screen can have one out of 256 colours. This range can be extended to *any* 256 colours out of a 'palette' of 2^{24} (16 million) by using an 8×24 bit look-up table (Figure 4.17). In this system the pixel intensity, instead of appearing directly on the screen, is used to address a row in the LUT. The fact that the entire contents of an LUT can be changed in real time leads to a number of uses in different areas of computer graphics.

An implication of the simplifications that reduce the reflected intensity to a function of N:

$$I = f(N)$$

is that it is possible to precalculate a set of I values, store these in a table and use the surface normal to index the table. An animation situation (perhaps fairly rare) in which this method can provide a real-time, or near real-time, sequence is where a three-dimensional scene is to remain static while the illumination sources move or change in some way; for example, in intensity or colour characteristics. If the scene remains static then the surface normals do not change with time. Here the scene is stored in the screen memory as a set of surface normals. Changing the way in which the scene is illuminated is then easily accomplished, in real time, by changing the contents of the table storing the set of I values.

Bass (1981) used this method with a 12-bit LUT. This means that a total of 4096 different normal vectors can be used. In this is embedded the

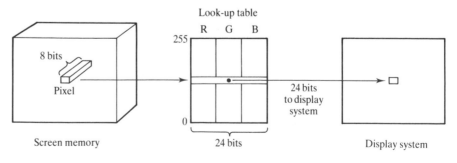

Figure 4.17
An 8-bit screen memory accessing an 8-bit × 24-bit look-up table.

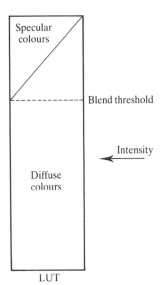

Figure 4.18
Using an LUT to blend
diffuse and specular
colours.

disadvantage of the method. 'Vector quantization noise' results, which manifests itself in coherent interference in the final image. The solution is, of course, to increase the entry dimension of the LUT at extra hardware cost.

The same basic idea can be used with a software table to reduce the calculation of I to an evaluation of the normalized surface normal. This has the disadvantage that a separate table must be stored for each object in the scene that has a different set of reflection coefficients. This will have the effect of considerably expanding the object database in most contexts. The method is useful in scenes consisting of many identical objects (for example, in rendering molecular models) where there will be a large number of occurrences of each possible surface normal.

A novel use of LUTs is described by Warn (1983). The idea here is to allow a degree of interactive control over the final appearance of the image; that is, the colour and the proportion of specular to diffuse reflection. Warn uses Phong's model but assumes that the intensity at a point on a surface consists of a diffuse and specular contribution, and that a particular intensity corresponds to exactly one combination of diffuse and specular components. (This is a simplification that appears to work in practice.) The calculated intensity is stored in a 10-bit frame buffer that is then used to access an LUT. The LUT is loaded with a set of diffuse colours of increasing intensity that blend into a set of specular colours (Figure 4.18). The diagonal line in Figure 4.18 represents the transition from diffuse colour to specular colour. Both the specular and diffuse colours can be changed interactively via a suitable user interface. (It will be shown later that it is not always a good approximation to have white specular highlights.) The 'blend' intensity, the threshold at which specular highlights start to occur, can also be changed interactively, altering the area of visible specular highlights and therefore the look of the image, without having to recalculate from the shading equation.

One disadvantage of this approach is that a separate partition is required in the LUT for each surface type. For a 10-bit table this places obvious restrictions on the number of surface types and the colour range within a surface type.

Plate 5 shows a demonstration of this process used in conjunction with a simple interactive technique for changing LUT contents. All three illustrations were obtained from one rendering process by changing LUT entries. Dividing the LUT into three columns, the red, green and blue components of the colour of an entry (the detailed use of the RGB colour model in computer graphics is dealt with extensively in Chapter 14) we 'rubber band' the RGB profiles to set the entire contents of the LUT. Changing entries below the blend threshold alters the colour of the object, changing entries above this threshold alters the colours of the highlights, and changing the value of the blend threshold alters the degree of specular reflection.

Each illustration shows an object together with its accompanying LUT profiles. The first illustration shows how both the colour of the object and the colour of the highlight are easily changed to simulate a metallic object – where the highlight colour is not necessarily white. In the second illustration the blend intensity is changed and the degree of specular to diffuse reflection altered. Special effects are easily obtained as shown in the final illustration.

This is a useful technique when a scene is being composed. Rerendering by changing coefficients in the Phong equation can take minutes and if colour aesthetics are important then real-time interaction is vital.

4.9   Empirical transparency

Simple transparency effects in computer graphics are almost as common as simple reflection models. If refraction is ignored then transparency can be grossly (but effectively) approximated using a linear parameter t to mix the object colour with the intensity of a single background. For partially transparent objects that are hollow, t can be 'modulated' by the z component of the normalized surface normal of the projected object (Kay, 1979). We are then saying that t is a transmission factor that attenuates anything behind the object (further z) according to an amount that can be approximated by multiplying by N_z. For the paths shown in Figure 4.19, P_1 is longer than P_2 and point s on the surface of the object should exhibit a lower intensity of background colour than point r. t is given by:

$$t = t_{min} + (t_{max} - t_{min})N_z \qquad\qquad \textbf{(4.5)}$$

The object colour I_o is computed in the normal way using a reflection

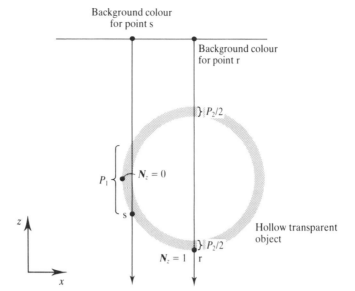

Figure 4.19
Mixing background
colour and object
colour as a function of
N_z, the z component of
the surface normal.

model. In the simplest case, background colour I_b can be a constant. The final intensity I is given by the mix:

$$I = tI_b + (1 - t)I_o \tag{4.6}$$

If refractive effects are to be taken into account and the scene is simple – say a single planar background – then a simple special-case ray tracing scheme (where rays terminate on the background) is easily implemented (see Chapter 8).

Finally, the main problem with transparency is that it cannot be easily integrated with the preferred rendering method – a Z-buffer based approach (see Section 5.5.9).

4.10 The Cook and Torrance model

The first significant development in reflection models after the Phong model involved a physically based rather than an empirical specular term. This was first proposed by Blinn (1977) and was based on a surface model introduced by Torrance and Sparrow (1967). Cook and Torrance (1982) then enhanced this model to account for energy equilibrium and the change of colour within a specular highlight. In particular they directed their attention to the accurate rendering of different metallic and non-metallic surfaces. This development is a good example of the continuing quandary that faces image renderers: is the pursuit of more and more accurate physical models (which inevitably incur higher processing costs) worth the extra computing expense? A computer graphics image is, after all, an artifice created, in the main, for

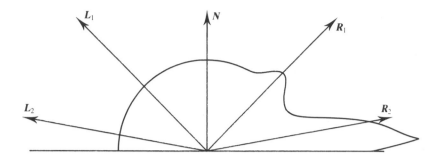

Figure 4.20
The value of the
specular intensity for
high and low angles of
incidence.

effect. Undoubtedly images that are accurately realistic have a place in computer graphics, but this does not imply that greater and greater realism is necessarily justified. Indeed, at the time of publication, it is almost certainly the case that most images are rendered with the Phong model.

The Cook and Torrance model is distinguished from the Phong model by the following factors:

- It is based on a consideration of incident energy rather than intensity.
- The specular term is based on a physical microfacet model.
- Colour change within the highlight is based on Fresnel's law and measured characteristics of the material.

The model contains Blinn's treatment (Blinn, 1977) which includes the second factor but excludes the third. The model consists of three terms: the specular and diffuse reflection due to direct illumination and the global ambient component. In this respect, and the fact that it models light due to direct illumination only, it is similar to Phong's approach. One of the original aims of the model was to render polished metallic surfaces correctly; the Phong model gives the impression of coloured plastic surfaces, also, it is inaccurate in the specular term for illumination at low angles of incidence. Physically the amplitude of the specular 'bump' is a function of the angle the light source makes with the surface. Figure 4.20 shows the value of the reflected intensity for a light source at a high and low angle of incidence (L_1 and L_2) obtained using the improved model described in this chapter. Using the Phong model, equal specular bumps would be produced at R_1 and R_2. That this behaviour occurs in reality is easily confirmed by viewing low incidence light reflected from a sheet of paper. In addition, for low angles of incidence, the maximum value of the specular bump is not coincident with the reflection vector R. (A rendered function illustrating this point is shown in Figure 4.21.) The Cook and Torrance model corrects this defect, and this results in a change in the shape of the specular highlights for illumination at low incidence angles. Modelling the specular highlight correctly is particularly important in animated sequences that involve specular reflection.

The surface model on which this improved specular term is based is given by Torrance and Sparrow (1967). Blinn (1977) used this new specular

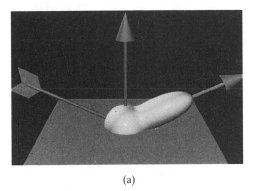
(a)

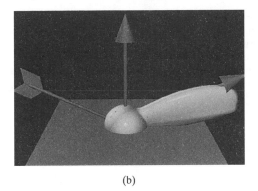
(b)

Figure 4.21
The Phong model (a) and the Cook and Torrance model (b) for low angles of incidence. Note the larger lobe in (b) and the non-coincidence of the lobe centre with the reflection vector R.

term to account for the dependence of the magnitude of the specular highlight on the angle of incidence, and retained the approximation that the colour of the highlight is that of the light source. Cook and Torrance include the wavelength dependency of the specular reflection coefficient in the model (Plate 6).

In general the colour of a specular highlight depends on physical characteristics of the material, except when the illumination is at a low angle of incidence. In the Phong model the highlight colour is the colour of the light source, usually white, and the change from a white highlight to a region exhibiting diffuse reflection means a change of colour that depends on the relative magnitude of the diffuse and specular terms. As the specular term reduces to zero, the colour surrounding the highlight would approach the colour given by the diffuse coefficients. Consider the spheres shown in Plate 4. As the intensity of the specular term reduces, the diffuse term predominates and the colour changes from white to green. This colour change is an effect that will only occur in practice for green-coloured plastic. Other materials will behave differently. In the Cook and Torrance model it is possible to represent, for example, highly polished metallic surfaces with a diffuse contribution of zero. A change in both the colour and the intensity of the highlight term is controlled by the value of the specular reflection coefficient.

In the model the BDRF is split into diffuse and specular contributions and we have:

$$BDRF = sR_s + dR_d \qquad \text{where } s + d = 1$$

This accounts for that component of illumination seen in a particular direction – the viewing direction, for example – originating from a direct source or a number of direct sources. To this must be added, as with the previous model, a term due to ambient illumination.

In the Phong model ambient illumination was modelled as a constant. In fact, ambient illumination can be viewed as the inverse of the diffuse illumination process. A perfect diffuser reflects light equally in all directions.

Figure 4.22
Microfacet model of a reflecting surface: a set of symmetric V-shaped grooves whose orientation can be modelled by a distribution about a particular direction.

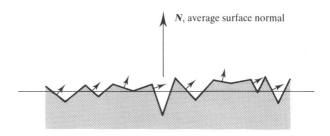

N, average surface normal

The combination reflected along the viewing direction is considered to be the same as that reflected in any other direction in the hemispherical reflection space. Conversely, ambient light is incident on a surface element from every direction in the hemispherical reflection space. The light reflected along the viewing direction from any particular incoming ambient direction is small, and is the incoming ambient intensity times R_a, the ambient reflectance for this direction. If we assume that R_a is a constant over the hemispherical space then the total ambient illumination reflected along a particular direction is R_a times the integral of I_a, the incoming ambient intensity. If we assume that I_a is a constant over the space then the ambient term is again a constant and equal to $I_a R_a$. Since the ambient term can be considered to be the reflected intensity (diffuse and specular) from an infinity of low-intensity direct light sources, R_a must be a linear combination of R_s and R_d. Such an approach reduces the model to a modified version of the Phong model – applicable to isolated objects floating in free space. In practice, I_a depends on the proximity of objects to each other. An approximation to accurate computation of the global ambient term is to include a **blocking fraction** f. This is the fraction of the hemisphere that is not blocked by nearby objects. We then have:

$$\text{Global ambient term} = I_a R_a f$$

and the complete model for the intensity at a point is:

$$I = I_a R_a f + \sum_n I_{i,n} (N \cdot L_n) \, d\omega_{i,n} (dR_d + sR_s)$$

and this should be compared with Equation 4.2.

This model is distinguished from the previous by the fact that it contains a reflectance definition that relates the brightness of an object to the intensity and size of the light source that illuminates it. The other major distinction of the Cook and Torrance model is incorporated in the specular term. In the Phong model the angular spread of the specular contribution about the reflection vector R was modelled empirically using an exponentiated cosine term. Here the model is a physical one based on a **microfacet** description of the surface introduced by Torrance and Sparrow (1967). This is based on the notion of a reflecting surface that consists of a large number of microfacets, each with perfectly reflecting or mirror faces (Figure 4.22).

Figure 4.23
Tangent plane approximation. The reflection behaviour at point **P** can be considered to be equal to that which would occur from a perfect plane positioned at **P**. The plane is the tangent plane.

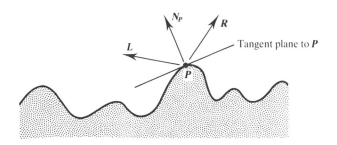

The geometric extent of a surface element – the unit of surface area from which a reflected intensity is calculated – means that it is made up of a collection of such microfacets. These can be described by a distribution function of the slope or orientation of the reflecting planes of the micro-facets. If we consider the component R_d to be a constant then the physics of the model are incorporated into the specular term which is given by:

$$R_s = \frac{FDG}{\pi(N \cdot V)(N \cdot L)} \tag{4.7}$$

From this it can be seen that there are three terms which act together to influence the value of R_s. We will first explain the overall philosophy of these terms and individually look at how each is modelled. F, the Fresnel term, can be viewed as a theoretical reflection coefficient. Based on classical wave theory, it applies to a perfect mirror-like surface. Its value for such a surface depends on wavelength, incidence angle and material. For any practical or rough surface we can consider points on the surface to be locally perfect. This approach is known as the **tangent plane approximation** (Figure 4.23). At a point the surface is considered to be a perfect plane whose orientation is given by the tangent to the surface at that point. This approximation is only valid if the local curvature of the surface is large compared to the wavelength of the incident light.

In computer graphics we are interested in the light directed along the **V** direction and this is the role of the second term D. D is a distribution function for microfacets on a surface that gives a statistical estimate of the proportion of microfacet slopes that are oriented in the **H** direction. We consider that the surface is made up of V-shaped grooves over whose surfaces the Fresnel term can be applied.

Finally, G accounts for the fact that at large incidence angles light incoming to a facet may be shadowed by adjacent surface irregularities, and outgoing light along a view angle that grazes the surface may be masked or interrupted in its passage to the viewer.

First, consider D. The function used by Torrance and Sparrow was a simple Gaussian:

$$D = k \exp\left[- (\alpha/m)^2\right]$$

where:

k is a constant

α is the angle of the microfacet with respect to the normal of the (mean) surface, that is, the angle between N and H

m is the root mean square slope of the microfacets

For low values of m the surface is shiny or glossy. (If m is 0 the surface is a perfect mirror and H must be equal to N for there to be any contribution to the specular reflection along V.) A high value for m implies that the surface is dull. D quantifies the dependence of R_s on the angle between N and H. The Cook and Torrance model uses a distribution proposed by Beckmann and Spizzichino (1963):

$$D = \frac{1}{m^2 \cos^4 \alpha} \exp\left[-\left(\tan^2 \alpha / m^2\right)\right]$$

This is computationally more expensive but is a function of m and α only and does not include an arbitrary constant. Lobes are shown in Figure 4.24 for Gaussian and Beckmann distributions for different values of m. The value of D is given as a distance from the surface element (to the outside of the lobe) and is a maximum along the reflection vector R.

The inverse dependence of R_s on $N \cdot V$ can now be considered. As the angle between N and V is increased, more of the surface is seen along the viewing direction. A greater proportion of the microfacets oriented in the H direction will be seen. If the surface is viewed normally then only a very small area will be seen. If, on the other hand, the surface is viewed at a low angle then a large number of microfacets will be seen along the surface. This effect is counteracted by the next factor.

The next term to be considered is G. This is an attenuation factor due to the effect of shadowing by the microfacets. Figure 4.25 shows the three possible cases which depend on the relative positions of L and V with respect to the microfacets oriented in the H direction. The term **shadowing** is used to describe interference in the incident light and **masking** to describe interference in the reflected light. The degree of masking and shadowing is dependent on the ratio l_1/l_2 (Figure 4.26) which describes the proportionate amount of the facets contributing to reflected light that is given by:

$$G = 1 - l_1/l_2$$

In the case where l_1 reduces to zero then all the reflected light escapes and

$$G = 1$$

A detailed derivation of the dependence of l_1/l_2 on L, V and H is given by Blinn (1977). For masking:

$$G_m = \frac{2(N \cdot H)(N \cdot V)}{V \cdot H}$$

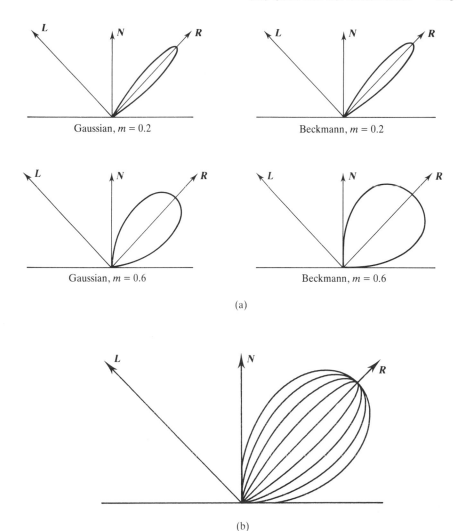

Figure 4.24
(a) Microfacet orientation distributions; (b) Gaussian distributions with m varying from 0.2 to 0.8.

For shadowing the situation is geometrically identical with the role of the vectors L and V interchanged. For shadowing we have:

$$G_s = \frac{2(N \cdot H)(N \cdot L)}{V \cdot H}$$

The value of G that must be used is the minimum of G_s and G_m. Thus:

$$G = \min\_\text{of}\ \{1, G_s, G_m\}$$

F, the Fresnel term in R_s, accounts for the colour change of the specular highlight as a function of the angle of incidence of the light source ϕ. This equation expresses the reflectance of a perfectly smooth mirror

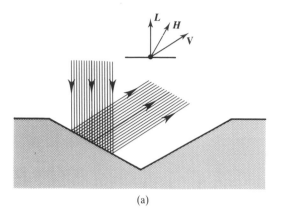

(a)

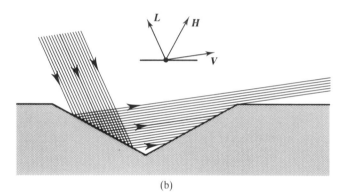

(b)

Figure 4.25
The interaction of light
with microfacet
reflecting surface (a)
No interference: angle
between *L* and *V* is
small – all light falling
on the microfacet
escapes. (b) Some
reflected light is
trapped – 'masking'.
(c) Some incident light
is 'shadowed' (inverse
of case b).

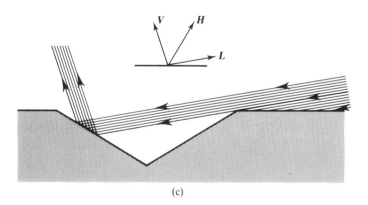

(c)

surface in terms of the refractive index of the material, η, and the angle of
incidence of the light source ϕ:

$$F = \frac{1}{2} \frac{\sin^2(\phi - \theta)}{\sin^2(\phi + \theta)} + \frac{\tan^2(\phi - \theta)}{\tan^2(\phi + \theta)} \tag{4.8}$$

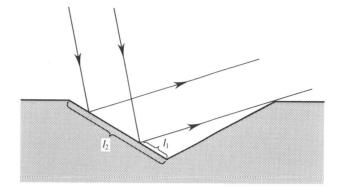

Figure 4.26
Amount of light which
escapes depends on
$(1 - l_1/l_2)$.

where:

ϕ is the angle of incidence, that is, $\cos^{-1}(\boldsymbol{L}\cdot\boldsymbol{H}) = \cos^{-1}(\boldsymbol{V}\cdot\boldsymbol{H})$

θ is the angle of refraction

$\sin \theta = \sin \phi/\eta \qquad$ where η is the refractive index of the material

These angles are shown in Figure 4.27. F is minimum, that is, most light is absorbed when $\phi = 0$ or normal incidence. No light is absorbed by the surface and F is equal to unity for $\phi = \pi/2$. The wavelength-dependent property of F comes from the fact that η is a function of wavelength. This dependence is not normally known and Cook and Torrance suggest a practical compromise, which is to fit the Fresnel equation to the measured normal reflectance for a polished surface.

Rewriting the Fresnel equation as:

$$F = \frac{1}{2}\frac{(g-c)^2}{(g+c)^2}\left\{1 + \frac{(c(g+c)-1)^2}{(c(g-c)+1)^2}\right\}$$

where:

$$c = \cos \phi = \boldsymbol{V}\cdot\boldsymbol{H}$$

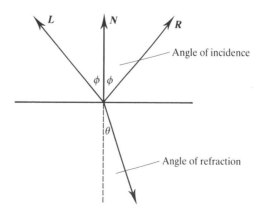

Figure 4.27
The angles used in the
Fresnel equation.

and:

$$g^2 = \eta^2 + c^2 - 1$$

for $\phi = 0$, that is, normal incidence:

$$F_0 = \frac{(\eta - 1)^2}{(\eta + 1)^2}$$

giving:

$$\mu = \frac{1 + F_0^{1/2}}{1 - F_0^{1/2}}$$

This then gives values for η as a function of wavelength from the measured values of F_0 and this can be substituted into Equation 4.8 to give F for any angle of incidence ϕ. A method to approximate the colour changes in the highlight as a function of ϕ is to proceed as follows:

(1) $F_{0,\text{red}}$, $F_{0,\text{green}}$ and $F_{0,\text{blue}}$ are obtained from measured values (Purdue University, 1970) giving η_{red}, η_{green} and η_{blue}.

(2) These values of μ are then substituted into Equation 4.8 to obtain $F_{\text{red}}(\phi)$, $F_{\text{green}}(\phi)$ and $F_{\text{blue}}(\phi)$. These slices through $F(\phi, \lambda)$ are shown in Figure 4.28.

(3) These values of F are used in the three $(\text{R}, \text{G}, \text{B})$ intensity

In general, both R_d and F (and thus R_s) vary with the geometry of reflection. Cook and Torrance assume that R_d is the bidirectional reflectance for normal illumination and restrict dependence on illuminating angle to F. The dependence of F on incidence angle ϕ and wavelength λ is shown in Figure 4.28 for a polished copper surface. From this it can be seen that significant colour changes only occur when ϕ approaches $\pi/2$. Also note that it is inaccurate to attempt to model 'realistic' colour by working with three sets of coefficients at the red, green and blue wavelengths. Accurate rendering of the colour and colour changes that simulate real metals requires consideration of the complete spectral variation of F and the spectral distribution of the light source. These considerations are described in detail in Chapter 14.

Plate 6 shows sets of three spheres obtained using this technique. The illustrations are exaggerated to show how the model controls the rendering of shiny metallic objects. In this respect the diffuse contributions have been deliberately set equal to zero. In practice, a non-zero diffuse contribution would produce a more 'recognizable' effect. The message is that shiny metallic objects behave almost as mirror spheres, the only difference being the colour of the specular highlight. In the illustration each sphere is illuminated by a perfect white illuminant at normal incidence and at an angle of 77°. The top sphere was produced by a form of Phong shading showing no change in intensity between the centre and edge highlight. The colour was controlled

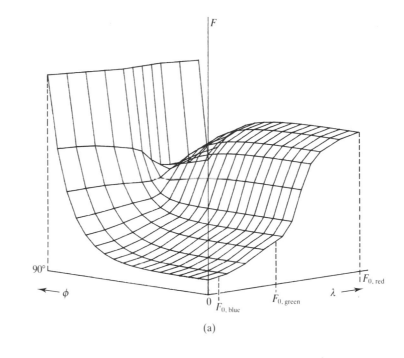

(a)

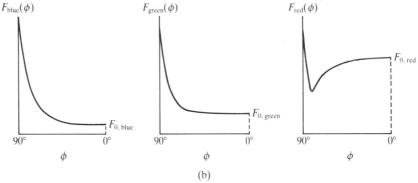

Figure 4.28
(a) Reflectance F as a function of wavelength (λ) and angle of incidence (polished copper). (b) The dependence of F on ϕ for red, green and blue wavelengths.

(b)

(given that k_d is zero) by setting the light source colours to the object colour. The centre sphere is rendered using the Cook and Torrance model but the F term dependence on the angle of incidence in R_s is omitted. This sphere exhibits an edge highlight of higher intensity than the centre highlight and is of markedly different shape to the Phong edge highlight. Finally, the bottom sphere includes the F term, which produces a distinct colour change – the edge highlight tending to white. Program 4.2 is straightforward code that rendered the bottom sphere in each case. It contains the data for copper (illuminated at normal incidence) defined at red, green and blue wavelengths.

Program 4.2   Code for rendering the bottom spheres in Plate 6.

```
program Fresnel (input, output);
    var
        dw, m, kd,ks, F0r, F0g, F0b: real;
        Rar, Rag, Rab, Rdr, Rdg, Rdb: real;
        V, L, H: vector;
        mur, mug, mub: real;
        Il, Ia: real;
        col: C;
    function GetMu (F0: real): real;
    begin
        GetMu := (1 + sqrt (F0))/(1 − sqrt (F0));
    end {GetMu};
    function GetF (phi, mu: real): real;
    var
        theta: real;
    begin
        {Fresnel curves are nearly horizontal for small phi}
        if phi < 0.005 then phi := 0.005;
        theta := arcsin (sin (phi)/mu);
        GetF := (sqr (sin (phi − theta))/sqr (sin (phi + theta))
                + sqr (tan (phi − theta))/sqr (tan (phi + theta)))/2;
    end {GetF};
    procedure EvalCol (N, L, H: vector; var col: C);
        var
            alpha, phi: real;
            D, Gs, Gm, G, F: real;
            Rs, Rsr, Rsg, Rsb: real;
            Ir, Ig, Ib: real;
    begin
        alpha := arccos (dot (N, H));
        D := 1/sqr (m)/sqr (sqr (cos (alpha)))*exp (− sqr (tan (alpha))/sqr (m));
        if alpha > pi/2 then D := 0;

        Gs := 2*dot (N, H)*dot (N, V)/dot (V, H);
        Gm := 2*dot (N, H)*dot (N, L)/dot (V, H);
        if Gs < Gm then G := Gs else G := Gm;
        if G > 1 then G := 1;
        if G < 0 then G := 0;
        Rs := D*G/pi/dot (N, V)/dot (N, L);
        phi := arccos (dot (N, L));

        F := GetF (phi, mur);
        Rsr := F*Rs;
        F := GetF (phi, mug);
        Rsg := F*Rs;
```

```
F := GetF (phi, mub);
Rsb := F*Rs;

Ir := Ia*Rar + Il*dot (N, L)*dw*(kd*Rdr + ks*Rsr);
Ig := Ia*Rag + Il*dot (N, L)*dw*(kd*Rdg + ks*Rsg);
Ib := Ia*Rab + Il*dot (N, L)*dw*(kd*Rdb + ks*Rsb);

if Ir < 0 then Ir := 0;
if Ig < 0 then Ig := 0;
if Ib < 0 then Ib := 0;

if Ir > 255 then Ir := 255;
if Ig > 255 then Ig := 255;
if Ib > 255 then Ib := 255;

with col do
    begin
    r := round (Ir);
    g := round (Ig);
    b := round (Ib);
    end
end {EvalCol};

procedure ShadeObject;

begin
    {
        This is specific to a particular object, see for example ShadeSphere in
        previous chapter. The procedure has to repeatedly call EvalCol
        supplying a surface normal. The value returned is the colour of the pixel.
    }
end {ShadeObject};

begin
    Il := 650000;
    dw := 0.0001;

    ks := 1.0;
    F0r := 0.755; {Fresnel coefficients for copper}
    F0g := 0.490;
    F0b := 0.095;
    m := 0.3;

    kd := 0.0;
    Rdr := F0r;
    Rdg := F0g;
    Rdb := F0b;

    Ia := 0.00001*Il;
    Rar := pi*Rdr;
    Rag := pi*Rdg;
    Rab := pi*Rdb;

    mur := GetMu (F0r);
```

```
mug := GetMu (F0g);
mub := GetMu (F0b);

with V do
   begin
      x := 0; y := 0; z := 1;
   end
with L do
   begin
      x := -5; y := 0; z := 10;
   end;
Normalize (L);
AddVector (V, L, H); Normalize (H);

ShadeObject;

end.
```

4.11   Illumination source models

Modelling the attributes of illumination sources is another neglected topic in computer graphics. This is because most scenes modelled consist of either a single object or a few objects and apparently different lighting conditions can be achieved by adjusting coefficients in the Phong reflection model. Also, the Phong reflection model functions ideally with simple point light sources. Consider the 20 spheres example used earlier. Visually these effects could result from changing the characteristics of the source, rather than altering the nature of the material, and it is likely that most people would identify changes in this example as being due to changes in lighting conditions.

In scenes of complex environments (such as interiors of rooms) realism can only be attained by taking into account the attributes of light sources. Rooms are lit either by artificial light or by daylight streaming in through a window. In either case we can identify the following attributes of a light source:

(1) its geometry – whether it is a fluorescent or incandescent source or a window,

(2) its luminous intensity distribution, which will be a function of the geometry, and

(3) its spectral distribution; fluorescent lights have a distinctly different spectral distribution from both incandescent lights and daylight.

The main problem with modelling light sources accurately is the computational expense. A different *L* vector must be calculated for each point

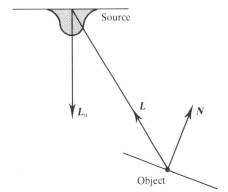

Figure 4.29
Warn's method of representing a light source as a specularly reflecting surface.

on the surface and an emitted intensity I calculated from $I(L)$, the luminous intensity distribution of the source. Certain empirical approaches have evolved that deal with the first two factors, the simplest of which is Warn's method (Warn, 1983).

The third factor is dealt with in depth in Chapter 14. For the moment we can note that a coloured light source can be approximately modelled by making I_i a function of wavelength.

4.11.1 Warn's method for modelling illumination sources

This is a simple method for modelling a spotlight as an empirical intensity distribution – the cosine model (Phong) of reflected light. Light is assumed to emanate from a source whose predominant direction is specified by a vector L_N. Given that L is the vector from the source to the object point, the intensity reflected from a point due to a source is:

$$I = \text{source intensity} \, [k_d(N \cdot L) + k_s(N \cdot H)^n]$$

The source intensity in this case is given by (Figure 4.29):

$$\text{Source intensity} = [I_i(L_N \cdot L)^s]$$

This illumination model provides control over the concentration and the direction of the light source. Warn points out that point light sources are difficult to position to produce highlights in a desired area of the object. In this model the light source is fixed in position, but its direction is changed by changing L_N. The concentration of the light source and hence the area (and generally the shape) of the highlight it produces is controlled by adjusting the index s. Low exponents simulate floodlights whereas high s values will tend to simulate spotlights. The model is exactly equivalent to representing the light source as a surface receiving light from a point light source and specularly reflecting it according to Phong's model.

Warn extends this model to generate special effects by limiting the spatial extent of the light to provide sharp cut-offs. This is equivalent to studio lights that have flaps or barn doors. Such devices can be used in practice to emphasize a crease in an object, by lining up a flap with the crease so that the object is illuminated above the crease, but not below. Rather than have the complex geometry of implementing these as actual flaps Warn models their effect as parallel extents in the X, Y and Z axes in world coordinate space, defining a rectangularly shaped illumination volume.

Another benefit that easily accrues from this model is that variable cone-shaped sources can be simulated. This can be implemented by comparing the angle that L makes with L_N against a cone threshold, simulating a point source with a conical intensity distribution.

4.11.2   Using goniometric diagrams

Verbeck and Greenberg (1984) introduced a comprehensive light source model in 1984. Although this is now somewhat overshadowed with Greenberg's radiosity method (Chapter 10) it is a model that uses the Phong diffuse component, modulated by an intensity value that is computed from a **goniometric diagram** of the source. Verbeck points out that the extensions to the standard intensity computations are quite simple, yet dramatic improvements in image quality can be achieved.

Luminous intensity distribution is a three-dimensional field and a goniometric diagram is a slice through this field. Generalizing the Phong diffuse term to include a reflection coefficient that is a function of wavelength, we have:

$$I = k_{\mathrm{d}}(\lambda) \sum_n (N \cdot L_n) I_{\mathrm{i},n}$$

the intensity due to n point light sources. To include the luminous intensity distribution $I_{\mathrm{i},n}$ is replaced with $I_{\mathrm{i}\theta,n}$ and we have:

$$I = k_{\mathrm{d}}(\lambda) \sum_n (N \cdot L_n) I_{\mathrm{i}\theta,n} S_n$$

where $I_{\mathrm{i}\theta,n}$ is the relative intensity of the nth light source which is now a function of θ specified by the goniometric diagram (Figure 4.30). Also included is S_n, a 0 or 1 valued occlusion factor.

This is an equation that extends the Phong reflection model to cope with point sources with particular intensity distributions expressed as goniometric diagrams. It can be used to simulate a light source of any geometry by treating the light source as a summation of m point sources.

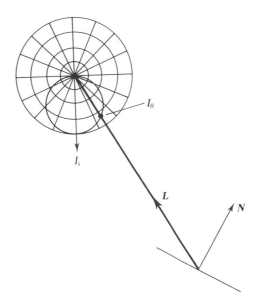

Figure 4.30
Using a goniometric
diagram to modulate
the calculated
intensity.

Projects, notes and suggestions ───────────

4.1 Shading spheres

Implement the program that shades spheres, for more than one light source. Alter Equation 4.3 so that different coloured light sources are possible (*I* now has red, green and blue components) and experiment with coloured light sources.

What are the problems involved in extending this scheme for shading spheres to any quadric surface and why is the general philosphy of combining a screen space procedure and a world space implicit definition unsatisfactory?

4.2 Light source interaction

Develop an interaction view port for Project 4.1, showing a view of a single sphere together with the light sources, that enables a user to change the position of each light source.

4.3 Reflection model representation

Write a program that generates a wireframe model of a three-dimensional version of Figure 4.12. This will show the variation in intensity over the hemispherical space surrounding a single point whose reflected intensity is calculated from Equation 4.3.

Ensure that the polygonal resolution is increased sufficiently in the region of the specular bump.

4.4   Transparency

Implement the empirical transparency scheme given by Equations 4.5 and 4.6 by shading a hollow transparent sphere in front of a suitable background.

4.5   Postprocessing shaded images

Write a program that postprocesses a shaded image using LUTs. Design an interface that allows a user to rubber-band LUT profiles as suggested by Plate 5.

4.6   Reflection model solid

Repeat Project 4.3 but this time use Equation 4.7 to determine the reflected intensity.

4.7   Cook and Torrance model

Investigate the visual effect of the Cook and Torrance model using a sphere and light sources at different angles as suggested by Plate 6.

5 | Rendering Algorithms

5.1 Introduction

Having considered the geometric processes in previous chapters, we shall now look at the 'non-geometric' algorithms required in the rendering pipeline. We will mainly be concerned with polygon mesh objects although occasionally techniques for other representations will be described.

Rendering is a general term that describes the overall process of going from a database representation of a three-dimensional object to a shaded two-dimensional projection on a view surface. It involves a number of separate processes:

(1) setting up a polygon model that will contain all the information which is subsequently required in the shading process;

(2) applying linear transformations to the polygon mesh model, for example, transformations to position objects within a scene, and viewing transformations;

(3) culling back-facing polygons;

(4) clipping polygons against a view volume;

(5) scan converting or rasterizing polygons, that is, converting the vertex-based model into a set of pixel coordinates;

(6) applying a hidden surface removal algorithm;

(7) shading the individual pixels using an interpolative or incremental shading scheme.

The first two processes were dealt with in earlier chapters and we now consider the remainder. In most popular rendering strategies operations 5, 6 and 7 are carried out simultaneously in a single interdependent algorithm. However, computer graphics textbooks normally fragment the rendering process. They usually contain a chapter comparing hidden surface removal algorithms without regard to how these algorithms are integrated with the other processes. In this text we have ignored the classification and description of the many hidden surface removal algorithms in favour of an integrated approach to the entire latter half of the rendering process. So rather than dealing with them as unconnected processes, we shall wherever possible try to show how they work together.

It would appear that most rendering systems have settled for some manifestation of the **Z-buffer** approach, and indeed graphics workstations are now available with hardware Z-buffers. Other hidden surface removal algorithms find applications in special contexts such as flight simulators. A complete rendering system based on this approach is given in Appendix C.

5.2 Culling and clipping

Culling or **backface elimination** was introduced in Chapter 2. It is an operation that compares the orientation of complete polygons with the view point or centre of projection and removes those polygons that cannot be seen. If a scene only contains a single convex object, then culling generalizes to **hidden surface removal**. A general hidden surface removal algorithm is always required when one polygon partially obscures another. On average, half of the polygons in a polyhedron are backfacing and the advantage of this process is that a simple test removes these polygons from consideration by a more expensive hidden surface removal algorithm.

The test for visibility is straightforward and is best carried out in view space. We calculate the outward normal for a polygon (Section 1.5.3) and examine the sign of the dot product of this and the vector from the centre of projection (Figure 5.1). Thus:

$$\text{visibility} := N_p \cdot N > 0$$

where:

N_p is the polygon normal
N is the 'line of sight' vector

In Chapter 3 we described the geometry and specification of the viewing frustum, which you will recall gave us the following limits in homogeneous coordinates:

$$-w \leqslant x \leqslant w$$
$$-w \leqslant y \leqslant w$$
$$0 \leqslant z \leqslant w$$

We will now look at how we can extend this definition, which tells us if a single point is inside the view frustum, to polygons.

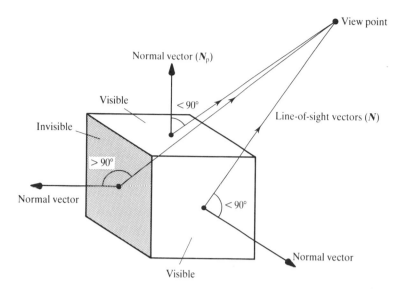

Figure 5.1
Culling or backface
elimination.

Objects that need to be clipped are most easily dealt with by the Sutherland–Hodgman re-entrant polygon clipper (Sutherland and Hodgman, 1974a). This is easily extended to three dimensions. A polygon is tested against a clip boundary by testing each polygon edge against a single infinite clip boundary. This structure is shown in Figure 5.2.

We consider the innermost loop of this algorithm, where a single edge is being tested against a single clip boundary. In this step the process outputs zero, one or two vertices to add to the list of vertices defining the clipped polygon. Figure 5.3 shows the four possible cases. An edge is defined by vertices *S* and *F*. In the first case the edge is inside the clip boundary and the existing vertex *F* is added to the output list. In the second case the edge

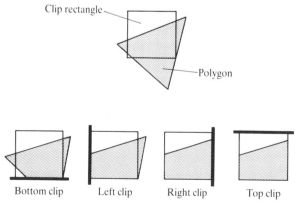

Figure 5.2
Sutherland–Hodgman
clipper clips each
polygon against each
edge of each clip
rectangle.

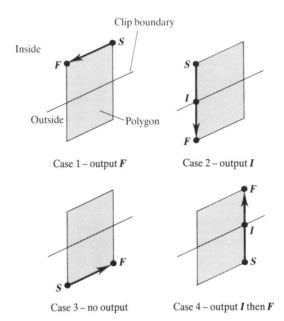

Figure 5.3
Sutherland–Hodgman
clipper – within the
polygon loop each
edge of a polygon is
tested against each clip
boundary.

crosses the clip boundary and a new vertex **I** is calculated and output. The
third case shows an edge that is completely outside the clip boundary. This
produces no output. (The intersection for the edge that caused the excursion
outside is calculated in the previous iteration and the intersection for the
edge that causes the incursion inside is calculated in the next iteration.) The
final case again produces a new vertex which is added to the output list.

To calculate whether a point or vertex is inside, outside or on the clip
boundary we use a dot product test. Figure 5.4 shows a clip boundary **C** with
an outward normal N_c and a line with end points **S** and **F**. We represent the
line parametrically as:

$$P(t) = S + (F - S)t \qquad (5.1)$$

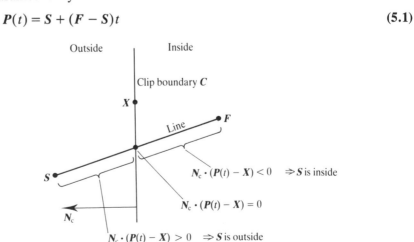

Figure 5.4
Dot product test to
determine whether a
line is inside or outside
a clip boundary.

where:

$$0 \leqslant t \leqslant 1$$

We define an arbitrary point on the clip boundary as X and a vector from X to any point on the line. The dot product of this vector and the normal allows us to distinguish whether a point on the line is outside, inside or on the clip boundary. In the case shown in Figure 5.4:

$$N_c \cdot (S - X) > 0 \qquad \Rightarrow S \text{ is outside the clip region}$$
$$N_c \cdot (F - X) < 0 \qquad \Rightarrow F \text{ is inside the clip region}$$

and:

$$N_c \cdot (P(t) - X) = 0$$

defines the point of intersection of the line and the clip boundary. Solving Equation 5.1 for t enables the intersecting vertex to be calculated and added to the output list.

In practice the algorithm is written recursively. As soon as a vertex is output the procedure calls itself with that vertex and no intermediate storage is required for the partially clipped polygon. This structure makes the algorithm eminently suitable for hardware implementation.

5.3 Incremental shading techniques

Most images currently generated in computer graphics apply the Phong reflection model, described in Chapter 4, to polygon mesh models. Polygon mesh models are distinguished by the fact that the geometric information is only available at the vertices of a polygon. Incremental or interpolative shading techniques apply simple reflection models to polygons, calculating intensities at the vertices, then interpolating values for interior points. Interior points are evaluated in scanline order (from left to right) and the schemes are easily integrated into a Z-buffer or a scanline hidden surface removal algorithm. Incidentally, on terminology: the term 'shading' is loosely used to signify the application of a 'point' reflection model over the entire surface of an object. The term 'rendering' appears to be used to mean the complete process of going from an object database to the final shaded object on a screen.

Two incremental shading techniques are common: Gouraud interpolation (Gouraud, 1971) and Phong interpolation (Phong, 1975a). Phong interpolation gives more accurate highlights and is generally the preferred model. The Gouraud method tends to be confined to applications where the diffuse component is sufficient, or to preview images prior to final rendering.

Phong shading is more expensive than Gouraud shading and obeys the first law of computer graphics, which appears to be that the required processing time grows exponentially with perceived image quality. However, Gouraud shading has become almost standard in recent graphics hardware and Phong shading is also available. This trend is reflected in the proposed standard PHIGS+ which contains Gouraud and Phong shading utilities (PHIGS, 1988).

This section deals with both these methods and we also look at how to combine these methods and speed up the shading process without losing quality. Doing shading calculations efficiently is a neglected topic in computer graphics. Phong calculations can greatly exceed more than 50% of the total rendering time; addressing the problem of shading using an efficient method should be considered just as important as the quality of the reflection model. It is mandatory in areas such as three-dimensional animation where large numbers of frames have to be generated.

Another problem that must be addressed by interpolative shading techniques is final polygon visibility. Polygon boundaries should be invisible in the final shaded version and some impression of the original surface that the polygon mesh approximates restored. We can thus identify two functions of a shading scheme for polygon meshes:

(1) to use some interpolative method for interior points, and

(2) to diminish the visibility of the polygon mesh approximation.

The first shading schemes to be used in computer graphics were developed by Bouknight (1970) and Wylie *et al.* (1967). Wylie's method calculated an intensity at the vertices of triangular facets on the basis of distance from the view point and then used linear interpolation to assign an intensity to interior points. In Bouknight's work the emphasis was on hidden surface removal and the polygons were 'constant' shaded; that is, a single intensity was calculated for each polygon and used over its entire area. This method, although it certainly imparts an impression of three-dimensionality (see Plate 7) leaves the polygon mesh structure glaringly obvious.

5.3.1   Gouraud shading

The generally acknowledged first scheme that overcame the disadvantages of constant shading of polygons uses bilinear intensity interpolation. This is known as **Gouraud shading** (Gouraud, 1971). It is a simple and economic scheme that does not entirely eliminate the visibility of polygons. It suffers from **Mach banding** – where piecewise linear intensity changes across a polygon boundary trigger the human visual system into perceiving the boundary as a bright band. The standard explanation for this is that the human visual system is sensitive to the first derivative of intensity because of our need to detect and enhance edges.

The Gouraud scheme is normally restricted to the diffuse component of the reflection model developed in Chapter 4. This is because the shape of

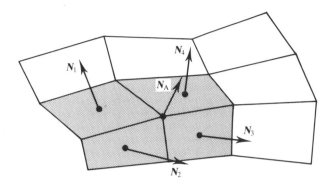

Figure 5.5
The vertex normal N_A is the average of the normals N_1, N_2, N_3 and N_4, the normals of the polygons that meet at the vertex.

the specular highlights, using this scheme, depends strongly on the underlying polygon mesh. An obvious highlight example that Gouraud shading misses altogether is the case of a highlight in the middle of a polygon. If there is no highlight component at any vertex then there is no way that the highlight will be recovered by the interpolation. The diffuse component from Equation 4.2 is:

$$I_i k_d \, (L \cdot N)/(r + k)$$

If we assume the light source is at infinity then $L \cdot N$ is constant over the surface of the polygon. The only variable is r, the distance to the view point. If we ignore the fact that the variation of r over the polygon is non-linear (or even ignore r altogether), then we can calculate intensities at the vertices and use bilinear interpolation to calculate all other intensities.

The technique first calculates the intensity at each vertex of the polygon by applying Equation 4.2. Note that this operation must be carried out in world coordinate space. The normal N used in this equation is the so-called **vertex normal** and this is calculated as the average of the normals of the polygons that share the vertex (Figure 5.5). This is an important feature of the method and the vertex normal is an approximation to the true normal of the surface (which the polygon mesh represents) at that point. Plate 7 shows a wireframe object with the vertex normals superimposed.

Now, as was implied in Chapter 2, it is usual to calculate vertex normals once only and to store these as part of the object database. What happens, however, if polygons have been clipped? We have to recalculate vertex normals and vertex intensities. Consider Figure 5.6 which shows a cross-section through three polygons. Before clipping the two vertex normals are N_1 and N_2. After clipping the new vertex normal N_2' can be calculated by interpolating between N_1 and N_2. Thus the object is shaded up to the clip boundary as if the clipped portion still existed. This effect is shown in Plate 2.

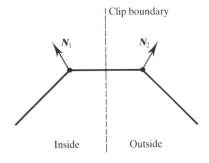

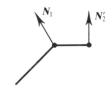

Figure 5.6
Vertex normals and
clipping: N_2' is
interpolated from N_1
and N_2.

A pass through the data structure storing the object will calculate an
intensity, I_v, for each vertex. The interpolation process that calculates the
intensity over a polygon surface can then be integrated with a scan conversion algorithm that evaluates the position of the edges of a polygon from the
vertices in the data structure. The intensities at the edge of each scan line
are calculated from the vertex intensities and the intensities along a scan line
from these (Figure 5.7). The interpolation equations are as follows:

$$I_a = \frac{1}{y_1 - y_2} \left(I_1(y_s - y_2) + I_2(y_1 - y_s) \right)$$

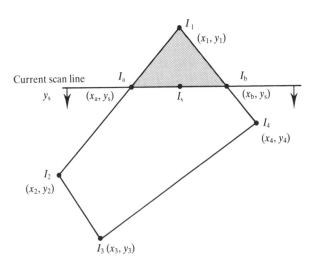

Figure 5.7
The notation used for
the intensity
interpolation
equations.

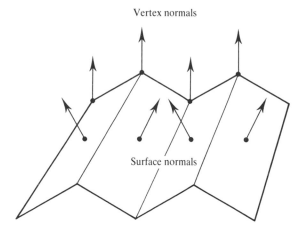

Vertex normals

Surface normals

Figure 5.8
A regularly corrugated surface producing identical vertex normals from non-identical surface normals.

$$I_b = \frac{1}{y_1 - y_4}\left(I_1(y_s - y_4) + I_4(y_1 - y_s)\right)$$

$$I_s = \frac{1}{x_b - x_a}\left(I_a(x_b - x_s) + I_b(x_s - x_a)\right)$$

For computational efficiency these equations are implemented as incremental calculations. This is particularly important in the case of the third equation, which is evaluated for every pixel. If we define Δx to be the incremental distance along a scan line then ΔI, the change in intensity, from one pixel to the next is:

$$\Delta I_s = \frac{\Delta x}{x_b - x_a}\left(I_b - I_a\right)$$

$$I_{s,n} = I_{s,n-1} + \Delta I_s$$

Apart from Mach banding, two well-known errors that can be introduced in Gouraud shading are:

- Anomalies can appear in animated sequences because the intensity interpolation is carried out in screen coordinates from vertex normals calculated in world coordinates. This is not invariant with respect to transformations such as rotation and in animated sequences frame-to-frame disturbances can be caused by this.

- The process of averaging surface normals to provide vertex normals for the intensity calculation can cause errors which result in, for example, corrugations being smoothed out. Figure 5.8 shows three normals all pointing in the same direction. This would result in a visually flat surface.

    At this stage it is useful to consider the position of the calculation of vertex intensities in the overall rendering pipeline. Refer again to Figure 2.22

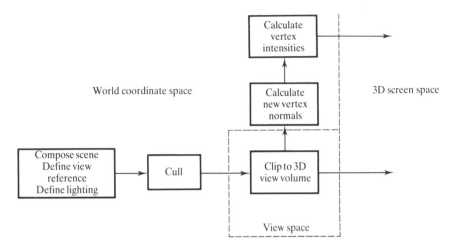

Figure 5.9
Elaborating the 3D
rendering pipeline
(Figure 2.22) for
Gouraud shading.

which showed a general three-dimensional rendering pipeline. Recall that
the vertex intensity calculations are carried out in world coordinate space. If
we perform culling also in world coordinate space, then the vertex intensities
can be calculated once only and are independent of any change in the view
transform. This strategy can be advantageous in, for example, 'walk
through' animation where only the view point is changing in consecutive
animation frames. However, bear in mind that any clipping that takes place
requires calculation of new vertex intensities. Thus our general three-dimensional pipeline can be elaborated for Gouraud shading, as shown in Figure
5.9.

5.3.2   Phong interpolation

A method due to Bui-Tuong Phong (1975a) overcomes some of the disadvantages of Gouraud shading, and specular reflection can be successfully
incorporated in the scheme. In particular we can now have a specular highlight in the middle of a polygon despite the fact that each of the vertex
normal angles would not produce a highlight. The features of the method
are:

- Bilinear interpolation is still used so that points interior to polygons can
  be calculated incrementally.
- The attributes interpolated are the vertex normals, rather than vertex
  intensities. These are calculated, as before, by averaging the normal vectors of the surfaces that share the vertex.
- A *separate* intensity is evaluated for each pixel from the interpolated
  normals.

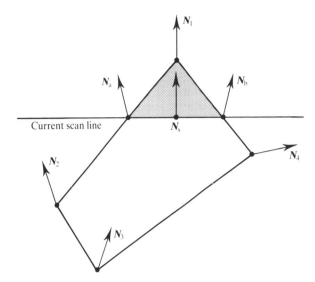

Figure 5.10
In the Phong method vector interpolation replaces intensity interpolation.

- Again we need to assume that both the light source and the view point are at infinity so that the intensity at a point is a function only of the interpolated normal.

    The first stage in the process is the same as for the Gouraud method – for any polygon we evaluate the vertex normals. For each scan line in the polygon we evaluate by linear interpolation the normal vectors at the end of each line (Figure 5.10). These two vectors, N_a and N_b, are then used to interpolate N_s. We thus derive a normal vector for *each* point or pixel on the polygon that is an approximation to the real normal on the curved surface approximated by the polygon. This feature accounts for the quality of Phong shading. N_s, the interpolated normal vector, is then used in the intensity calculation. The vector interpolation is, of course, carried out in world coordinates. This idea is represented in Figure 5.11, which shows that vector interpolation tends to restore the curvature of the original surface that has been approximated by a polygon mesh.

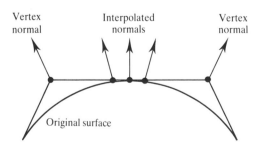

Figure 5.11
Vector interpolation tends to 'restore' curvature.

Referring to the notation used in Figures 5.7 and 5.10 we have:

$$N_a = \frac{1}{y_1 - y_2} (N_1(y_s - y_2) + N_2(y_1 - y_s))$$

$$N_b = \frac{1}{y_1 - y_4} (N_1(y_s - y_4) + N_4(y_1 - y_2)) \qquad (5.2)$$

$$N_s = \frac{1}{x_b - x_a} (N_s(x_b - x_s) + N_b(x_s - x_a))$$

These are vector equations that would each be implemented as a set of three equations, one for each of the components of the vectors in world space. This makes the interpolation phase three times as expensive as Gouraud shading. In addition, there is an application of the Phong model intensity equation at every pixel. Incremental computations can be employed as with intensity interpolation, and Equations 5.2, for example, would be implemented as:

$$N_{sx,n} = N_{sx,n-1} + \Delta N_{sx}$$
$$N_{sy,n} = N_{sy,n-1} + \Delta N_{sy}$$
$$N_{sz,n} = N_{sz,n-1} + \Delta N_{sz}$$

where N_{sx}, N_{sy} and N_{sz} are the components of a general scanline normal vector N_s and

$$\Delta N_{sx} = \frac{\Delta x}{x_b - x_a} (N_{bx} - N_{ax})$$

$$\Delta N_{sy} = \frac{\Delta x}{x_b - x_a} (N_{by} - N_{ay})$$

$$\Delta N_{sz} = \frac{\Delta x}{x_b - x_a} (N_{bz} - N_{az})$$

Plate 7 is a composite illustration showing the same object after constant shading, Gouraud shading and Phong shading.

5.3.3   Comparison of Gouraud and Phong shading

Gouraud shading is effective for shading surfaces which reflect light diffusely. Specular reflections can be modelled using Gouraud shading, but the shape of the specular highlight produced is dependent on the relative positions of the underlying polygons. The advantage of Gouraud shading is that it is computationally the less expensive of the two models, only requiring the evaluation of the intensity equation at the polygon vertices, and then bilinear interpolation of these values for each pixel.

Phong shading produces highlights which are much less dependent on the underlying polygons. However, more calculations are required involving the interpolation of the surface normal and the evaluation of the intensity function for each pixel. These facts suggest a straightforward approach to speeding up Phong shading by combining Gouraud and Phong shading.

5.3.4 Speeding up Phong shading

In any practical context, such as the production of an animated sequence, the application of a speed-up method to Phong shading is a vital adjunct to a Phong reflection and interpolation scheme. This section describes two useful speed-up techniques.

Speed-up techniques generally fall into one of two categories: geometric and numerical. Geometric approaches are to be found in (Phong, 1975a) and (Bergman *et al.*, 1986) Phong's method is based on the reflection vector and an extra coordinate transformation to align the light source (assuming there is only one) along the z axis. Bergman uses a simple test which compares the directions of the polygon's vertex normals with the direction of maximum highlight. This will detect only those specular highlights which correspond to the simplest case (case 1) given below. Although most highlighted polygons fall into this category the remainder are aesthetically significant. It is particularly important in animated sequences to detect all highlighted polygons otherwise highlights may 'switch' on and off. The emphasis in (Bergman *et al.*, 1986) is on the high-speed interactive development of single images, where a simple highlight test will suffice.

A numerical approach to efficient shading has been investigated by Duff (1979) and Bishop and Weimar (1986). These are mathematical optimizations of the basic Phong method. Bishop, for example, uses a two-dimensional Taylor series to approximate the Phong equation, claiming that no visual penalty is incurred in doing this since the Phong normal interpolation is itself an approximation. The technique results in a method that evaluates an ambient, diffuse and specular term for each pixel with five additions plus one memory access per pixel.

We now describe two methods that speed up shading by combining Gouraud and Phong shading. The first is an extremely simple technique that results in approximately 35% saving in the shading phase. The second method – the H test – is a far more elaborate geometric approach that detects those polygons in which a highlight will appear. This results in even greater savings as will be described. Both methods are effectively combinations of Gouraud and Phong shading.

Simple Phong shading speed up
In Phong shading one vertex normal is linearly interpolated towards the other, one pixel step at a time. At each pixel it is normalized, and an intensity calculated from the standard Phong intensity equation.

There is virtually no loss of image quality if double-step interpolation is used, with intermediate pixels being calculated from simple averaging.

Note that this is equivalent to Gouraud interpolative shading where each polygon projects onto a three-pixel-wide screen area. At this resolution, of course, the disadvantages of using Gouraud shading disappear. You will recall that Gouraud shading cannot be used for highlights, in general, because the large polygon areas over which the interpolation is performed lead to bad highlights.

Highlight detection – the H test

Generally, an object will have relatively few highlighted polygons, so it would be computationally more efficient to Phong shade the highlighted polygons, and to Gouraud shade the remainder (Harrison, Mitchell and Watt, 1988). In practice, however, the diffuse components produced for a particular pixel by the two interpolation methods differ slightly, and it is necessary to Gouraud shade the entire object. The Phong specular term is then evaluated on the highlighted polygons, and combined with the Gouraud diffuse value.

To enable the implementation of the combined shading algorithm, a test has to be determined to ascertain which of the polygons are partially or fully within an area of specular highlight. This test is known as the **highlight test** or **H-test** (Harrison, Mitchell and Watt, 1988).

The highlight detection is based on a hierarchy of simple tests that predict the value of the highlight function on the line between two vertices. For there to be a contribution from the specular term ($N \cdot H$) (vector H is the halfway vector described in Chapter 4) we can say:

$$N \cdot H \geq T$$

where T is a threshold term. The value of this term is examined at pairs of vertices to predict the variation in its magnitude along the edge. A hierarchy of five simple tests performs this prediction:

- Test A determines whether $N \cdot H$ at any vertex is greater than the threshold value.
- Test B determines if $N \cdot H$ reaches a maximum along any polygon edge.
- Test C determines whether the maximum of test B is greater than zero.
- Test D determines if this maximum is greater than the threshold value.
- Test E is performed once per polygon, and determines if a polygon has a maximum along each of its edges.

Figure 5.12 shows the four distinct highlight possibilities for a polygon:

(1) A highlight can cover one or more vertices, intersecting the lines between this vertex and its two neighbouring vertices.

(2) A highlight can spread over a single line between two vertices, but not over any vertices.

(3) A highlight can be contained within a polygon, or

(4) There is no highlight associated with the polygon.

The five tests (A–E) are used to ascertain which of the four highlight cases has occurred. The way in which the tests are organized to do this is shown in Figure 5.13. Code for the algorithm in the form of a function is given in Program 5.1.

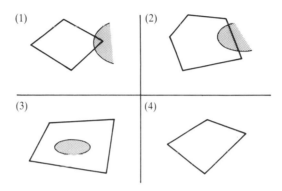

Figure 5.12
Highlight possibilities with respect to a single polygon.

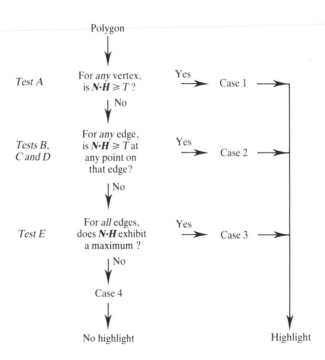

Figure 5.13
Testing for highlights.

Program 5.1   The H test algorithm.

```
function H_test (T: real; Hv: vector): boolean;

   type vector = record
                       xc, yc, zc: real;
                   end;
   var
      a, b, c, d, e, f, g, h: real;
      all_edges_max: boolean;
      highlight: boolean;
      Av, Bv, Hv: vector;

begin
   all_edges_max := true;
   highlight := false;

   while more_vertices and not highlight do
      begin
         get_next_normal (Av);
         if dot (Av, Hv) > T then    {the current vertex is within the}
            highlight := true           {range of a specular highlight}
      end;
   reset_polygon_data;

   while more_vertices and not highlight do
      begin
         get_next_pair_of_normals (Av, Bv);
         a := dot (Av, Hv); b := dot (Bv, Hv);
         c := dot (Av, Bv);
         d := b*c − a; e := a*c − b;
         f := d*e;

         if f > 0 then    {the specular intensity reaches a maximum along}
                            {the current edge}

            begin
               g := a*d + b*e;
               if d*g > 0 then    {the maximum is greater than zero}
                  if g*g >= T*T*(d*d + 2*c*f + e*e) then    {the maximum
                     highlight := true                        is greater
                                                              than the
                                                              threshold}

            end
         else    {the current edge did not have a maximum}
            all_edges_max := false
      end;
   H_test := highlight or all_edges_max;
end {H_test};
```

5.4   Rasterization

Having looked at how general points within a polygon can be assigned intensities that are determined from vertex values, we now look at how we determine the actual pixels for which we require intensity values. The process is known as **rasterization** or **scan conversion**. We consider this somewhat tricky problem in two parts. First, how do we determine the pixels which the edge of a polygon straddles? Second, how do we organize this information to determine the interior points?

5.4.1   Rasterizing edges

There are two different ways of rasterizing an edge, based on whether line drawing or solid area filling is being used. Line drawing is not covered in this book, since we are interested in solid objects. However, the main feature of line-drawing algorithms (such as Bresenham's algorithm (Bresenham, 1965)) is that they must generate a linear sequence of pixels with no gaps (Figure 5.14). For solid area filling, a less rigorous approach suffices. We can fill a polygon using horizontal line segments; these can be thought of as the intersection of the polygon with a particular scan line. Thus, for any given scan line, what is required are the left- and right-hand limits of the segment, that is, the intersections of the scan line with the left- and right-hand polygon edges. This means that, for each edge, we need to generate a sequence of pixels corresponding to the edge's intersections with the scan lines (Figure 5.14b). This sequence may have gaps, when interpreted as a line, as shown by the right-hand edge in the diagram.

The conventional way of calculating these pixel coordinates is by use of what is grandly referred to as a 'digital differential analyser', or DDA. All this really consists of is finding how much the x coordinate increases per scan line, and then repeatedly adding this increment.

Let (xs, ys), (xe, ye) be the start and end points of the edge (we

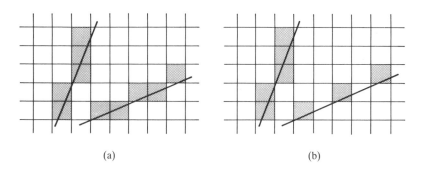

Figure 5.14
Pixel sequences required for (a) line drawing and (b) polygon filling.

(a)   (b)

assume that $ye > ys$) The simplest algorithm for rasterizing sufficient for polygon edges is:

$$x := xs$$
$$m := (xe - xs)/(ye - ys)$$
for $y := ys$ **to** ye **do**
  $output \ (round(x), y)$
  $x := x + m$

The main drawback of this approach is that m and x need to be represented as floating-point values, with a floating-point addition and real-to-integer conversion each time round the loop. A method due to Swanson and Thayer (1986) provides an integer-only version of this algorithm. It can be derived from the above in two logical stages. First, we separate out x and m into integer and fractional parts. Then each time round the loop, we separately add the two parts, adding a carry to the integer part should the fractional part overflow. Also, we initially set the fractional part of x to -0.5 to make rounding easy, as well as simplifying the overflow condition. In pseudocode:

$$xi := xs$$
$$xf := -0.5$$
$$mi := (xe - xs) \ \textbf{div} \ (ye - ys)$$
$$mf := (xe - xs)/(ye - ys) - mi$$

for $y := ys$ **to** ye **do**
  $output \ (xi, y)$
  $xi := xi + mi$
  $xf := xf + mf$
  if $xf > 0.0$ **then** $\{xi := xi + 1; xf := xf - 1.0\}$

Because the fractional part is now independent of the integer part, it is possible to scale it throughout by $2(ye - ys)$, with the effect of converting everything to integer arithmetic:

$$xi := xs$$
$$xf := -(ye - ys)$$
$$mi := (xe - xs) \ \textbf{div} \ (ye - ys)$$
$$mf := 2*[(xe - xs) \ \textbf{mod} \ (ye - ys)]$$

for $y := ys$ **to** ye **do**
  $output \ (xi, y)$
  $xi := xi + mi$
  $xf := xf + mf$
  if $xf > 0$ **then** $\{xi := xi + 1; xf := xf - 2*(ye - ys)\}$

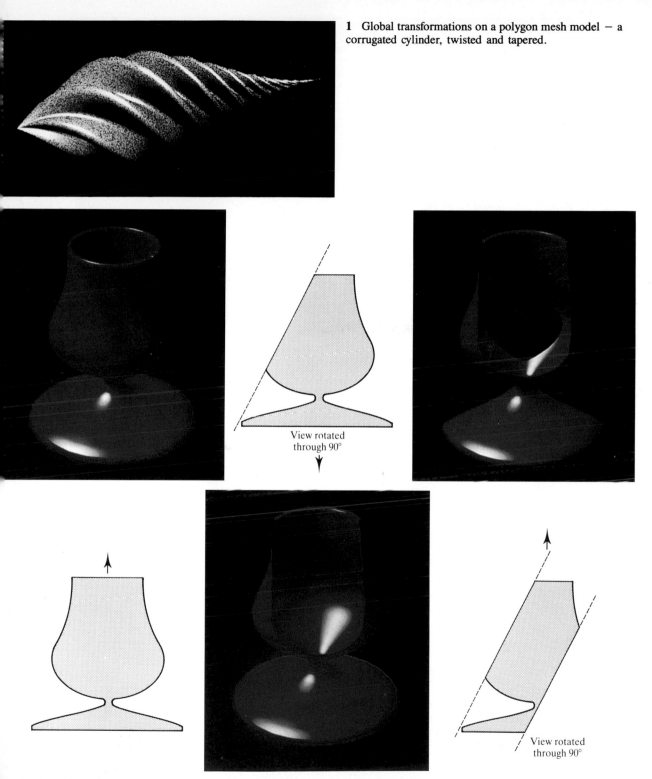

1 Global transformations on a polygon mesh model − a corrugated cylinder, twisted and tapered.

View rotated through 90°

View rotated through 90°

A view volume interacting with a shaded object. Bringing near and far planes into coincidence with an object; *(centre)* near plane coincides; *(right)* both planes coincide with the object.

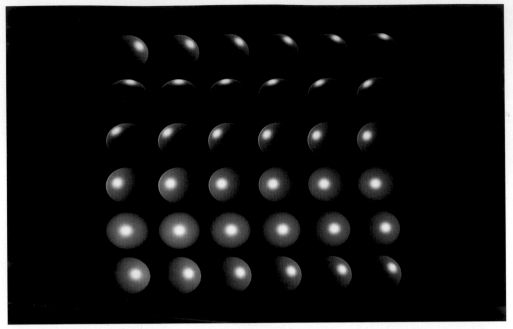

3 Using Phong's reflection model with no ambient term, a distant point light source is moved around an orange sphere. ('Oranges of confusion' courtesy of Steve Maddock)

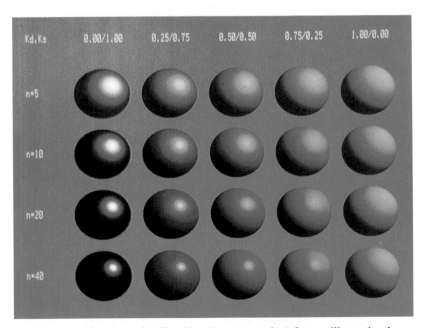

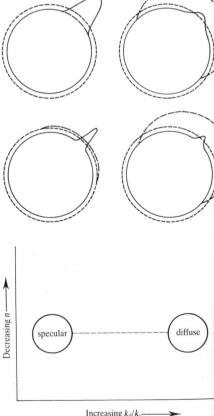

4 *(Above and bottom right)* The 20 spheres example (after an illustration by Roy Hall). *(top right)* Slices through the specular bump showing the variation in magnitude of the diffuse, specular and ambient components over the surface of each of the following spheres: top row, spheres 1 and 4; bottom row, spheres 1 and 4.

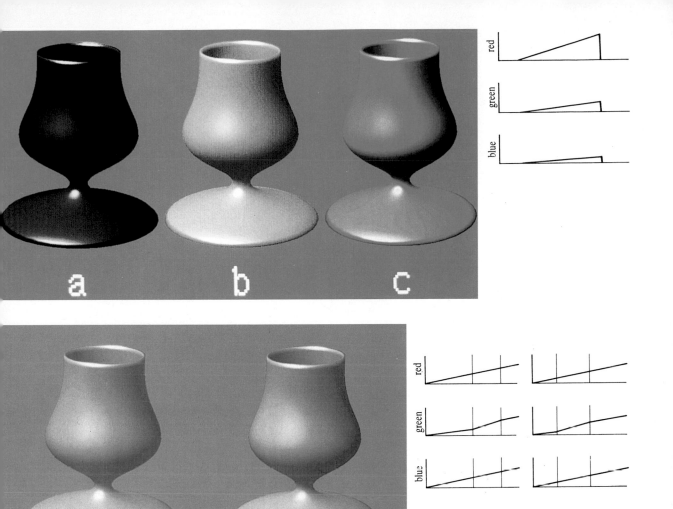

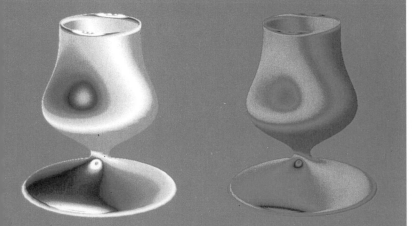

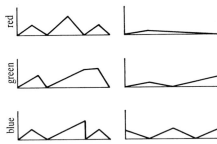

5 Using LUT profiles to control the colour and the degree of specularity of an object. *(top)* All objects have a similar profile, copper (object a) is shown. *(centre)* Varying the position of the blend region. *(bottom)* Special effects.

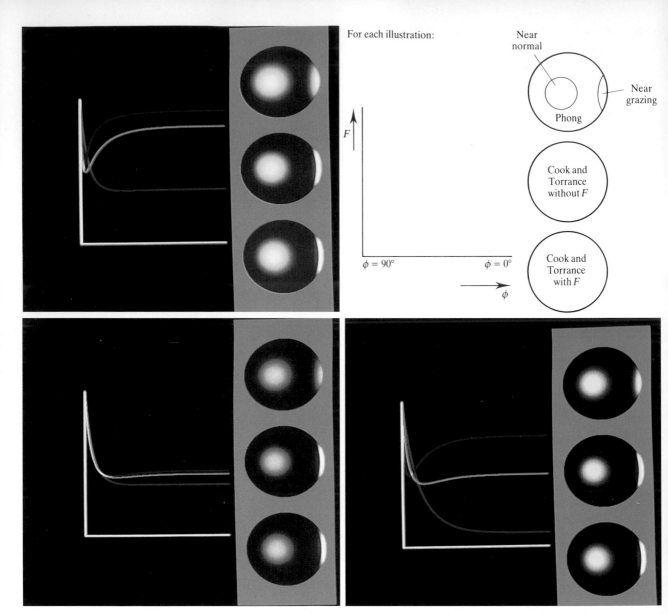

6 The Cook and Torrance model used to simulate different materials. Each RGB profile shows the dependence of F on ϕ for the material: *(top left)* gold; *(bottom left)* silver; *(bottom right)* copper.

7 The Utah teapot and shading options. Note the visibility of piecewise linearities along silhouette edges since this representation contains only 512 polygons. *(top left)* Wireframe plus vertex normals. *(top right)* Constant shaded polygons. *(bottom left)* Gouraud shading. *(bottom right)* Phong shading.

8 Parametric patch rendering at different levels of uniform subdivision (128, 512, 2048 and 8192 polygons). (Courtesy of Steve Maddock)

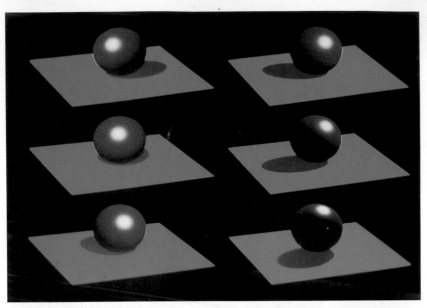

9 Varying light source position in a shadow algorithm.

10 Two-dimensional texture mapping methods. *(top)* Recursive teapots: conventional two-dimensional texture wrapping using mip-map filtering. *(bottom)* Bump mapping (courtesy of J. Blinn).

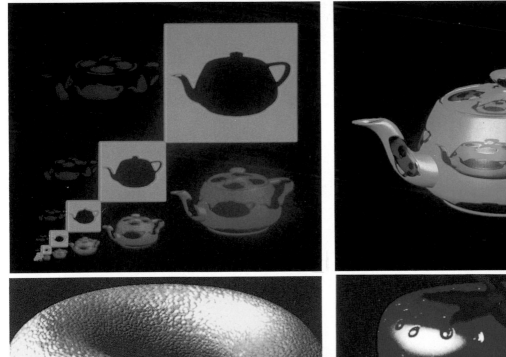

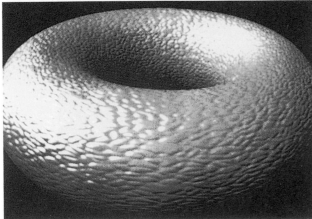

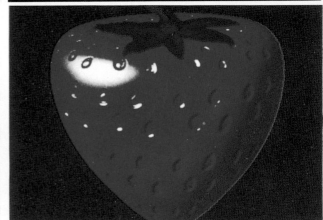

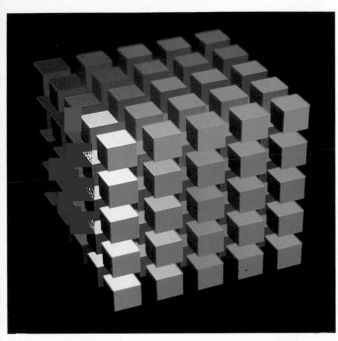

11 Surfaces modulated by three-dimensional texture fields. *(left)* Cube of cubes: the centre point of each cube is used to obtain a colour from the RGB cube. *(below)* Wood grain: harmonic functions (Fourier synthesis). *(bottom left)* Marble texture: equivalent to harmonic function plus noise. *(bottom right)* Using a three-dimensional noise function.

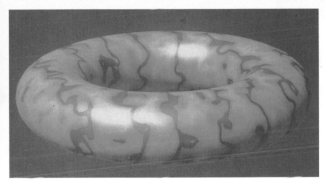

12 Environment mapping: *(right)* an environment-mapped teapot produced from the synthetic environment map shown on the left.

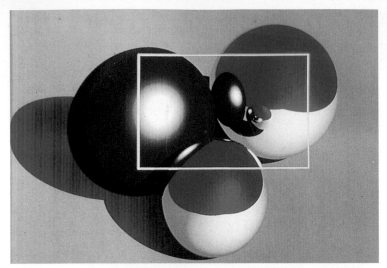

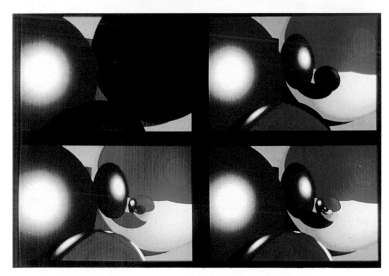

13 Ray tracing spheres. *(top)* Ray tracing to a depth of 6. *(centre)* Part of the above image traced to a depth of 1, 2, 3 and 4. *(bottom)* Reflective and refractive spheres against a striped background (after an illustration by Apollo Computers).

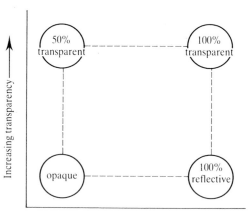

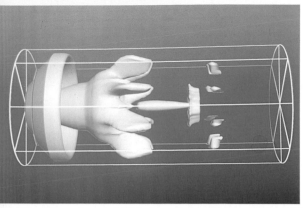 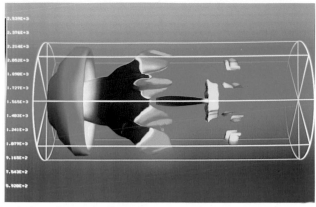

14 Marching cubes and CFD data. *(left)* a Navier−Stokes CFD simulation of a reverse flow pipe combuster. Flow occurs from left to right and from right to left. The interface between these flows defines a zero velocity isosurface. The marching cubes algorithm is used to extract this surface which is then conventionally rendered. *(right)* A texture-mapped zero velocity surface. A pseudocolour scale that represents field temperature is combined with the colour used for shading in the illustration on the left. (Courtesy of Mark Fuller)

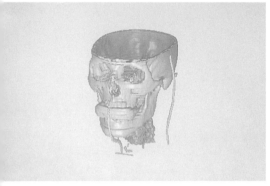 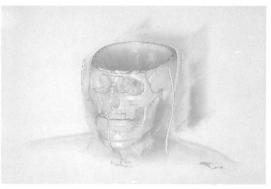

15 A volume-rendered version of a skull. The bone opacity is set to 1 and all other material opacities are set to zero. (Courtesy of Klaus de Geuss)

16 As Plate 15 except that a non-zero opacity has been assigned to non-bony material. (Courtesy of Klaus de Geuss)

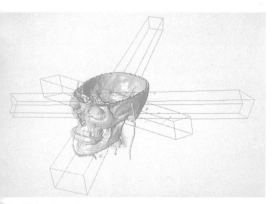 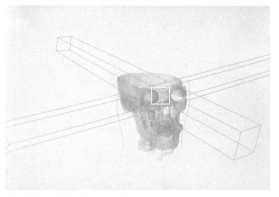

17 This plate shows the skull together with other superimposed information. The critical structures are detected in the data as separate objects. These objects are stylized as bounding volumes – spheres for the eyeballs and generalized cylinders for the spinal cord. They are rendered as normal using the colour orange. The idea is that the stylized bounding volumes are guaranteed to contain the actual object. A brain tumour is shown in green and three treatment beams are shown as wireframe objects. The blue on the skull shows the intersection of each beam with the skin surface. (Courtesy of Klaus de Geuss)

18 Plates 18 to 21 are all rendered with the bone opacity set to a value less than unity and are all views looking down a treatment beam. This plate shows a beam intersecting an eyeball. (Courtesy of Klaus de Geuss)

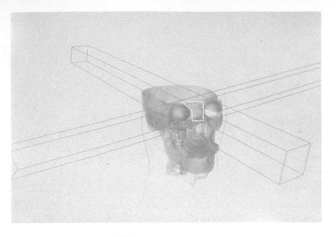

19 The beam in Plate 18 is re-shaped to avoid the eyeball. (Courtesy of Klaus de Geuss)

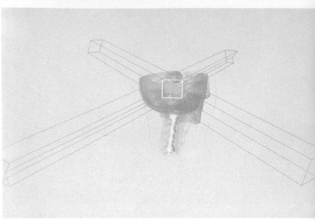

20 Another beam intersects an eyeball. (Courtesy of Klaus de Geuss)

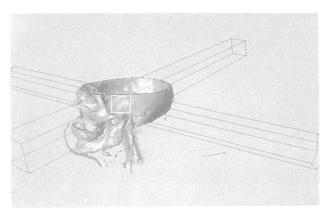

21 A beam that does not intersect any critical structures. (Courtesy of Klaus de Geuss)

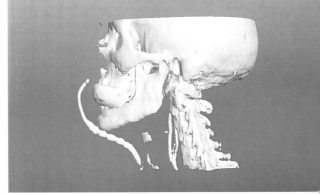

22 The marching cubes algorithm applied to CT data. The isosurface is defined by the X-ray absorption coefficient for bone.

23 Radiosity illustrations. *(top)* Dutch interior, after Vermeer. This image was inspired by the work of the 17th century Dutch painter, Jan Vermeer, whose sensitivity to the interplay of light and surfaces helped to give his painting a dramatic effect. The radiosity method was used to compute the global diffuse illumination during a view-independent preprocess. After the view was determined, a Z-buffer based algorithm similar to distributed ray tracing was used to compute the specular reflection on the marble floor. (Courtesy of John Wallace. © 1987 by Cornell University, Program of Computer Graphics). *(bottom)* Simulated steel mill. The image was created using a modified version of the hemicube radiosity algorithm, computed on a VAX 8700 and displayed on a Hewlett-Packard Renaissance Display. The environment consists of approximately 55,000 elements, and is one of the most complex environments computed to date. (Courtesy of Stuart Feldman and John Wallace, Program of Computer Graphics, Cornell University)

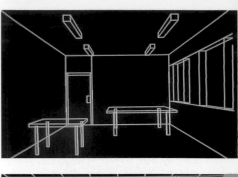

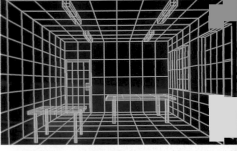

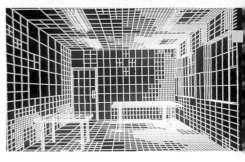

24 Radiosity method for diffuse interaction. *(above)* The result from the window lit scene using subdivision of the patches to produce the elements shown: *(top right)* Original surfaces; *(centre right)* Surfaces divided up into patches; *(bottom right)* Patches subdivided into elements using the substructuring method.

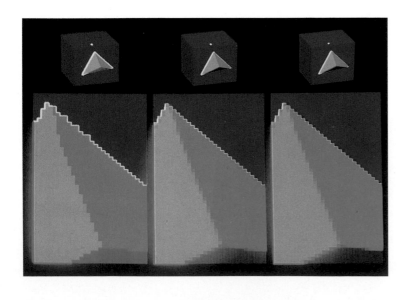

25 Supersampling and filtering. Top row: full size images. Bottom row: ×10 images, from left to right an unfiltered image, a 3 × 3 filter; a 5 × 5 filter.

26　Recursively generated tree shapes. *(top)* Two runs of the program using the same 'skeletal' parameters. *(bottom)* Two runs of the program using 'bushy' parameters.

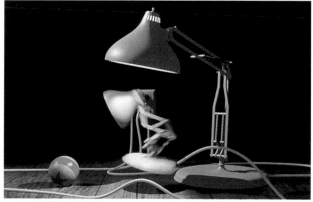

(Left) A frame from *Luxo Jr.* produced by John Lasseter, Bill Reeves, Eben Ostby and Sam Leffler; © 1986 Pixar; Luxo™ is a trademark of Jak Jacobson Industries. The film was animated by a keyframe animation system with procedural animation assistance, and frames were rendered with multiple light sources and procedural texturing techniques. *(right)* This frame from *Luxo Jr.* exhibits motion blur as described in Chapter 13.

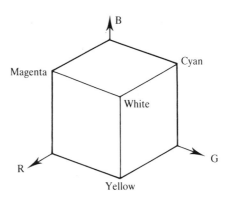

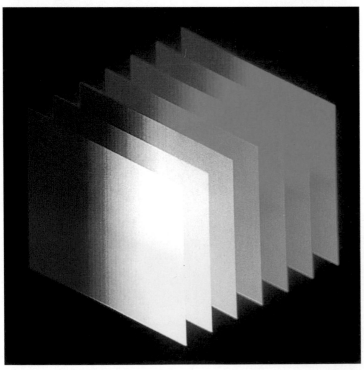

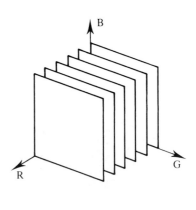

28 *(Top)* The RGB cube. *(bottom)* Planes in the RGB cube parallel to the BG plane.

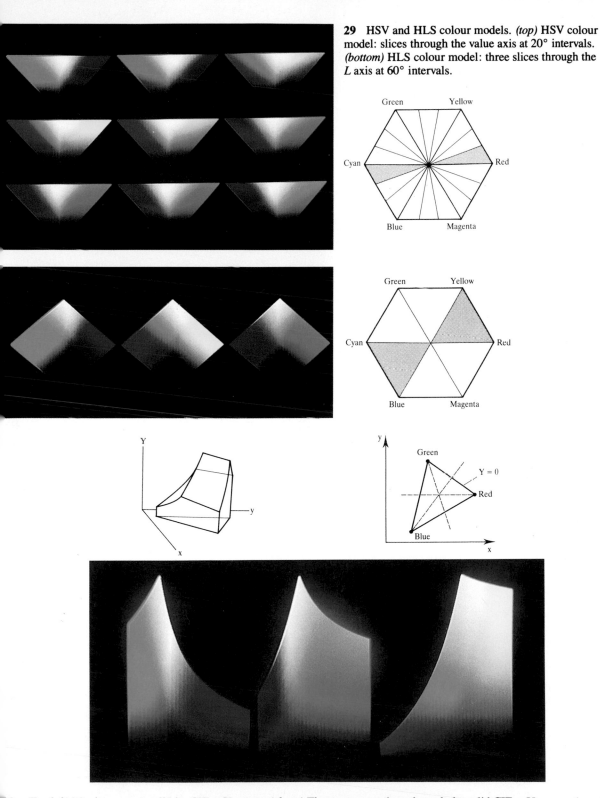

29 HSV and HLS colour models. *(top)* HSV colour model: slices through the value axis at 20° intervals. *(bottom)* HLS colour model: three slices through the L axis at 60° intervals.

30 *(Top left)* Monitor gamut solid in CIE xyY space; *(above)* Three cross-sections through the solid CIE xyY space; *(top right)* The position of the cross-sections on the plane Y=0.

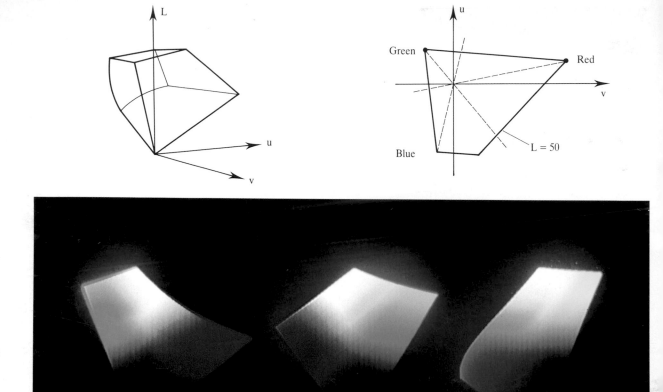

31 *(Top left)* Monitor gamut solid in L*u*v* space; *(above)* Three cross-sections through the solid in L*u*v* space; *(top right)* T[...] position of the cross-sections in a plane of constant L.

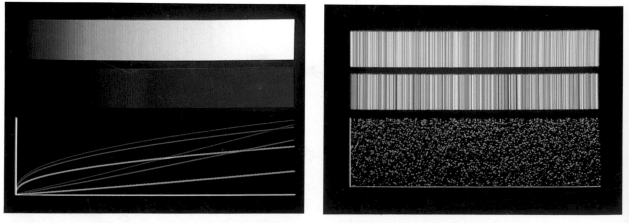

32 Gamma correction showing contrast and chromaticity shift. The top bar in each illustration is gamma corrected. *(left)* Colou[...] ramp showing a chromaticity shift. *(right)* Random colours showing a contrast shift.

Although this appears now to involve two divisions rather than one, they are both integer rather than floating point. Also, given suitable hardware, they can both be evaluated from the same division, since the second (**mod**) is simply the remainder from the first (**div**). Finally, it remains only to point out that the $2(ye - ys)$ within the loop is constant and would in practice be evaluated just once outside it.

5.4.2 Rasterizing polygons

Now that we know how to find pixels along the polygon edges, it is necessary to turn our attention to filling the polygons themselves. Since we are concerned with shading, 'filling a polygon' means finding the pixel coordinates of interior points and assigning to these a value calculated using one of the incremental shading schemes described in Section 5.3. We need to generate pairs of segment end points and fill in horizontally between them. This is usually achieved by constructing an **edge list** for each polygon. In principle this is done using an array of linked lists, with an element for each scan line. Initially, all the elements are set to **nil**. Then each edge of the polygon is rasterized in turn, and the x coordinate of each pixel (x, y) thus generated is inserted into the linked list corresponding to that value of y. Each of the linked lists is then sorted in order of increasing x. The result is something like that shown in Figure 5.15. Filling in of the polygon is then achieved, for each scan line, by taking successive pairs of x values and filling in between them (because a polygon has to be closed, there will always be an even number of elements in the linked list). Note that this method is powerful enough to cope with concave polygons with holes.

In practice, the sorting of the linked lists is achieved by inserting values in the appropriate place in the first place, rather than by a big sort at the end. Also, as well as calculating the x value and storing it for each pixel on an edge, the appropriate shading values would be calculated and stored at the same time (for example, intensity value for Gouraud shading; x, y and z components of the interpolated normal vector for Phong shading).

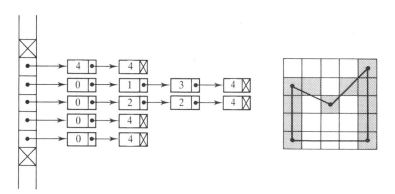

Figure 5.15
An example of a linked list maintained in polygon rasterization.

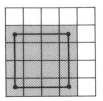

Figure 5.16
Problems with polygon
boundaries – a 9-pixel
polygon fills 16 pixels.

If the object contains only convex polygons then the linked x lists will only ever contain two x coordinates; the data structure of the edge list is simplified and there is no sort required. It is not a great restriction in practical computer graphics to constrain an object to convex polygons.

One thing that has been slightly glossed over so far is the consideration of exactly where the borders of a polygon lie. This can manifest itself in adjacent polygons either by gaps appearing between them, or by them overlapping. For example, in Figure 5.16, the width of the polygon is 3 units, so it should have an area of 9 units, whereas it has been rendered with an area of 16 units. The traditional solution to this problem, and the one usually advocated in textbooks, is to consider the sample point of the pixel to lie in its centre, that is, at $(x + 0.5, y + 0.5)$. (A pixel can be considered to be a rectangle of finite area with dimensions 1.0×1.0, and its sample point is the point within the pixel area where the scene is sampled in order to determine the value of the pixel.) So, for example, the intersection of an edge with a scan line is calculated for $y + 0.5$, rather than for y, as we assumed above. This is messy, and excludes the possibility of using integer-only arithmetic. A simpler solution is to assume that the sample point lies at one of the four corners of the pixel; we have chosen the top right-hand corner of the pixel. This has the consequence that the entire image is displaced half a pixel to the left and down, which in practice is insignificant. The upshot of this is that it provides the following simple rasterization rules:

(1) Horizontal edges are simply discarded.

(2) An edge which goes from scan line y_{bottom} to y_{top} should generate x values for scan lines y_{bottom} through to $y_{\text{top}} - 1$ (that is, missing the top scan line), or if $y_{\text{bottom}} = y_{\text{top}}$ then it generates no values.

(3) Similarly, horizontal segments should be filled from x_{left} to $x_{\text{right}} - 1$ (with no pixels generated if $x_{\text{left}} = x_{\text{right}}$).

Incidentally, in rules 2 and 3, whether the first or last element is ignored is arbitrary, and the choice is based around programming convenience. The four possible permutations of these two rules define the sample point as one of the four corners of the pixel. The effect of these rules can be demonstrated in Figure 5.17. Here we have three adjacent polygons A, B and C, with edges a, b, c and d. The rounded x values produced by these edges for the scan shown are 2, 4, 4 and 7 respectively. Rule 3 then gives pixels 2 and 3 for polygon A, none for polygon B, and 4 to 6 for polygon C.

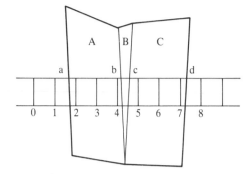

Figure 5.17
Three polygons
intersecting a scan line.

overall, there are no gaps, and no overlapping. The reason why horizontal edges are discarded is because the edges adjacent to it will have already contributed the x values to make up the segment (for example, the base of the polygon in Figure 5.15 – note also that for the sake of simplicity, the scan conversion of this polygon was not done strictly in accordance with the rasterization rules mentioned above).

5.4.3   Order of rendering

There are two basic ways of ordering the rendering of a scene. These are: on a polygon-by-polygon basis, where each polygon is rendered in turn, in isolation from all the rest; and in scanline order, where the segments of all polygons in that scene which cross a given scan line are rendered, before moving on to the next scan line. In standard textbooks, this classification has the habit of becoming hopelessly confused with the classification of hidden surface removal algorithms. In fact, the order of rendering a scene places restrictions upon which hidden surface algorithms can be used, but is of itself independent of the method employed for hidden surface removal. To skip ahead briefly, these are the common hidden surface removal algorithms that are compatible with the two methods:

- by polygon   z-buffer
- by scan line   z-buffer; scanline z-buffer,
            spanning scan line algorithm

By-polygon rendering has a number of advantages. It is simple to implement, and it requires little data active at any one time. Because of this, it places no upper limit on scene complexity, unlike scanline rendering, which needs to hold simultaneously in memory rasterization, shading, and perhaps texture information for all polygons which cross a particular scan line. The main drawback of by-polygon rendering is that it does not make use of possible efficiency measures such as sharing of information between polygons (for example most edges in a scene are shared between two polygons). The method can only be used with the Z-buffer hidden surface algorithm, which, as we shall see, is rather expensive in terms of memory usage. Also, scanline-based algorithms possess the property that the completed image is generated in scanline order, which has advantages for hardware implementation and anti-aliasing operations.

An important difference between the two rendering methods is in the construction of the edge list. This has been described in terms of rendering on a polygon-by-polygon basis. If, however, rendering is performed in scanline order, two problems arise. One is that rasterizing all edges of all polygons in advance would consume a vast quantity of memory, setting an even lower bound on the maximum complexity of a scene. Instead, it is usual to maintain a list of 'active edges'. When a new scan line is started, all edges which start on that scan line are added to the list, while those which end on it are removed. For each edge in the active list, current values for x, shading information, and so on are stored, along with the increments for these values. Each time a new edge is added, these values are initialized; then the increments are added for each new scan line.

The other problem is in determining segments, since there are now multiple polygons active on a given scan line. In general, some extra information will need to be stored with each edge in the active edge list, indicating to which polygon it belongs. The exact details of this depend very much upon the hidden surface removal algorithm in use. Usually an active polygon list is maintained that indicates the polygons intersected by the current scan line, and those therefore that can generate active edges. This list is updated on every scan line, new polygons being added and inactive ones deleted.

The outline of a polygon-by-polygon renderer is thus:

> **for** each polygon **do**
>   construct an edge list from the polygon edges
>   **for** $y := ymin$ to $ymax$ **do**
>   **for** each pair (x_I, x_{I+1}) in $EdgeList[y]$ **do**
>   shade the horizontal segment (x_I, y) **to** (x_{I+1}, y)

while that of a scanline renderer is:

> clear active edge list
> **for** each scan line **do**
>   **for** each edge starting on that scan line **do**
>   add edge to active edge list
>   initialize its shading and rasterization values and their increments
>   remove edges which end on that scan line
>   parse active edge list to obtain and render segments
>   add the increments to all active edges

Finally, it is worth pointing out that it is possible to achieve a hybrid of these two methods. Often it is possible to split a scene up into a number of unconnected objects. If the scene is rendered on an object-by-object basis, using scanline ordering within each object, then the advantage of shared information is realized within each object, and there is no upper limit on scene complexity, only on the complexity of each individual object.

5.5 Hidden surface removal

The major hidden surface removal algorithms are described in most computer graphics textbooks and are classified in an early, but still highly relevant, paper by Sutherland, Sproull and Schumacker (1974). In this paper, algorithms are characterized as to whether they operate primarily in object space or image (screen) space, and the different uses of 'coherence' that the algorithms employ. **Coherence** is a term used to describe the process where geometrical units, such as areas or scanline segments, instead of single points, are operated on by the hidden surface removal algorithm.

There are two popular approaches to hidden surface removal. These are scanline-based systems and Z-buffer based systems. Other approaches to hidden surface removal such as area subdivision (Warnock, 1969), or depth list schemes (Newell, Newell and Sancha, 1972) are not particularly popular or are reserved for special-purpose applications such as flight simulation.

5.5.1 Depth comparisons

Hidden surface removal eventually comes down to a point-by-point depth comparison. Certain algorithms operate on area units, scanline segments or even complete polygons, but they must contain a provision for the worst case, which is a depth comparison between two points. Most hidden surface algorithms perform this comparison in three-dimensional screen space. This space is defined in Section 3.7 and we repeat, for convenience, the equation for z_s

$$z_s = \frac{f(1 - d/z_v)}{f - d}$$

This transforms, for example, a box in view space as shown in Figure 5.18. The perspective projection of the box in view space is now equivalent to the parallel projection of the transformed box in three-dimensional screen space. $z_v = 0$ is transformed to $z_s = -\infty$ and rays from the view point or centre of projection are now parallel. The depth test in view space to determine if P_1 is nearer to the centre of projection than P_2 involves the complication that this only has meaning if both points are on the same projector. Now if we make comparisons in screen space we know that *all* points with the same (x_s, y_s) coordinates lie on the same projector. There is, however, a price to be paid. Equal intervals in z_v do not map into equal intervals in z_s. As z_v approaches the far clipping plane, z_s approaches 1 more rapidly. In

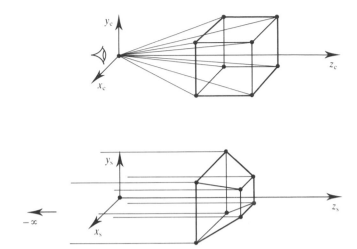

Figure 5.18
Transformation of box
and light rays from eye
space to screen space.

effect, objects are compressed as a function of their z_v value and this has ramifications for precision – particularly important in the case of the Z-buffer algorithm.

5.5.2   The Z-buffer algorithm

The Z-buffer algorithm, developed by Catmull (1975), is as ubiquitous in computer graphics as the Phong reflection model and interpolator, and the combination of these represents the most popular rendering option. Using Sutherland's classification scheme (Sutherland, Sproull and Schumacher, 1974), it is an algorithm that operates in image (screen) space.

Pixels in the interior of a polygon are shaded, using an incremental shading scheme, and their depth is evaluated by interpolation from the z values of the polygon vertices as described in the previous section.

The Z-buffer algorithm is equivalent, for each point (x_s, y_s) to a search through the associated z values of each interior polygon point, to find that point with the minimum z value. This search is conveniently implemented by using a Z-buffer that holds for a current point (x, y) the smallest z value so far encountered. During the processing of a polygon we either write the intensity of a point (x, y) into the frame buffer, or not, depending on whether the depth z, of the current point, is less than the depth so far encountered as recorded in the Z-buffer.

One of the major theoretical advantages of the Z-buffer is that it is independent of object representation form. Although we see it used most often in the context of polygon mesh rendering, it can be used with any representation – all that is required is the ability to calculate a z value for each point on the surface of an object. It can be used with CSG objects, and separately rendered objects can be merged into a multiple object scene using Z-buffer information on each object. These aspects are examined shortly.

The overwhelming advantage of the Z-buffer algorithm is its simplicity of implementation. Its main disadvantage is the amount of memory required for the Z-buffer. The size of the Z-buffer depends on the accuracy to which the depth value of each point (x,y) is to be stored, which is a function of scene complexity. Between 20 and 32 bits is usually deemed sufficient and the scene has to be scaled to this fixed range of z so that accuracy within the scene is maximized. Recall in Section 5.5.1 that we discussed the compression of z_s values. This means that a pair of distinct points with different z_v values can map into identical z_s values. Note that for frame buffers with less than 24 bits per pixel, say, the Z-buffer will in fact be *larger* than the frame buffer. In the past, Z-buffers have tended to be part of the main memory of the host processor, but now graphics terminals are available with dedicated Z-buffers and this represents the best solution.

The memory problem can be alleviated by dividing the Z-buffer into strips or partitions in screen space. The price paid for this is multiple passes through the geometric part of the renderer. Polygons are fetched from the database and rendered if their projection falls within the Z-buffer partition in screen space.

An interesting use of the Z-buffer is suggested by Foley *et al.* (1989). This involves rendering selected objects but leaving the Z-buffer contents unmodified by such objects. The idea can be applied to interaction where a three-dimensional cursor object can be moved about in a scene. The cursor is the selected object, and when it is rendered in its current position, the Z-buffer is not written to. Nevertheless the Z-buffer is used to perform hidden surface removal on the object and will move about the scene obscuring some objects and being obscured by others.

5.5.3   Z-buffer and CSG representation

The Z-buffer algorithm can be used to advantage in rendering CSG objects. As you will recall from Section 2.6.3, that describes a ray tracing algorithm for rendering such objects, rendering involves calculating a boundary representation of a complex object that is made up of primitive objects combined with boolean operators and described or represented by a construction tree.

The problem with the ray tracing method is expense. A normal recursive ray tracer is a method that finds intersections between a ray of arbitrary direction and objects in the scene. This model operates recursively to any depth to evaluate specular interaction. However, with CSG objects, all rays are parallel and we are only interested in the first hit, so in this respect ray tracing is inappropriate and a Z-buffer approach is easier to implement and less expensive (Rossignac and Requicha, 1986). The Z-buffer algorithm is driven from object surfaces rather than pixel-by-pixel rays. Consider the overall structure of both algorithms:

- Ray tracing

  for each pixel **do**
  generate a ray and find all object surfaces that intersect the ray
  evaluate the CSG tree to determine the boundary of the
  first surface along the ray

- Z-buffer

  for each primitive object **do**
  for primitive surface *F* **do**
  for each point *P* in a sufficiently dense grid on *F* **do**
  Project *P* and apply Z-buffer
  if currently visible **then**
  if by evaluating the CSG tree *P* is on boundary surface **then**
  render into frame buffer

Both algorithms have to apply a test that descends the CSG tree and evaluates the boolean set operations to find the boundary of the object, but the Z-buffer avoids the intersection tests associated with each pixel ray.

5.5.4 Z-buffer and compositing

An important advantage of Z-buffer based algorithms is that the z value associated with each pixel can be retained and used to enable the compositing or merging of separately generated scene elements.

Three-dimensional images are often built up from separate subimages. A system for compositing separate elements in a scene, pixel by pixel, was proposed by Porter and Duff (1984) and Duff (1985). This simple system is built round an RGBαZ representation for pixels in a subimage. At the time of writing, 24-bit frame stores with associated 16-bit z memories are becoming increasingly common – hardware confirmation of the popularity of Z-buffer based rendering systems. Also, at least one company (Pixar) has now incorporated an α memory or channel allowing this fifth parameter to be associated with each pixel. This parameter allows subimages to be built up separately and combined, retaining subpixel information that may have been calculated in the rendering of each subimage.

Composites are built up by using a binary operator that combines two subimages:

$$c = f \ \mathbf{op} \ b$$

For example, consider the operator $\mathbf{Z}_{min}$. We may have two subimages, say of single objects, that have been rendered separately, the Z values of each pixel in the final rendering contained in the Z channel. Compositing in this context means effecting hidden surface removal *between* the objects and is defined as:

$$RGB_c = (\mathbf{if} \ Z_f < Z_b \ \mathbf{then} \ RGB_f \ \mathbf{else} \ RGB_b)$$

$$Z_c = \min(Z_f, Z_b)$$

for each pixel.

The α parameter $(0 \leqslant \alpha \leqslant 1)$ is the fraction of the pixel area that the object covers. It is used as a factor that controls the mixing of the colours in the two images. The use of the α channel effectively extends area anti-aliasing across the compositing of images. Of course this parameter is not normally calculated by a basic Z-buffer renderer and, because of this, the method is only suitable when used in conjunction with the A-buffer hidden surface removal method (Carpenter, 1984), an anti-aliased extension to the Z-buffer described in Chapter 11.

The operator **over** is defined as:

$$RGB_c = RGB_f + (1 - \alpha_f)RGB_b$$
$$\alpha_c = \alpha_f + (1 - \alpha_f)\alpha_b$$

This means that as α_f decreases more of RGB_b is present in the pixel.

The compositing operator **comp** combines both the above operators. This evaluates pixel results when Z values at the corners of pixels are different between RGB_f and RGB_b. Z_f is compared with Z_b at each of the four corners. There are 16 possible outcomes to this and if the Z values are not the same at the four corners, then the pixel is said to be confused. Linear interpolation along the edges takes place and a fraction β computed (the area of the pixel of which f is in front of b). We then have the **comp** operator:

$$RGB_c = \beta(f \text{ over } b) + (1 - \beta)(b \text{ over } f)$$

Another example of compositing in three-dimensional image synthesis is given in by Nakamae *et al.* (1986). This is a montage method, the point of which is to integrate a three-dimensional computer-generated image of, say, a new building, with a real photograph of a scene. The success of the method is due to the fact that illuminance for the generated object is calculated from measurements of the background photograph and because atmospheric effects are integrated into the finished image.

5.5.5 Z-buffer and rendering

The Z-buffer imposes no constraints on database organization (other than those required by the shading interpolation) and in its simplest form can be driven on a polygon-by-polygon basis, with polygons being presented in any convenient order.

In principle, for each polygon we compute:

(1) the (x, y) value of the interior pixels,
(2) the z depth for each point (x, y), and
(3) the intensity, I, for each point (x, y).

Thus we have three concurrent bilinear interpolation processes and a triple nested loop. The z values and intensities, I, are available at each vertex and the interpolation scheme for z and I is distributed between the two inner loops of the algorithm.

An extended version of the by-polygon algorithm with Z-buffer hidden surface removal is as follows:

for all x,y **do**
   Z-buffer$[x,y] := $ maximum_depth

for each polygon **do**
   construct an edge list from the polygon edges (that is, for each edge, calculate the values of x, z and I for each scan line by interpolation and store them in the edge list)

   for $y := ymin$ **to** $ymax$ **do**

      for each segment in *EdgeList*$[y]$ **do**
      get *Xleft,Xright, Zleft,Zright, Ileft,Iright*
         for $x := Xleft$ **to** *Xright* **do**
            linearly interpolate z and I between *Zleft,Zright* and *Ileft, Iright* respectively
            if $z < Z\_Buffer[x,y]$ **then**
               $Z\_Buffer[x,y] := z$
               $frame\_buffer[x,y] := I$

The structure of the algorithm reveals the major inefficiency of the method, in that shading calculations are performed on hidden pixels which are then either ignored or subsequently overwritten.

If Phong interpolation is used then the final reflection model calculations, which are a function of the interpolated normal, should also appear within the innermost loop; that is, interpolate N rather than I, and replace the last line with:

$frame\_buffer[x,y] := ShadingFunction(N)$

Procedures that implement the above techniques are given in Appendix C. Adding these procedures to the code in Appendix B results in a complete rendering system.

5.5.6   Scanline Z-buffer

There is a variation of the Z-buffer algorithm for use with scanline-based renderers, known (not surprisingly) as a **scanline Z-buffer**. This is simply a Z-buffer which is only one pixel high, and is used to solve the hidden surface problem for a given scan line. It is reinitialized for each new scan line. Its chief advantage lies in the small amount of memory it requires relative to a full-blown Z-buffer; in fact it is very common to see a scanline Z-buffer based program running on systems which do not have sufficient memory to support a full Z-buffer.

5.5.7   Spanning hidden surface removal

A spanning hidden surface removal algorithm attempts, for each scan line, to find **spans** across which shading can be performed. The hidden surface removal problem is thus solved by dividing the scan line into lengths over which a single surface is dominant. This means that shading calculations are performed only once per pixel, removing the basic inefficiency inherent in the Z-buffer method. Set against this is the problem that spans do not necessarily correspond to polygon segments, making it harder to perform incremental shading calculations (the start values must be calculated at an arbitary point along a polygon segment, rather than being set to the values at the left-hand edge). The other major drawback is in the increase in complexity of the algorithm itself, as will be seen.

It is generally claimed that spanning algorithms are more efficient than Z-buffer based algorithms, except for very large numbers of polygons (Foley *et al.*, 1989; Sutherland, Sproull and Schumacker, 1974). However, since extremely complex scenes are now becoming the norm, it is becoming clear that, overall, the Z-buffer is more efficient, unless a very complex shading function is being used.

5.5.8   A spanning scanline algorithm

The basic idea, as has been mentioned, is that rather than solving the hidden surface problem on a pixel-by-pixel basis using incremental z calculation, the spanning scanline algorithm uses spans along the scan line over which there is no depth conflict. The hidden surface removal process uses coherence in x and deals in units of many pixels. The processing implication is that a sort in x is required for each scan line and the spans have to be evaluated.

The easiest way to see how a scanline algorithm works is to consider the situation in three-dimensional screen space (x_s, y_s, z_s). A scanline algorithm effectively moves a scanline plane, that is, a plane parallel to the (x_s, z_s) plane, down the y_s axis. This plane intersects objects in the scene and reduces the hidden surface problem to two-dimensional space (x_s, z_s). Here the intersections of the scanline plane with object polygons become lines (Figure 5.19). These line segments are then compared to solve the hidden surface problem by considering spans. A span is that part of a line segment that is contained between the edge intersections of all active polygons. A span can be considered a coherence unit, within the extent of which the hidden surface removal problem is 'constant' and can be solved by depth comparisons at either end of the span. Note that a more complicated approach has to be taken if penetrating polygons are allowed.

It can be seen from this geometric overview that the first stage in a spanning scanline algorithm is to sort the polygon edges by y_s vertex values. This results in an active edge list which is updated as the scan line moves

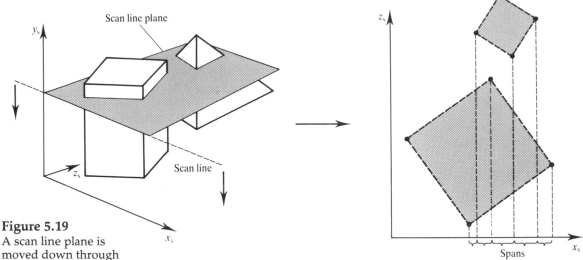

Figure 5.19
A scan line plane is
moved down through
the scene producing
line segments and
spans.

down the y_s axis. If penetrating polygons are not allowed then each edge
intersection with the current scan line specifies a point on the scan line
where 'something is changing', and so these collectively define all the span
boundary points.

By going through the active edge list in order, it is possible to generate a set of line segments, each of which represents the intersection of the
scanline plane with a polygon. These are then sorted in order of increasing x_s.

The innermost loop then processes each span in the current scan line.
Active line segments are clipped against span boundaries and are thus subdivided by these boundaries. The depth of each subdivided segment is then
evaluated at one of the span boundaries and hidden surface removal is
effected by searching within a span for the closest subdivided segment. This
process is shown in Figure 5.20.

In pseudocode the algorithm is:

> **for** *each polygon* **do**
>   *Generate and bucket sort in y_s the polygon edge information.*
>
> **for** *each scanline* **do**
>   **for** *each active polygon* **do**
>   *Determine the segment or intersection of the scan plane and polygon.*
>   *Sort these active segments in x_s.*
>   *Update the rate of change per scan line of the shading parameters.*
>   *Generate the span boundaries.*
>   **for** *each span* **do**
>   *Clip active segments to span boundaries.*
>   *Evaluate the depth for all clipped segments at one of the span*
>   *boundaries.*

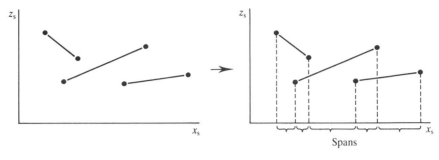

Active line segments produce span boundaries

Which are used to subdivide a line

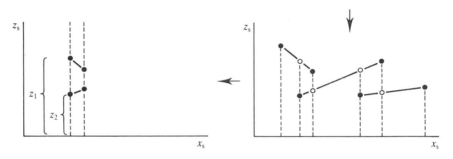

Within a span the hidden
surface problem is resolved by
considering depths along one of
the span boundaries.

Figure 5.20
Processing spans.

*Solve the hidden surface problem for the span by finding the
segment with minimum z_s.*
Shade the visible clipped line segment.
*Update the shading parameters for all other line segments by the
rate of change per pixel times the span width.*

Note that integrating shading information is far more cumbersome than with
the Z-buffer. Records of values at the end of clipped line segments have to
be kept and updated. This places another scene complexity overhead (along
with the absolute number of polygons overhead) on the efficiency and memory requirements of the process.

5.5.9 Comparative points

From an ease of implementation point of view the Z-buffer is best. It has
significant memory requirements, particularly for high-resolution frame buffers. However, it places no upward limit on the complexity of scenes, an
advantage that is now becoming increasingly important. It renders scenes
one object at a time and for each object one polygon at a time. This is both

a natural and a convenient order as far as database considerations are concerned.

An important restriction it places on the type of object that can be rendered by a Z-buffer is that it cannot deal with transparent objects without costly modification. A partially transparent polygon may:

● be completely covered by an opaque nearer polygon, in which case there is no problem, or

● be the nearest polygon, in which case a list of all polygons behind it must be maintained so that an appropriate combination of the transparent polygon and the next nearest can be computed. (The next nearest polygon is not of course known until all polygons are processed.)

Compared with scanline algorithms, anti-aliasing solutions, particularly hardware implementations, are more difficult.

Cook (Cook, Carpenter and Catmull, 1987) points out that a Z-buffer has an extremely important 'system' advantage. It provides a 'back door' in that it can combine point samples with point samples from other algorithms that have other capabilities such as radiosity or ray tracing.

If memory requirements are too prodigious then a scanline Z-buffer is the next best solution. Unless a renderer is to work efficiently on simple scenes, it is doubtful if it is worth contemplating the large increase in complexity that a spanning scanline algorithm demands.

Historically there has been a shift in research away from hidden surface problems to realistic image synthesis. This has been motivated by the easy availability of high spatial and colour resolution terminals. All of the 'classic' hidden surface removal algorithms were developed prior to the advent of shading complexities and it looks as if the Z-buffer will be the most popular survivor for conventional rendering.

Projects, notes and suggestions ───────────

The following projects inevitably require a rendering system described in this chapter. They are mostly concerned with the quality–speed trade-off in incremental shading techniques. As usual each project is classified with a heading and those marked (*) are longish and can be used as a major course assignment or project.

5.1   Phong shading

Extend the code given in Appendix C to include Phong shading and, for an object, produce a display similar to Plate 7 which shows:

(1) a wireframe plus vertex normals,

(2) a flat or constant shaded version,

(3) a Gouraud-shaded object, and

(4) a Phong-shaded object.

Isolate the time your program spends in actual shading and compare timings for (2), (3) and (4).

5.2 Mach band visualization (*)

Investigate the relationship between Mach band visibility and polygonal resolution. This can be done by generating a variable number of polygons, for, say, a toroid by volume sweeping, Gouraud shading the object and postprocessing the image so that the Mach bands can be visualized.

Mach bands can be highlighted by spatially differentiating the image twice and thresholding the high intensity values. To differentiate once, we can use the following approximation. For all pixels:

$$E' := \{[(A + B + C) - (G + H + I)]^2 + [(A + D + G) \\ - (C + F + I)]^2\}^{1/2}$$

where E' is the new value for pixel E and $A, B, \ldots, I$ are a 3×3 array of pixels centred on E:

$A\,B\,C$

$D\,E\,F$

$G\,H\,I$

You should find that the 'strength' of the Mach bands increases as the 'polygonal resolution' decreases. Why is this so?

5.3 Simple Phong speed up

Implement the double-step interpolation method for Phong speed up as described in Section 5.3.4 and investigate the efficacy of the method by doing a comparison of timing and image quality between the speed-up method and the standard method.

For image quality comparisons, generate a normal Phong-shaded image and an image of the same scene using the speed-up technique. Subtract the two images and display a difference image.

5.4 Vertex intensity

For a polygon mesh object with a regular quadrilateral structure, a useful texture effect can be achieved by reducing the vertex intensities in diagonally opposite vertices to zero as shown in Figure 5.21. The non-zero vertex intensities can be set up to equal values and Gouraud shading used to render the object.

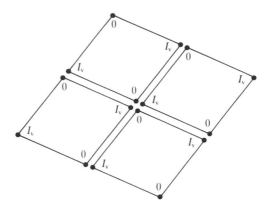

Figure 5.21
Using Gouraud
shading and the
polygon mesh
structure as a texture
effect.

5.5   Vertex intensity

In a Gouraud-shaded object, map the variation in intensity into a hue variation using a suitable path in HSV space (see Chapter 14). Note that this should be done by precalculating the HSV path, storing the results in an LUT and using a single-equation Gouraud scheme to index into the LUT.

5.6   Phong speed up

Implement the H test (see Section 5.3.4) and compare its performance against numeric methods (Bishop and Weimar, 1986).

5.7   Reflection model soild

Produce a rendered version of the wireframe reflection model solids (Projects 4.3 and 4.6). Add thin cylinders and cones in a different colour to represent the vectors *L*, *N* and *R* (see, for example, Figure 4.13).

5.8   Illumination source model (*)

Implement Warn's method (Warn, 1983) for controlling the nature and direction of a light source. Use the Phong reflection model together with a suitable light source interaction view port.

Extend the scheme to include light flaps and cones.

5.9   Z-buffer by-polygram renderer

Implement the rendering system described in Appendix C. If you are short of memory shape for the Z-buffer a possibility is to use half the screen memory as a Z-buffer for the other half. If the screen memory is used for depth, the Z-buffer image can be displayed using a pseudocolour enhancement technique (Chapter 14). That is, map the depth variations in the Z-buffer into colour changes so that the depth variations are more visible than they would otherwise be if they were left as intensity variations in the screen memory.

5.10   Simple rendering using flat-shaded polygons

Implement a simple rendering scheme that flat-shades polygons with an average intensity, using a fast polygon fill utility. Handle surface removal by building up a polygon list that contains an average intensity and average depth and sorts the list by depth. The polygons are then shaded in order of depth – the furthest polygon being dealt with first.

What constraints does this method of hidden surface removal place on the nature of the scene or the objects?

5.11   Transparency

The rendering method employed in Project 5.10 can easily be adapted to handle partially transparent surfaces. Adapt the program of Project 5.10 to do this.

5.12   Z-buffer resolution

Investigate the relationship between scene complexity and Z-buffer resolution (that is, element resolution, not spatial resolution). You could do this by setting up an object formed from the intersection of two objects (say, for example, a sphere and a cylinder) and observing the effect of truncating the Z-buffer to lower and lower ranges on the curve of intersection between the two objects.

5.13   Scanline Z-buffer (*)

A scanline Z-buffer is a particular form of the general Z-buffer algorithm where the rendering proceeds one scan line at a time. All those polygons that cover the current scan line must be processed and this means maintaining a list of active polygons together with the current state of the intensity and depth interpolation for each polygon. When the intersection of a scan line and an active polygon is initiated, the interpolations are restarted and the Z-buffer comparison is made.

Implement this approach and find out the extent of the extra processing over the conventional Z-buffer method.

6 Parametric Representation and Practice

6.1 Parametric representation of three-dimensional solids

Although data representation was reviewed in Chapter 2, parametric representation requires consideration in more detail; this chapter is devoted entirely to this representational form.

The parametric representation of solids and curves is now an established tool in computer graphics, particularly in computer-aided design (CAD). Techniques that were originally developed to model car bodies and aircraft shapes are now applied in the many diverse branches of computer graphics. For example, the techniques are used in object modelling and subsequent interactive design and in animation key-framing.

One of the most popular parametric formulations is the Bézier patch, developed in the 1960s by Pierre Bézier for use in the design of Renault car bodies. His CAD system, UNISURF, in use by 1972, was no doubt responsible for the many varied models emerging from Renault's factories in the 1970s. In fact Bézier's work may have been preceded by the efforts of P. de Casteljau at Citroën in the early 1960s. However his internal reports lay undiscovered until 1975. We may not be referring to de Casteljau patches today, but his name is none the less familiar in an algorithm that is widely used to design and display curves and surfaces.

The usual approach in considering parametric representations is to begin with a description of three-dimensional curves and then to generalize to surfaces. We shall adopt this trend, concentrating on Bézier and B-spline formulations. The behaviour of curves and the associated notation is less cumbersome than that for surfaces, and we shall study in detail the behaviour of curves in the knowledge that all the properties of curves extend to surfaces. In addition, curves are used in computer graphics in their own right. We can 'script' the path of an object through defined points in three-space by interpolating a parametric curve through these points. Also, we can define or model a 'ducted' solid by sweeping a constant or varying cross-section along the curve. In the latter half of the chapter the de Casteljau algorithm is used to display Bézier curves and the different rendering techniques employed for visualizing parametrically defined surfaces are discussed.

6.1.1   Overview of parametric curves

As we shall see, a **parametric curve** is defined by a set of discrete points known as **control points** or **control vertices**, together with a set of **basis** or **blending functions**. This is completely different from the 'normal' way of specifying a curve which is in the form of an implicit function. The idea is demonstrated in Figure 6.1. Four control points P_0 to P_3 are supplied to an algorithm that generates the curve. Note that in this case the curve goes through two of the points. There is a basis function defined over the range of the parameter u for each control point and a curve $Q(u)$ is formed by using the control points to scale the basis functions. In Figure 6.1 the basis functions are Bézier functions. Thus:

$$x(u) = \sum_{i=0}^{3} P_{xi} B_i(u)$$

specifies that we derive the x component of $Q(u)$ by summing the x component of each control point scaled by the value of the basis function at u. Similarly:

$$y(u) = \sum_{i=0}^{3} P_{yi} B_i(u)$$

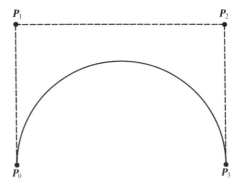

Figure 6.1
A curve defined by four control points. In this case the curve is a cubic Bézier.

and:

$$z(u) = \sum_{i=0}^{3} P_{zi} B_i(u)$$

or more precisely:

$$Q(u) = \sum_{i=0}^{3} P_i B_i(u)$$

The basis functions that are used to scale or blend the control points into a curve segment can be any set of a number of different basis functions that have evolved in CAD and computer graphics. Different basis functions have different properties; principally whether they interpolate the control points or approximate them. The other main distinguishing characteristics are the continuity properties of the curves and the parameters that are used to control the shape of a curve through an interactive interface. In this chapter we concentrate on Bézier and B-spline basis functions. Bézier curves are popular because of their simplicity and because objects can be easily rendered if they are represented by Bézier patches. Bézier curves have certain disadvantages that can be overcome by using B-splines.

The specification of a curve segment (or surface patch) by a set of control points is the foundation of an interactive design method in CAD. A set of points or polygons is specified interactively by a designer. A curve is constructed from these points and viewed. If it is not satisfactory a new set of points is specified and so on.

We distinguish between a curve and a curve segment. Generally, a curve is made up of a number of curve segments joined together with some continuity constraint. Each curve segment is defined by four control points. We define the convex hull of control points as follows. If we consider all the control points as a point set, the **convex hull** of these points (in a plane) can be thought of as the region formed by stretching a rubber band around the control points (Figure 6.2). Note that the convex hull is not the same as the polygon formed by joining successive control points. Convex hulls are important in rendering contexts. For example, in ray tracing surface patches, convex hulls can be used as bounding volumes.

In computer graphics, cubic curves tend to be used. This is because they exhibit sufficient shape flexibility for most practical applications and because higher order curves result in higher order costs and other difficulties. Also, cubic polynomials are true space curves – they are not planar. Quadratic curves are functions of three control points and in three-space are confined to a plane. A curve made up of quadratic segments can only be a set of piecewise two-dimensional segments. This will almost certainly not be satisfactory when such segments are used to model three-dimensional shapes. Thus in this chapter we concentrate on cubic polynominial definitions.

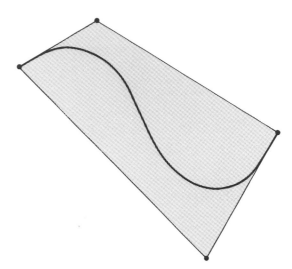

Figure 6.2
Convex hull property
for a cubic spline. The
curve is contained in
the shaded area
formed from the
control points.

Curve segments exhibit continuity properties. When a composite
curve is made up of curve segments these properties may change depending
on how the segments have been joined. Simply joining two segments
together at a common end point implies G^0 geometric continuity. If the
tangent vectors to each curve segment at the common end point match to
within a constant (directions equal, magnitudes not equal) then the curve
has G^1 geometric continuity. If the tangent vectors match, the curve exhibits
first degree or C^1 continuity. Tangent vectors to a curve are shown in Figure
6.5. In general, parametric continuity C^n is defined as follows. If the direction and magnitude of $d^n/dt^n[Q(u)]$ are equal at the join point between
segments then the curve exhibits C^n continuity.

6.2   Parametric representation of three-dimensional curves

We will now look in detail at the derivation of the basis function curve
definitions discussed in Section 6.1.

A simple practical example of a three-dimensional space curve is a
point moving in space (Figure 6.3). Its position is defined by a vector r, a
function of time t. This gives a so-called parametric description of the curve
as a set of three equations in t:

$$x = x(t)$$
$$y = y(t)$$
$$z = z(t)$$

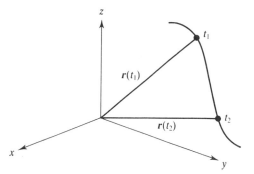

Figure 6.3
A point moving in
three-dimensional
space.

Following from this we can describe any space curve parametrically, using any parameter u, say, and a **cubic curve** is given by:

$$x(u) = a_x u^3 + b_x u^2 + c_x u + d_x$$
$$y(u) = a_y u^3 + b_y u^2 + c_y u + d_y \qquad\qquad \textbf{(6.1)}$$
$$z(u) = a_z u^3 + b_z u^2 + c_z u + d_z$$

where $0 \leqslant u \leqslant 1$, and each of x, y and z is a cubic polynomial of the parameter u.

There are a number of reasons for using parametric descriptions in computer graphics rather than implicit functions. (An implicit function is $f(x,y,z) = 0$; for example, the implicit function description of a sphere is $x^2 + y^2 + z^2 - r^2 = 0$.) First, points on a curve can be computed sequentially, rather than by solving non-linear equations for each point in an implicit definition. Parametric curves (and surfaces) are easily transformed. Applying a linear transform to the parametric representation of the curve transforms the curve itself. Most design applications involve complex curves (and/or surfaces) which cannot be described by simple functions, whereas a parametric representation allows piecewise descriptions and a curve or a surface can be a set of piecewise polynomials. (Polynomials of high degree can describe complex curves but require a large number of coefficients and may introduce unwanted oscillations into the curve.)

6.2.1 Bézier cubic curves

We now look at a particular form of parametric representation: the Bézier cubic curve. The Bezier formulation of a cubic curve involves specifying a set of control points from which the cubic polynomial is derived. This form is derived, in most texts, by starting with blending or basis functions (see below). Foley *et al.* (1989) give a comprehensive derivation showing the relationship between the Bézier formulation and Hermite or Ferguson cubics.

Rewriting Equations 6.1 as a single vector equation gives:

$$Q(u) = au^3 + bu^2 + cu + d$$

and this is the normal way to express a parametric cubic polynomial. Using the Bézier basis or Bernstein blending functions (these are discussed more fully below):

$$(1 - u)^3$$
$$3u (1 - u)^2$$
$$3u^2(1 - u)$$
$$u^3$$

the polynomial is expressed in terms of these functions and four control points:

$$Q(u) = P_0(1 - u)^3 + P_1 3u(1 - u)^2 + P_2 3u^2(1 - u) + P_3 u^3$$

or in matrix notation:

$$Q(u) = UBP$$

$$= [u^3 \ u^2 \ u \ 1] \begin{bmatrix} -1 & 3 & -3 & 1 \\ 3 & -6 & 3 & 0 \\ -3 & 3 & 0 & 0 \\ 1 & 0 & 0 & 0 \end{bmatrix} \begin{bmatrix} P_0 \\ P_1 \\ P_2 \\ P_3 \end{bmatrix}$$

From an intuitive point of view the matrix formulation is not particularly useful, the blending function definition, given below, is preferred; however a matrix formulation is useful when considering hardware implementation.

P_0, P_1, P_2 and P_3 are four control points that specify the curve, P_0 and P_3 being the end points. They are called control points because moving them around in space controls or influences the shape of the curve. The polygon formed by joining the control points together is called the **characteristic** or **control polygon**. Figure 6.1 shows a curve and its characteristic polygon.

The Bézier form is an ingenious reformulation of a Hermite cubic polynomial form. It allows the shape of the curve to be determined entirely from the position of the four control points. In particular, the user does not have to specify or control the tangent vectors, or first derivatives, required for the Hermite specification. A geometric interpretation of the way in which the control points work now follows. This can easily be omitted if you are only interested in the practical use of Bézier segments.

By differentiating the basis functions with respect to u it can be shown that:

$$Q_u(0) = 3(P_1 - P_0)$$
$$Q_u(1) = 3(P_2 - P_3)$$

These are the tangent vectors to the curve at the end points and it can be

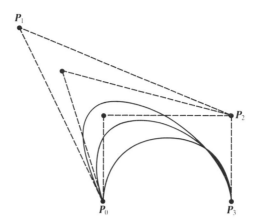

Figure 6.4
Effects of moving
control point P_1.

seen that P_1 and P_2 lie on these vectors. Altering the four control points will thus allow the position and shape of the curve to be controlled as they effectively alter the end points and the two tangent vector values.

Figure 6.4 attempts to show the way in which the control points influence the curve shape and Figure 6.5 shows a curve and its tangent vectors. Writing a short interactive program and experimenting with the position of the control points will give an intuitive appreciation of this geometric interpretation. In particular, you will see that the middle two control points appear to exercise a 'pull' on the curve. Say, for example, that we required a design method that reproduced the shape of a 'simple' hand-drawn curve. We could proceed as follows:

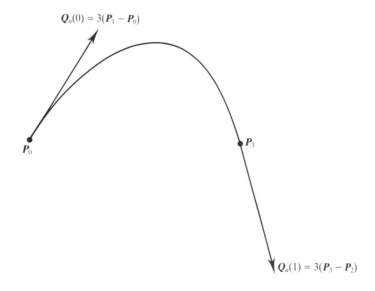

Figure 6.5
The relationship
between Bézier control
points and tangent
vectors.

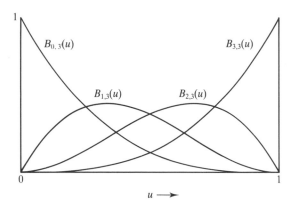

Figure 6.6
Cubic Bézier basis
functions.

(1) Approximate the shape of the curve by forming a control polygon.
(2) Use this to draw the associated Bézier curve.
(3) Adjust the control points.
(4) Repeat 2 and 3 until satisfied with the shape.

We now return to the basis or blending function discussed at the beginning of the chapter. The four basis functions are shown in Figure 6.6 and for this interpretation the curve is specified by:

$$Q(u) = \sum_{i=0}^{3} P_i B_{i,3}(u)$$

where each term in the sum is a product of a control point P_i and a blending function $B_{i,3}$ which in this case is a polynomial of degree three. These curves show the 'influence' that each control point has on the final curve form. For a particular value of u we sum the values obtained from each of the four blending functions. P_0 is most influential at $u = 0$ ($B_{1,3}$, $B_{2,3}$ and $B_{3,3}$ are all zero at this point). As u is increased 'towards' P_1, B_0 and B_1 mainly determine the curve shape, with $B_{2,3}$ and $B_{3,3}$ exerting some influence. The control points P_1 and P_2 have most effect when $u = 1/3$ and $2/3$ respectively. Note that moving any control point will influence, to a greater or lesser extent, the shape of all parts of the curve. This is a disadvantage of a Bézier curve – the control is global. Another important point is that parametric representations allow multiple-valued curves. For example, if $P_0 = P_3$ then the resulting curve will be a closed loop.

The set of basis or blending functions given for cubic polynomials:

$$B_{0,3}(u) = (1 - u)^3$$
$$B_{1,3}(u) = 3u(1 - u)^2$$
$$B_{2,3}(u) = 3u^2(1 - u)$$

$$B_{3,3}(u) = u^3$$

is a particular case of basis function of any degree n, where:

$$Q(u) = \sum_{i=0}^{n} P_i B_{i,n}(u)$$

and:

$$B_{i,n}(u) = C(n,i)u^i(1 - u)^{n-i}$$

and $C(n,i)$ is the binomial coefficient:

$$C(n,i) = n!/(i!(n - i)!)$$

Note that this increases the number of control points to $n + 1$ in general. There are, however, problems associated with increasing the number of control points by increasing the degree of the blending functions, and these difficulties are one reason for preferring B-splines.

At this point it is useful to consider all the ramifications of representing a curve with control points. The most important property, as far as interaction is concerned, is that moving the control points gives an intuitive change in curve shape. Another way of putting it is to say that the curve mimics the shape of the control polygon. An important property from the point of view of the algorithms that deal with curves (and surfaces) is that a curve is always enclosed in the convex hull formed by the control polygon. This follows from the fact that the basis functions sum to unity for all u. Considering transformations, since the curves are defined as linear combinations of the control points, the curve is transformed by any affine transformation (rotation, scaling, translation and so on) in three-dimensional space by applying the appropriate transformations to the set of control points. Thus to transform a curve we transform the control points then compute the points on the curve. In this context note that it is not easy to transform a curve by computing the points then transforming (as we might do with an implicit description). For example, it is not clear in scaling how many points are needed to ensure smoothness when the curve has been magnified. Note here that perspective transformations are non-affine, so we cannot map control points to screen space and compute the curve there.

Although we have discussed the cubic Bézier form, this is only a special case of a set of Bernstein–Bézier polynomial curves. Cubics are used most often because they are reasonably simple, but are still sufficiently flexible for interactive design work. The advantages of higher order curves relate to the degree of continuity that can be achieved between curve segments (see Section 6.2.2). Apart from the computational expense, as higher order curves are used the relationship between the characteristic polygons formed by the control points and the curve becomes weaker.

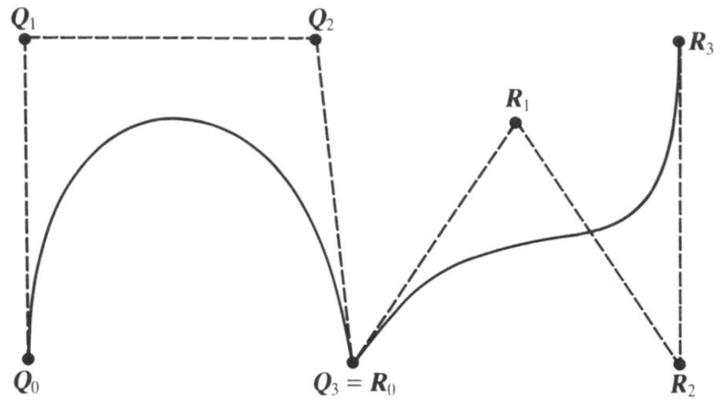

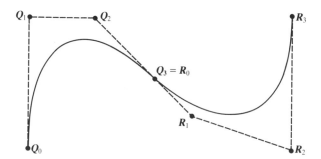

Figure 6.7
Positional continuity
between Bézier curves.

6.2.2   Joining Bézier curve segments

Curve segments defined by a set of four control points can be joined to
make up 'more complex' curves than those obtainable from a cubic polynomial form. This results in a piecewise polynomial curve. An alternative
method of representing more complex curves is to increase the order of the
polynomial, but this has computational and mathematical disadvantages and
it is generally considered easier to split the curve into cubic segments. Connecting curve segments implies that constraints must apply at the joins. The
default constraint is G^0. The difference between G^0 and G^1 continuity for a
Bézier curve is shown in Figures 6.7 and 6.8. G^0 continuity means that the
end point of the first segment is coincident with the start point of the
second. G^1 continuity means that the edges of the characteristic polygon are
collinear as shown in the figure. This means that the tangent vectors at the
end of one curve and the start of the other match to within a constant. In
shaded surfaces, maintaining only G^0 continuity would possibly result in the
joins being visible in the final rendered object.

   If the control points of the two segments are Q_i and R_i then G^1
continuity is maintained if:

$$(Q_3 - Q_2) = k(R_1 - R_0)$$

Using this condition, a composite Bézier curve is easily built up by adding a
single segment at a time. However, the advantage of being able to build up a

Figure 6.8
Tangential continuity
between Bézier curves.

composite form from segments is somewhat negated by the constraints on local control that now apply because of the joining conditions. This can only be alleviated by increasing the degree of the polynomial or by splitting a segment into two or more smaller segments.

6.2.3 Summary of Bézier curve properties

- The degree of the polynomial is always one less than the number of control points. In computer graphics we generally use degree three.
- The curve 'follows' the shape of the control point polygon and is constrained within the convex hull formed by the control points.
- The control points do not exert 'local' control. Moving any control point affects all of the curve to a greater or lesser extent. This can be seen by examining Figure 6.6, which shows that all the basis functions are everywhere non-zero except at the points $u = 0$ and $u = 1$.
- The first and last control points are the end points of the curve segment.
- The tangent vectors to the curve at the end points are coincident with the first and last edges of the control point polygon.
- The curve does not oscillate about any straight line more often than the control point polygon – this is known as the variation diminishing property.
- The curve is transformed by applying any affine transformation (that is, any combination of linear transformations) to its control point representation. The curve is invariant (does not change shape) under such a transformation.

6.3 B-spline curves

Two drawbacks associated with Bézier curves that are overcome by using B-spline curves are their non-localness and the relationship between the degree of the curve and the number of control points. The first property – non-localness – implies that although a control point heavily influences that part of the curve most close to it, it also has some effect on all the curve and this can be seen by examining Figure 6.6. All the basis functions are non-zero over the entire range of u. The second disadvantage means that we cannot use a Bézier cubic curve to approximate or represent n points without the inconvenience of using multiple curve segments (or by increasing the degree of the curve).

Originally, a spline was a draughtsman's aid. It was a thin metal (or wooden) strip that was used to draw curves through certain fixed points by adding weights at points called nodes or 'knots'. The resulting curve is smooth and minimizes the internal strain energy in the splines. The mathematical equivalent is the cubic polynomial spline.

Like a Bézier curve, a B-spline curve does not pass through the control points. A B-spline is a complete piecewise cubic polynomial consisting of any number of curve segments. (For notational simplicity we will only consider cubic B-splines. We can, however, have B-splines to any degree.) It is a cubic segment over a certain interval, and going from one interval to the next, the coefficients change. For a single segment only, we can compare the B-spline formulation with the Bézier formulation by using the same matrix notation.

The B-spline formulation is:

$$Q_i(u) = UB_sP$$

$$= [u^3 \ u^2 \ u \ 1]\frac{1}{6}\begin{bmatrix} -1 & 3 & -3 & 1 \\ 3 & -6 & 3 & 0 \\ -3 & 0 & 3 & 0 \\ 1 & 4 & 1 & 0 \end{bmatrix}\begin{bmatrix} P_{i-3} \\ P_{i-2} \\ P_{i-1} \\ P_i \end{bmatrix}$$

where Q_i is the ith B-spline segment and P_i is a set of four points in a sequence of control points. Alternatively, we can write:

$$Q_i(u) = \sum_{k=0}^{3} P_{i-3+k}B_{i-3+k}(u) \tag{6.2}$$

where i is the segment number and k is the **local control point index**, that is, the index for the segment i. The value of u over a single curve segment is $0 \leqslant u \leqslant 1$. Using this notation we can describe u as a local parameter – locally varying over the parametric range of 0 to 1 – to define a single B-spline curve segment.

Thus using this notation we see that a B-spline curve is a series of $m - 2$ curve segments that we conventionally label $Q_3, Q_4, \ldots, Q_m$ defined or determined by $m + 1$ control points $P_0, P_1, \ldots, P_m, m \geqslant 3$. Each curve segment is defined by four control points and each control point influences four and only four curve segments. This is the local control property of the B-spline curve – the main advantage over Bézier curves. (Here we must be careful. Barsky (Bartels, Beatty and Barsky, 1988) points out that comparing Bézier curves and B-spline curves is misleading because it is not a comparison of like with like but a comparison of a single-segment Bézier curve (which may have the control vertex set extended and the degree of the curve raised) with a piecewise or composite B-spline curve. A single-segment Bézier curve is subject to global control because moving a control point affects the complete curve. In a composite B-spline curve, moving a control point only affects a few segments of the curve. The comparison should be between multisegment Bézier curves and B-splines. The difference here is that to maintain continuity between Bézier segments the movement of the control points must satisfy constraints, while the control points of a B-spline composite can be moved in any way.)

A B-spline exhibits positional, first derivative and second derivative (C^2) continuity and this is achieved because the basis functions are themselves C^2 piecewise polynominials. A linear combination of such basis functions will also be C^2 continuous. We define the entire set of curve segments as one B-spline curve in u:

$$Q(u) = \sum_{i=0}^{m} P_i B_i(u)$$

In this notation i is now a non-local control point number and u is a global parameter discussed in more detail in the next section.

6.3.1 Uniform B-splines

Equation 6.2 shows that each segment in a B-spline curve is defined by four basis functions and four control vertices. Hence there are three more basis functions and three more control vertices than there are curve segments. The join point on the value of u between segments is called the **knot value** and a uniform B-spline means that knots are spaced at equal intervals of the parameter u. Figure 6.9 shows a B-spline curve that is defined by (the position of) six control vertices or control points P_0, P_1, ..., P_5. It also shows the effect of varying the degree of the polynomials, and curves are shown for degree 2, 3 and 4. We are generally interested in cubics and this is a curve of three segments with the left-hand end point of Q_3 near P_0 and the right-hand end point of Q_5 near P_5. (Thus we see that a uniform B-spline does not, in general, interpolate the end control points, unlike a Bézier curve.)

The notation gives us the following organization:

Q_3 is defined by $P_0 P_1 P_2 P_3$ which are scaled by $B_0 B_1 B_2 B_3$
Q_4 is defined by $ P_1 P_2 P_3 P_4$ which are scaled by $B_1 B_2 B_3 B_4$
Q_5 is defined by $ P_2 P_3 P_4 P_5$ which are scaled by $B_2 B_3 B_4 B_5$

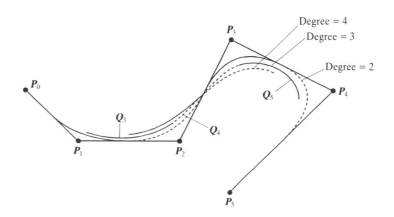

Figure 6.9
A three-segment B-spline cubic curve defined by six control points.

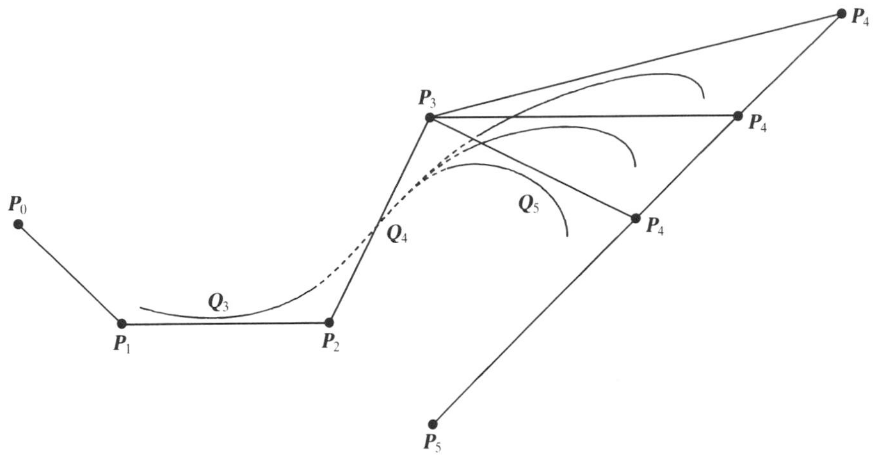

Figure 6.10
Demonstrating the
locality property of
B-spline curves.
Moving P_1 changes Q_5
and Q_4 to a lesser
extent. Q_3 is
unchanged.

The fact that each curve segment shares control points is the underlying mechanism whereby C^2 continuity is maintained between curve segments. Figure 6.10 shows the effect of changing the position of control point P_4. This pulls the segment Q_5 in the appropriate direction and also affects, to a lesser extent, segment Q_4 (which is also defined by P_4). However, it does not affect Q_3 and this figure demonstrates the important locality property of B-splines. In general, of course, a single control point influences four curve segments.

We now consider the underlying basis functions that define the curve. Each basis function is non-zero over four successive intervals in u (Figure 6.11). It is, in fact, a cubic composed itself of four segments. The B-spline is non-zero over the intervals u_i, u_{i+1}, ..., u_{i+4} and centred on u_{i+2}. Now each control point is scaled by a single basis function, and if we assume that our knot values are equally spaced, then each basis function is a copy or translate and the set of basis functions used by the curve in Figure 6.9 is shown in Figure 6.12.

The basis functions sum to unity in the range $u = 3$ to $u = 6$ in this case, the values of the parameter u over which the curve is defined. A consequence of this is that the entire B-spline curve is contained within the convex hull of its control points. If we consider a single segment in the curve

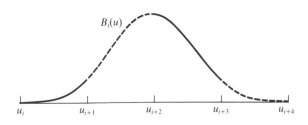

Figure 6.11
The uniform cubic
B-spline $B_i(u)$.

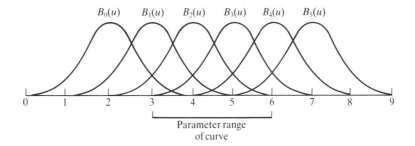

Figure 6.12
The six B-splines used in constructing the curve of Figure 6.9. They are all translates of each other.

then this defines a parameter range u_i to u_{i+1}. The basis functions that are active in the ith parametric interval, u_i to u_{i+1}, that is, the functions that define a single curve segment, are shown highlighted in Figure 6.13. This gives a useful interpretation of the behaviour of the functions as u is varied. In general, for values of u that are not knot values, four basis functions are active and sum to unity. When a knot value $u = u_i$ is reached, one basis function 'switches off' and another 'switches on'. At the knot value there are three basis functions that sum to unity.

At this stage we can summarize and state that a B-spline curve is made up of $m - 2$ segments defined by the position of $m + 1$ basis functions over $m + 5$ knot values. Thus in Figure 6.9 we have three segments, six control points and six basis functions over ten knot values.

Now consider again Figure 6.13. In the parameter range $u_i \leqslant u \leqslant u_{i+1}$ we evaluate the four B-splines, B_i, B_{i-1}, B_{i-2} and B_{i-3}, by substituting $0 \leqslant u \leqslant 1$ and computing:

$$
\begin{aligned}
B_i &= 1/6\, u^3 \\
B_{i-1} &= 1/6\,(-3u^3 + 3u^2 + 3u + 1) \\
B_{i-2} &= 1/6\,(3u^3 - 6u^2 + 4) \\
B_{i-3} &= 1/6\,(1 - u)^3
\end{aligned}
\tag{6.3}
$$

It is important to note that this definition gives a single segment from each of the four B-spline basis functions over the range $0 \leqslant u \leqslant 1$. It does *not* define a single B-spline basis function which consists of four segments over the range $0 \leqslant u \leqslant 4$.

We now come to consider the end control vertices and note again that the curve does not interpolate these points. In general, of course, a B-spline

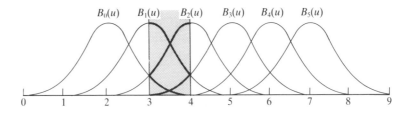

Figure 6.13
The four B-splines that are non-zero or active for the first curve segment in Figure 6.9.

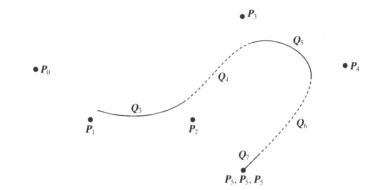

Figure 6.14
Demonstrating the effect of multiple end control points. P_5 is repeated three times forcing the curve to interpolate it.

curve does not interpolate *any* control points. We can make a B-spline curve interpolate control points by introducing multiple vertices. However, this involves a loss of continuity as we shall see. Intuitively we can think of increasing the influence of a control point by repeating it. The curve is attracted to the repeated point. A segment is made by basis functions scaling control points. If a control point is repeated it will be used more than once in the evaluation of a single segment. Such a technique can be used to make the curve interpolate both the intermediate control points and the end points – where the loss of continuity may not be of the same significance. For example, consider Figure 6.14 and compare it with Figure 6.9. The last control point in the example in Figure 6.9 is now repeated three times. There are now five segments and P_5 is used once in the determination of Q_5, twice in Q_6 and three times in Q_7. The curve now ranges over $3 \leqslant u \leqslant 8$. At $u = 8$ the curve is concident with P_5.

Figure 6.15(a) shows the effect of introducing multiple intermediate control points. In this figure P_3 has been doubled. P_3 is almost interpolated and an extra segment is introduced. The continuity changes from C^2G^2 to C^2G^1. Figure 6.15(b) shows P_3 made into a triple control point. This time the curve interpolates the control point and the curve becomes a straight line on either side of the control point. The continuity reduces now to C^2G^0.

6.3.2   Non-uniform B-splines

A non-uniform B-spline is a curve where the parametric intervals between successive knot values are not necessarily equal. This implies that the blending functions are no longer translates of each other but vary from interval to interval. The most common form of a non-uniform B-spline is where some of the intervals between successive knot values are reduced to zero by inserting multiple knots. This facility is used to interpolate control points (both end points and intermediate points) and it possesses certain advantages over the method used in the previous section – inserting multiple control points.

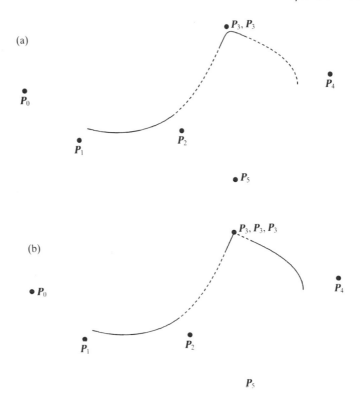

Figure 6.15
Demonstrating the
effect of multiple
intermediate control
points. (a) P_3 is
duplicated. (b) P_3 is
triplicated.

In particular, a control point can be interpolated without the effect that occurred with multiple control vertices, namely, straight-line curve segments on either side of the control point.

Consider the curve generated in Figure 6.9. The knot values for this curve are $u = 3,4,5,6$. We define a useful parametric range (within which the basis functions sum to unity) as $3 \leqslant u \leqslant 6$. The interval between each knot value is 1. If non-uniform knot values are used, then the basis functions are no longer the same for each parametric interval, but vary over the range of u. Consider Figure 6.16. This uses the same control points as Figure 6.9 and the B-spline curve is still made up of three segments. However, the curve now interpolates the end points because multiple knots have been inserted at each end of the knot vector. The knot vector used is $[0,0,0,0,1,2,3,3,3,3]$. The basis functions are also shown in the figure. The curve now possesses nine segments, Q_0 to Q_8. However, Q_0, Q_1 and Q_2 are reduced to a single point. Q_3, Q_4 and Q_5 are defined over the range $0 \leqslant u \leqslant 3$. Q_6, Q_7 and Q_8 are reduced to a single point $u = 3$. A second example showing the flexibility of a B-spline curve is given in Figure 6.17. Here we have nine control points and thirteen knots. The knot vector is $[0,0,0,0,1,2,3,4,5,6,6,6,6]$.

In general, a knot vector is any non-decreasing sequence of knot values u_0 to u_{m+4}. As we have seen, successive knot values can be equal and

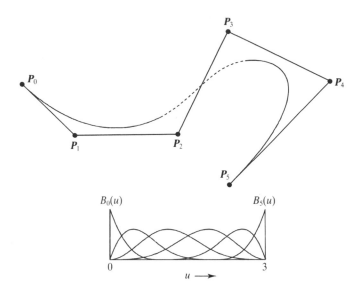

Figure 6.16
A non-uniform
B-spline that
interpolates the end
points by using a knot
vector [0,0,0,0,1,2,3,
3,3,3].

the number of identical values is called the **multiplicity** of the knot. Causing a curve to interpolate the end points by using multiple control vertices does not have precisely the same effect as using multiple control vertices, and Figure 6.18 shows the final control point P_5 in our standard example interpolated using both a multiple control point and a knot vector with multiplicity 4 on the final knot value.

If we use the knot vector [0,0,0,0,1,1,1,1] then we have single segment curve interpolating P_0 and P_3. In this instance the basis functions are the Bézier basis functions (Figure 6.6) and the resulting curve is a Bézier curve. Thus we see that a Bézier curve is just a special case of a non-uniform B-spline.

The effect of a multiple knot on the shape of a basis function is easily seen. Consider Figure 6.19. Part (a) shows the uniform B-spline basis function defined over the knots 0,1,2,3,4. As explained in the previous section, this is itself made up of four cubic polynomial seqments defined over the given ranges. These are generated by using Equation 6.3 and translating each cubic segment by 0,1,2,3 and 4 units in u. Alternatively we can use:

$$B_0(u) = \begin{cases} b_{-0}(u) = 1/6\, u^3 & 0 \leqslant u \leqslant 1 \\ b_{-1}(u) = -1/6(3u^3 - 12u^2 + 12u - 4) & 1 \leqslant u \leqslant 2 \\ b_{-2}(u) = 1/6(3u^3 - 24u^2 + 60u - 44) & 2 \leqslant u \leqslant 3 \\ b_{-3}(u) = -1/6(u^3 - 12u^2 + 48u - 64) & 3 \leqslant u \leqslant 4 \end{cases}$$

Compared with Equation 6.3 note that this defines a single B-spline basis function over the range $0 \leqslant u \leqslant 4$. If we double the second knot and use [0,1,1,2,3], $b_{-1}(u)$ shrinks to zero length and the function becomes asymmetric as shown in Figure 6.19(b). The double knot eliminates second derivative continuity but first derivative continuity remains. Tripling the

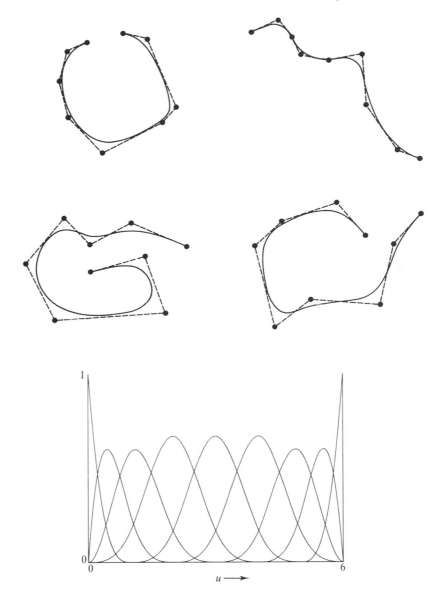

Figure 6.17
Showing the flexibility
of B-spline curves. The
knot vector is [0,0,0,0,
1,2,3,4,5,6,6,6,6].

second knot by using knot vector [0,1,1,1,2] gives the symmetrical function shown in Figure 6.19(c) which now only has positional continuity. Quadrupling this knot [0,1,1,1,1] produces the function shown in Figure 6.19(d) where even positional continuity is eliminated.

If we now return to the context shown in Figure 6.16, the first basis function is defined over 0,0,0,0,1 and is asymmetric with no positional continuity. The second is defined over a set of knot values that contains a triple knot – 0,0,0,1,2. The third is defined over the sequence 0,0,1,2,3 and is also

Figure 6.18
Comparing multiple
knots with multiple
control points. (a) The
curve is generated by a
knot vector with
multiplicity 4 on the
start and end values.
(b) P_5 is repeated three
times.

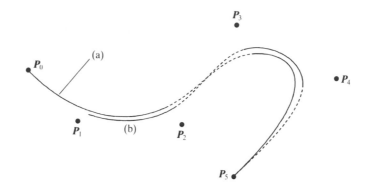

asymmetric. In this case all functions are asymmetric and summarizing we
have:

Knot vector	Basis function
00001	B_0
00012	B_1
00123	B_2
01233	B_3
12333	B_4
23333	B_5

We can further see from this set of basis functions that they sum to unity
over the entire range of u and that at $u = 0$ and $u = 3$ the only non-zero
basis functions are B_0 and B_5 (both unity) which cause the end points to be
interpolated by Q_3 and Q_5 respectively.

We now consider altering the knot multiplicity for interior knots
where the issue of continuity changes becomes apparent. Consider the
examples given in Figure 6.20. This is the same example as we used in
Figure 6.9 except that an extra control point has been added to give us a
four-segment curve. The knot vector is [0,1,2,3,4,5,6,7,8,9,10] and Figure
6.20(a) shows the curve. Figure 6.20(b) shows the effect of introducing a
double knot using vector [0,1,2,3,4,4,5,6,7,8,9]. The number of segments is
reduced to three. Q_4 shrinks to zero. The convex hulls containing Q_3 and Q_5
meet on edge P_2P_3 and the join point between Q_3Q_4 and Q_5 is forced to lie
on this line. In Figure 6.20(c) a triple knot is introduced –
[0,1,2,3,4,4,4,5,6,7,8]. The curve is reduced to two segments. Q_4 and Q_5
shrink to zero at P_3. There is only positional continuity between Q_3 and Q_6
but the segments on either side of the control point P_3 are curved. This
should be compared with Figure 6.15, produced using a triple control vertex.
In Figure 6.20(d) a quadruple knot is introduced – [0,1,2,3,4,4,4,4,5,6,7,8].
Positional continuity is destroyed. The curve reduces to a single segment. To
see what this means, we have introduced another control point so that
another segment, Q_7, now appears. There is now a gap between the end of
Q_3 and the start of Q_7. They have no control points in common.

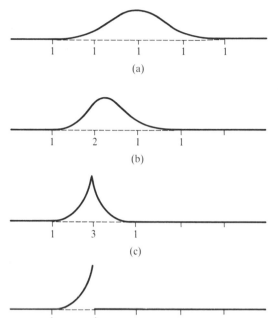

Figure 6.19
The effect of knot
multiplicity on a single
cubic B-spline basis
function. (a) All knot
multiplicities are unity:
[0,1,2,3,4]. (b) Second
knot has multiplicity 2:
[0,1,1,2,3]. (c) Second
knot has multiplicity 3:
[0,1,1,1,2]. (d) Second
knot has multiplicity 4:
[0,1,1,1,1].

We now consider a recursive method for generating the basis or blending functions for non-uniform B-splines. The method, known as the **Cox–deBoor algorithm** (De Boor, 1972; Cox, 1972), remarkably is able to generate uniform or non-uniform B-splines of any degree using a single recursive formula. Because the functions are no longer translates of one another the computation is more expensive. For a cubic (fourth order) curve we can define the recursion in its unwound form. Extending the notation of a B-spline to include order as the second subscript, we define the basis function for weighting control point P_i as $B_{i,j}(u)$ and the recurrence relationships for a cubic B-spline is:

$$B_{i,1}(u) = \begin{cases} 1 & u_i \leqslant u \leqslant u_{i+1} \\ 0 & \text{otherwise} \end{cases}$$

$$B_{i,2}(u) = \frac{u - u_i}{u_{i+1} - u_i} B_{i,1}(u) + \frac{u_{i+2} - u}{u_{i+2} - u_{i+1}} B_{i+1,1}(u)$$

$$B_{i,3}(u) = \frac{u - u_i}{u_{i+2} - u_i} B_{i,2}(u) + \frac{u_{i+3} - u}{u_{i+3} - u_{i+1}} B_{i+1,2}(u)$$

$$B_{i,4}(u) = \frac{u - u_i}{u_{i+3} - u_i} B_{i,3}(u) + \frac{u_{i+4} - u}{u_{i+4} - u_{i+1}} B_{i+1,3}(u)$$

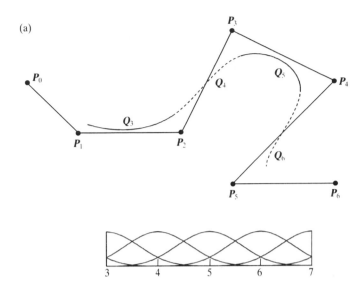

Figure 6.20
The effect of interior
knot multiplicity on a
B-spline curve.

(a) A four-segment
B-spline curve. The
knot vector is
[0,1,2,3,4,5,6,7,8,9,10].
All B-splines are
translates of each
other.

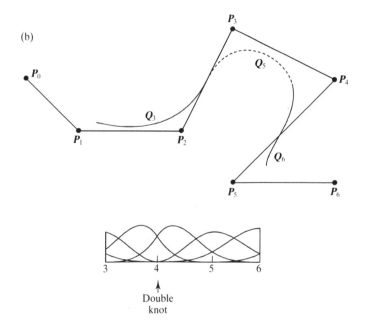

(b) Knot vector is
[0,1,2,3,4,4,5,6,7,8,9].
Q_4 shrinks to zero.

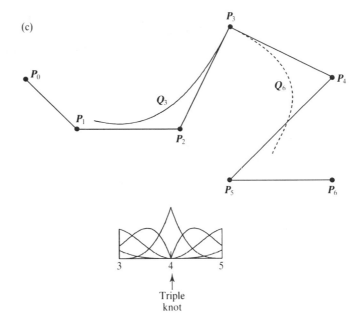

(c) Knot vector is [0,1,2,3,4,4,5,6,7,8]. Q_4 and Q_5 shrink to zero. Continuity between Q_3 and Q_6 is positional.

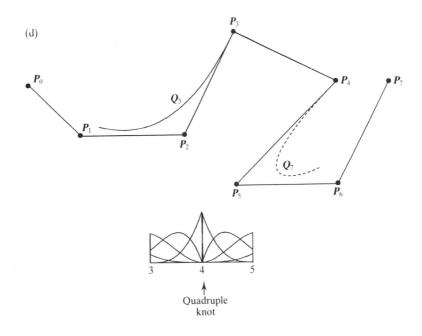

(d) Knot vector is [0,1,2,3,4,4,4,4,5,6,7,8]. The curve reduces to a single segment Q_3. Another control point has been added to show that the curve now 'breaks' between P_3 and P_4.

When knots are repeated a quotient of 0/0 can occur in the Cox–deBoor definition and this is deemed to be zero. Computationally the numerator is always checked for zero and the result set to zero irrespective of the denominator value. The choice of a particular knot set in commercial CAD systems that use B-splines is usually a predefined part of the system.

6.3.3   Summary of B-spline curve properties

Some of the properties that we listed for Bézier curves apply to B-spline curves. In particular:

- The curve follows the shape of the control point polygon and is constrained to lie in the convex hull of the control points.
- The curve exhibits the variation diminishing property.
- The curve is transformed by applying any affine transformation to its control point representation.

In addition, B-splines possess the following property:

- A B-spline curve exhibits local control – a control point is connected to four segments (in the case of a cubic) and moving a control point can influence only these segments.

6.4   Biparametric cubic surfaces

The treatment of parametric cubic curve segments given in the foregoing sections is easily generalized to biparametric cubic surface patches. A point on the surface patch is given by a biparametric function and a set of blending or basis functions is used for each parameter. A cubic Bézier patch is defined as:

$$Q(u, v) = \sum_{i=0}^{3} \sum_{j=0}^{3} P_{ij} B_i(u) B_j(v)$$

Mathematically, the three-dimensional surfaces are said to be generated from the cartesian product of two curves. A Bézier patch and its control points are shown in Figure 6.21 where the patches are displayed using isoparametric lines. The 16 control points form a characteristic polyhedron and this bears a relationship to the shape of the surface in the same way that the characteristic polygon relates to a curve segment. From Figure 6.21(a) it can be seen intuitively that 12 of the control points are associated with the boundary edges of the patch (four of them specifying the end points) and the four interior points specify the internal shape. Only the corner vertices lie in the surface.

The properties of the Bézier curve formulation are extended into the surface domain. Figure 6.22 shows a patch being deformed by 'pulling out' a

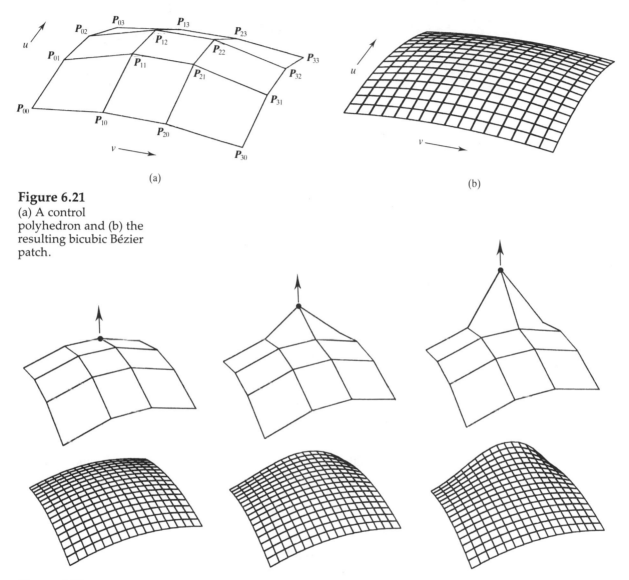

Figure 6.21
(a) A control polyhedron and (b) the resulting bicubic Bézier patch.

Figure 6.22
The effect of 'lifting' one of the control points of a Bézier patch.

single control point. The intuitive feel for the surface through its control points, and the ability to ensure first-order continuity are maintained. The surface patch is transformed by applying transformations to each of the control points.

The way in which the control points work can be seen by analogy with the cubic curve. The geometric interpretation is naturally more difficult than that for the curve and, of course, the purpose of the Bézier formulation is to protect the designer against having to manipulate tangent vectors and so on, but it is included for completeness.

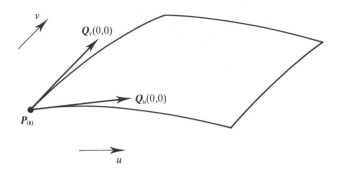

Figure 6.23
Tangent vector at P_{00}.

The matrix specification is:

$$P(u, v) = [u^3 \ u^2 \ u \ 1] \, [BPB^{\mathrm{T}}] \begin{bmatrix} v^3 \\ v^2 \\ v \\ 1 \end{bmatrix}$$

where:

$$B = \begin{bmatrix} -1 & 3 & -3 & 1 \\ 3 & -6 & 3 & 0 \\ -3 & 3 & 0 & 0 \\ 1 & 0 & 0 & 0 \end{bmatrix}$$

$$P = \begin{bmatrix} P_{00} & P_{01} & P_{02} & P_{03} \\ P_{10} & P_{11} & P_{12} & P_{13} \\ P_{20} & P_{21} & P_{22} & P_{23} \\ P_{30} & P_{31} & P_{32} & P_{33} \end{bmatrix}$$

It is instructive to examine the relationship between control points and derivative vectors at the corner of a patch. For example, consider the corner $u = v = 0$. The relationship between the control points and the vectors associated with the vertex P_{00} is as follows:

$$\begin{aligned} Q_u(0,0) &= 3(P_{10} - P_{00}) \\ Q_v(0,0) &= 3(P_{01} - P_{00}) \\ Q_{uv}(0,0) &= 9(P_{00} - P_{01} - P_{10} + P_{11}) \end{aligned}$$

(6.4)

Figure 6.23 shows these vectors at a patch corner. $Q_u(0,0)$ is a constant times the tangent vector at $Q(0,0)$ in the u parameter direction. Similarly $Q_v(0,0)$ relates to the tangent vector in the v parameter direction. The cross derivatives at each end point, sometimes called **twist vectors**, specify the rate of change of the tangent vectors with respect to u and v. It is a vector normal to the plane containing the tangent vectors.

Analogous to the control points in Bézier curves – which we saw are a reformulation of Hermite curves – the net of 16 control points is a reformulation of Hermite surface patches which are patches specified in terms of

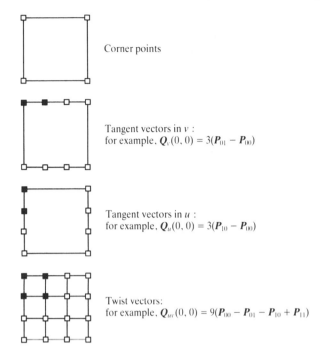

Corner points

Tangent vectors in v :
for example, $Q_v(0, 0) = 3(P_{01} - P_{00})$

Tangent vectors in u :
for example, $Q_u(0, 0) = 3(P_{10} - P_{00})$

Twist vectors:
for example, $Q_{uv}(0, 0) = 9(P_{00} - P_{01} - P_{10} + P_{11})$

Figure 6.24
Control point matrix
elements.

four end points, eight tangent vectors (two at each corner) and four twist vectors. Consider Figure 6.24 that shows the elements of the control point polyhedron that are involved in the derivatives. Four pairs of points specify the tangent vectors in u at each corner (two rows in the matrix), four pairs specify tangent vectors in v (two columns in the matrix) and all 16 elements specify the twist vectors.

For shading calculations we need to calculate certain surface normals. One of the easiest ways to shade a patch is to subdivide it until the products of the subdivision are approximately planar (this technique is discussed fully later in the chapter). The patches can then be treated as planar polygons and Gouraud or Phong shading applied. Vertex normals are calculated from the cross product of the two tangent vectors at the vertex. For example:

$$a = (P_{01} - P_{00})$$
$$b = (P_{10} - P_{00})$$
$$N = a \times b$$

A normal can be computed at any point on the surface from the cross product of the two partial derivatives $\partial Q/\partial u$ and $\partial Q/\partial v$ but shading a patch by exhaustive calculation of internal points from the parametric description is computationally expensive and is subject to other problems (described below). The advantages of using a parametric patch description of a surface are not contained in the fact that a *precise* world coordinate is available for every point in the surface – the cost of this information is generally too high – but in the advantages that patch representation has to offer in object modelling.

6.4.1   Joining Bézier surface patches

Maintaining first-order continuity across two patches is a simple extension of the curve-joining constraints and is best considered geometrically. Figure 6.25 shows two patches, Q and R, sharing a common edge. For positional or zero-order continuity:

$$\mathbf{Q}(1,v) = \mathbf{R}(0,v) \qquad \text{for } 0 \leqslant v \leqslant 1$$

This condition implies that the two patches require a common boundary edge characteristic polygon and:

$$\mathbf{Q}_{33} = \mathbf{R}_{03}$$
$$\mathbf{Q}_{30} = \mathbf{R}_{00}$$
$$\mathbf{Q}_{32} = \mathbf{R}_{02}$$
$$\mathbf{Q}_{31} = \mathbf{R}_{01}$$

or

$$\mathbf{Q}_{3i} = \mathbf{R}_{0i} \qquad i = 0, \ldots, 3$$

To satisfy first-order continuity the tangent vectors at $u = 1$ for the first patch must match those at $u = 0$ for the second patch for all v. This implies that each of the four pairs of control polyhedron edges that straddle the boundary must be collinear (Figure 6.26). That is:

$$(\mathbf{Q}_{3i} - \mathbf{Q}_{2i}) = k(\mathbf{R}_{1i} - \mathbf{R}_{0i}) \qquad i = 0, \ldots, 3$$

Faux and Pratt (1979) point out that in CAD contexts, this constraint is severe if a composite surface is constructed from a set of Bézier patches. For example, a composite surface might be designed by constructing a single patch and working outwards from it. Joining two patches along a common boundary implies that 8 of the control points for the second patch are already fixed and joining a patch to two existing patches implies that 12 of the control points are fixed.

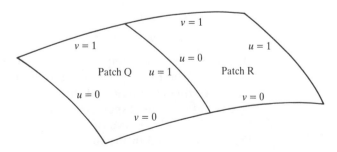

Figure 6.25
Joining two patches.

(a)

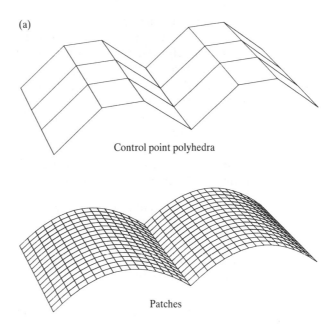

Control point polyhedra

Patches

(b)

Four sets of three control points must be collinear

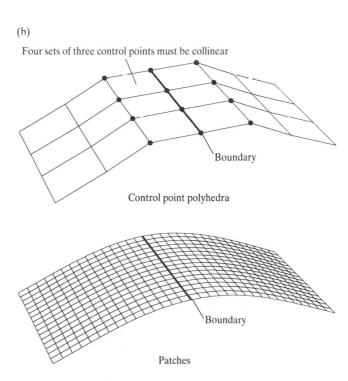

Boundary

Control point polyhedra

Boundary

Patches

Figure 6.26
(a) Positional continuity between bicubic Bézier patches and (b) tangential continuity between bicubic Bézier patches.

A slightly less restrictive joining condition was developed by Bézier in 1972 (Bézier, 1972). In this patch, corners have positional but not gradient continuity. However, tangent vectors of edges meeting at a corner must be coplanar. Even with this marginally greater flexibility, there are still problems with the design of composite surfaces and one solution is to use patches of higher degree than cubic.

It should be mentioned that although the foregoing treatment has dealt with rectangular patches, such patches cannot represent all shapes. Consider, for example, a spherically shaped object. Rectangular patches must degenerate to triangles at the poles. Triangular patches do not suffer from such degeneracies and are a more appropriate choice for complex shapes.

Farin (1988) points out that perhaps the main reason for the predominance of rectangular patches in most CAD systems is that the first applications of patches in car design were to the design of the outer body panels. Those parts have a rectangular geometry and it is natural to break them down into smaller rectangles and to use rectangularly shaped patches.

6.4.2   B-spline surface patches

To form a bicubic B-spline surface patch we need to evaluate:

$$Q(u,v) = \sum_{i=0}^{n} \sum_{j=0}^{m} P_{ij} B_{i,j}(u,v)$$

where P_{ij} is an array of control points and $B_{i,j}(u,v)$ is a bivariate basis function. We can generate $B_{i,j}(u,v)$ from:

$$B_{i,j}(u,v) = B_i(u) B_j(v)$$

where $B_i(u)$ and $B_j(v)$ are the previously defined univariate cubic B-splines. A basis function formed in this way is called a **tensor product surface**. Thus we have:

$$Q(u,v) = \sum_{i=0}^{n} \sum_{j=0}^{m} P_{ij} B_i(u) B_j(u)$$

Analogous to B-spline curves, we consider a B-spline patch to be made up of several rectangular surface patch segments. We now have two knot sequences in u and v, which taken together form a grid in parameter space.

We consider uniform B-spline patches where the grid of knot values exhibits equal intervals in the u and v parametric directions. First, consider a single patch segment. We shall use the phrase 'single patch segment' to mean the entity in two-parameter space that is analogous to a curve segment in single parameter space. Thus we say that a B-spline surface patch is made up of several patch segments. In the case of a single B-spline curve segment we required four control points to define the segment. Extending into two-parameter space we now require a grid, P_{ij}, of 4×4 control points to form a

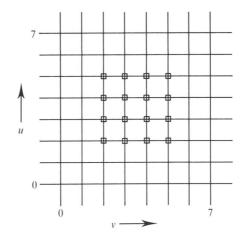

Figure 6.27
The 16 bivariate
B-splines peak at the
points shown in
parametric space.

single patch segment. These control points are blended with 4×4 bivariate basis functions. Recall from Figures 6.12 and 6.13 that a single B-spline segment requires a vector of eight knot values $u_0, \ldots, u_7$. Thus a single patch segment requires a grid or knot array of 8×8 knot values (Figure 6.27). The bivariate basis functions peak at the knot values shown with a square.

Consider a simple example. Figure 6.28 shows a single B-spline patch segment determined by 16 control points. Note that the patch is confined to the region nearer the central four control points. Just as with B-spline

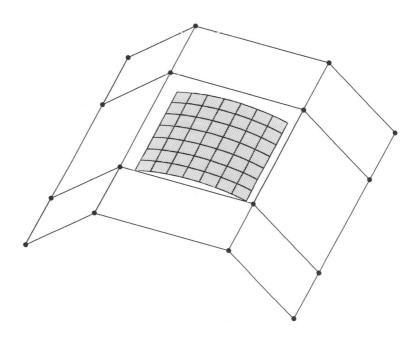

Figure 6.28
A single B-spline patch
segment.

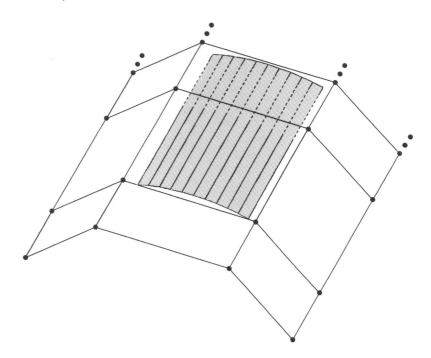

Figure 6.29
Triplicating a row of
control points for the
example in Figure 6.28.

curves, which do not interpolate their control points, a B-spline patch segment does not interpolate the inner 4 control points or any of the outer 12.

We can control the behaviour of patches at the edges of the control
point polyhedron by using multiple vertices (just as we controlled curves by
using multiple end points). This is easily demonstrated by using a simple
example. Consider Figure 6.29. Here we have triplicated a set of boundary
vertices forming a control point matrix made up of 24 points. This causes a
three-segment patch to be formed that is pulled to the boundary vertices.
Note that none of the boundary vertices is actually interpolated.

In the second example (Figure 6.30) we triplicate two sets of boundary vertices, one of which forms a collinear set. This results in a nine-
segment patch where the collinear vertices are interpolated. If we triple all
boundary vertices then we end up with a 25-patch segment surface which, in
general, will only interpolate the corner points.

Duplicating and triplicating interior control points can be used to
produce modelling effects that are more powerful than those available with a
Bézier patch. Figure 6.31 is an example. The control point polyhedron is as
in the previous example except that an inner point has been lifted. A row
and a column of control points have been triplicated. In the case of the
column, three of the control vertices are collinear and this results in a
surface with a crease aligned along the corresponding edge in the control
point polyhedron. Now consider the triplicated row. Here the points are not
collinear and the creasing effect is less sharp. Clearly, these effects can be

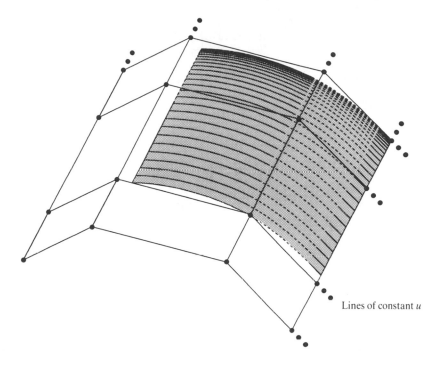

Lines of constant *u*

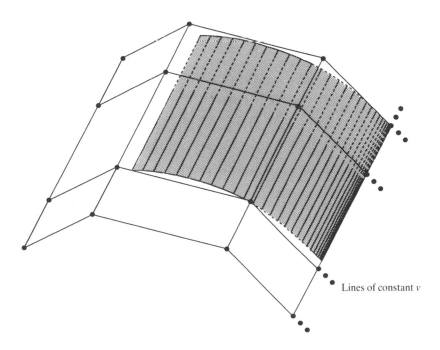

Lines of constant *v*

Figure 6.30
A nine-segment
B-spline patch formed
by triplicating a row
and a column of
control points.

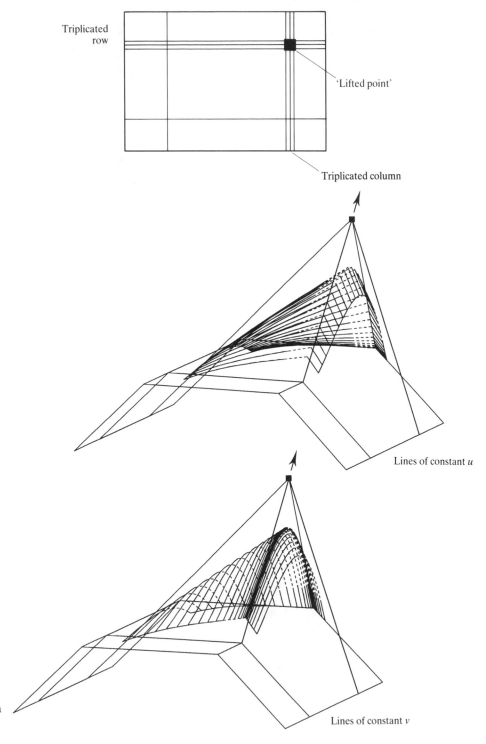

Triplicated row

'Lifted point'

Triplicated column

Lines of constant *u*

Lines of constant *v*

Figure 6.31
Triplicating interior
control points
produces a patch with
creases.

built into a modelling program where rows and columns are triplicated and the entire edge of the control point polyhedron is moved interactively to define or drag a crease in the surface. Surfaces that contain creases are common, for example, in car bodies.

6.5   Rendering parametric surfaces

Algorithms that scan convert surfaces represented by bicubic parametric patches divide naturally into two categories:

- those that render directly from the parametric description, and
- those that approximate the surface by a polygon mesh and use a planar polygon scan converter to render this approximation.

Currently the second approach appears to be the more popular. It is certainly the easier to implement and is computationally less expensive. Examples of the first are to be found in Blinn (1978a), Whitted (1978), Schweitzer and Cobb (1982) and Griffiths (1984). Lane *et al.* (1980) give a comparative description of these methods and describe an implementation of the second approach.

Scan conversion of parametrically defined surfaces is difficult because attributes of a polygon mesh, used in 'standard' polygon scan conversion, are not available from parametrically defined patches. Those attributes of a polygon that make for simple scan conversion are:

- The maximum and minimum Y coordinates are easily obtained from the vertex list.
- Incremental equations can be used to track each of the polygon edges as functions of Y.
- Incremental equations can be used to calculate the screen depth Z as a function of X.

A parametrically defined surface has none of these properties. The maximum and minimum Y coordinates will not, in general, be on the boundary or edges of the surface and a patch will often exhibit a silhouette edge. Silhouette edges are difficult because they are not necessarily the actual patch edges but, say, part of a central bump obscuring an actual edge. With parametrically defined surfaces both the boundary edge and the silhouette edge need to be tracked. A further complication is that a silhouette edge and a boundary edge may intersect. Finally, in general, neither the boundary nor the silhouette edges will be monotonic in X or Y.

We recall that a parametrically defined surface, or surface patch, is specified by three bivariate functions:

$$x = X(u,v)$$
$$y = Y(u,v)$$
$$z = Z(u,v)$$

where both u and v vary between 0 and 1. The boundaries of a surface patch are defined by the values $u = 0$, $u = 1$, $v = 0$ and $v = 1$. This results in a four-sided patch.

One way of looking at scan conversion in the context of bicubic parametric patches is that it is an algorithm which operates on curves formed by the intersection of the XZ scan plane with the surface. In general, the curve is between two boundary points or between a boundary point and a silhouette edge. With planar polygons this curve is a straight line and it is only necessary to store the end points. In the case of parametric surfaces, all points on the intersection curve need to be determined.

Blinn's algorithm (Blinn, 1978a) for parametric scan conversion is a straightforward algebraic approach and involves solving equations (using iterative techniques) for the intersection of the boundary curves and the silhouette edge with each scan line. The intersection of a scan line Y_s with the boundary of a patch is given by:

$$Y_s = Y(0,v)$$
$$Y_s = Y(1,v)$$
$$Y_s = Y(u,0)$$
$$Y_s = Y(u,1)$$

The silhouette edge intersections are given by:

$$Y_s = Y(u,v)$$
$$0 = N_z(u,v)$$

where N_z is the z component of the surface normal to the patch. A silhouette edge is defined by those points on the surface that exhibit a surface normal with zero z component. Local maxima and minima are determined from:

$$Y_u(u,v) = 0$$
$$Y_v(u,v) = 0$$

The points on the curve between these points are given by:

$$Y(u,v) - Y_s = 0$$
$$X(u,v) - X_s = 0$$

Solving these equations yields a set of points (u,v) in parameter space that can be substituted into the X and Z functions to yield the X and Z values of the edge on the current scan plane. This procedure is followed for each patch or surface, yielding successive pairs of boundaries representing areas to be shaded. As the scan plane moves down the screen, the boundary and silhouette edges must be tracked and their connectivity maintained. This is not an easy process and Blinn gives an instructive example using saddle points. Detection of a local maximum implies that a new intersection curve is added to an intersection curve list. Curves are deleted at Y minima. The effect of this process is to partition the surface patch into regions that are monotonically decreasing in Y and single valued in Z. It is pointed out in Lane *et al.* (1980) that there are numerous problems with this approach, but that for most shapes the algorithm is robust. Thus, as with planar polygon scan conversion, the outer Y scan loop tracks boundary and silhouette edges and the inner X scan loop 'fills in' points on the intersection curve in the Y scan plane. Blinn further modifies this process by trading off accuracy against speed, approximating the intersection curve by straight-line segments.

Whitted's, Schweitzer's and Griffith's methods are all variations of this basic approach.

6.6 Approximation to a surface patch using a polygon mesh

In Chapter 2 we overviewed the process of patch splitting as a rendering strategy for objects modelled from bicubic parametric patches. We now investigate this process in more detail.

A planar polygon mesh is easily generated from a surface patch. The patch can be divided using isoparametric curves. (Splitting up a patch into isoparametric curves is a common method of display in CAD systems, permitting a wireframe visualization of the surface sufficient for the requirements of such systems.) This yields a net or mesh of points at the intersection of these curves with each other and the boundary edges. This net of points can be used to define the vertices for a mesh of planar polygons which can then be rendered using a planar polygon renderer. There are two basic flaws in this rudimentary approach. Visible boundary edges and silhouette edges may exhibit discontinuities. In general, a finer polygon resolution will be necessary to diminish the visibility of piecewise linear discontinuities on edges than is necessary to maintain smooth shading within the patch. Also, internal silhouette edges in the patch will generally be of a higher degree than cubic.

Connected with this is the question: how fine should the isoparametric division be? Too fine a subdivision is computationally expensive; too coarse implies visible discontinuities. A possible approach is to relate the number of divisions to the area projected by the patch on the screen.

A subtler approach is a varying 'resolution'. Areas of the patch that are 'flattish' are subject to few subdivisions. Areas where the local curvature is high are subject to more subdivisions. Effectively, the patch is subdivided

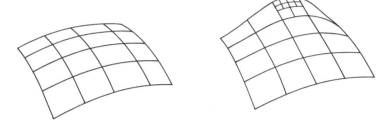

Figure 6.32
Uniform and
non-uniform
subdivision of a Bézier
patch.

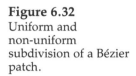

to a degree that depends on local curvature. This is the approach adopted by Lane *et al.* (1989). It is demonstrated in Figure 6.32.

Patches are subdivided until the products of the subdivision submit to a flatness criterion. Such patches are now considered to be approximately planar polygons and are scan converted by a normal polygon renderer using the corner points of the patches as vertices for rectangles in the polygon mesh. The set of patches representing the surface can be preprocessed, yielding a set of polygons which are then scan converted as normal. This is the approach adopted by Clark (1979). Lane integrates this patch splitting approach with a scan conversion algorithm.

There are two significant advantages to patch splitting:

(1) it is fast, and

(2) the speed can be varied by altering the depth of, the subdivision. This is important for interactive systems.

A disadvantage of non-uniform subdivision is that holes can appear between patches owing to the approximation of a patch boundary by a straight line. An example of this degenerative process is shown in Figure 6.33.

Subdivision algorithms are best considered for a curve. These are then easily extended or generalized to deal with a patch. The crux of the method is that rather than evaluate points along a curve, the curve is *approximated* by a piecewise linear version obtained by subdividing the control points recursively. This gives a finer and finer approximation to the curve. The level of subdivision/recursion terminates when a linearity criterion is satisfied. Lane and Riesenfeld (1980) show that the piecewise linear approximation to the curve will eventually 'collapse' onto the curve, provided that enough subdivisions are undertaken.

A subdivision formula for the Bézier basis (or, in general, the Bernstein basis) is given in Lane *et al.* (1980) and derived in Lane and Riesenfeld

Figure 6.33
Tears produced by
non-uniform
subdivision of patches.

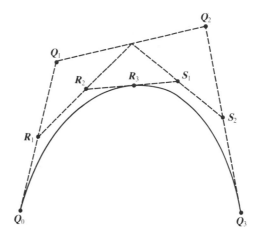

Figure 6.34
Splitting a bicubic
Bézier curve.

(1980). (This process can be used for any basis by first converting the representation to the Bézier basis as described in Section 6.9.1.) This is, in effect, the de Casteljau algorithm mentioned at the beginning of the chapter. A Bézier curve is subdivided into two curves by subdividing the control points, forming two new sets of control points R_i and S_i. The point R_3/S_0 is the end point of the first curve and the start of the second. The formula is:

$$
\begin{aligned}
R_0 &= Q_0 & S_0 &= R_3 \\
R_1 &- (Q_0 + Q_1)/2 & S_1 &= (Q_1 + Q_2)/4 + S_2/? \\
R_2 &= R_1/2 + (Q_1 + Q_2)/4 & S_2 &= (Q_2 + Q_3)/2 \\
R_3 &= (R_2 + S_1)/2 & S_3 &= Q_3
\end{aligned}
$$

Figure 6.34 shows how, after a single subdivision, the piecewise linear curve joining the two new sets of control points is a better approximation to the curve than the original. The approximation after three levels of subdivision is shown in Figure 6.35.

Figure 6.35
Drawing the control
points at each level of
subdivision.

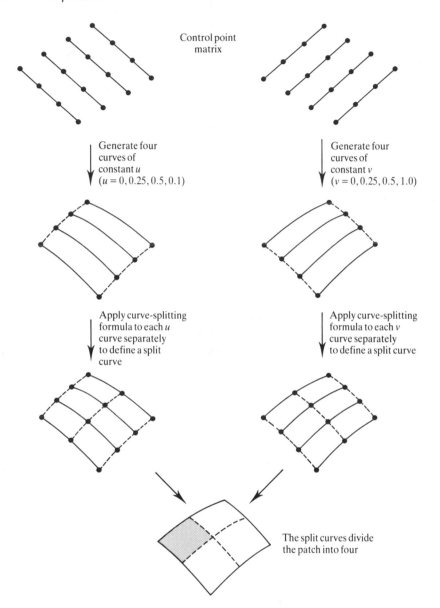

Control point matrix

Generate four curves of constant u ($u = 0, 0.25, 0.5, 0.1$)

Generate four curves of constant v ($v = 0, 0.25, 0.5, 1.0$)

Apply curve-splitting formula to each u curve separately to define a split curve

Apply curve-splitting formula to each v curve separately to define a split curve

The split curves divide the patch into four

Figure 6.36
Using curve splitting to subdivide a patch into four subpatches.

The curve-splitting process is easily extended to patches, as illustrated in Figure 6.36. We consider the patch to be made up of four curves of constant u and four curves of constant v, whose control points are consecutive rows and consecutive columns of the control point matrix. We apply the curve-splitting formula separately to each of the four curves in u yielding two subpatches of the original patch. Repeating the process for the curves in v again produces two subpatches and putting these divisions together divides the patch into four.

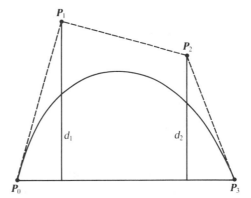

Figure 6.37
A cubic Bézier curve
with control points P_0,
P_1, P_2, P_3.

The depth of the sub-division is easily controlled using a linearity criterion. The Bézier basis functions sum identically to 1:

$$\sum_{i=0}^{3} B_{i,n}(u) = 1$$

This means that the curve lies in the convex hull formed by the control points P_i. The piecewise linear subdivision product will coincide with the curve when it 'merges' with the line joining the two end points. The degree to which this is achieved, that is, the linearity of the line joining the four control points, can be tested by measuring the distance from the middle two control points to the end point joining line (Figure 6.37).

The philosophy of this test is easily extended to surface patches. A plane is fitted through three non-collinear control points. The distance of each of the other 13 control points from this plane is then calculated. If one of these distances lies outside a prespecified tolerance, then the patch is further subdivided.

A practical problem that occurs when considering non-uniform subdivision (subdivision until a flatness criterion is satisfied) compared with uniform subdivision to some predetermined level, is the cost of the flatness test. It is debatable if it is a simpler and better, but less elegant approach, simply to adopt uniform subdivision and ignore the fact that some areas are going to be unnecessarily subdivided (because they are already flat). Plate 8 shows a uniform subdivision approach for the Utah teapot at subdivisions of one, two and three. This shows predictably that the difference in quality between the rendered images is mainly visible along silhouette edges.

If uniform subdivision is adopted then rendering bicubic patches can reduce to a preprocessing phase of a normal Z-buffer renderer. This method requires a large database for the subdivision products. If sufficient memory is not available, and the extra complexity of a scanline algorithm is to be introduced, then it is not a big step to use non-uniform subdivision.

The overall structure of a scanline algorithm such as the Lane–Carpenter algorithm is as follows:

(1) Sort the patches by maximum possible Y value. This value, as already stated, may be a corner point, a point on a boundary edge, or a point on a silhouette edge. The only quick way to an estimate of this value is to take the maximum Y value of the convex hull of the control points.

(2) For each scan line an inactive and active list of patches is updated. For each active patch, subdivision is performed until either a flatness criterion is satisfied, or until any one subdivision product no longer straddles a scan line. 'Flat' polygons are added to an active polygon list and scan converted in the normal way. Subdivision products that no longer overlap the scan line can be added to the inactive patch list. Thus we have an active and inactive list of parametric patches together with an active list of flat polygons.

One of the practical points that has to be dealt with is the problem of **tears**. Tears are a natural consequence of recursive or non-uniform subdivision. If one part of a surface patch is subdivided along a boundary shared by another patch that requires no further subdivision, then a gap between the two parts will naturally result. This 'tear' is then an unrepresented area and will appear as a gap or hole in the final rendering phase (Figure 6.33). The Lane–Carpenter algorithm does not deal with this problem. It can be minimized by making the flatness criterion more rigorous, but herein lies the normal computational paradox. The philosophy of the subdivision approach is that areas of a surface are subdivided to a degree that corresponds to local curvature. Large flat areas are minimally subdivided. Areas exhibiting fast curvature changes will be subdivided down to sufficiently small polygons. Tightening the flatness criterion means that many more polygons are generated and the final rendering phase takes much longer.

Clark's method deals with this problem in a more elegant way by adopting a subdivision method that is initially constrained to the boundary curves. There are three steps involved:

(1) The convex curve hull criterion is applied to the boundary edges $u = 1$ and $u = 0$ and the patch is subdivided along the v direction until this is satisfied.

(2) The same method is then applied to the $v = 1$ and $v = 0$ boundaries.

(3) Finally, the normal convex hull test is applied to the subdivision products and the process is continued, if necessary, along either the u or v directions.

Once a boundary satisfies the convex hull criterion it is assumed to be a straight line. Any further subdivision along this boundary will thus incur no separation.

A possible advantage of subdividing in the direction of the u or v boundaries is that with some objects this will result in fewer patches. Consider, for example, subdividing a 'ducted' solid – a cylinder is a trivial example of such an object. Subdividing the cylinder along a direction parallel to its long axis will lead this algorithm to converge more quickly and with fewer patches than if the subdivision proceeds in both parametric directions. A disadvantage with this approach is that it is difficult to integrate with a scanline algorithm. A scanline algorithm 'drives' or controls the order of subdivision depending on how the patches lie with respect to the scan lines.

Another aspect that requires consideration is the calculation of surface normals. These are, of course, required for shading. They are easily obtainable from the original parametric description at any point (u,v) on the surface by computing the cross-product of the u and v derivatives. However, if a subdivision method is being used to scan convert then the final polygon rendering is going to utilize a Phong interpolation method and the vertex normals are easily calculated by taking the cross products of the tangent vectors at the corner points. This will, in general, depending on the level of the subdivision, give non-parallel vertex normals for the 'flat' polygons, but all polygons contributing to a vertex will have the same normal. Two consequences can result from the fact that 'flat' polygons are being sent to a shader with non-parallel vertex normals. First, erroneous shading effects can occur at low levels of subdivision. Second, the question of which vertex normal to use for culling arises. Problems occur because not all the polygons surrounding a vertex may be available, since subdivision is taking place on the fly, and an average vertex normal cannot be calculated as in polygon meshes. Cases can obviously result where one normal subtends an angle of greater than 90° with the view vector and one with an angle less than 90°. The only safe course of action is to cull a polygon by testing each of its vertex normals. If any vertex normal is 'visible' the polygon is not culled.

An earlier approach by Catmull (1974) subdivided patches until they approximated the size of a single pixel, writing the results into a Z-buffer. This straightforward but computationally expensive approach sidesteps yet another problem – relating the extent of the subdivision to the projected screen size of the patch. Clearly there is no point in subdividing to a greater and greater depth if, when projected into screen space, the patch only covers a few pixels. Clark relates the subdivision test to the depth coordinates of the control points of the patches.

Finally, these subdivision methods differ in the basis used. The Lane–Carpenter algorithm uses a cubic Bernstein or Bézier basis. Clark uses a Taylor series expansion and central differences to derive more efficient subdivision formulae and to utilize a flatness test that is available directly from the subdivision components. We describe these representations for curves only but, as usual, the theory extends to patches.

6.7   Extending the control: NURBS and β-splines

Two important surface representation schemes exist that extend the control of shape beyond movement of control vertices. These are NURBS (non-uniform rational B-splines) and β-splines. In the case of NURBS, a control vertex is extended to a four-dimensional coordinate, the extra 'parameter' being a weight that allows a subtle form of control which is different in effect to moving a control vertex. In the simplest form of β-spline control, two 'global' parameters are introduced that affect the whole curve. These are 'bias' and 'tension' controls.

6.7.1   NURBS

A non-uniform B-spline curve is a curve defined on a knot vector where the interior knot spans are not equal. For example, we may have interior knots with multiplicity greater than 1 (that is, knot spans of length zero). Some common curves and surfaces, such as circles and cylinders, require non-uniform knot spacing, and the use of this option generally allows better shape control and the ability to model a larger class of shapes.

A rational B-spline curve is defined by a set of four-dimensional control points:

$$P_i^w = (w_i x_i, w_i y_i, w_i z_i, w_i)$$

The perspective map of such a curve in three-dimensional space is called a rational B-spline curve:

$$P(u) = H\left[\sum_{i=0}^{n} P_1^w B_{i,k}(u)\right]$$

$$= \frac{\sum\limits_{i=0}^{n} P_i w_i B_{i,k}(u)}{\sum\limits_{i=0}^{n} w_i B_{i,k}(u)}$$

$$= \sum_{i=0}^{n} P_i R_{i,k}(u)$$

where:

$$R_{i,k}(u) = \frac{B_{i,k}(u) w_i}{\sum\limits_{j=0}^{n} B_{j,k}(u) w_j}$$

Rational B-splines have the same analytical and geometric properties as non-rational B-splines and if:

$$w_i = 1 \qquad \text{for all } i$$

then:

$$R_{i,k}(u) = B_{i,k}(u)$$

The w_i associated with each control point are called **weights** and can be viewed as extra shape parameters. It can be shown that w_i affects the curve only locally. If, for example, w_j is fixed for all $j \neq i$, a change in w_i only affects the curve over k knot spans (just as moving a control point only affects the curve over k spans). w_i can be interpreted geometrically as a coupling factor. The curve is pulled towards a control point P_i if w_i increases. If w_i is decreased the curve moves away from the control point.

A specialization of rational B-splines is the generalized conic segment important in CAD. Faux and Pratt (1979) show that a rational quadratic form can produce a one-parameter (w) family of conic segments.

6.7.2 β-splines

β-splines are a formulation (Barsky and Beatty, 1983) of B-spline curve segments. Barsky introduced two new degrees of freedom – bias and tension – which can be applied either uniformly to the whole curve (uniformly shaped B-splines) or non-uniformly by varying their values along the curve (continuously shaped B-splines). For appropriate values of bias and tension, the β-spline formulation reduces to a uniform cubic B-spline.

A β-spline curve is defined by a sequence of $m - 2$ curve segments, the ith of which is:

$$P_i(u) = \sum_{r=-2}^{1} P_{i+r} b_r(\beta_1, \beta_2, u)$$

where:

P_i is a set of control points $[P_0, P_1, \ldots, P_m]$

$0 \leq u \leq 1$

$i = 2, \ldots, m - 1$

$b_r(\beta_1, \beta_2, u)$ is a cubic polynomial called the rth β-spline basis function. By relaxing the first and second derivative continuity requirement (C^2) for B-spline curves to unit tangent and curvature vector continuity (G^2), Barsky gives the following formulae for the value of the four basis functions for each curve segment as:

$$b_{-2}(\beta_1, \beta_2, u) = (2\beta_1^3/\delta)(1 - u)^3$$

$$\begin{aligned} b_{-1}(\beta_1, \beta_2, u) = (1/\delta)[&2\beta_1^3 u(u^2 - 3u + 3) \\ &+ 2\beta_1^2(u^3 - 3u^2 + 2) \\ &+ 2\beta_1(u^3 - 3u + 2) \\ &+ \beta_2(2u^3 - 3u^2 + 1)] \end{aligned}$$

$$\begin{aligned} b_0(\beta_1, \beta_2, u) = (1/\delta)[&2\beta_1^2 u^2(-u + 3) + 2\beta_1 u(-u^2 + 3) \\ &+ \beta_2 u^2(-2u + 3) + 2(-u^3 + 1)] \end{aligned}$$

$$b_1(\beta_1, \beta_2, u) = (2u^3)/\delta$$

where:

$$\delta = 2\beta_1^3 + 4\beta_1^3 + 4\beta_1 + \beta_2 + 2$$

When $\beta_1 = 1$ the curve is said to be unbiased. Increasing β_1 causes the curve to skew to one side approaching the control polygon in an unsymmetric way. Replacing β_1 by a reciprocal value causes the curve to be skewed in the opposite manner. The β_2 parameter affects the curve symmetrically and is called **tension**. As β_2 is increased the curve approaches the control polygon. When $\beta_1 = 1$ and $\beta_2 = 0$ the β-spline reduces to the uniform cubic B-spline. Barsky categorized such a B-spline curve, in terms of his definition, as an unbiased, untensed β-spline.

Because the β-spline is a generalization of B-splines, it behaves in a similar manner when multiple control points or multiple knots are introduced.

Both these curve methods can be extended to tensor product surfaces in the same way that the Bézier and B-spline curve definitions were used as a surface basis.

6.8   Interpolation using B-splines

Fitting a B-spline curve (or surface) through existing data points finds two major applications in computer graphics. First, in modelling: a set of sample data points can be produced by a three-dimensional digitizing device, such as a laser ranger. The problem is then to fit a surface through these points so that a complete computer graphics representation is available for manipulation (for, say, animation or shape change) by a program. Second, in computer animation: we may use a parametric curve to represent the path of an object that is moving through three-space. Particular positions of the object (key frame positions) may be defined, and we require to fit a curve through these points. A B-spline curve is commonly used for this purpose because of its C^2 continuity property. In animation we are normally interested in smooth motion and a B-spline curve representing the position of an object as a function of time will guarantee this.

In this section we will concentrate on curve interpolation. Although the theory of curves normally extends to surfaces, this is not the case when one wishes to extend curve fitting to surface fitting. There are significant problems, unique to surface fitting, that make this topic a research area. The principle of surface fitting was introduced in Chapter 2 and is described in more detail in the next section.

We state the problem of B-spline interpolation informally as follows: given a set of data points we require to derive a set of control points for a B-spline curve that will define a 'fair' curve that represents the data points. We may require the curve to interpolate all the points or to interpolate a subset of the points and pass close to the others. For example, in the case where data points are known to be noisy or slightly unreliable we may not require an exact interpolation through all the points. Different methodologies for fitting a B-spline curve to a set of data points are given by Bartels, Beatty and Barsky (1988).

We can state the problem formally for the case where we require the curve to interpolate all the data points. If we consider the data points to be knot values in u then we have for a cubic:

$$
\begin{aligned}
Q(u_p) &= \sum_{i=0}^{m} P_i B_i(u_p) \\
&= D_p \qquad \text{for all } p = 3, \ldots, m+1
\end{aligned}
$$

where:

D_p is a data point

u_p is the knot value corresponding to the data point

The problem we now have is to determine u_p. The easiest solution, and the one we will adopt here, is to set u_p to p. This is called **uniform parametrization** and it completely ignores the geometric relationship between data points and is usually regarded as giving the poorest interpolant in a hierarchy of possibilities described in detail by Farin (1990). The next best solution, **chord length parametrization**, sets the knot intervals proportional to the distance between the data points. An advantage of uniform parametrization, however, is that it is invariant under affine transformation of the data points.

Here we are specifying a B-spline curve through the data points. There are $m - 1$ data points to be interpolated and the curve is defined by $m + 1$ control points. If we consider a single component, say x, then we have:

$$
x(u_p) = \sum_{i=0}^{m} P_{xi} B_i(u_p) = D_{xp}
$$

where:

D_{xp} is the x component of the data point

This defines a system of equations that we solve for P_{xi}:

$$
\begin{bmatrix}
B_0(u_3) & \cdots & B_m(u_3) \\
\vdots & & \vdots \\
B_0(u_{m+1}) & \cdots & B_m(u_{m+1})
\end{bmatrix}
\begin{bmatrix}
P_{x0} \\
\vdots \\
P_{xm}
\end{bmatrix}
=
\begin{bmatrix}
D_{x3} \\
\vdots \\
D_{xm+1}
\end{bmatrix}
$$

This scheme results in $m - 1$ equations in $m + 1$ unknowns. For example, for $m = 5$ we have six control points to find from four data points. Various possibilities exist. The easiest approach is to select two additional points, P_2

and P_7, to be interpolated on extensions to the curve at $Q(u_2)$ and $Q(u_{m+2})$ giving:

$$
\begin{bmatrix}
B_0(u_2) & \cdots & B_m(u_2) \\
B_0(u_3) & \cdots & B_m(u_3) \\
\vdots & & \vdots \\
B_0(u_{m+1}) & \cdots & B_m(u_{m+1}) \\
B_0(u_{m+2}) & \cdots & B_m(u_{m+2})
\end{bmatrix}
\begin{bmatrix}
P_{x0} \\
\vdots \\
\\
P_{xm}
\end{bmatrix}
=
\begin{bmatrix}
D_{x2} \\
D_{x3} \\
\vdots \\
D_{xm+1} \\
D_{xm+2}
\end{bmatrix}
$$

In this equation the matrix will have zero entries except in a band three entries wide along the main diagonal, and for uniform cubic B-splines the matrix is:

$$
\frac{1}{6}
\begin{bmatrix}
4 & 1 & & & & & \\
1 & 4 & 1 & & & & \\
& 1 & 4 & 1 & & & \\
& & & \cdot & & & \\
& & & & \cdot & & \\
& & & & \cdot & & \\
& & & & 1 & 4 & 1 \\
& & & & & 1 & 4
\end{bmatrix}
$$

6.9   Modelling objects with bicubic parametric nets

In Chapter 2 we overviewed modelling techniques that allowed objects to be represented by a net of parametric patches. We will now look at these processes in more detail.

Modelling issues embrace both building up a parametric net description from scratch and editing or changing the shape of an existing description. One of the motivations for using a patch description is the ability to 'sculpt' an existing surface by altering its shape. Whereas modelling with a single patch, for example a Bézier patch, is straightforward, significant difficulties arise when dealing with a mesh of patches. The subject area is still very much a research topic and for that reason much of the material is outside the scope of this text. It is, however, an extremely important area and we will cover it as comprehensively as possible.

6.9.1   Surface fitting

The first technique means that we wish to interpolate a set of three-dimensional data points with a parametrically defined surface. As outlined in Chapter 2, we do this by first fitting a network of uv curves through the data points. Each data point is interpolated by a curve of constant u and v.

These curves are B-splines interpolated through the data points using a standard B-spline curve interpolation technique. In the next stage, the B-spline curves are converted to Bézier curves. This curve network is partitioned into individual mesh elements formed from four Bézier curve segments (see Figure 2.10). These curve segments are the boundary edge of a Bézier patch and given these we can then derive the control points for the patch. Thus a set of points in three-space is converted to a net of Bézier patches using a net of B-spline curves as an intermediary.

Now let us consider the first stage – deriving a net of curves that interpolate the data points. The main problem here is that we may have no knowledge of the topology of the points. (In curve interpolation we know that the points are sequential.) This is a problem that can only be solved in context and one approach is given by Watt and Watt (1992). Consider the case where the points have been obtained from a real object using a manual digitizer and the sequence of which points to interpolate with curves is known. This is quite a common context and we will proceed with the second stage – that of deriving a net of Bézier patches from a B-spline curve network.

First we need to convert the B-spline curves into multisegment Bézier curves. If we first consider a single B-spline then the conversion to Bézier form is straightforward and is given by:

$$[P_0\ P_1\ P_2\ P_3] = B^{-1}B_s[Q_0\ Q_1\ Q_2\ Q_3]$$

$$= \frac{1}{6}\begin{bmatrix} 1 & 4 & 1 & 0 \\ 0 & 4 & 2 & 0 \\ 0 & 2 & 4 & 0 \\ 1 & 4 & 1 & 0 \end{bmatrix}\begin{bmatrix} Q_0 \\ Q_1 \\ Q_2 \\ Q_3 \end{bmatrix}$$

where:

P are the Bézier control points
Q are the B-spline control points
B is the Bézier matrix
B_s is the B-spline matrix

(Note that a change of basis matrix can only be used for uniform B-splines. If the curve network consists of non-uniform B-splines then conversion has to proceed by knot insertion. This more general approach is described by Watt and Watt (1992).)

For a multisegment B-spline curve we apply this formula repeatedly to the appropriate control points. For example, consider a two-segment B-spline curve defined by five control points $[Q_0\ Q_1\ Q_2\ Q_3\ Q_4]$. The conversion formula is applied twice for the control points sets $[Q_0\ Q_1\ Q_2\ Q_3]$ and $[Q_1\ Q_2\ Q_3\ Q_4]$.

Now consider a net of 5×5 two-segment B-spline curves with control points shown in Figure 6.38(a). Application of the above scheme on

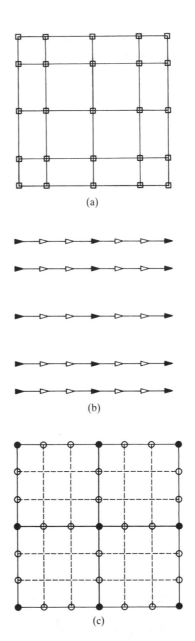

Figure 6.38
Converting a B-spline curve network to Bézier patches (after Farin (1990)). (a) 5×5 two-segment B-spline curve network. (b) Curve network converted row-wise to 5 two-segment Bézier curves. (c) Curve network converted to 7×7 two-segment Bézier curves forming the boundaries of four Bézier patches.

row-by-row basis yields five two-segment Bézier curves (Figure 6.38b). We now interpret these, column by column, and consider each column to be the control points of a B-spline curve. Each column is converted to a two-segment Bézier curve. This yields a net of 7×7 two-segment Bézier curves (Figure 6.38c). We know that the boundary edge of a Bézier patch is a

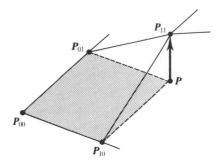

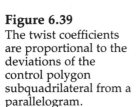

Figure 6.39
The twist coefficients are proportional to the deviations of the control polygon subquadrilateral from a parallelogram.

Bézier curve and we interpret the unbroken lines in Figure 6.38(c) as the boundaries of four Bézier patches. Thus we have converted a network of 5×5 two-segment B-spline curves into 2×2 Bézier patches. However, we have only defined the boundaries of each patch, that is, we have only determined 12 out of the 16 control points for each patch.

The question that now arises is: how are we to determine the inner four control points? We first consider their significance by reproducing Equation 6.4:

$$Q_{uv}(0,0) = 9(P_{00} - P_{01} - P_{10} + P_{11})$$

This defines the twist of a surface as a mixed partial derivative and can be interpreted as a vector which is the deviation of the corner quadrilateral of the control polyhedron from a parallelogram (Figure 6.39). When the twist is zero this vector reduces to zero and the corner quadrilateral is a parallelogram. An intuitive grasp of the effect of non-zero twist is difficult. It is easier to look at the geometric significance when a patch has zero twist at all four corners. Then we have a translational surface where every quadrilateral of the control polyhedron is a parallelogram. The parallelograms are also translates of each other. Such a patch is called a **translational surface** because it is generated by two curves, $C_1(u)$ and $C_2(v)$. Any isoparametric line in u is a translate of C_1 and any isoparametric line in v is a translate of C_2.

Thus the easiest solution to estimating the inner four control points is to assume that the patch is a translational surface, then the inner points are derivable from the boundary points. The implication of this, in terms of surface fitting, is that the boundary curves of the patch should more or less be translates of each other. In any practical situation this will depend on two factors: the shape of the object and the resolution of the uv curve network. You can see, for example in Figure 2.11, how the validity of this assumption varies across the surface of the object. The method gives us a correct surface with C^1 continuity overall, but it does not guarantee a 'good' shape. Alternative methods for determining the twist of a surface patch are given by Farin (1990).

6.9.2   Cross-sectional design

Cross-sectional design means constructing a 'ducted' solid by specifying consecutive cross-sections at intervals along a sweep or spine curve. We start by listing a hierarchy of possibilities that depend on the underlying shape constraints. These are:

- Linear axis: surfaces of revolution (circular cross-sections) – the sweep curve is a straight line.
- Linear axis: generalized cross-sections – the sweep curve is a straight line, the cross-section is a closed parametric curve.
- Curved axis: generalized cross-sections – both the sweep curve and the cross-section are parametric curves.

Linear axis design: surfaces of revolution
If we constrain the axis or sweep curve to be a straight line, then two straightforward possibilities are immediately suggested. First, surfaces of revolution. Here cross-sections are circular and normal to the axis. The variation in the cross-section is controlled by a profile curve that we define as a parametric curve. To design the object a user simply defines and edits the profile curve. This, if it is not already a Bézier curve, is converted to the Bézier representation and subdivided to an appropriate piecewise linear resolution. The curve is swept around the axis to generate a polygon mesh representation directly.

Linear axis design: generalized cross-sections
We now consider the case where we have a cross-segment defined by a multisegment Bézier curve which is allowed to vary proportionally as it is swept along the axis. For example, consider one segment of a curve with four-fold rotational symmetry about the z axis (Figure 6.40a). This is defined by the control points $[S_0 \, S_1 \, S_2 \, S_3]$. Further consider that the cross-section dimension is allowed to vary according to a curve $r = r(v)$ that is also a Bézier curve (Figure 6.40b) defined by the control points $[R_0 \, R_1 \, R_2 \, R_3]$. From this description we need to generate four patches as shown in Figure 6.40(c). Each patch is generated by moving the cross-section curve along the z axis, scaling according to $r(v)$. That is, the patch is a surface of the form:

$$Q(u,v) = r(v)Q(u,0)$$

It is easily seen (Figure 6.40d) that the 16 control points are given by:

$$
\begin{bmatrix}
P_{00} & P_{01} & P_{02} & P_{03} \\
P_{10} & P_{11} & P_{12} & P_{13} \\
P_{20} & P_{21} & P_{22} & P_{23} \\
P_{30} & P_{31} & P_{32} & P_{33}
\end{bmatrix}
=
\begin{bmatrix}
S_{00} \\
S_{10} \\
S_{20} \\
S_{30}
\end{bmatrix}
\begin{bmatrix} r_0 & r_1 & r_2 & r_3 \end{bmatrix}
+
\begin{bmatrix}
k \\
k \\
k \\
k
\end{bmatrix}
\begin{bmatrix} z_0 & z_1 & z_2 & z_3 \end{bmatrix}
$$

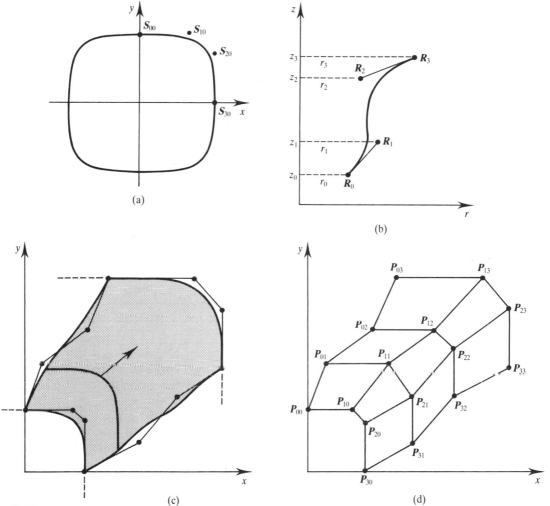

Figure 6.40
Linear axis design with generalized cross-sections. (a) Four Bézier curves defining a cross-section with four-fold symmetry. (b) A scaling curve for the cross-sections. (c) Generating a patch by sweeping a curve along z and scaling it at the same time. (d) The control point polyhedron for the patch.

Curved axis design

First note that in Chapter 2 we dealt with a special case of this category. There the sweep or spine curve was a parametric curve but the cross-section was a piecewise linear curve, and the model generated as the cross-section was swept along the spine was a polygon mesh object. In Chapter 2 we dealt with the problem of how to position or orient each cross-section using a local coordinate system defined at every point along the curve. We also looked at problems that arose owing to the curvature of the sweep curve.

The general case of a ducted solid is a variable curve moved along a variable spine. Although this appears to be a special case of the surface-fitting methodology, where we generate a *uv* network there is a problem.

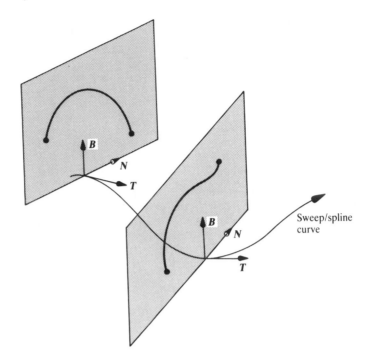

Figure 6.41
Sweeping a general
curve along a general
spine.

Consider Figure 6.41 which shows two curve segments of constant v drawn in planes defined by a local coordinate system on the curve (see Chapter 2). The curves are cross-sectional segments which are defined by the designer at appropriate intervals along the spine. Each instance of a curve segment defines a boundary of the required patch ($v = 0$, $v = 1$). This defines eight control points for the patch. The inner four control points can eventually be calculated for non-zero or zero twist as described earlier. The problem comes in determining the other four control points which define the curves swept out by the end points of the curve segments (Figure 6.42). Because the cross-section curve varies, these curves are not translates of the spine curve. A solution to this problem, in terms of a designer-specified parameter – 'flare angle' – is given by Goss (1976).

Figure 6.42
Showing the problem
of determining the
control points of the
curves swept out by
the cross-section end
points.

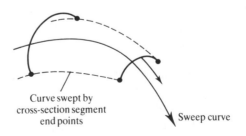

Curve swept by
cross-section segment
end points

Sweep curve

6.9.3   Control polyhedron design: basic technique

This approach to modelling with a parametric patch object is the one described in most textbooks. The idea is that, given an existing patch model, a designer interacts with a loop which enables the control points to be moved, and the result of the movement displayed as a new surface. Sometimes it is described as 'free-form sculpting'. The designer can move one or a number of control points at will, modelling a surface as if it is some malleable material such as modelling clay. Leaving aside the practical problem of providing a three-dimensional editing system to faciliate control point movement, two fundamental problems arise.

First, what do we do when we are interacting with a mesh of patches rather than a single patch? Although single patch design can cope with a number of practical problems, car body panels, for example, we may need to work with a net of patches. The problem is that we cannot move the control points of a single patch without regard to maintaining continuity with surrounding patches. For example, if we consider an object made up of Bézier patches, then one way of moving control points and maintaining adjoining patch continuity is to move groups of nine control points as a single unit, as shown in Figure 6.43(a). This automatically ensures patch continuity but it has the effect of introducing plateaux into the surface. This is clearly seen with curves. Figure 6.43(b) shows a two-segment Bézier curve. If we move control points in collinear groups of three then we get a curved step effect (Figure 6.43c). What we may require is a deformation as shown in Figure 6.43(d).

Figure 6.43
(a) Four adjoining Bézier patches and their control points. Continuity constraints imply that the central control point cannot be moved without considering its eight neighbours. All nine points can be moved together and continuity maintained.
(b) Undeformed two-segment curve.
(c) Deformed curve by moving control points in collinear groups.
(d) Desired deformation.

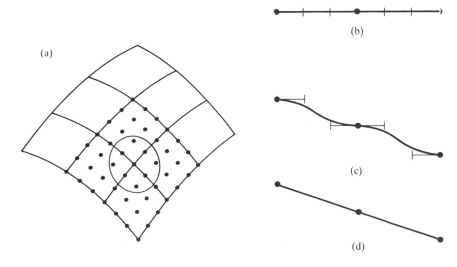

6.9.4   Control polyhedron design: fine control

The other problem that arises is locality of control. We have already discussed this with respect to a Bézier versus B-spline patch and we now consider the B-spline case in more detail. The difficulty centres around the need to be able to vary the *scale* of the deformation. Although moving a control point only changes those patches that share the point, the scale of the deformation in object space is related to the size of the patches. This suggests that we can control the scale by locally subdividing the patches in the region of the deformation if a fine change is required. This is the basis of a technique called **hierarchical B-spline deformation** (Forsey and Bartels, 1988).

Consider the definition of a B-spline patch:

$$Q(u,v) = \sum_{i=0}^{n} \sum_{j=0}^{m} P_{ij} B_i(u) B_j(u)$$

This can be redefined by knot insertion (Farin, 1990) to a patch:

$$Q(u,v) = \sum_{i=0}^{N} \sum_{j=0}^{M} R_{ij} B_i(u) B_j(u)$$

where:

$$N > n \quad \text{and} \quad M > m$$

The new control points are derived as described by Forsey and Bartels (1988). The problem is how to apply this strategy to the region of a surface that interests us. Forsey and Bartels do this by defining a minimal surface – the smallest section of the surface that this refinement of control points can be applied to. This minimal surface satisfies two constraints:

- Movement of the new control points produce deformations that are localized to this minimal surface.

- The derivatives at the boundary of the minimal surface remain unchanged.

This means that deformations within the refined surface will not affect the surface from which it is derived and continuity is everywhere maintained. The motivation for such an elaborate approach is to affect control point refinement only where required. The alternative would be control point refinement over the entire surface. This process can be repeated within the refined surface until a satisfactory level of fine control is achieved – hence the term 'hierarchical'.

A minimal surface is 16 patches defined by a 7×7 control point matrix (Figure 6.44a). The control points that are required if the centre 4 patches are refined to 16 are shown in Figure 6.44(b). Here we note that that 3×3 of the original control points are shared with the refined patches. A dynamic data structure of control points is created with the original surface at the root of a tree of overlays of control points. Editing the surface

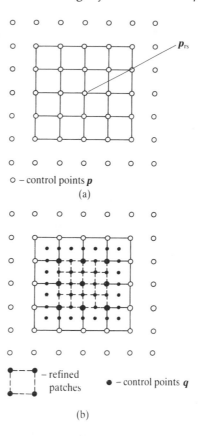

$\circ$ – control points p

(a)

$\boxed{\vphantom{x}}$ – refined patches $\bullet$ – control points q

(b)

Figure 6.44
(a) Sixteen patch minimal surface with 49 control points. (b) Central 4 patches refined to 16 patches (after Forsey and Bartels (1988)).

invokes a tree traversal and one of the important points of the scheme is that traversal can occur in either direction. Coarse refinement will carry previous fine refinements in the same surface region, owing to the representation of control points in terms of offsets relative to a local reference frame.

6.9.5 Control polyhedron design: coarse control

We now consider the opposite of the previous case – coarse control. Say that we are interested in global shape deformation, for example, taking a cylinder or tubular object and bending it into a toroidal-like body. Here we may need to operate, to some degree, on all the control points simultaneously.

Consider the strategy applied to a curve $Q(t)$ defined by four control points P_i. First, we enclose the curve in a unit square and divide this region into a regular grid of points R_{ij} ($i = 0, \ldots, 3$; $j = 0, \ldots, 3$) as shown in Figure 6.45. If we consider the square to be uv space then we can write:

$$(u,v) = \sum_{i=0}^{3} \sum_{j=0}^{3} R_{ij} B_i(u) B_j(v)$$

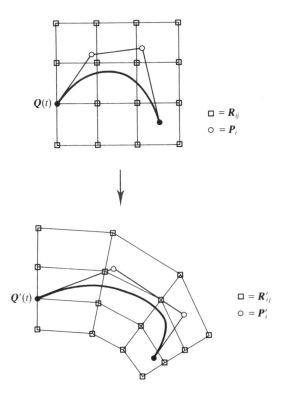

Figure 6.45
Global distortion of a
planar curve (after
Farin (1990)).

Compare this identity with the equation for a bicubic parametric Bézier patch. This identity follows from the linear precision property of the polynomials $B_i(u)$ and $B_j(v)$ and it is expressing the fact that a set of coplanar control points will define a planar patch. If the grid of points R_{ij} is now distorted into the grid R'_{ij} (Figure 6.45) then the point (u,v) will be mapped into the point (u',v')

$$(u',v') = \sum_{i=0}^{3} \sum_{j=0}^{3} R'_{ij} B_i(u) B_j(v)$$

and we can use this equation to derive a new set of control points, P'_i, for the new curve $Q'(t)$.

This is a method of changing the shape of the curve globally and indirectly. We are embedding the curve in a planar patch, distorting the patch by moving the control points of the patch and, at the same time, changing the shape of the curve.

Now to extend this principle to operate globally on patches we embed the control points, P_{ij}, of the patch that we wish to deform in a **trivariate Bézier hyperpatch**, itself specified by a three-dimensional grid of control points, R_{ijk}, forming a unit cube. Thus we have:

$$(u',v',w') = \sum_{i=0}^{3} \sum_{j=0}^{3} \sum_{k=0}^{3} R'_{ijk} B_i(u) B_j(v) B_k(w) \qquad \text{(6.5)}$$

The unit cube grid is distorted globally in any way that we require and the new patch control points, P'_{ij}, are calculated.

An important aspect of this technique is that it can be applied to an object with any parametric representation. Thus we can embed B-spline patches in the trivariate Bézier space. We can also embed polygon mesh vertices in the same way. This gives us the concept of any point x embedded in a trivariate hyperpatch volume and then mapped to point x' by globally distorting the control grid of the trivariate patch. To use Equation 6.5 to do this we need to map x into (u,v,w) space and (u',v',w') back into cartesian space. The conversions are:

$$x = x_0 + uu + vv + ww$$

and:

$$u = u \cdot (x - x_0)$$
$$v = v \cdot (x - x_0)$$
$$w = w \cdot (x - x_0)$$

x_0 defines the origin of (u,v,w) space and u,v and w define the space. These values are set by the designer, who positions the unit cube with respect to the object to be distorted.

The technique was originally developed by Bézier (1972) but most graphics-oriented treatments refer to a paper by Sederberg and Parry (1986) wherein the strategy is termed **free form deformation** (FFD).

Projects, notes and suggestions ────────

6.1   A patch editor (*)

Write an interactive editor that facilitates the deformation of a Bézier curve or a Bézier surface patch. The editor should allow the user to grab and manipulate control points. Project 1.3 discusses the general problems of using a two-dimensional locator device in three-dimensional space.

6.2   Control point animation (*)

By using a suitable interpolation procedure with the control points that specify a shape made up, say, of piecewise Bézier segments, write a program to 'in-between' the transformation of one arbitrary shape into another. For example, Figure 6.46 shows a multisegment Bézier curve forming the letter 'E' changing into a curve forming the letter 'Z'. Repeat this procedure using B-splines. Extend the procedure to deal with surfaces.

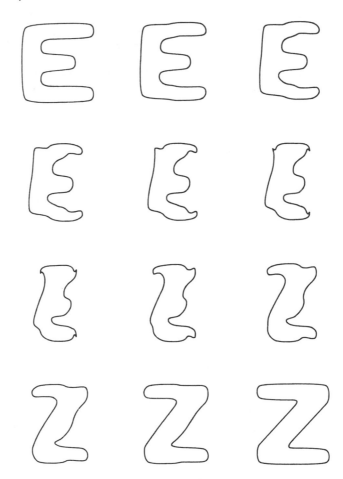

Figure 6.46
A multisegment Bézier
curve representing the
letter 'E' changing into
a curve representing
the letter 'Z'.

6.3 Rendering bicubic patches

Using the rendering software of Chapter 5, write a uniform subdivision algorithm that converts bicubic parametric patches into polygons. Compare the cost of the uniform subdivision with non-uniform subdivision.

6.4 Modelling and representational methods – a comparison (*)

Consider an example of a non-trivial solid, such as, say, that formed from the union of three mutually perpendicular cylinders. Use a solid such as this in a study that compares the following representational methods.

(1) A polygon mesh model:
The polygon mesh model adopted in this text is just one of a number of possible schemes generally known as boundary representations. Such schemes differ in the way in which edges and vertices are represented

and connected, and in the entities, other than polygons, that appear in the representation.

(2) Quadric surfaces:
Use a set of implicit equations for a library of quadric functions (Project 2.4).

(3) A bicubic parametric patch model:
Use a net of an appropriate number of bicubic parametric patches to represent the surface.

(4) A CSG tree:
CSG denotes constructive solid geometry and is a form used mainly in CAD applications.

(5) Octrees:
Discussed in Chapter 2, octrees are used extensively, for example, in medical imaging, where consecutive cross-sectional images are merged to form a three-dimensional data field represented by an octree.

Points that you may consider in the comparison are:

- The generality of the representation. What are the limitations on the type of three-dimensional shape that can be represented?

- The relative difficulty in building or specifying the structure initially.

- The ability to derive a representation from automatically collected data such as an object scanned by a laser ranger.

- The data storage requirements.

- The ability of the method to accommodate an interactive editing scheme.

- The ease of rendering the object. For example, how would you go about extracting a surface from an octree representation? Clearly a Z-buffer renderer can cope with a union operator in a CSG representation, but how well can a Z-buffer renderer generally cope with a CSG tree?

- The generality of the method with respect to applications. For example, can CSG methods be applied in 'creative' three-dimensional graphics where the polygon mesh model tends to predominate?

This project should involve a wide search through the literature and references have been deliberately omitted.

6.5 Generalized cylinder modelling (*)

Design a system that implements a generalized cylinder method (Chapter 2) for modelling polygon mesh objects. Three view ports should appear on the screen: one for the profile curve, one for the cross-section and one for the object. The profile curve and the object should be interactively generated Bézier curves and the scheme for ensuring polygonal resolution as a function of the curvature of the sweep curve should be implemented.

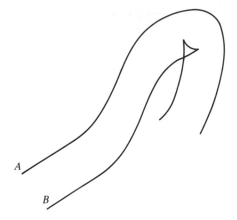

Figure 6.47
A swept object that has
crimped. Curve *A* is
the main axis curve.
Curve *B* is the profile
of the swept object
(that is, it represents
the cross-section size
along *A*) and at the top
right the cross-section
size is too large.

Note that there is an important practical problem, an example of
which is shown in Figure 6.47. Here *A* is the sweep curve. Consider a flat
profile curve. If the curvature of the sweep curve is too tight a crimp can
occur because the object profile offset is too large for the bend.

7 | Shadows and Textures

7.1 Introduction

Shadow generation and texture mapping are two common additions to simple shading that attempt to increase the realism of three-dimensional shaded objects. Both elaborations are implemented by a variety of ad hoc algorithms and, with the exception of shadow computation in ray tracing and radiosity, neither phenomenon has been incorporated in a theoretical reflection/illumination model. Unlike shading, no particular technique predominates and choice of a suitable method, particularly with texture algorithms, is motivated by the desired visual effect. Shadow algorithms are distinguished both by the method used and by the type of shadow produced. The methods used in texture algorithms are so diverse that they can only really be categorized according to the end effect. Although some overview of both areas will be given, this chapter will concentrate on the implementation of methods that have gained some popularity.

7.2 Shadows: their function

Shadows are an important, and somewhat neglected, addition to the repertoire of techniques used to visualize three-dimensional objects in computer graphics. Simple shadows (see Section 7.3) can be used to dissolve the perceptual effect of objects floating above the ground, and they are far less expensive to compute and are more necessary for simple images than, for example, the accurate modelling of ambient illumination.

Plate 9 demonstrates this effect, where the shadows appear to serve two functions. First, they 'anchor' the spheres to the green planes, negating the computer graphics 'look' of objects floating in space; second, they emphasize the changing direction of the light source.

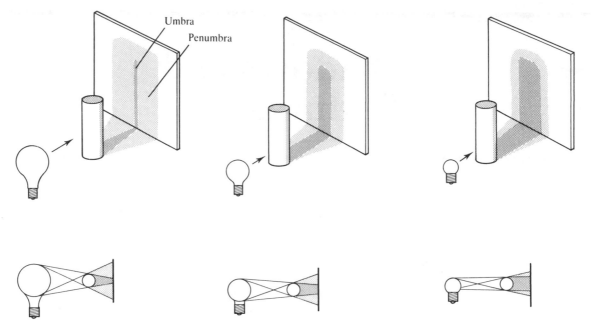

Figure 7.1
Intensity of reflected light in a shadow area: the umbra–penumbra effect due to the relative sizes of a light source and an object.

Shadows vary tremendously as a function of the lighting environment. They can be hard edged or soft edged and contain both an **umbra** and a **penumbra** area. The relative size of the umbra/penumbra is a function of the size and the shape of the light source and its distance from the object (Figure 7.1). The umbra is that part of a shadow that is completely cut off from the light source, whereas the penumbra is an area that receives some light from the source. A penumbra surrounds an umbra and there is always a gradual change in intensity from a penumbra to an umbra. In computer graphics, if we are not modelling illumination sources, then we usually consider point light sources at large distances, and assume in the simplest case that objects produce umbrae with sharp edges. This is still only an approximation. Even although light from a large distance produces almost parallel rays, there is still light behind the object because of diffraction and the shadow grades off. This effect also varies over the distance a shadow is thrown. These effects, that determine the quality of a shadow, enable us to infer information concerning the nature of the light source, and they are clearly important to us as human beings perceiving a three-dimensional environment. For example, the shadows that we see outdoors depend on the time of day and whether the sky is overcast or not.

So far we have only talked about single primary sources. Once we have multiple sources, all at different intensities, and reflecting surfaces (that can be treated as secondary sources), then shadows should be considered as part of the global illumination problem. Indeed, an elegant, but extremely expensive, method for shadow generation is given as part of a simple ray tracing algorithm in Chapter 8.

7.2.1 Computer graphics and shadows

A number of aspects of shadows are exploited in the computer generation of the phenomenon. These are now discussed.

A shadow from polygon A that falls on polygon B because of a point light source can be calculated by projecting polygon A onto the plane that contains polygon B. The position of the point light source is used as the centre of projection.

No shadows are seen if the view point is coincident with the (single) light source. An equivalent form of this statement is that shadows can be considered to be areas hidden from the light source, implying that modified hidden surface algorithms can be used to solve the shadow problem.

If the light source, or sources, are point sources then there is no penumbra to calculate and the shadow has a hard edge.

For static scenes, shadows are fixed and do not change as the view point changes. If the relative position of objects and light sources change, the shadows have to be recalculated. This places a high overhead on three-dimensional animation where shadows are important for depth and movement perception.

Because of the high computational overheads, shadows have been regarded in much the same way as texture mapping – as a quality add-on. They have not been viewed as a necessity and, compared with shading algorithms, there has been little consideration of the quality of shadows. Most shadow generation algorithms produce hard edge, point light source shadows.

With the exception of shadow generation in ray tracing programs, most algorithms deal only with polygon mesh models.

7.3 Simple shadows on a ground plane

An extremely simple method of generating shadows is reported by Blinn (1988). It suffices for single object scenes throwing shadows on a flat ground plane. The method simply involves drawing the projection of the object on the ground plane. It is thus restricted to single object scenes, or multi-object scenes where objects are sufficiently isolated so as not to cast shadows on each other. The ground plane projection is easily obtained from a linear transformation and the projected polygon can be treated as a polygon (at an appropriate dark intensity) by a Z-buffer algorithm.

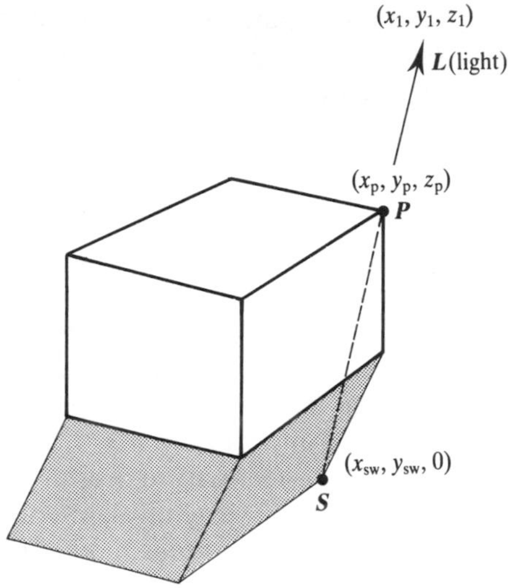

Figure 7.2
Ground plane shadows
for single objects.

If the usual illumination approximation is made – a single point source at an infinite distance – then we have parallel light rays in a direction $L = (x_1, y_1, z_1)$ as shown in Figure 7.2. Any point on the object $P = (x_p, y_p, z_p)$ will cast a shadow at $S = (x_{sw}, y_{sw}, 0)$. Considering the geometry in the figure, we have:

$$S = P - \alpha L$$

and given that $z_{sw} = 0$, we have:

$$0 = z_p - \alpha z_1$$
$$\alpha = z_p / z_1$$

and:

$$x_{sw} = x_p - (z_p/z_1)\, x_1$$
$$y_{sw} = y_p - (z_p/z_1)\, y_1$$

As a homogeneous transformation this is:

$$[x_{sw} \; y_{sw} \; 0 \; 1] = [x_p \; y_p \; z_p \; 1]
\begin{bmatrix}
1 & 0 & 0 & 0 \\
0 & 1 & 0 & 0 \\
-x_1/z_1 & -y_1/z_1 & 0 & 0 \\
0 & 0 & 0 & 1
\end{bmatrix}$$

Note from this that it is just as easy to generate shadows on a vertical back or side plane. Blinn also shows (Blinn, 1988) how to extend this idea to handle light sources that are at a finite distance from the object.

This type of approximate shadow (on a flat ground plane) is beloved of traditional animators and its use certainly enhances movement in three-dimensional computer animation.

7.4 Shadow algorithms

Unlike hidden surface removal algorithms, where one or two algorithms now predominate and other methods are only used in special cases, no popular candidate has emerged as the top shadow algorithm. In fact, shadow computation is a rather neglected area of computer graphics. What follows, therefore, is a brief description of four major approaches. Shadow generation in ray tracing is separately described in Chapter 8.

7.4.1 Projecting polygons/scan line

This approach was developed by Appel (1968) and Bouknight and Kelley (1970). Adding shadows to a scanline algorithm requires a preprocessing stage that builds up a secondary data structure which links all polygons that may shadow a given polygon. **Shadow pairs** – a polygon together with the polygon that it can possibly shadow – are detected by projecting all polygons onto a sphere centred at the light source. Polygon pairs that cannot interact are detected and discarded. This is an important step because for a scene containing n polygons the number of possible projected shadows is $n(n-1)$.

The algorithm processes the secondary data structure simultaneously with a normal scan conversion process to determine if any shadows fall on the polygon that generated the visible scanline segment under consideration. If no shadow polygon(s) exist then the scanline algorithm proceeds as normal. For a current polygon, if a shadow polygon exists then, using the light source as a centre of projection, the shadow is generated by projecting onto the plane that contains the current polygon. Normal scan conversion then proceeds simultaneously with a process that determines whether a current pixel is in shadow or not. Three possibilities now occur:

(1) The shadow polygon does not cover the generated scanline segment and the situation is identical to an algorithm without shadows.

(2) Shadow polygon(s) completely cover the visible scanline segment and the scan conversion process proceeds, but the pixel intensity is modulated by an amount that depends on the number of shadows that are covering the segment. For a single light source the segment is either in shadow or not.

(3) A shadow polygon partially covers the visible scanline segment. In this case the segment is subdivided and the process is applied recursively until a solution is obtained.

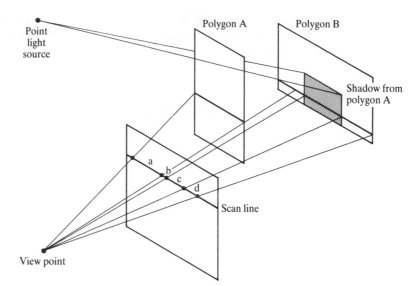

Figure 7.3
Polygons that receive a shadow from another polygon are linked in a secondary data structure. Scan line segments are now delineated by both view point projection boundaries and shadow boundaries.

A representation of these possibilities is shown in Figure 7.3. These are, in order along the scan line:

(a) Polygon A is visible, therefore it is rendered.

(b) Polygon B is visible and is rendered.

(c) Polygon B is shadowed by polygon A and is rendered at an appropriately reduced intensity.

(d) Polygon B is visible and is rendered.

7.4.2 Shadow volumes

The shadow volume approach was originally developed by Crow (1977) and subsequently extended by others. In particular, Brotman and Badler (1984) used the idea as a basis for generating 'soft' shadows, that is, shadows produced by a distributed light source.

A **shadow volume** is the invisible volume of space swept out by the shadow of an object. It is the infinite volume defined by lines emanating from a point light source through vertices in the object. Figure 7.4 conveys the idea of a shadow volume. A finite shadow volume is obtained by considering the intersection of the infinite volume with the view volume. The shadow volume is computed by first evaluating the contour or silhouette edge of the object, as seen from the light source. The contour edge of a simple object is shown in Figure 7.4(a). A contour edge of an object is the edge made up of one or more connected edges of polygons belonging to the object. A contour edge separates those polygons that can see the light source from those that cannot.

(a)

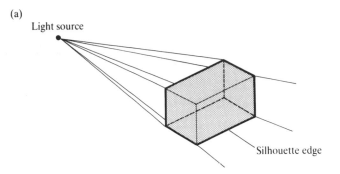

Light source

Silhouette edge

(b)

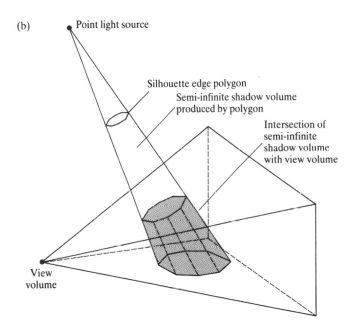

Point light source

Silhouette edge polygon
Semi-infinite shadow volume
produced by polygon

Intersection of
semi-infinite
shadow volume
with view volume

View
volume

Figure 7.4
Illustrating the
formation of a shadow
volume. (a) Silhouette
edge of an object. (b)
Finite shadow volume
defined by a silhouette
edge polygon, a point
light source and a view
volume.

Polygons defined by the light source and the contour edges define the bounding surface of the shadow volume as shown in Figure 7.4(b). Thus each object, considered in conjunction with a point light source, generates a shadow volume object that is made up of a set of shadow polygons. Note that these shadow polygons are 'invisible' and should not be confused with the visible shadow polygons described in the next section. These shadow polygons are themselves used to determine shadows – they are not rendered.

This scheme can be integrated into a number of hidden surface removal algorithms and the polygons that define the shadow volume are processed along with the object polygons, except that they are considered invisible. A distinction is made between 'front-facing' polygons and

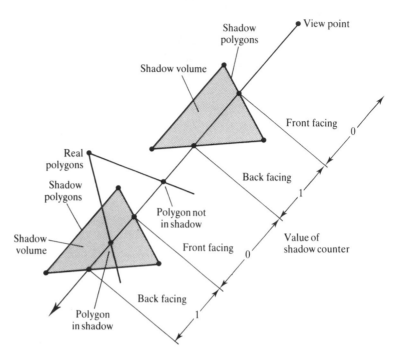

Figure 7.5
Front-facing and
back-facing shadow
polygons and the
shadow counter value.

'back-facing' polygons and the relationship between shadow polygons labelled in this way and object polygons is examined. A point on an object is deemed to be in shadow if it is behind a front-facing shadow polygon and in front of a back-facing polygon. That is, if it is contained within a shadow volume. Thus a front-facing shadow polygon puts anything behind it in shadow and a back-facing shadow polygon cancels the effect of a front-facing one.

As it stands, the algorithm is most easily integrated with a depth-priority hidden surface removal algorithm. Consider the operation of the algorithm for a particular pixel. We consider a vector or ray from the view point through the pixel and look at the relationship between real polygons and shadow polygons along this vector. For a pixel a counter is maintained. This is initialized to 1 if the view point is already in shadow, 0 otherwise. As we descend the depth-sorted list of polygons, the counter is incremented when a front-facing polygon is passed and decremented when a back-facing polygon is passed. The value of this counter tells us, when we encounter a real polygon, whether we are inside a shadow volume. This is shown schematically in Figure 7.5.

Brotman and Badler use an enhanced Z-buffer algorithm and this approach has two significant advantages:

(1) the benefits of the Z-buffer rendering approach are retained, and

(2) their method is able to compute soft shadows or umbra/penumbra effects.

The price to be paid for using a shadow volume approach in conjunction with a Z-buffer is memory cost. The Z-buffer has to be extended such that each pixel location is a record of five fields. As shadow polygons are 'rendered' they modify counters in a pixel record and a decision can be made as to whether a point is in shadow or not.

Soft shadows are computed by modelling distributed light sources as arrays of point sources and linearly combining computations due to each point source.

The original shadow volume approach places heavy constraints on the database environment; the most serious restriction is that objects must be convex polyhedrons. Bergeron (1986) developed a general version of Crow's algorithm that overcomes these restrictions and allows concave objects and penetrating polygons.

7.4.3 Derivation of shadow polygons from light source transformations

This approach was developed by Atherton, Weiler and Greenberg (1978) and relies on the fact that applying hidden surface removal to a view from the light source produces polygons or parts of polygons that are in shadow. It also relies on the object space polygon clipping algorithm (to produce shadow polygons that are *parts* of existing polygons) by Weiler and Atherton (1977).

A claimed advantage of this approach is that it operates in object space. This means that it is possible to extract numerical information on shadows from the algorithm. This finds applications, for example, in architectural CAD.

The algorithm enhances the object data structure with shadow polygons to produce a 'complete shadow data file'. This can then be used to produce any view of the object with shadows. It is thus a good approach in generating animated sequences where the virtual camera changes position, but where the relative positions of the object and the light source remain unchanged. The working of the algorithm is shown for a simple example in Figure 7.6. A single shadow polygon is shown for clarity. Referring to Figure 7.6, the first step in the algorithm is to apply a transformation such that the object or scene is viewed from the light source position. Hidden surface removal then produces *visible* polygons, that is, polygons that are visible to the light source and are therefore *not* in shadow. These are either complete or clipped as the illustration implies. This polygon set can then be combined with the original object polygons, providing both data sets are in the same coordinate system. The process of combining these sets results in a complete shadow data file – the original polygon set enhanced by shadow polygons for a particular light source. Transforming the database to the required view point and applying hidden surface removal will then result in

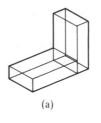

(a)

(b)

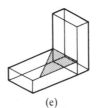

(c)

Figure 7.6
Derivation of shadow
polygons from
transformations. (a)
Simple polygonal
object in modelling
coordinate system. (b)
Plan view showing the
position of the light
source. (c) Hidden
surface removal from
the light source as a
view point. (d) Visible
polygons from (c)
transformed back into
the modelling
coordinate system. (e)
Parts (a) and (d)
merged to produce a
database that contains
shadow polygons. (f)
Part (e) can produce
any view of the object
with shadows.

(d)

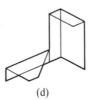

(e)

(f)

an image with shadows. This algorithm exploits the fact that shadow polygons are view point independent. Essentially, the scene is processed twice for hidden surface removal; once using the light source as a view point, which produces the shadow polygons, and once using normal hidden surface removal (from any view point).

7.4.4 Shadow Z-buffer

Possibly the simplest approach to the shadow computation, and one that is easily integrated into a Z-buffer based renderer, is the shadow Z-buffer developed by Williams (1978). This technique requires a separate shadow Z-buffer for each light source and, in its basic form, is only suitable for a scene illuminated by a single light source. Alternatively, a single shadow Z-buffer could be used for many light sources and the algorithm executed for each light source, but this would be somewhat inefficient and slow.

The algorithm is a two-step process. A scene is 'rendered' and depth information stored into the shadow Z-buffer using the light source as a view point. No intensities are calculated. This computes a 'depth image' from the light source, of those polygons that are visible to the light source.

The second step is to render the scene using a Z-buffer algorithm. This process is enhanced as follows. If a point is visible, a coordinate transformation is used to map (x,y,z), the coordinates of the point in three-dimensional screen space (from the view point), to (x',y',z'), the coordinates of the point in screen space from the light point as a coordinate origin. The (x',y') are used to index the shadow Z-buffer and the corresponding depth value is compared with z'. If z' is greater than the value stored in the shadow Z-buffer for that point, then a surface is nearer to the light source than the point under consideration and the point is in shadow, thus a shadow 'intensity' is used; otherwise the point is rendered as normal.

Apart from extending the high memory requirements of the Z-buffer hidden surface removal algorithm, the algorithm also extends its inefficiency. Shadow calculations are performed for surfaces that may be subsequently 'overwritten' – just as shading calculations are.

Anti-aliasing and the shadow Z-buffer
In common with the Z-buffer algorithm, the shadow Z-buffer is susceptible to aliasing artefacts due to point sampling. Two aliasing opportunities occur. First, straightforward point sampling in the creation phase of the shadow Z-buffer produces artefacts. These will be visible along shadow edges – we are considering a hard-edged shadow cast by a point light source. The second aliasing problem is created when accessing the shadow Z-buffer. It is somewhat analogous to the problem created in texture mapping (described in Section 7.5). This problem arises because we are effectively projecting a pixel extent onto the shadow Z-buffer map. This is shown schematically in Figure 7.7. If we consider the so-called pre-image of a square pixel in the

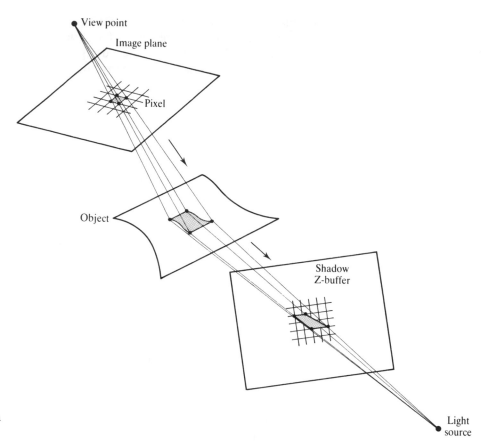

Figure 7.7
'Pre-image' of a pixel in
the shadow Z-buffer.

shadow Z-buffer map then this will, in general, be a quadrilateral that encloses a number of shadow Z-buffer pixels. It is this many map pixels to one screen pixel problem that we have to deal with. It means that a pixel may be partly in shadow and partly not and if we make a binary decision then aliasing will occur. We thus consider the fraction of the pixel that is in shadow by computing this from the shadow Z-buffer. This fraction can be evaluated by the z' comparisons over the set of shadow Z-buffer pixels that the screen pixel projects onto. The fraction is then used to give an appropriate shadow intensity. The process in summary is:

(1) For each pixel calculate four values of $(x'y')$ corresponding to the four corner points. This defines a quadrilateral in shadow Z-buffer space.

(2) Integrate the information over this quadrilateral by comparing the z value for the screen pixel with each z' value in the shadow Z-buffer quadrilateral. This gives a fraction that reflects the area of the pixel in shadow.

(3) Use this fraction to give an appropriate attenuated intensity. The visual effect of this is that the hard edge of the shadow will be softened for those pixels that straddle a shadow boundary.

Full details of this approach are given by Reeves, Salesin and Cook (1987). The price paid for this anti-aliasing is a considerable increase in processing time. Prefiltering techniques (see Section 7.9.2) cannot be used and a stochastic sampling scheme for integrating within the pixel pre-image in the shadow Z-buffer map is suggested by Reeves, Salesin and Cook (1987).

7.5 Texture

Texture mapping was one of the first developments towards making images of three-dimensional objects more interesting and apparently more complex. The original motivation for texture mapping was to diminish the 'shiny plastic' effects produced by using the simple Phong reflection model and to enable different objects to exhibit different surface properties (apart from the trivial distinction of colour).

In one sense the term 'texture' is somewhat misleading; with the exception of bump mapping ((Blinn, 1978a) and below), which gives the impression of actual surface perturbation, the normal semantics associated with the term 'texture', most methods modulate the colour of a surface using repeating motifs or a frame-grabbed image. Textures on real objects usually exhibit both surface and colour modulation – the bark on a tree or the texture of a woven fabric, for example.

There are three major considerations in texture mapping:

(1) What attribute or parameter of the model or object is to be modulated to produce the desired textural effect?

(2) How is the texture mapping to be carried out? Given that a texture is defined in a texture **domain** and an object exists as world space data, we need to define a mapping between these domains.

(3) Texture mapping requires special anti-aliasing treatment because it tends to produce worse aliasing artefacts than other techniques associated with image synthesis.

These three considerations are dealt with in order.

7.5.1 Object attributes modulated for texture

In a review paper, Heckbert (1986) categorizes the parameters that can be modulated to provide a textural impression. A modified version of this categorization is as follows:

- *Surface colour (diffuse reflection coefficient(s))* This is the most commonly used parameter for texture mapping and involves, for example in a simple reflection model, modulating the diffuse coefficient. The first example of this was by Catmull (1974).

- *Specular and diffuse reflection (environment mapping)* This method is now known as environment mapping and has come to be regarded as a separate technique rather than as a category of texture mapping. It is described in Section 7.10 and was first developed by Blinn and Newell (1976).

- *Normal vector perturbation* This is an elegant device, developed again by Blinn (1978a), that 'tricks' a simple reflection model into producing what appears to be a perturbed surface. An extension to this technique is given by Kajiya (1985) which Kajiya calls 'frame mapping'. In this method a 'frame bundle' rather than just a normal vector is perturbed. A frame bundle for a surface is a local coordinate system given by the tangent, binormal and normal to the surface. Kajiya points out that this approach allows a mapping of the directionality of surface features such as hair and cloth.

- *Specularity* Although this effect was reported by Blinn (1978b) (yet again) it does not seem to have been used to any great extent. The attribute modulated is the surface roughness function in the Cook–Torrance reflection model (Chapter 4). An example of a surface with variable shininess is an object painted with textured paint.

- *Transparency* An example of the modulation of transparency is given by Gardener (1985). This particular example is interesting in that it is not strictly a method of applying texture to an object, but a method of generating a complete object – a cloud – using a mathematical texture function to modulate the transparency of an ellipsoid. A real-life example of this case is chemically etched glass.

One can further distinguish among these methods by noting that all except environment mapping 'cement' a texture onto the object and the texture then becomes a 'permanent' part of the object, invariable under object transformations and viewing conditions. Environment mapping, on the other hand, depends on where the object is placed in an environment, and this is a further justification to considering environment mapping as a technique distinct from texture mapping.

7.6   Two-dimensional texture mapping

By far and away the most common form of texture mapping involves the use of a two-dimensional texture domain, $T(u,v)$. This is because an almost infinite variety of textures is readily available. Texture images can be frame grabbed or can be generated procedurally.

Figure 7.8
An overall texture mapping consists of a surface parametrization followed by the normal geometric transformations (after Heckbert (1986)).

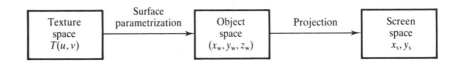

Consider Figure 7.8. This shows the overall process from the texture domain $T(u,v)$ to screen space. The overall mapping can be described either by two transformations as shown or as a single combined transformation. The first transformation, sometimes known as surface parametrization, takes the two-dimensional texture pattern and 'glues' it on the object. The second transformation is the standard object to screen space mapping. Two major difficulties arise in texture mapping: inventing a suitable surface parametrization and anti-aliasing. The difficulty with the first transformation is because we normally wish to stick a texture pattern on a polygon mesh object – itself a discontinuous approximation to a real object. For such objects, surface parametrizations are not defined. They have to be invented. This contrasts with quadric and cubic surfaces where parametrizations are readily available. If we use the analogy of wallpaper pasting: how are we going to paste the wallpaper onto the polygon mesh object? This is a problem to which there is no good solution and a variety of ad hoc techniques has evolved.

Now as we have seen the 'standard' object representation and 'standard' rendering regime imply algorithms driven from screen space. Interpolative shading and Z-buffer hidden surface removal imply a pixel-by-pixel ordering for each polygon. This means that we have to find a single texture value for each pixel to insert into the interpolative shading scheme. The easiest way to do this is by **inverse mapping** – we find the **pre-image** of the current pixel in the texture domain (Figure 7.9a). Because the overall transform is non-linear, the pixel maps into an area in texture space that in general is a curvilinear quadrilateral. To perform the inverse transformation we need to take the four pixel corner points, invert the object to screen space transformation, and invert the surface parametrization. Another reason for adopting this methodology is that it facilitates anti-aliasing.

The use of an anti-aliasing method is mandatory with texture mapping. This is easily seen by considering an object retreating away from a viewer so that its projection in screen space covers fewer and fewer pixels. As the object size decreases, the pre-image of a pixel in texture space will increase, covering a larger area. If we simply point sample at the centre of the pixel and take the value of $T(u,v)$ at the corresponding point in texture space then grossly incorrect results will follow (Figure 7.9b,c,d). Another example of this effect is shown in Figure 11.2. Here as the chequerboard

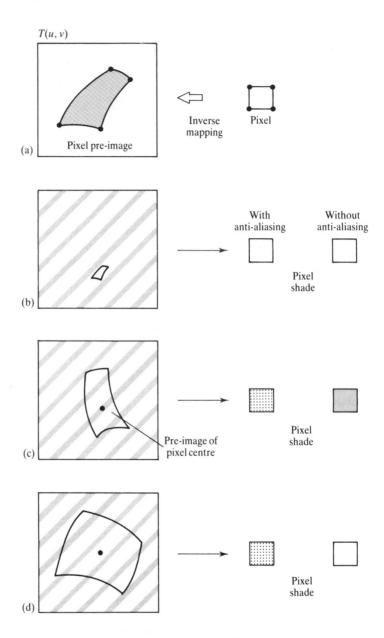

Figure 7.9
Pixels and pre-images
in $T(u,v)$ space.

pattern recedes into the distance it begins to break up in a disturbing manner. These problems are highly visible and move when animated. Consider Figure 7.9(c,d). Say, for example, that an object projects onto a single pixel and moves in such a way that the pre-image translates across the $T(u,v)$. As the object moves it would switch colour from black to white.

Anti-aliasing in this context then means integrating the information over the pixel pre-image and using this value in the shading calculation.

7.6.1   Surface parametrization

This transformation associates a point on the object (x_w, y_w, z_w) with a point (u,v) in texture space. We can split the problem into two parts. For a certain polygon, how do we map each interior point in the polygon into a point in $T(u,v)$ space? Then, for a number of connected polygons making up an entire object, how do we map each polygon into $T(u,v)$ space? This is a global mapping problem. As we have hinted, the second problem tends to predominate and we will now look at a method that combines both these requirements into a single algorithm. Common methods that parametrize with surface definitions are reviewed by Heckbert (1986). These distort the pattern $T(u,v)$ from, say, a rectangle on to a quadrilateral, but their usefulness is limited. In the method described in the next section the parametrization is the direction of a normal or reflection vector at the point on the object under consideration.

7.6.2   Polygon mesh texture mapping: two-part mapping

Two-part texture mapping is a recently developed technique that overcomes the global mapping problem by using an 'easy' intermediate surface onto which the texture is initially projected. Introduced by Bier and Sloan (1986) it is a method that will map two-dimensional texture onto unconstrained polygon mesh models. The method can also be used to implement environment mapping and is thus a method that unifies texture mapping and environment mapping. The texture is projected onto the surface in a way that depends only on the geometry of the object, known as a 'target' object, and not on its parametrization.

The process is known as two-part mapping because the texture is mapped onto an intermediate surface before being mapped onto the object. The intermediate surface is in general non-planar, but it possesses an analytic mapping function and the two-dimensional texture is mapped onto this surface without difficulty. Finding the correspondence between the object point and the texture point then becomes a three-dimensional to three-dimensional mapping and the surface parametrization is replaced by a normal vector parametrization. Thus we can use this method to implement both local and global mapping simultaneously. The price that we pay for this generality is double distortion – the texture is distorted by two mappings.

The basis of the method is as follows:

(1) The first stage is a mapping from two-dimensional texture space to a *simple* three-dimensional intermediate surface such as a cylinder:

$$T(u,v) \rightarrow T'(x_i, y_i, z_i)$$

This is known as the S mapping.

(2) A second stage maps the three-dimensional texture pattern onto the object surface:

$$T'(x_i, y_i, z_i) \rightarrow O(x_w, y_w, z_w)$$

This is referred to as the O mapping.

These combined operations can distort the texture pattern onto the object in a 'natural' way, for example, one variation of the method is a 'shrinkwrap' mapping, where the planar texture pattern shrinks onto the object in the manner suggested by the eponym.

For the S mapping Bier describes four intermediate surfaces: a plane at any orientation, the curved surface of a cylinder, the faces of a cube and the surface of a sphere. Although it makes no difference mathematically, it is useful to consider that $T(u,v)$ is mapped onto the interior surfaces of these objects. For example, consider the cylinder. Given a parametric definition of the curved surface of a cylinder as a set of points (θ, h), we transform the point (u,v) onto the cylinder as follows:

$$S_{\text{cylinder}}: (\theta, h) \rightarrow (u,v)$$

$$= \left(\frac{r}{c}(\theta - \theta_0), \frac{1}{d}(h - h_0) \right)$$

where c and d are scaling factors and θ_0 and h_0 position the texture on the cylinder of radius r.

When using a sphere as the intermediate surface, the standard problem of high distortion at the poles must be considered. As is well known, there are no zero-distortion mappings from a plane to a sphere and the standard projection (Mercator) has unbounded distortion at the poles. In practice, if such a mapping is used, obvious discontinuities occur when a point on the object maps onto a point in the polar region of the sphere. Bier and Sloan suggest using the stereographic projection that maps two circular patterns with low distortion onto the two hemispheres (with a discontinuity at the equator):

$$S_{\text{sphere}}: (\theta, \phi) \rightarrow (u,v)$$

$$= \left(\frac{2p}{1 + (1 + p^2 + q^2)^{1/2}}, \frac{2q}{1 + (1 + p^2 + q^2)^{1/2}} \right)$$

where

$$p = \tan \phi \cos \theta$$
$$q = \tan \phi \sin \theta$$

θ and ϕ are the azimuth and elevation angles that define a point on the surface of a sphere. p and q define the gnomic projection that maps circles in the plane to lines of latitude on the sphere.

The box is the topological equivalent of the sphere. Figure 7.10 shows diagrammatically how a planar texture pattern is mapped onto a box.

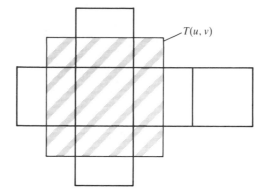

Figure 7.10
Box mapping.

Whereas we have to tolerate distortion in the sphere mapping, there is no distortion in mapping onto an unfolded box. However the pattern is cut or clipped. (Note that there will still be pattern distortion introduced by the other mapping – going from the object to the box surface.) Despite the clipping, Bier and Sloan consider there are useful applications. For example, if the texture contains a few foreground figures on a constant colour background it may be possible to position the pattern so that the figures are not clipped, or if the texture is homogeneous and invariant to 90° rotation, it may be possible to orient the texture to hide the seams. In environment mapping the pattern *must* be designed to fit exactly on the unfolded box. Finally, we must remember that the pre-image of a pixel may occur over a number of box sides. This is discussed in more detail in the case of environment mapping (Section 7.10).

Various possibilities occur for the O mapping where the texture values for $O(x_w, y_w, z_w)$ are obtained from $T'(x_i, y_i, z_i)$, and these are best considered from a ray tracing point of view. The four O mappings are shown in Figure 7.11 and are:

(1) The intersection of the reflected view ray with the intermediate surface, T' (this is in fact environment mapping).
(2) The intersection of the surface normal at (x, y, z) with T'.
(3) The intersection of a line through (x, y, z) and the object centroid with T'.
(4) The intersection of the line from (x, y, z) to T' whose orientation is given by the surface normal at (x_i, y_i, z_i).

Excluding the first, which is concerned with environment mapping (rather than mapping texture onto a surface) we have three O mappings and four S mappings giving a total of 12 possible combinations. These, together with an indication of their usefulness, are shown in Figure 7.12. For example, Bier and Sloan state that the object normal/cylinder mapping and the object centroid/cylinder mapping are eliminated because they inherit the

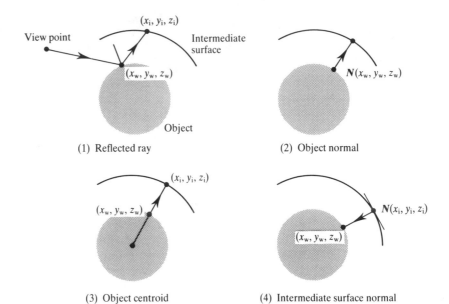

Figure 7.11
The four possible O mappings that map the intermediate surface texture T' onto the object.

topological problem of the cylinder – there is no texture defined at either end. If the intermediate surface normal is employed then every point on the object can be given a texture.

Let us now consider the complete inverse mapping process for the shrinkwrap case. We break the process into three stages (Figure 7.13):

(1) Inverse map four pixel points to four points (x_w, y_w, z_w) on the surface of the object.

(2) Apply the O mapping to find the point (θ, h) on the surface of the cylinder. In the shrinkwrap case we simply join the object point to the centre of the cylinder and the intersection of this line with the surface of the cylinder gives us (x_i, y_i, z_i):

$$x_w, y_w, z_w \rightarrow (\theta, h)$$
$$= (\tan^{-1}(y_w/z_w), z_w)$$

(3) Apply the S mapping to find the point (u, v) corresponding to (θ, h).

	Cylinder	Box	Sphere	Plane	
	Environment mapping				Reflected vector
		Normal/box	Normal/sphere	Redundant	Object normal
		Centroid/box	Centroid/sphere	Redundant	Object centroid
	Shrink wrap	ISN/box	Redundant	Slide projector	Intermediate surface normal (ISN)

■ Very inappropriate   ▨ Somewhat inappropriate

Figure 7.12
O mapping combinations (after Bier and Sloan (1986)).

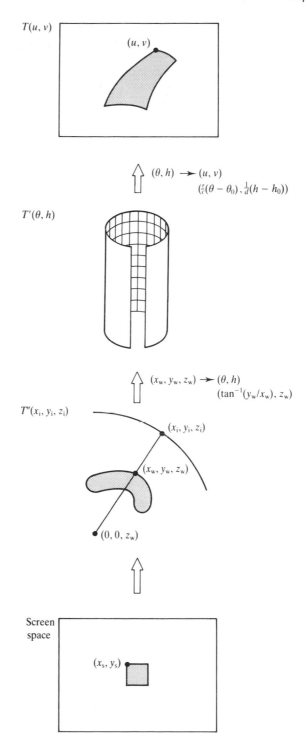

Figure 7.13
Inverse mapping using the shrinkwrap method.

7.6.3   Two-dimensional texture domain techniques: mapping onto bicubic parametric patches

If an object is a quadric or a cubic then surface parametrization is straightforward. In Section 0.0 we used quadrics as intermediate surfaces because of this property. If the object is a bicubic parametric patch, texture mapping is trivial since a parametric patch by definition already possesses u,v values everywhere on its surface.

The first use of texture in computer graphics was a method developed by Catmull (1974). This technique applied to bicubic parametric patch models; the algorithm subdivides a surface patch in object space, and at the same time executes a corresponding subdivision in texture space. The idea is that the patch subdivision proceeds until it covers a single pixel (a standard patch rendering approach described in detail in Chapter 6). When the patch subdivision process terminates, the required texture value(s) for the pixel is (are) obtained from the area enclosed by the current level of subdivision in the texture domain. This is a straightforward technique that is easily implemented as an extension to a bicubic patch renderer. A variation of this method has been used by Cook, Carpenter and Catmull (1987) where object surfaces are subdivided into 'micropolygons' and flat shaded with values from a corresponding subdivision in texture space.

An example of this technique is shown in Plate 10. Here *each* patch on the teapot causes subdivision of a single texture map, which is itself a rendered version of the teapot. For each patch, the u,v values from the parameter space subdivision are used to index the texture map whose u,v values also vary between 0 and 1. This scheme is easily altered, say, to map four patches into the entire texture domain by using a scale factor of two in the u,v mapping.

7.7   Three-dimensional texture domain techniques

A method that neatly circumvents the mapping problem is to employ a three-dimensional texture domain. We can imagine that a texture value exists everywhere in the object domain. Ignoring object scale problems (the texture 'size' will not vary as the size of the object changes) we can then say that, given a point on the surface of an object, (x_w, y_w, z_w), its texture is given by the **identity mapping** $T(x_w, y_w, z_w)$. This is equivalent to sculpting or carving an object out of a solid block of material. The colour of the object is determined by the intersection of its surface with the predefined three-dimensional texture field. This method was reported simultaneously by Perlin (1985) and Peachey (1983) wherein the term 'solid texturing' was coined.

A fairly obvious requirement of this technique is that the three-dimensional texture field is obtained by procedural generation. Storing a complete three-dimensional field would be prohibitively expensive in memory requirements. Thus the coordinates (x_w, y_w, z_w) are used to index a procedure that defines the three-dimensional texture field for that point.

A significant advantage of the elimination of the mapping problem is that objects of arbitrary complexity can receive a texture on their surfaces in a 'coherent' fashion. No discontinuities occur when the texture appears on the object.

An interesting possibility occurs when using this technique in an animated sequence. The correct approach is to subject the texture field to the same transformations as the object, such that the texture remains static on the surface of the object. However, the 'incorrect' approach – moving the object through a static texture field – can produce unique effects.

An 'easy' example of this technique is shown in Plate 11. Here 125 cubes are shaded and the colour of each cube is obtained by an identity mapping between (x_w, y_w, z_w), the coordinate of a reference vertex on each cube, and the corresponding point RGB (x_w, y_w, z_w) in an RGB cube defined over the domain of the object (see Chapter 14 for further details on the RGB cube).

Further examples of this technique demonstrate the idea. First, wood grain can be simulated by a set of concentric cylinders whose reference axis is, in general, tilted with respect to one of the reference axes of the object. This approach is shown in Plate 11 where the three-dimensional texture field is a set of functionally defined concentric cylinders modulated with a harmonic function. The example demonstrates how you can build up a three-dimensional texture definition in stages, each step further elaborating the definition. First, we make the field a modular function of r, the radius of the cylinder. For a particular cylinder we have:

$$r_1 = (u^2 + w^2)^{1/2}$$

Second, we can perturb r with a sinusoidal function, or with any function that simulates the deviation of wood growth away from a perfect cylinder:

$$r_2 = r_1 + 2\sin(a\theta)$$

then we can apply a small twist along the axis of the cylinders:

$$r_2 = r_1 + 2\sin(a\theta + v/b)$$

where:

a,b are constants

$\theta = \tan^{-1}(u/w)$

Program 7.1   A procedure for representing wood grain.

```
procedure wood_grain(u, v, w: real; var r, g, b: real);

  var radius, angle: real;
      grain: integer;
begin
  radius := sqrt(sqr(u) + sqr(w));
  if w = 0 then angle := pi/2
  else angle := arctan(u, w);
  {arctan evaluates arctan (u/w), but uses quadrant information to
   return a value in the range 0..2π}
  radius := radius + 2*sin(20*angle + v/150);
  grain := round(radius) mod 60;
  if grain < 40 then
    begin
      r := r_light;
      g := g_light;
      b := b_light;
    end else
  begin
      r := r_ dark;
      g := g_ dark;
      b := b_ dark;
    end;
end {of wood_grain};
```

We can then index the texture by:

$$(x, y, z) = \text{tilt}(u, v, w)$$

where 'tilt' is any desired tilt function implementing any rotation between the two coordinate systems.

Program 7.1 returns a colour (r, g, b) given a texture space coordinate (u, v, w). In this example we have used a three-dimensional texture field to model an effect that would in reality be a three-dimensional texture. In Plate 11 the visible texture on the ends of the wood is circular – the end grain – whereas the grain tends to run along the side faces of the block. This effect would be tedious to model using two-dimensional texture mapping.

An extension of this basic idea is to use a general three-dimensional noise function to perturb the basic field, rather than use a context-dependent perturbation, as we did for the wood grain. This approach is now well established in three-dimensional computer graphics because it works well visually. An example of marble texture is shown in Plate 11. The

Program 7.2 A procedure for representing marble.

```
procedure marble(u, v, w: real; var r, g, b: real);

    const
        width = 0.02;

    var
        d, dd: real;
        i: real;

begin
    d := (u + 15000)*width + 7*noise(u/100, v/200, w/200);
    dd := trunc(d) mod 17;
    if dd < 4 then
        i := 0.7 + 0.2*noise(u/70, v/50, w/50)
    else
        if (dd < 9) or (dd > = 12) then
        begin
            d := abs(d − trunc(d/17)*17 − 10.5)*0.1538462;
            i := 0.4 + 0.3*d + 0.2*noise(u/100, v/100, w/100);
        end
        else
            i := 0.2 + 0.2*noise(u/100, v/100, w/100);
    r := 0.9*i;
    g := 0.8*i;
    b := 0.6*i;
end {marble};
```

texture field in this case is a set of alternating black, grey, white and grey slabs. A three-dimensional noise function, fully described in Chapter 12, is used to modulate the basic black/grey stripes to give an impression of turbulent flow. In the procedure shown in Program 7.2, *width* defines the overall width in object space of a full cycle of marble texture (that is from dark to light). *dd* is used to define the relative widths of the different coloured stripes (that is, four bands [0..3], [4..8], [9..11] and [12..16]).

Another way of looking at this particular example is that it is the combination of two procedurally defined texture fields. One field is the low-frequency black, grey and white slabs, the other is a three-dimensional noise function.

The final example, (see Plate 11) uses a similar technique but the amplitude of the three-dimensional noise perturbation is increased to such an extent that the marble effect is destroyed. These two examples show the power of the method in being able to generate visually different effects from the same procedural basis.

7.8   Bump mapping

Bump mapping, a technique developed by Blinn (1978b), is an elegant device that enables a surface to appear wrinkled or dimpled without the need to model these depressions geometrically. Instead, the surface normal is angularly perturbed according to information given in a two-dimensional **bump map** and this 'tricks' a local reflection model, wherein intensity is a function mainly of the surface normal, into producing local variations on a smooth surface. The only problem with bump mapping is that because the pits or depressions do not exist in the model, a silhouette edge that appears to pass through a depression will not produce the expected cross-section. In other words the silhouette edge will follow the line of the model.

It is an important technique because it appears to texture a surface in the normal sense of the word rather than modulate the colour of a flat surface. Plate 10 shows two examples of this technique.

Texturing the surface in the rendering phase, without perturbing the geometry, bypasses serious modelling problems that would otherwise occur. If the object is polygonal the mesh would have to be fine enough to receive the perturbations from the texture map – a serious imposition on the original modelling phase, particularly if the texture is to be an option.

In implementing bump mapping, a scheme is required that perturbs the normal vector in a way that is independent of the orientation and position of the surface. For a particular point on the surface, the normal at that point must always receive the same perturbation. If this is not the case, then in an animation sequence, the bump-mapped detail will animate as the object moves. This is achieved by basing the perturbation on a coordinate system based on local surface derivatives.

If $O(u,v)$ is a parametrized function representing the position vectors of points O on the surface of an object, then the normal to the surface at a point is given by:

$$N = O_u \times O_v$$

where O_u and O_v are the partial derivatives of the surface at point O lying in the tangent plane.

We define two other vectors that lie in the tangent plane. These are:

$$A = N \times O_v$$

and:

$$B = N \times O_u$$

D is a vector derived from components of these two vectors, and summing D and N gives N', the perturbed vector:

$$N' = N + D$$

The vectors A, B and N form a coordinate system in which D is defined independent of the orientation and position of the surface.

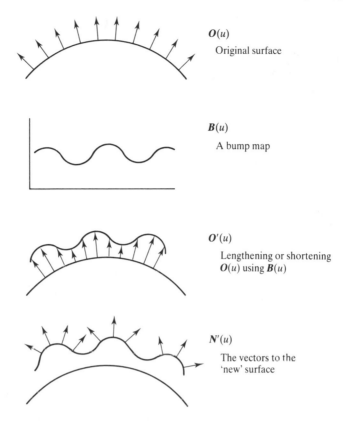

$O(u)$

Original surface

$B(u)$

A bump map

$O'(u)$

Lengthening or shortening
$O(u)$ using $B(u)$

$N'(u)$

The vectors to the
'new' surface

Figure 7.14
A one-dimensional
example of the stages
involved in bump
mapping (after Blinn
(1978b)).

We now address the problem of the value of D. The components of D
are given by:

$$D = B_u A - B_v B$$

where B_u and B_v are the partial derivatives of the bump map $B(u,v)$. Thus
we define a bump map as a displacement function or height field but use its
derivatives at the point (u,v) to calculate D. This can be shown as follows.
Consider Figure 7.14 that shows a one-dimensional analogy or cross-section
of the process. We first add a small increment, derived from the bump map
$B(u,v)$ to $O(u,v)$ to define $O'(u,v)$:

$$O'(u,v) = O(u,v) + B(u,v)\frac{N}{|N|}$$

Now differentiating this equation gives:

$$O_u' = O_u + B_u \frac{N}{|N|} + B\left(\frac{N}{|N|}\right)_u$$

$$O_v' = O_v + B_v \frac{N}{|N|} + B\left(\frac{N}{|N|}\right)_v$$

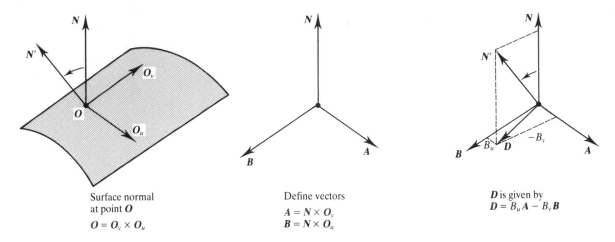

Surface normal at point O	Define vectors	D is given by
$O = O_v \times O_u$	$A = N \times O_v$ $B = N \times O_u$	$D = B_u A - B_v B$

Figure 7.15

Geometric interpretation of bump mapping.

If B is small (that is, the bump map displacement function is small compared with its spatial extent), the last term in each equation can be ignored and:

$$N'(u,v) = O_u \times O_v + B_u\left(\frac{N}{|N|} \times O_v\right) + B_v\left(O_u \times \frac{N}{|N|}\right)$$
$$+ \ B_u B_v\left(\frac{N \times N}{|N|^2}\right)$$

The first term is the normal to the surface and the last term is zero, giving:

$$D = B_u(N \times O_v) - B_v(N \times O_u)$$

where $N/|N|$ is written as N, or

$$D = B_u A - B_v B$$

A geometric interpretation of this is given in Figure 7.15. D is a vector in the plane of A and B whose components are given by B_u and $-B_v$. N' is then given by:

$$N' = N + D$$

which is the required result.

One of the problems of bump mapping examined by Blinn is its dependence on the scale of the object. If the surface definition function is scaled by a factor of two then the length of the normal vector is scaled by four, but the length of D is only scaled by two. This is because the object is scaled but the displacement function B is not. The effect of this is to smooth out the wrinkles as the surface is stretched – clearly undesirable. Blinn suggests deriving a D which is scale invariant:

$$D' = aD \frac{|N|}{|D|}$$

A choice for the value of a is given as:

$$a = (B_u{}^2 + B_v{}^2)^{1/2}$$

Blinn also discusses the anti-aliasing problem, pointing out that the normal techniques for anti-aliasing texture mapping, described later in this chapter, are not relevant because the bump map displacement values are not linearly related to the final intensity values. Filtering the bump map will simply smooth out the bumps and the only alternative is to map at subpixel resolution and average. However, this is clearly a very expensive operation and Blinn does claim that some improvement can be obtained by area filtering the bump map.

Another approach to wrinkling a surface is to use displacement maps where a two-dimensional height field is used to perturb a surface point along the direction of its surface normal. The major practical difference between this method and bump mapping is the difficulty in incorporating it in a standard polygon mesh renderer. Bump mapping can be merged into a normal interpolation scheme and the same polygonal model can be used to produce both a smooth object and a bump-mapped object. For polygonal objects, displacement mapping is most easily incorporated into the modelling phase. Displacement mapping need only be considered when the detail must be made visible on silhouette edges, otherwise bump mapping is preferable.

7.9   Anti-aliasing and texture mapping

As we discussed in Section 7.5 aliasing artefacts are extremely problematic in texture mapping. Texture mapping is generally unsuccessful unless it is integrated with an anti-aliasing procedure. Artefacts are highly noticeable, particularly in texture that exhibits coherence or periodicity and originates from point sampling (see Chapter 11 for a more theoretical discussion on general anti-aliasing techniques). For example, unless inverse mapping is accurately performed then neither the shape nor the area of the mapped pixel area in the texture domain is known. Accurate mapping produces, in general, a curvilinear quadrilateral. In extreme cases, point sampling without filtering will lead to extreme errors. A large number, perhaps thousands, of texels (an element that is the smallest square area in the texture domain) will map into a single pixel (see Figure 7.9). This case can arise when a number of texels map onto a surface, but the projection of the surface in screen space is small, either because of its depth, or because of its orientation with respect to the viewing direction.

We can informally define anti-aliasing in texture mapping as the process of integrating the information within the pixel pre-image in texture space. A single value has to be returned from the parameter used in the shading equation at the pixel under consideration. This integration process is known as **filtering**. Because the shape of the pre-image changes as the pixels change, we require filters whose shape changes. Approaches to anti-aliasing in texture mapping are based on approximations to this ideal.

7.9.1 Approximations to space-variant filters

There are a number of empirical approaches to the space-variant filtering problem. In the previously mentioned subdivision patch renderer Catmull (1974) computes an unweighted average of the texels corresponding to a screen pixel. The shape of the area mapped in the texture domain is deemed to be a quadrilateral. Blinn and Newell (1976) use a similar approach using a pyramid weighting function with the pyramid distorted to fit the approximating quadrilateral. These simple schemes demonstrate the two essential requirements of space-variant filtering:

- The area in $T(u,v)$ space over which the filter operates must be defined or approximated.
- The integration has to be performed by weighting and summing values of $T(u,v)$ that fall within the filter kernel.

Consider Figure 7.16. Here a pixel pre-image is approximated with a quadrilateral. The weighting function that enables us to integrate the information into a single value is deemed to be a pyramid shape with the apex at the pre-image of the pixel centre. Each value of $T(u,v)$ is weighted by the corresponding value of the pyramid function and included in the weighted sum over the domain of the filter.

Feibush, Levoy and Cook (1980) and Ganget, Perry and Coueignoux (1982) also describe empirical approaches to space-variant filtering.

A method that is claimed to be both economical and accurate is the elliptical weighted average (EWA) filter proposed by Greene and Heckbert (1986). The basis of this method is to approximate square pixel areas in screen space with a circle. The reason for this is that the inverse mapping of a circle is *always* an ellipse. Even though the size, eccentricity and orientation of the ellipse change, the shape is invariant and this fact is exploited in the method. A function $q(u,v)$ is defined. This is an elliptical paraboloid – a function whose 'iso-Q' contours are concentric ellipses. The elliptical contours are used to evaluate the extent of the filter. $T(u,v)$ points are tested to see if they lie within the elliptical filter extent. The value of Q is used as a filter weighting. More precisely, it is used to index into a look-up table of precalculated values. The function is defined as:

$$Q(u,v) = Au^2 + Buv + Cv^2$$

where $(0,0)$ is the centre of the concentric ellipses.

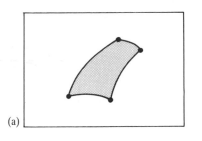

(a)

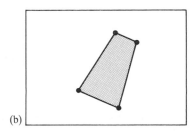

(b)

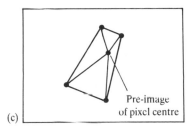

(c)

Figure 7.16
Approximating a pixel pre-image with a quadrilateral. (a) Pre-image of pixel. (b) Filter extent is approximated using a quadrilateral. (c) Filter kernel is approximated using a pyramid.

Pre-image
of pixel centre

This function is shown in Figure 7.17 as a set of 'iso-Q' contours. The algorithm is as follows:

(1) We perform the inverse mapping to determine the correspondence between the pixel corner points and points (u,v) in texture space. This enables us to compute an approximation to the partials $(\partial u/\partial x, \partial v/\partial x)$ and $(\partial u/\partial y, \partial v/\partial y)$. These quantify the distortion of the pixel pre-image and are used to estimate the eccentricity and orientation of the elliptical paraboloid which is then centred at (u_0, v_0) the inverse mapping of the pixel centre. The ellipse that corresponds to the circular approximation of the pixel is given by:

$$A = v_x^2 + v_y^2$$
$$B = -2(u_x v_x + u_y v_y)$$
$$C = u_x^2 + u_y^2$$

where u_x, u_y and v_x, v_y are the above partials.

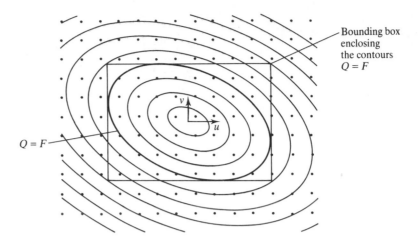

Figure 7.17
'Iso-Q' contours in the texture domain. (After Greene and Heckbert (1986)).

(2) This ellipse is then enclosed in a bounding box.

(3) This space is scanned and Q is efficiently evaluated using finite differences. Points satisfying:

$$Q(u,v) < F \quad \text{for some threshold } F$$

are used to index a look-up table that stores a filter function which may, for example, be a Gaussian or sinc function. Q therefore serves to provide inclusion testing and an index function for the prestored look-up table. This method is claimed to be twice as fast as methods of similar quality.

7.9.2   Prefiltering techniques

The computational cost of the above filtering techniques is always some function of the area of the inverse-mapped pixel in texture space. Using such methods in a context where, for example, large texture areas are mapped into small screen areas is costly. Prefiltering techniques are approaches where cost does not grow in proportion to mapped texture area.

An elegant prefiltering technique that has achieved some popularity is Williams' 'mip-mapping' scheme (Williams, 1983). Instead of a texture domain comprising a single image, Williams uses many images, all derived by averaging down the original image to successively lower resolutions. Each image in the sequence is exactly half the resolution of the previous. A possible texture domain layout is shown in Figure 7.18 and is effectively a three-dimensional database with a third parameter, D, used to select the particular image resolution required. For example, using this organization a $T(u,v)$ of resolution 512×512 would require a 1024×1024 array. Plate 10 shows a mip-map that was used in conjunction with Catmull's mapping method, described earlier, to produce the textured teapot.

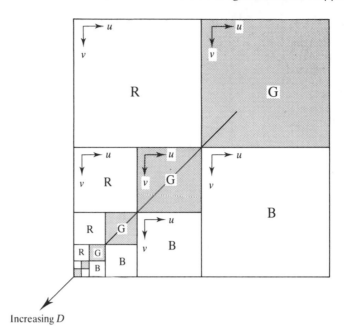

Figure 7.18
Organization of a
prefiltered
mip-mapped texture
domain.

The term 'mip' is derived from *multum in parvo* or many things in a small place. In a low-resolution version of the image each texel represents the average of a number of texels. By a suitable choice of D, an image at appropriate resolution is selected and the filtering cost remains constant – the many-texels-to-one-pixel cost problem being avoided. The centre of the pixel is mapped into that map determined by D and this single value is used. In this way the original texture is filtered and, to avoid discontinuities between the images at varying resolutions, different levels are also blended. Blending between levels occurs when D is selected. The images are discontinuous in resolution but D is a continuous parameter. Linear interpolation is carried out from the two nearest levels.

Williams selects D from:

$$D = \text{max\_of} \left[\text{sqrt}((\partial u/\partial x)^2 + (\partial v/\partial x)^2), \text{sqrt}((\partial u/\partial y)^2 + (\partial v/\partial y)^2) \right]$$

A 'correct' or accurate estimation of D is important. If D is too large then the image will look blurred, too small and aliasing artefacts will still be visible. Detailed practical methods for determining D depending on the mapping context are given in Watt and Watt (1992).

This method of indexing into a particular level with the parameter D is equivalent to approximating a texture quadrilateral with a square. Figure 7.19, based on an illustration by Heckbert, graphically highlights the approximation implicit in this technique, and compares this method to the more accurate methods described in the previous section. Anti-aliasing is

Figure 7.19
A representation of filtering errors that occur when a square, rectangle and suitably oriented ellipse are used to approximate a quadrilateral area in the texture domain. (After Heckbert.)

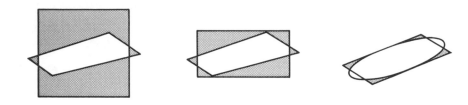

always a compromise. Aliasing artefacts persist if the areas filtered are too small; blurring occurs if the areas are too large.

Another implication of square filtering is that it presupposes that the required compression is symmetric. Since, in this scheme, the addressing is based on the axis of maximum compression, for surfaces that curve away from the viewer fuzziness may result (although Williams claims that in animated sequences where areas collapse into long thin edges the quality of the mapping is not noticeably degraded).

Crow (1984) proposes a generalization of Williams' technique that uses a single table from which a virtually continuous range of texture densities can be drawn. It is pointed out by Crow that his method is equivalent to mip-mapping where each texture intensity is replaced by a value representing the sum of the intensities of all texels contained in the rectangle defined by the texel of interest. This table is sampled in four places for any rectangle and a sum of texel intensities found from a sum and two differences taken from the table.

Mip-mapping can also be extended into a three-dimensional domain and used as a filtering method for three-dimensional or solid textures. This approach is, however, somewhat limiting because the power of three-dimensional textures is that they are generally a procedural technique that does not require prefiltered maps to be precalculated and stored prior to mapping.

7.9.3   Anti-aliasing and three-dimensional texture mapping

We have seen that the use of a three-dimensional texture field produces convincing texture and eliminates many of the difficulties associated with two-dimensional mapping methods. An associated advantage that emerges from the procedural nature of the method is that points can be calculated at any level of detail. Effectively, the texture field can be sampled as finely or as coarsely as required. This compares with precalculated or fixed two-dimensional maps, which either have to be stored at different levels of detail (mip-mapping) or careful anti-aliasing has to be employed. Simple anti-aliasing techniques, such as supersampling, are easily extended to three-dimensional texture fields and the aliasing problems that occur with two-dimensional texture mapping (that are a function of the mapping itself) are avoided. Anti-aliasing three-dimensional texture fields is discussed in detail by Peachey (1988). Peachey points out that it is often possible with procedurally generated textures to integrate anti-aliasing into the generation method by averaging the texture field over a spherical region of appropriate diameter, rather than point sampling the function.

7.10 Environment mapping

This term refers to the process of reflecting the surrounding environment in a shiny object. It tends to be classified as a texture technique, although it is distinguished from 'normal' texture mapping in that the pattern seen on an object is a function of the view vector V. A particular detail in the environment will move across the object as V changes. Environment mapping can also be considered as a simplification of ray tracing (see Chapter 8), where only the reflected ray is traced and the process is terminated at a depth of two. We introduced the notion of environment mapping in Section 0.0 where a box or sphere could be used as an intermediate surface.

The principle of the technique is shown in Figure 7.20. For a perfect mirror object, the view ray V is reflected from the surface of the object. The intersection of this ray with a surface, such as the interior of a sphere that contains an image of the environment to be reflected in the object, gives the shading attributes for the point O on the object surface.

In practice, four rays through the pixel point define a reflection 'cone' with a quadrilateral cross-section (Figure 7.21). The region that subtends the environment map is then filtered to give a single shading attribute for the pixel.

Figure 7.20
Environment mapping: using the reflected view ray V_r to index an environment map.

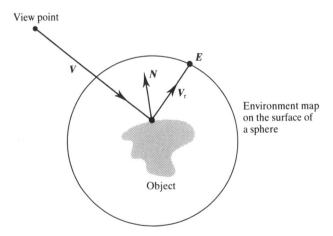

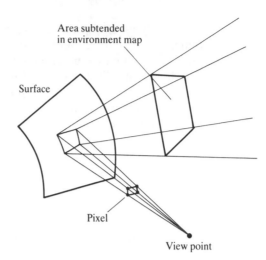

Area subtended
in environment map

Surface

Pixel

View point

Figure 7.21
Reflection 'cone'
subtends a
quadrilateral area in
the environment map.

Environment maps are usually prefiltered and transformed into two-dimensional images. Here we are effectively reducing a three-dimensional problem to a two-dimensional one. This reduction is precomputed and stored as an environment map. The illumination as seen from a point on an object surface is then given by a single indexing operation into the map rather than as a three-dimensional object space calculation – as in ray tracing. Environment mapping can also be seen as a technique that extends the limited illumination possibilities in the n (small integer) point light source Phong shading technique. An environment can be viewed as an infinity of light sources and a map can represent any arbitrary geometry of light sources such as an indoor or outdoor scene. From this point of view geometrically distributed light sources, such as striplights, are just rectangles of high intensity white values in the environment map.

The first use of environment mapping was by Blinn and Newell (1976) wherein the sphere interior technique was used and a latitude–longitude map created. The practical difficulty with this approach is in the production of the environment map. Predistorting an environment to fit the interior surface of a sphere is difficult. Another disadvantage of this technique is that it is only geometrically accurate for small objects based on the centre of the sphere. As the object size becomes large with respect to the environment sphere, or the object is positioned a long way from this centre, the geometric distortion increases.

Using the reflected view vector, V_r, it is a simple matter to index into a latitude–longitude environment map. If $E(u,v)$ is a point on the map $(0 \leqslant u \leqslant 1, 0 \leqslant v \leqslant 1)$ and the reflected view vector is:

$$V_r = (V_{rx}, V_{ry}, V_{rz})$$

then:

$$u = \tfrac{1}{2}[1 + 1/\pi \tan^{-1}(V_{rx}, V_{rz})]$$

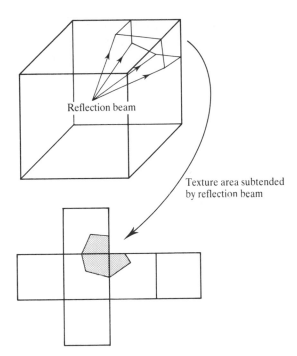

Reflection beam

Texture area subtended
by reflection beam

Figure 7.22
Texture area subtended
by reflection beam for
environment mapping.

$$\text{and} \quad v = \frac{V_{ry} + 1}{2}$$

Developments in environment mapping (for example, Miller and Hoffman (1984) and Greene and Heckbert (1986)) treat the environment as a set of two-dimensional projections. Using the interior of a cube as an environment map is more convenient than a sphere. It means, for example, that a map can be created from a real environment by photographing or frame-grabbing the environment in six directions using a flat field lens with a 90° view field. Alternatively, six views of a simulated environment can be generated by a rendering system. Miller and Hoffman use the cube projection as an intermediate step in creating a single latitude–longitude map. The trade-off between using a latitude–longitude map and a six-component cube map are concerned with the nature of the shapes that are projected by the reflection cone in each domain. These are fully discussed by Greene. Figure 7.22 shows that in general the four reflection vectors will spread over more than one of the cube sides. Plate 12 shows an example of an environment map and the image created using it.

Greene points out that although environment mapping is a less versatile technique than ray tracing, it eliminates certain ray tracing problems. It is far less expensive, handles diffuse illumination 'correctly', and can use texture filtering to overcome the ray tracing aliasing artefacts that arise from point sampling. In particular, diffuse and specular surface illumination is found by prefiltering regions of two-dimensional diffuse and specular environment maps. Integration over a two-dimensional environment map projection, rather than over a three-dimensional environment (which is what anti-aliasing operations in ray tracing do) can produce gross errors, but Greene points out that 'the subjective quality of reality cues produced by environment mapping may be superior to those produced by a naive ray tracer'. An obvious disadvantage of environment mapping is that an object will not normally be able to contain reflections of itself, since the object will not appear in the environment map.

The above discussion applies to specular illumination environment maps. Miller and Hoffman have shown how to create a diffuse illumination environment map. The shading attributes obtained for a point on the surface then consist of both a diffuse and a specular component and the diffuse component gives an approximate solution to the global interaction of diffuse light that is not catered for in ray tracing. The specular/diffuse surface attributes or coefficients then select the proportion of the contribution from each map. A perfect diffuse surface would only have a contribution from the diffuse map and a perfect mirror object would only access the specular map:

$$I = k_d D(N) + k_s S(V_r)$$

where D is the contribution from the diffuse map, indexed by the surface normal, and S is the contribution from the specular map, indexed by the reflected view vector.

A diffuse environment map is effectively a highly blurred version of the specular environment map. It is created by convolving an illumination map with a Lambert's law cosine function. Each point on the diffuse map is a weighted sum of all illumination on the surface of a hemisphere centred at that point. The diffuse map is indexed by the surface normal N. A useful attribute of the diffuse map is that it contains no high-frequency components and can thus be stored at extremely low resolution.

Projects, notes and suggestions ━━━━━━━

7.1 Shadows on side or ground planes

Implement Blinn's method of projecting shadows onto a ground plane for planes parallel to the x_w, y_w plane, the x_w, z_w plane and the y_w, z_w plane. Develop the technique to calculate 'perspective' shadows for local light sources. Here we have:

$$S = P - \alpha(P - L)$$

7.2 Shadow Z-buffer

Implement the shadow Z-buffer algorithm described in the text.

7.3 Shadow algorithm investigation

The disadvantages of most shadow algorithms that deal with polygon mesh models is that their geometric coding complexity is high and they can only generate hard-edged shadows. An expensive, but simple, method is to use shadow feelers (see Chapter 8) and to apply them to polygon mesh objects. Experiment with this idea. Note that shadow feeler rays on the interior of polygons can be interpolated from vertex values. Can this method be adapted to model fuzzy shadows, and if so how?

How can intersection testing be optimized if the constraints that shadow feelers either intersect one object or none is made?

What is wrong with the idea of saying that a polygon does not contain a shadow if none of the vertex shadow feelers intersects an object (and conversely that it does have a shadow if any of its vertex shadow feelers do intersect)?

7.4 Texture mapping of bicubic patches

Implement a simple two-dimensional texture mapping technique for bicubic patches using subdivision. Extend the method to include mip-mapping as a filtering technique.

7.5 Two-part texture mapping (*)

Using an appropriate test pattern such as a grid, implement the two-part texture mapping scheme described in this chapter. Bier and Sloan (1986) state that only five out of the twelve intermediate/O mappings are appropriate. Find these mappings and investigate their properties.

7.6 Solid texture

Implement the three-dimensional or solid texture method and investigate the efficacy of the following methods of solid texture definition:

- Concentric cylinders perturbed in various ways.
- A 'bubble' texture formed by placing spheres of random radii at random locations.
- The three-dimensional noise function (Chapter 12).
- Three-dimensional Fourier synthesis (Chapter 12).
- A distorted colour solid such as the RGB cube that has undergone a linear or non-linear transformation.
- A two-dimensional texture function repeated along one axis. Say, for example, we have a frame-grabbed image $T(u,v)$: we could use this to generate a three-dimensional texture field as follows:

$$O(x_w, y_w, z_w) = T(x_w, y_w)$$

7.7   Texture anti-aliasing

Compare the efficacy of the two texture anti-aliasing methods described in the text; mip-mapping (Wilhems, 1987) and EWA filtering (Greene and Heckbert, 1986).

7.8   Environment mapping (*)

Implement an environment mapping scheme using any predeveloped ray tracing software to trace V rays from each pixel into the environment.

You can build an environment map for a simulated interior by rendering the interior six times from the point of view of the object that is to be mapped, that is, six viewing planes on the faces of a cube that surround the object.

How can light sources be incorporated into the environment map?

7.9   Environment mapping and anti-aliasing

Anti-aliasing operations in environment mapping are just as important as they are in texture mapping. If a surface has a high curvature, adjacent pixels in the view plane can produce reflected view vectors that map into non-adjacent pixels in the environment maps. An obvious solution is to find the area subtended by the rays through each pixel corner (Figure 7.21) and to obtain an average value. Implement this scheme.

A short note on diffuse and specular tables

Miller and Hoffman (1984) generalize environment mapping to include specular and diffuse reflection tables. Tables are precomputed, reducing the mapping process to table look up indexed by the surface normal N and V_r, the reflected view vector. These tables are dependent on the properties of specific objects and this specificity is one of the disadvantages of the methods. This work is also reported in Greene and Heckbert (1986).

Miller and Hoffman start with a simulated or photographed environment map on six faces of a cube. This they refer to as an illumination table. It is from this basic map that the diffuse and specular tables are precomputed. Theses tables are essentially two-dimensional look-up tables. They are indexed by vectors that are converted into a two-dimensional form (for example, by converting into polar coordinates, or into a point on the surface of the enclosing cube).

To create the diffuse table the illumination map is convolved with a Lambert's law cosine function. The diffuse map is given by:

$$D(N) = \sum_L I(L)\,\text{Area}(L)f_\text{d}(N \cdot L)$$

where, for a particular value of N, L ranges over all possible directions into the illumination table $I(L)$, Area is the angular area subtended by sampling with L and f_d is the diffuse convolution function. Miller and Hoffman give the following examples of this convention for f_d:

- Lambertian reflection: k_d is the diffuse reflection coefficient and

$$f_d(N \cdot L) = \begin{cases} k_d(N \cdot L) & \text{for } N \cdot L > 0 \\ 0 & \text{for } N \cdot L \leq 0 \end{cases}$$

- Light sources:

$$f_d(N \cdot L) = k_d \text{ for all } N \cdot L$$

From this it can be seen that the diffuse table is a blurred version of the illumination map that is to be indexed by N, the surface normal, and this scheme reduces finding diffuse illumination to a single table look up. The diffuse table is computed and stored at very low resolution (by definition it contains no high-frequency components). Miller and Hoffman quote 36×72 pixels (equivalent to Gouraud-shaded spheres with facets at every $5°$).

The specular table indexed by V_r is given by:

$$S(V_r) = \sum_L I(L) \, \text{Area}(L) f_s(V_r \cdot L)$$

where f_s is the specular convolution function, for example:

$$f_s(V_r \cdot L) = k_s(V_r \cdot L)^n$$

In this case, by raising $V_r \cdot L$ to a power, there is no weighting given to elements where V_r and L are more than a few degrees apart, giving the effect of near-mirror-like reflections with a small amount of scattering. This is similar to the way the specular term is evaluated in Phong shading.

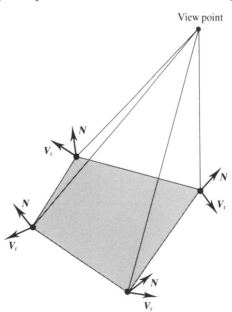

Figure 7.23
Vertex normals and vertex reflected view vectors are calculated for each vertex in the model and then interpolated.

7.10   Environment mapping – diffuse and specular tables

Compute diffuse and specular tables as outlined above and with a ray tracing scheme use V_r to index the specular table and N to index the diffuse table.

7.11   Environment mapping – polygon mesh objects

Implement the diffuse and specular table approach for polygon mesh objects using a conventional renderer. Do this by calculating a vertex normal (as in Phong shading) and using this normal to calculate a V_r for each vertex (Figure 7.23). During scan conversion both the vertex normals and the V_r are interpolated in the usual way. This gives for each pixel in each polygon an interpolated N and V_r to index the diffuse and specular table respectively.

8 | Ray Tracing

8.1 Introduction

It is often stated that ray tracing has produced the most realistic images to date in computer graphics. It is more the case that ray tracing has produced extremely impressive images of scenes that are carefully chosen to demonstrate the attributes of the ray tracing model; for example, the ability of the technique to deal with specular interaction between objects. Thus most examples contain mixtures of highly reflective and highly transparent procedurally defined objects. These scenes, examples of which abound in the literature on ray tracing, are also characterized by the frequent occurrence of spheres – for reasons that will later become clear. Both the choice of objects that tend to appear in ray-traced scenes, and the fact that ray tracing is only a partial solution to the global illumination–reflection problem, result in images that are indisputably impressive but which exhibit a ray-traced 'signature'. The nature of and reasons for this signature will become apparent as this chapter proceeds, and the difficulties and limitations of ray tracing are revealed.

Ray tracing is currently the most complete simulation of an illumination–reflection model in computer graphics. The local reflection models introduced earlier can be seen as simplifications of ray tracing. In both simple local reflection models and in ray tracing, light is simulated as infinitely thin rays travelling in a straight line through homogeneous media. The difference between a simple reflection model and a ray-traced model is the 'depth' to which interaction between light rays and objects in the scene is examined.

The basic philosophy of ray tracing is that an observer sees a point on a surface as a result of the interaction of the surface at that point with rays emanating from elsewhere in the scene. In simple surface reflection models, only the interaction of surface points with direct illumination from light sources is considered. In general, however, a light ray may reach the surface indirectly via reflection in other surfaces, transmission through partially transparent objects, or a combination of these. This is often referred to as **global illumination** – light that originates from the scene environment rather than from local interaction of the surface with direct illumination from the light source or sources.

The method possesses a number of disadvantages, the most important being extremely high processing overheads. Ray-traced images typically take many minutes, hours or even days to compute. Its significant advantage is that it is a partial solution to the global illumination problem, elegantly combining in a single model:

- hidden surface removal,
- shading due to direct illumination,
- shading due to global illumination, and
- shadow computation.

We look first at the theoretical and practical details necessary to implement a very simple ray tracing program. Next we look at various established extensions to ray tracing.

8.2   Basic algorithm

Ray tracing is an algorithm that works entirely in object space. At a point in the image plane, the surfaces visible and hence colour and intensity at that point are obtained by tracing a ray backwards from the eye through the point into the scene. If this ray intersects an object, then local calculations will determine the colour that is the result of direct illumination at that point. This is light from a light source directly reflecting from the surface. If the object is partially reflective, partially transparent or both, the colour of the point in the image plane will include a contribution from reflected and transmitted rays. These must be traced backwards to discover their contribution. Determining a colour for each of these rays may itself require the tracing of further rays at other intersections with objects. To determine the colour of the original point in the viewing plane completely, this set of rays must be traced backwards through the scene. The trace of a particular ray in the set terminates when no more objects are intersected (the ray is allotted a background colour), or if so many surface intersections separate it from the observer that its colour contribution to the image is likely to be negligible.

A ray is started from the observer through each point that is to be defined in the viewing plane, or image plane. In a simple program a ray is traced through the centre of each pixel in the image plane. This means that the scene is sampled in object space by infinitesimally thin rays. The process uses zero spatial coherence (all rays are traced independently – no informa-

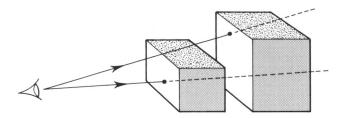

Figure 8.1
Terminating a ray trace
at the first intersection
gives hidden surface
removal.

tion discovered by neighbouring rays is used) and the sampling produces aliasing. On the other hand, the fact that each ray calculation is independent of all others makes implementation in parallel processing hardware trivial. The process is easily distributable. For example an implementation of a standard ray tracing program on transputers is given by Atkin (1986).

Ray tracing was originally used in computer graphics by Appel (1968). Here it was used only as a solution to the hidden surface problem in a general rendering system for three-dimensional objects. The ray tracing in this case stops at the first intersection of the ray and a surface (Figure 8.1). Such intersections are then categorized as visible points in the screen image. A simple implementation of this algorithm would search for an intersection between the ray and all surfaces in the scene, the intersection nearest to the viewer being the one required. These initial rays are sometimes called viewer rays, hidden surface rays or first-level rays.

Note at this point that in a scene containing highly reflective objects the 'conventional' hidden surface solution is no longer apt. Surfaces of an object, which would be back surfaces if the object was isolated, may be reflected in the front surfaces of an adjacent object (Figure 8.2). Culling or depth-sorting techniques cannot be used for such scenes.

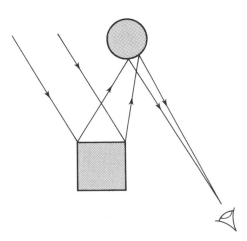

Figure 8.2
In a ray-traced scene
'back' surfaces of an
object may be visible.
Here a back surface of
the cube is reflected in
the sphere.

The first use of a ray tracing model to trace beyond the initial ray–surface intersection and incorporate reflection, refraction and shadows was developed in 1979 (Kay, 1979; Whitted, 1980) and most simple ray tracing procedures use the model detailed in these reports.

8.3   A historical digression – the optics of the rainbow

Many people associate the term 'ray tracing' with a novel technique but in fact it has always been part of geometric optics. For example, an early use of ray tracing in geometric optics is René Descartes' treatise, published in 1637, explaining the shape of the rainbow. From experimental observations involving a spherical glass flask filled with water, Descartes used ray tracing as a theoretical framework to explain the phenomenon. Descartes used the already known laws of reflection and refraction to trace rays through a spherical drop of water.

Rays entering a spherical water drop are refracted at the first air–water interface, internally reflected at the water–air interface and finally refracted as they emerge from the drop. As shown in Figure 8.3, horizontal rays entering the drop above the horizontal diameter emerge at an increasing angle with respect to the incident ray. Up to a certain maximum the angle of the exit ray is a function of the height of the incident ray above the horizontal diameter. This trend continues up to a certain ray, when the behaviour reverses and the angle between the incident and exit ray decreases. This ray is known as the Descartes ray, and at this point the angle between the incident and exit ray is 42°. Incident rays close to the Descartes ray emerge close to it and Figure 8.3 shows a concentration of rays around the exiting Descartes ray. It is this concentration of rays that makes the rainbow visible.

Figure 8.4 demonstrates the formation of the rainbow. An observer looking away from the sun sees a rainbow formed by '42°' rays from the sun. The paths of such rays form a 42° 'hemi-cone' centred at the observer's eye. (An interesting consequence of this model is that each observer has his/her own personal rainbow.)

This early, elegant use of ray tracing did not, however, explain that magical attribute of the rainbow – colour. Thirty years would elapse before Newton discovered that white light contained light at all wavelengths. Along with the fact that the refractive index of any material varies for light of different wavelength, Descartes's original model is easily extended. About 42° is the maximum angle for red light, while violet rays emerge after being reflected and refracted through 40°. The model can then be seen as a set of concentric hemicones, one for each wavelength, centred on the observer's eye.

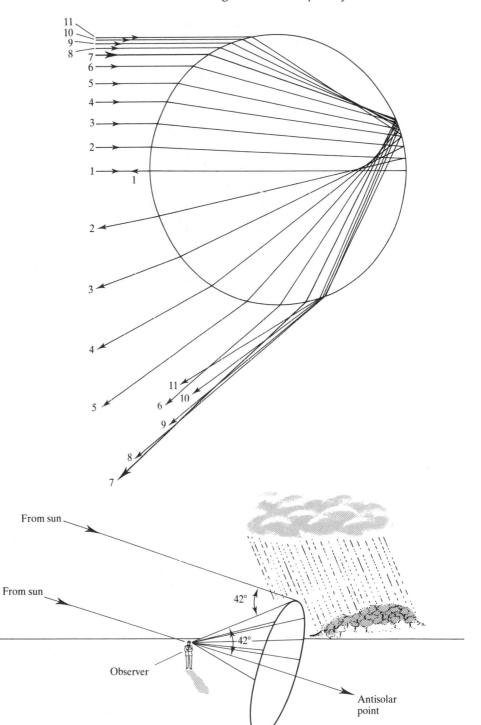

Figure 8.3
Tracing rays through a
spherical water drop
(ray 7 is the Descartes
ray).

Figure 8.4
Formation of a
rainbow.

This simple model is also used to account for the fainter secondary rainbow. This occurs at 51° and is due to two internal reflections inside the water drops.

8.4   Recursive implementation of ray tracing

The implementation of a general ray tracing algorithm is quite difficult for two reasons: the geometrical calculations are elaborate and the execution time is long. Execution time can be reduced for test runs by generating images at a lower spatial resolution than finally required, but this process may mask errors whose effect is slight and only visible in the final resolution image. A simple ray tracer for scenes of restricted geometry is straightforward.

In this section, we discuss the implementation of a simple ray tracing model in a language that supports recursion. Since the ray tracing procedure is purely recursive there is little point in implementation in a non-recursive language. A (recursive) procedure activation has its own private copy of the workspace required for its parameters and local variables and this, together with the recursive control mechanism of a language like Pascal, relieves the user of many of the bookkeeping tasks that would otherwise be associated with an implementation of ray tracing.

In Figure 8.5, a ray (ray 1) is being traced backwards from the eye through a pixel on the screen into an environment containing semi-transparent spheres (that is, objects that reflect and refract transmitted light). The colour to be seen along this ray will be the result of an analysis of its intersection with the first object surface encountered during the backwards trace of the ray. The colour seen coming along the ray from the surface (and hence the colour required at the pixel) is made up of three contributions: local colour due to illumination of the surface by direct and ambient light; a colour contribution from the reflection of a ray (ray 2) coming from the reflection direction; and a colour contribution from the transmission of a ray (ray 3) coming from the refraction direction.

The colour contribution from the reflection ray (ray 2) can be discovered by tracing this ray backwards to its first intersection (if any) with an object. The colour at this intersection will itself be made up of three contributions: local, reflected and transmitted. The reflected and transmitted contributions at this intersection are obtained by backward tracing rays 4 and 5, and so on. The transmitted contribution to ray 1 needs to be calculated in the same way by tracing ray 3 back to its next intersection, and so on.

Figure 8.6 shows the analysis that takes place at each intersection of a ray with a surface. The tree of Figure 8.7 shows the complete pattern of intersection analyses that need to be done to discover the colour perceived

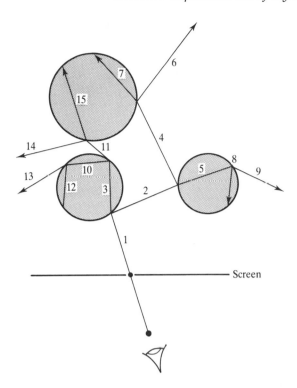

Figure 8.5
A simple example
demonstrating the
recursive nature of ray
tracing.

along ray 1. In Figure 8.7, we have assumed a trace depth of 4. This implies the assumption that, beyond four intersections, any colour contribution to the first-level ray will be negligible. Whether or not this is a reasonable assumption is discussed in Section 8.10.1.

In order to discover the colour of the pixel corresponding to ray 1 in Figure 8.5, a call of a recursive procedure would be made with parameters representing the start point and direction of this ray, together with a depth value to indicate the depth to which the trace should be carried out. An outline of such a procedure is given as Program 8.1.

Figure 8.8 shows the tree of procedure calls that takes place as a result of the above top-level call. The activation of the procedures in this tree takes place depth first and left to right. Thus, for example, the procedure calls for ray 2 and all its subsidiary rays are obeyed before the call for ray 3 is entered.

The procedure outline describes the situation at one intersection point and this model is used at every intersection point involved in the trace started by ray 1 in Figure 8.5.

Plate 13 (*bottom*) shows a ray-traced image of a rather contrived scene containing a mix of reflective and refractive spheres against a striped background. The background colour in all other directions is blue. Each

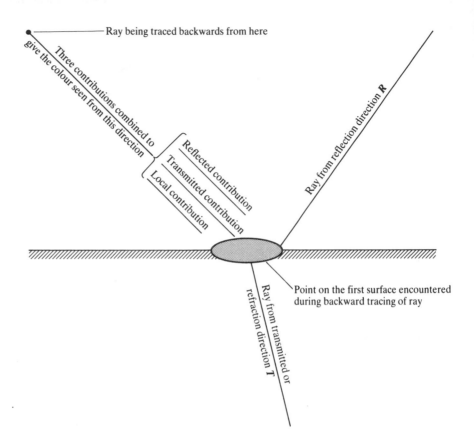

Figure 8.6
Details of three
contributions to the
intensity of a point on
a surface.

sphere displays a different mix of local colour, reflection and refraction. The
sphere at the bottom left is red. The spheres in the bottom row become
increasingly reflective from left to right. The sphere at the bottom right is
wholly reflective. Moving upwards, the spheres become more transparent.

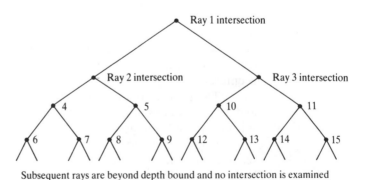

Figure 8.7
Ray tracing as a tree.

Program 8.1   An outline of a simple recursive ray tracing procedure.

```
procedure TraceRay (start, direction: vectors;
                         depth: integer; var colour: colours);

var intersection-point, reflected-direction,
     transmitted-direction: vectors;
     local-colour, reflected-colour,
     transmitted-colour: colours;

begin
   if depth > maxdepth then colour := black
   else
   begin
      {Intersect ray with all objects and find intersection point (if any)
       that is closest to start of ray}
      if {no intersection} then colour := background-colour
      else
      begin
         local-colour := {contribution of local colour model
                            at intersection-point}
         {Calculate direction of reflected ray}
         TraceRay(intersection-point, reflected-direction,
             depth + 1, reflected-colour);
         {Calculate direction of transmitted ray}
         TraceRay(intersection-point, transmitted-direction,
             depth + 1, transmitted-colour);
         Combine(colour,
             local-colour, local-weight-for-surface, reflected-colour,
             reflected-weight-for-surface, transmitted-colour,
             transmitted-weight-for-surface)
      end
   end
end {TraceRay};
```

The sphere at the top left is partially (50%) transparent and completely non-reflective. The sphere at the top right is completely transparent and looks rather strange. Perfectly transparent objects are not encountered in real life. The other spheres illustrate intermediate cases.

The trace depth used to produce Plate 13 was 6. The full effect of this can best be seen in the reflective sphere at the bottom right. This sphere contains an image of the rest of the scene (constructed with a trace depth of 5).

Note that with respect to the horizontal variation 'increasing reflectivity' actually refers to the relative proportions of local and global contributions controlled by the final process in the procedure outline. This, for

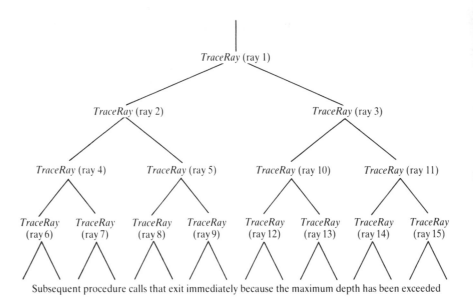

Figure 8.8
Tree of procedure calls.

example, changes the glossy red sphere into a perfect mirror sphere. On the left the local weight is 1 and the global weight is 0. On the right these proportions are reversed. In practice going along the bottom row, we should still always see the light source and it should end up as a point in the perfectly reflecting sphere. Problems like this arise in this simple approach to ray tracing and are entirely due to the hybrid nature of the model and the incorrect mixing of a spreading term (local illumination) with a non-spreading term (global illumination). (This particular deficiency can be overcome by enhancing the algorithm so that the traced rays are checked for intersection with the light source.)

8.4.1 A remark on efficiency

The structure of the procedure of Program 8.1 has certain drawbacks in terms of efficiency. In many recursive procedures, the simplest structure is obtained by making the test for the terminating condition at the start of the procedure and exiting immediately if this condition is satisfied. At the terminal branches of the tree of procedure calls, this involves unnecessary calls that terminate immediately. If the overheads in making the redundant calls are not too high then this is often an acceptable price to pay for program simplicity and transparency. In this case, making these extra calls involves doing the reflection and refraction geometry calculations for the calls. These calculations involve substantial real arithmetic.

Program 8.2   Improved efficiency in a naive ray tracing procedure.

```
procedure TraceRay (start, direction: vectors; depth: integer;
                        var colour: colours);

var intersection-point, reflected-direction,
    transmitted-direction: vectors;
    local-colour, reflected-colour,
    transmitted-colour: colours;

begin
    {Intersect ray with all objects and find intersection point (if any) that is
    closest to start of ray}
    if {no intersection} then colour := background-colour
    else
    begin
        local-colour := {contribution of local colour model at
                            intersection-point}
        if depth = maxdepth then
        begin
            reflected-colour := black; transmitted-colour := black
        end
        else
        begin
            {Calculate direction of reflected ray}
            TraceRay(intersection-point, reflected-direction,
                depth + 1, reflected-colour);
            {Calculate direction of transmitted ray}
            TraceRay(intersection-point, transmitted-direction,
                depth + 1, transmitted-colour);
        end;
        Combine(colour,
            local-colour, local-weight-for-surface, reflected-colour,
            reflected-weight-for-surface, transmitted-colour,
            transmitted-weight-for-surface)
    end
end {TraceRay};
```

The unnecessary procedure calls, and hence these calculations, can be eliminated by using the alternative structure of Program 8.2. An activation of this procedure does the local colour calculations first and then checks the current depth value to see if it is appropriate to make the calculations and procedure calls for the reflected and transmitted rays. This is the version of the ray tracing procedure that would be used in practice.

8.5   Ray tracing geometry

8.5.1   Intersections

Originally a ray traced backwards from the eye is tested against all objects in the scene for an intersection. The coordinates of the intersection points are retained and the one nearest the view point will be on the surface that is nearest to the viewer. This is the first intersection of the initial ray with the scene. This ray spawns (possibly) two more rays and each of these needs to be tested against all objects in the scene for intersection. Each node in the ray history tree is obtained in this way and it is easily seen that the program will spend a large proportion of its time testing for intersections between a ray and an object. Whitted (1980) estimated that, for scenes of moderate complexity, up to 95% of the processing time is spent in intersection calculations.

Whitted originally used a scheme of bounding volumes to speed up intersection calculations. First suggested by Clark (1976), each object in the scene has a bounding volume associated with it. An object of arbitrary complexity can be enclosed by a simple bounding volume whose intersections with a straight line are easily calculated. If a ray does not intersect the bounding volume, it cannot intersect the object. For an object represented by a large number of polygons this saves testing every polygon in the object against the ray.

Spheres have mostly been used as bounding volumes, although their suitability is critically dependent on the nature of the object. For example, long thin objects (Figure 8.9) will result in a situation where most rays that intersect the bounding sphere do *not* intersect the object. Because spherical objects and their bounding volumes coincide, early ray-traced images tend to contain only spheres. Bounding volumes are discussed further in Section 8.10.2.

Intersections: ray–sphere

As a simple initial example of an intersection calculation we now deal with the case of the sphere. The intersection between a ray and a sphere is easily calculated. If the end points of the ray are (x_1, y_1, z_1) and (x_2, y_2, z_2) then the first step is to parametrize the ray (Figure 8.10):

$$x = x_1 + (x_2 - x_1)t = x_1 + it$$
$$y = y_1 + (y_2 - y_1)t = y_1 + jt \qquad \qquad (8.1)$$
$$z = z_1 + (z_2 - z_1)t = z_1 + kt$$

A sphere at centre (l, m, n) of radius r is given by:

$$(x - l)^2 + (y - m)^2 + (z - n)^2 = r^2 \qquad \qquad (8.2)$$

Substituting for x, y and z gives a quadratic equation in t of the form:

$$at^2 + bt + c = 0 \qquad \qquad (8.3)$$

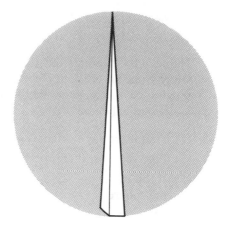

Figure 8.9
A sphere is an
inefficient bounding
volume for a long thin
object.

where:

$$a = i^2 + j^2 + k^2$$
$$b = 2i(x_1 - l) + 2j(y_1 - m) + 2k(z_1 - n)$$
$$c = l^2 + m^2 + n^2 + x_1{}^2 + y_1{}^2 + z_1{}^2 + 2(-lx_1 - my_1 - nz_1) - r^2$$

If the determinant of this quadratic is less than 0 then the line does not intersect the sphere. If the determinant equals 0 then the line grazes or is tangential to the sphere. The real roots of the quadratic give the front and back intersections. Substituting the values for t into the original parametric equations yields these points. Figure 8.10 shows that the value of t also gives the position of the points of intersection relative to (x_1, y_1, z_1) and (x_2, y_2, z_2). Only positive values of t are relevant and the smallest value of t corresponds to the intersection nearest to the start of the ray.

Other information that is usually required from an intersection is the surface normal (so that the reflected and refracted rays may be calculated) although, if the sphere is being used as a bounding volume, only the fact that an intersection has occurred, or not, is required.

If the intersection point is (x_i, y_i, z_i) and the centre of the sphere is (l, m, n) then the normal at the intersection point is:

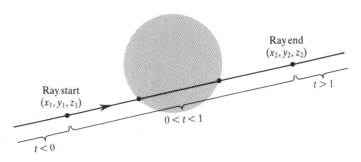

Figure 8.10
Values of parameter t
along a ray.

$$N = \left(\frac{x_i - l}{r}, \frac{y_i - m}{r}, \frac{z_i - n}{r} \right)$$

Haines (1989) points out that the special case of a sphere is worth further study from an efficiency point of view, and rather than just evaluating the quadratic, he suggests the following strategy, summarized here without mathematical detail:

(1) Find if the ray's origin is outside the sphere.

(2) Find the closest approach of the ray to the sphere's centre.

(3) If the ray is outside and points away from the sphere, the ray must miss the sphere.

(4) Else, find the squared distance from the closest approach to the sphere surface.

(5) If the value is negative, the ray misses the sphere.

(6) Else, from above, find the ray–surface distance.

(7) Calculate the intersection coordinates.

(8) Calculate the normal at the intersection point.

Intersections: ray–convex polyhedron

If an object is represented by a set of polygons and is convex then the straightforward approach is to test the ray individually against each polygon. We do this as follows:

(1) Obtain an equation for the plane containing the polygon.

(2) Check for an intersection between this plane and the ray.

(3) Check that this intersection is contained by the polygon.

For example, if the plane containing the polygon is:

$$ax + by + cz + d = 0$$

and the line is defined parametrically as before, then the intersection is given by:

$$t = -\frac{ax_1 + by_1 + cz_1 + d}{ai + bj + ck}$$

We can exit the test if $t < 0$. This means that the ray is in the half space defined by the plane that does not contain the polygon (Figure 8.11). We may also be able to exit if the denominator is equal to 0 which means that the line and plane are parallel. In this case the ray origin is either inside or outside the polyhedron. We can check this by examining the sign of the numerator. If the numerator is positive then the ray is in that half space

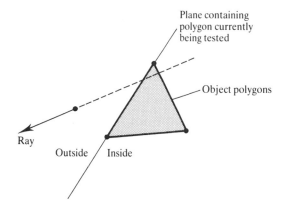

Figure 8.11
A ray in the half space that does not contain the object ($t < 0$).

defined by the plane that is outside the object and no further testing is necessary (Figure 8.12). A straightforward method that tests a point for containment by a polygon is simple but expensive. The sum of the angles between lines drawn from the point to each vertex is 360° if the point is inside the polygon, but not if the point lies outside.

There are three disavantages or inadequacies in this direct approach. We cannot stop when the first intersection emerges from the test unless we also evaluate whether the polygon is front- or back-facing with respect to the ray direction. The containment test is particularly expensive. (A fast direct containment test is given by Badouel (1990).) It is also possible for errors to occur when a ray and a polygon edge coincide. All of these disavantages can be overcome by a single algorithm developed by Haines (1991).

Again we use the concept of a plane that contains a polygon defining a half space. All points on one side of the plane are outside the polyhedron. Points on the other side may be contained by the polyhedron. The logical intersection of all inside half spaces is the space enclosed by the polyhedron.

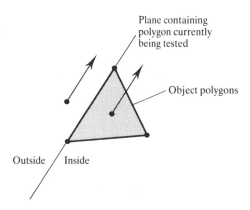

Figure 8.12
A possible exit condition. The ray is parallel to the plane containing the polygon currently being tested. It is either inside or outside the object.

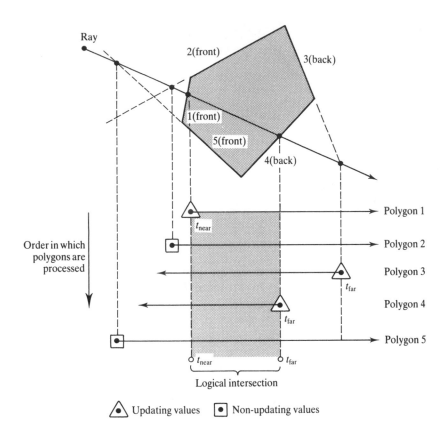

Figure 8.13
Ray–convex
polyhedron
intersection testing
(after Haines (1991)).

A ray that intersects a plane creates a directed line segment (unbounded in the direction of the ray) defined by the intersection point and the ray direction. It is easily seen that the logical intersection of all directed line segments gives the line segment that passes through the polyhedron. Proceeding as before, we exit from the test when a parallel ray occurs with an 'outside' origin. Otherwise the algorithm considers every polygon and evaluates the logical intersection of the directed line segments. Consider the example shown in Figure 8.13. For each plane we categorize it as front-facing or back-facing with respect to the ray direction. This is given by the sign of the denominator in the equation that appears towards the foot of p. 280 (positive for back-facing, negative for front-facing). The conditions that form the logical intersection of directed line segments are embedded in the algorithm which is:

{initialize t_{near} to large negative value
t_{far} to large positive value}

if *{plane is back-facing}* **and** $(t < t_{far})$ **then** $t_{far} = t$

if {*plane is front-facing*} **and** ($t > t_{near}$) **then** $t_{near} = t$

if ($t_{near} > t_{far}$) **then** {*exit – ray misses*}

Intersections: ray–box

Ray–box intersections are important because boxes may be more useful bounding volumes than spheres, particularly in hierarchical schemes. Also, generalized boxes can be used as an efficient bounding volume (Kay and Kajiya, 1986).

Generalized boxes are formed from pairs of parallel planes, but the pairs of planes can be at any angle with respect to each other. In this section we consider the special case of boxes forming rectangular solids, with the normals to each pair of planes aligned in the same direction as the ray tracing axes or the object space axes.

To check if a ray intersects such a box is straightforward and the algorithm is a special case of the ray–convex polyhedron example. We treat each pair of parallel planes in turn, calculating the distance along the ray to the first plane (t_{near}) and the distance to the second plane (t_{far}). The larger value of t_{near} and the smaller value of t_{far} are retained between comparisons. If the larger value of t_{near} is greater than the smaller value of t_{far}, the ray cannot intersect the box. This is shown for an example in the xy plane in Figure 8.14. If a hit occurs then the intersection is given by t_{near}.

A more succinct statement of the algorithm comes from considering the distance between the intersection points of a pair of parallel planes as intervals: if the intervals intersect, the ray hits the volume; if they do not intersect, the ray misses.

Again, because our convex polygon is reduced to a rectangular solid, we can define the required distances in terms of the box extent. Distances along the ray are given for the x plane pairs as follows. If the box extent is (x_{b1}, y_{b1}, z_{b1}) and (x_{b2}, y_{b2}, z_{b2}) then:

$$t_{1x} = \frac{x_{b1} - x_1}{x_2 - x_1}$$

is the distance along the ray from its origin to the intersection with the first plane, and:

$$t_{2x} = \frac{x_{b2} - x_1}{x_2 - x_1}$$

The calculations for t_{1y}, t_{2y} and t_{1z}, t_{2z} are similar. The largest value out of the t_1 set gives the required t_{near} and the smallest value of the t_2 set gives the required t_{far}. The algorithm can exit at the y plane calculations.

Intersections: ray–quadrics

The sphere example given earlier is a special case of rays intersecting with a general quadric. Ray–quadric intersections can be dealt with by considering

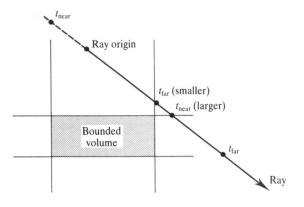

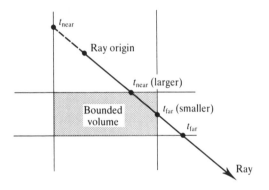

Figure 8.14
Ray–box intersection.

either the general case, or 'special' objects, such as cylinders, which can be treated individually for reasons of efficiency.

The general implicit equation for a quadric is:

$$Ax^2 + Ey^2 + Hz^2 + 2Bxy + 2Fyz + 2Cxz + 2Dx + 2Gy + 2Iz + J = 0$$

which is equivalent to:

$$[x \; y \; z \; 1] \begin{bmatrix} A & B & C & D \\ B & E & F & G \\ C & F & H & I \\ D & G & I & J \end{bmatrix} \begin{bmatrix} x \\ y \\ x \\ 1 \end{bmatrix} = 0$$

Following the same approach as we adopted for the case of the sphere, we substitute Equation 8.1 into the above and obtain the coefficients a, b and c for the quadratic as follows:

$$a = Ax_d^2 + Ey_d^2 + Hz_d^2 + 2Bx_dy_d + 2Cx_dz_d + 2Fy_dz_d$$
$$b = 2(Ax_1x_d + B(x_1y_d + x_dy_1) + C(x_1z_d + x_dz_1) + Dx_d + Ey_1y_d$$
$$+ F(y_1z_d + y_dz_1) + Gy_d + Hz_1z_d + Iz_d)$$

$$c = Ax_1{}^2 + Ey^2 + Hz_1{}^2 + 2Bx_1y_1 + 2Cx_1z_1 + 2Dx_1 + 2Fy_1z_1 \\ + 2Gy_1 + 2Iz_1 + J$$

where (x_d, y_d, z_d) is the normalized ray direction.

The equations for the quadrics are:

- Sphere

$$(x - l)^2 + (y - m)^2 + (z - n)^2 = r^2$$

where (l, m, n) is, as before, the centre of the sphere.

- Infinite cylinder

$$(x - l)^2 + (y - m)^2 = r^2$$

- Ellipsoid

$$\frac{(x - l)^2}{\alpha^2} + \frac{(y - m)^2}{\beta^2} + \frac{(z - n)^2}{\Gamma^2} - 1 = 0$$

where α, β and Γ are the semi-axes.

- Paraboloid

$$\frac{(x - l)^2}{\alpha^2} + \frac{(y - m)^2}{\beta^2} - z + n = 0$$

- Hyperboloid

$$\frac{(x - l)^2}{\alpha^2} + \frac{(y - m)^2}{\beta^2} + \frac{(z - n)^2}{\Gamma^2} - 1 = 0$$

If the objects are procedurally defined then the method used depends on the type of the definition. Kajiya (1983) gives efficient methods for three procedurally defined types: fractal surfaces, prisms and surfaces of revolution. A prism is a surface defined by translating a plane curve orthogonally and Kajiya points out that many objects used in computer graphics can be defined as (collections of) prisms, for example, block letters, machine parts formed by extrusion and simple models of urban architecture.

Details on intersecting a ray with bicubic patches are to be found in Joy and Bhetanabhotla (1986), Barr (1986), Steinberg (1984), Hanrahan (1983), Kajiya (1982), Potmesil and Chakrarvarty (1981) and Whitted (1980). Whitted uses an expensive approach which extends the bounding sphere approach to bicubic patches. Each patch on a surface is enclosed in a bounding sphere. If the sphere is intersected by a ray the patch is subdivided using a standard patch subdivision algorithm and each patch subdivision product is enclosed in a bounding sphere. This process is continued until either a bounding sphere, of preset minimum radius, is reached or the ray does not intersect the sphere. This recursive process of subdivision, enclosure in a bounding sphere and checking for intersection between the ray and the sphere will eventually produce a point of intersection whose accuracy is determined to within the radius of the minimum bounding sphere.

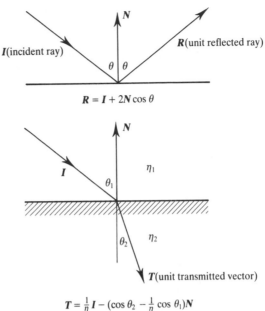

Figure 8.15
Reflection and
refraction geometry.

In contrast, Kajiya (1982) uses a direct numerical approach to ray–patch intersection.

8.5.2 Reflection and refraction

The formulae presented in this section are standard formulae in a form that is suitable for incorporation into a simple ray tracer.

Each time a ray intersects a surface it produces, in general, a reflected and refracted ray. The reflection direction, a unit vector, is given by:

$$R = I + 2N \cos \theta$$

where I and N are unit vectors representing the incident ray direction, which is the same as the light vector, and the surface normal respectively. L, R and N are coplanar. This is equivalent to Equation 1.2 where

$$I = -L$$

These vectors are shown in Figure 8.15.

A ray striking a partially or wholly transparent object is refracted owing to the change in the velocity of light in different media. The angles of incidence and refraction are related by Snell's law:

$$\frac{\sin \theta_1}{\sin \theta_2} = \frac{\eta_2}{\eta_1}$$

where the incident and transmitted rays are coplanar with N. The transmitted ray is represented by T and this is given by:

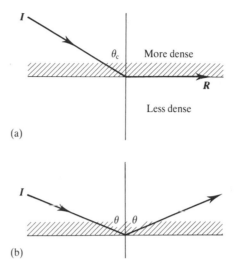

Figure 8.16
Internal reflection in an object. (a) θ_c = critical angle, (b) $\theta > \theta_c$.

$$T = \frac{1}{\eta} I - \left(\cos \theta_2 - \frac{1}{\eta} \cos \theta_1 \right) N$$

$$\eta = \frac{\eta_2}{\eta_1}$$

$$\cos \theta_2 = \eta \left(1 - \frac{1}{\eta^2} (1 - \cos^2 \theta_1) \right)^{1/2}$$

as shown in Figure 8.15. These formulae are given in Heckbert and Hanrahan (1984). They are equivalent to those used by Whitted (1980) but the formulae for the refracted ray are simpler.

If a ray is travelling from a more to a less dense medium then it is possible for the refracted ray to be parallel to the surface (Figure 8.16). θ_c is known as the critical angle. If θ is increased beyond θ_c then total internal reflection occurs.

8.6 Reflection–illumination model

At this stage it is useful to reiterate the difference between direct and global illumination and to look at how these considerations can be built in to a model that calculates intensity at a surface element. Direct illumination is light incident on a scene from a light source or a number of light sources. A surface element receives light directly from a source. On the other hand, if illumination from direct sources 'enters' a scene, and is incident on a surface element *after* interaction with another object or objects then that illumination is categorized as global. Global illumination arises from the interaction of direct light with reflective and transparent objects.

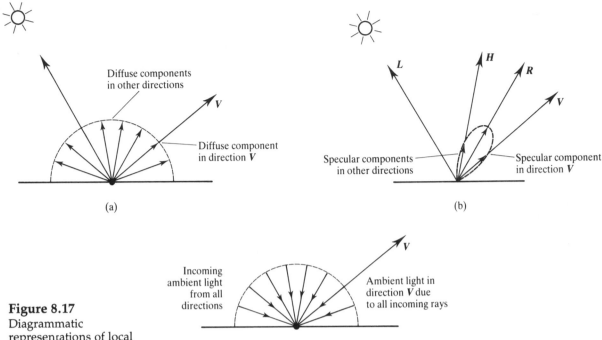

Figure 8.17
Diagrammatic
representations of local
reflection components.

In the Phong model for direct illumination, three terms are used:

$$I_{\text{phong}} = \frac{\text{diffuse}}{\text{term}} + \frac{\text{specular}}{\text{term}} + \frac{\text{ambient}}{\text{term}}$$

Each term in this equation is, of course, a vector of three RGB values.

The diffuse term and the specular term result from direct illumination and the ambient term results from diffuse light originating from the rest of the scene. In the Phong model the ambient term is modelled as a constant.

Figure 8.17 shows schematically how these reflection contributions are considered in computer graphics. A surface element exhibiting diffuse reflection radiates light equally in all directions, and specular reflection is concentrated around the reflection vector. The ambient term can be considered to originate from an infinity of incoming rays (or equivalently elemental light sources). Each one of these rays is reflected from the surface, and the overall summation of the reflections gives the ambient term. It is important to realize that although these effects are simulated in the local contribution, they are not in the global contribution. No diffuse interaction between objects is considered and the specular interaction involves simply tracing infinitesimally thin rays that are not spread (as are the rays from light sources in the local contribution).

The local component is calculated as before, using the Phong reflec-

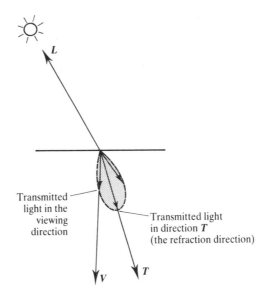

Figure 8.18
Extending the Phong model to account for the spread of transmitted light in a transparent object.

tion model, which is extended by another term that accounts for transparent objects. This is light that is seen through a transparent object due to a light source located at the other side of it. This term generalizes the direct illumination component of the model. The scattering of light transmitted through a medium blurs the image of a point light source, just as a surface that is not perfectly smooth reflects a highlight that is a spread or blur of a point source. The scattering can be modelled in the same empirical manner:

$$I_{\text{direct transmsitted}} = k_{\text{t}}(N \cdot H')^n$$

Recall that H, the bisector of the angle between the light source vector and the viewer, is the angle at which the surface microfacets have to be oriented to reflect light maximally to the viewer. Similarly, H' is the orientation that surface microfacets must possess to refract light maximally to the viewer (Figure 8.18). H' is thus a function of I, V and the relative index of refraction:

$$H' = \frac{-L - (\eta_2/\eta_1)V}{\eta_2/\eta_1 - 1} = \frac{-L - \eta V}{\eta - 1}$$

In ray tracing models it is useful to forget that the ambient term (which is anyway modelled as a constant) is technically a global term, and categorize all these terms as local. Local terms are those that are calculated at each surface intersection owing to direct illumination and ambient light. Our comprehensive local model is now:

$$I_{\text{local}} = I_{\text{a}}k_{\text{a}} + I_{\text{i}}[k_{\text{d}}(N \cdot L) + k_{\text{s}}(N \cdot H)^{n_{\text{s}}} + k_{\text{t}}(N \cdot H')^{n_{\text{t}}})] \qquad (8.4)$$

Note that for a given light source only one of the last two terms can be active. H and H' are calculated by using V, the view vector. To see the local specular reflection component we would have to be above the surface, but to see the local transmitted specular component the viewer would have to be positioned below the surface. In ray tracing, to this model are added two more terms, described as global. These are the contributions from a reflected ray incident on the surface element and from a transmitted ray incident on the surface element (if the object is transparent), originating from elsewhere in the scene. Both these are traced rays whose colour contributions are returned by the recursive ray tracing procedure:

$$I = I_{\text{local}} + k_{\text{rg}} I_{\text{reflected}} + k_{\text{tg}} I_{\text{transmitted}}$$

It is important to realize that this expresses the summation of the three values at a particular point in the recursive process. $I_{\text{transmitted}}$ invokes an equivalent expression at the next surface intersected by the transmitted ray, and $I_{\text{reflected}}$ invokes an equivalent expression at the next surface intersected by the reflected ray. Thus in any multi-object scene we can consider that reflection from a visible surface element will originate from three sources:

(1) ambient light – a surface element will always receive ambient light;

(2) direct light source(s) – a surface element will receive illumination from such a source if it is visible to the source; in our treatment 1 and 2 are considered as local terms;

(3) traced rays of light concentrated along particular directions because of interaction between objects.

Ray tracing is essentially a hybrid model – some rays are traced others are not. In the direct specular term, spread is calculated empirically, rather than by ray tracing. On the other hand, in ray-traced global terms, the transmitted and reflected rays are not spread (even although the direct reflection term *is* spread). Thus rays from direct illumination are spread (empirically) but rays from the eye (traced rays) are not. This is an inherent contradiction in the model and again underlines the fact that models in computer graphics are a combination of theoretical and empirical 'fixes' that are tuned until an acceptable image-generation tool is achieved. Reflections in an object, from other items in the scene, appear as if that object was a perfect mirror. Similarly, rays traced through objects appear as if the object was a perfect transmitter. This effect is somewhat diminished, because the image of one object in the other is usually less in size and intensity than the original, but it does contribute to the ray-traced signature of sharp reflections, refractions and shadows.

The final expression for a simple ray tracing model is:

$$\begin{aligned} I &= I_{\text{local}} + I_{\text{global}} \\ &= I_{\text{a}} k_{\text{a}} + I_{\text{i}} (k_{\text{d}} (N \cdot L) + k_{\text{s}} (N \cdot H)^n + k_{\text{t}} (N \cdot H')^n) + k_{\text{tg}} I_{\text{t}} + k_{\text{rg}} I_{\text{r}} \end{aligned}$$

$$\text{(8.5)}$$

k_a and k_d are functions of wavelengths, as before, and the local contribution would be evaluated for RGB components. Note that I_t and I_r are, in fact, RGB vectors since they are returning intensities that may have a local component. Also note that this equation does not explicitly reflect the recursive nature of the process used to obtain the I_t and I_r values, but gives a value for I at one stage in the recursive process. To emphasize the recursive nature of the process we could write Equation 8.5 as

$$I(P) = I_{local}(P) + k_{rg}I(P_r) + k_{tg}(P_t)$$

where:

P is the intersection point under consideration

P_r is the first hit of the reflected ray from P

P_t is the first hit of the transmitted ray from P

Finally note that Equation 8.5 also reflects the different theoretical domains of the two contributions. In practice, k_s should equal k_{rg}, but in this simple model it is convenient to use k_s to control the intensity of any highlight due to direct illumination, and k_{rg} to control the mirror reflectivity of objects in any multiple reflecting path. This point was discussed in relation to Plate 13 and accounts for the inconsistent appearance in a specularly reflecting object of sharp reflections of objects but blurred reflection of point light sources. Exactly the same considerations apply to k_t and k_{tg}.

A useful abstraction that puts the above model in perspective is Figure 8.19 which is based on an illustration by Wallace, Cohen and Greenberg (1987). In the model just described only 'mechanism' (d) is implemented, but without the spread. Mechanism (b) is partially contained in the model in that diffuse spread from direct illumination is modelled in the local part of the equation.

Finally, consider a simple example. Figure 8.20 shows a two-dimensional slice of a simple scene consisting of two opaque background surfaces, a semitransparent surface and a totally reflecting surface. The calculation will proceed recursively to a depth of 3.

$$I = I_{local\ surface1} + k_{r1}I_{r1} + k_{t1}I_{t1}$$

I_{r1} and I_{t1} are then calculated using the same expression giving:

$$I_{r1} = I_{local\ background2} + 0 + 0$$
$$I_{t1} = I_{local\ surface2} + k_{r2}I_{r2} + 0$$

The recursion now terminates with the evaluation of I_{r2}:

$$I_{r2} = I_{local\ background1} + 0 + 0$$

The contribution made to an image by the different levels of the trace can be seen in Plate 13. This contains four images of the portion of the scene marked in Plate 13. These four images were produced with maximum trace depths of 1, 2, 3 and 4. A black region in one of these images represents an

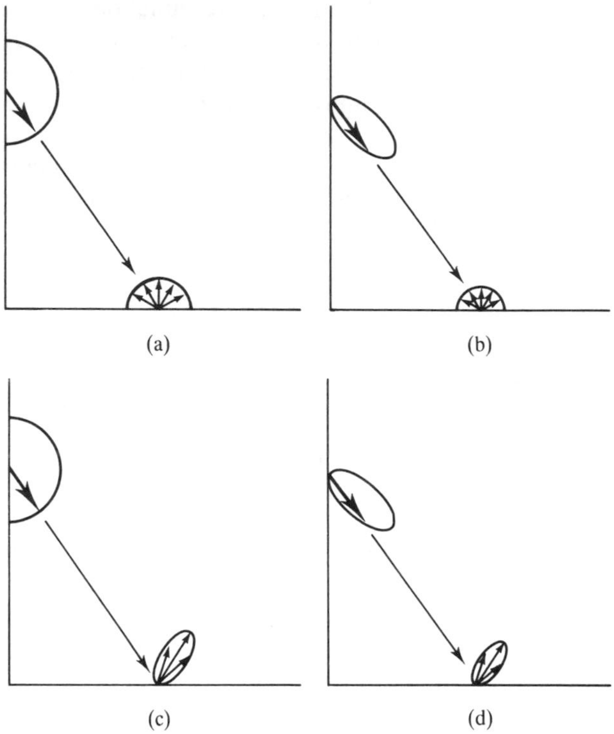

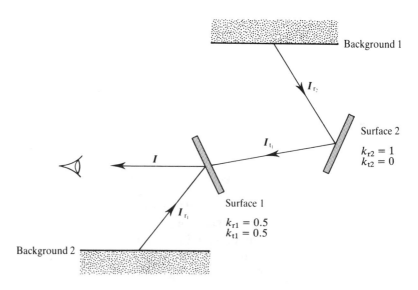

Figure 8.19
The four 'mechanisms' of light transport: (a) diffuse to diffuse; (b) specular to diffuse; (c) diffuse to specular; (d) specular to specular. (After Wallace, Cohen and Greenberg (1987)).

Figure 8.20
Ray tracing a simple two-dimensional scene.

object at which the trace was terminated 'prematurely' at a reflective surface (for the purpose of demonstration we have set the local specular reflection coefficient in the reflective spheres to zero). Tracing to depth 1 results in both reflective spheres appearing dark. All the detail that should be seen in the spheres has to be obtained by tracing rays that have been reflected (rays at depth 2 or beyond). Similarly, with maximum trace depth set to 2, reflections of mirror spheres appear black, and so on. A satisfactory level of detail in the reflected images is obtained for this scene with a maximum trace depth of 4.

With the adaptive depth modification discussed in Section 8.10.1, the depth of trace would vary for different parts of the scene. In some places, a depth of 1 would be adequate, in others a depth of 4 or more might be necessary.

8.7 Shadows

Shadows are easily incorporated into the reflection–illumination model described above. At each ray intersection I_{local} is computed. As described in the previous section this assumes that L, the light source vector (or vectors if there is more than one light source), is not interrupted by any objects in the path of this vector. If L is so interrupted then the current surface point lies in shadow. Whether other objects lie in the path of L is determined by creating an additional ray (called a **shadow feeler**) from the point to the light source (or to each light source in turn). If a wholly opaque object lies in the path of the shadow feeler then I_{local} is reduced to the ambient value. An attenuation in I_{local} is calculated if the intersecting object is partially transparent. Note that it is no longer appropriate to consider L as a constant vector (light source at infinity) and the so-called shadow feelers are rays whose direction is that of L.

Strictly speaking, a shadow feeler intersecting partially transparent objects should be refracted. It is not possible to do this, however, in the simple scheme described. The shadow feeler is initially calculated as the straight line between the surface intersection and the light source. This is an easy calculation and it would be difficult to trace a ray from this point to the light source and include refractive effects.

Finally note that, as the number of light sources increases from one, the computational overheads for shadow testing rapidly predominate. This is because the 'main' rays are only traced to an average depth of between 1 and 2 (see adaptive depth control in Section 8.10.1). However, each ray–surface intersection spawns n shadow feelers (where n is the number of light sources) and the object intersection costs for a shadow feeler are exactly the same as for a main ray.

A recent development (Haines and Greenberg (1986)) uses a 'light buffer' as a shadow testing accelerator. Shadow testing times were reduced using this procedure by a factor of between 4 and 30.

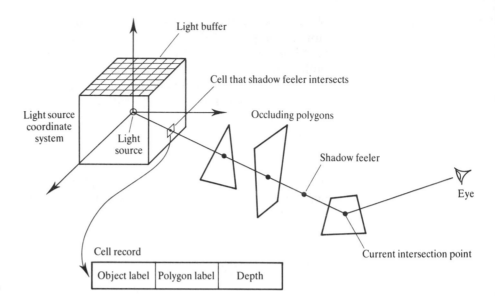

Figure 8.21
Shadow testing
accelerator of Haines
and Greenberg (1986).

The method precalculates, for each light source, a light buffer which is a set of cells or records, geometrically disposed as two-dimensional arrays on the six faces of a cube surrounding a point light source (Figure 8.21). To set up this data structure all polygons in the scene are cast or projected onto each face of the cube, using as a projection centre the position of the light source. Each cell in the light buffer then contains a list of polygons that can be seen from the light source. The depth of each polygon is calculated in a local coordinate system based on the light source, and the records are sorted in ascending order of depth. This means that for a particular ray from the eye, there is immediately available a list of those object faces that *may* occlude the intersection point under consideration.

Shadow testing reduces to finding the cell through which the shadow feeler ray passes, accessing the list of sorted polygons, and testing the polygons in the list until occlusion is found, or the depth of the potentially occluding polygon is greater than that of the intersection point (which means that there is no occlusion because the polygons are sorted in depth order).

The method deals with point light sources and the resulting images do not contain soft shadows or penumbrae. Storage requirements are prodigious and depend on the number of light sources and the resolution of the light buffers.

8.8   Distributed ray tracing

Earlier it was pointed out that there are inherent contradictions in the reflection–illumination model that is used in standard ray tracing algorithms. In particular, the traced rays are not spread but continue from intersection to intersection as infinitely thin beams. This results in standard aliasing artefacts together with sharp shadows, sharp reflection and sharp refraction, resulting in a super-real signature for conventional ray-traced images.

Some of these problems can be overcome by both increasing the number of initial rays and spawning extra rays at intersections but this approach very soon becomes completely impractical because of the overheads. Distributed ray tracing, developed by Cook, Porter and Carpenter (1984), is an elegant method that circumvents the straightforward solution of adding a large number of extra rays. Both the anti-aliasing problem and the modelling of what Cook calls 'fuzzy phenomena' are solved by distributed ray tracing. Algorithmically, the anti-aliasing function is inherent to the process and is described in this section. However, the underlying theory of stochastic anti-aliasing – the method used – is presented in Chapter 11.

The motivation for distributed ray tracing can easily be seen by examining a conventional ray-traced image (see for example, Plate 13). The ray-traced surreal signature originates from the assumption of perfect reflection and transmission for the global component. Reflecting surfaces produce, in general, blurred reflections because of surface imperfections, similarly transmitting surfaces blur transmitted rays because of scattering in the material. As discussed above, the hybrid nature of a naive ray tracer allows reflections from a direct light source to cause a blurred reflection (or specular highlight), but global reflection/transmission is deemed to be perfect. In Cook, Porter and Carpenter (1984) these problems are overcome by causing the rays to follow paths other than that predicted by the *exact* reflection and transmission direction. This produces blurred reflection and transmission. The same model incorporates new effects – blurred shadows, depth of field, motion blur and anti-aliasing Cook (1986). The method uses 16 rays per pixel and its main attributes are:

- The process of distributing rays means that stochastic anti-aliasing becomes an integral part of the method.
- Distributing reflected rays produces blurry reflections.
- Distributing transmitted rays produces translucency.
- Distributing shadow rays results in penumbrae.
- Distributing ray origins over the camera lens area produces depth of field.
- Distributing rays in time produces motion blur (temporal anti-aliasing).

Consider, for example, reflection and transmission. Essentially the algorithm provides an estimate of the entire reflection and transmission lobe. As well as generating an estimate for the integral over a pixel by spawning 16 initial rays, we have to sample the reflection/transmission characteristic at each hit. Consider first how the method deals with reflected rays. Figure 8.22 shows a single ray from a pixel hitting two objects. At the first hit the

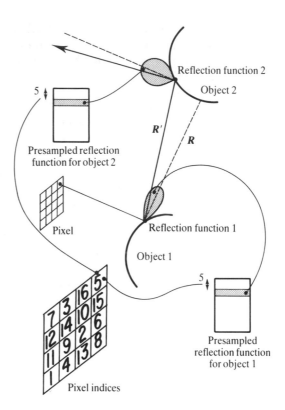

Figure 8.22
Distributed ray tracing
and reflected rays.

direction of the reflected ray is not necessarily the 'true' reflected direction, R, (and this deviation, of course, gives blurred reflections). Instead, jitter is used to implement 'importance' sampling. Here an emerging reflected direction is chosen on the basis of a precalculated importance-sampled reflection function. Given the angle between the reflected ray and the surface normal, a look-up table stores a range of reflection angles and a jitter magnitude.

The fact that rays emerge at some direction other than the previous reflected direction means that the second hit will occur at a different position to that given by the hit of the precise reflected direction (dotted line in Figure 8.22). Each object may exhibit a different specular reflection function and so the second object may index into a different table.

So far we have said nothing about how each look-up table index is chosen. Each ray derives an index as a function of its position in the pixel. The primary ray and all its descendants have the same index. This means that a ray emerging from a first hit along a direction relative to R will emerge from all other hits in the same relative R direction for each object. This ensures that each pixel intensity, which is finally determined from 16 samples, is based on samples that are distributed, according to the importance-sampling criterion, across the complete range of the specular reflection functions associated with each object. Note that there is nothing to prevent a look-up table from being two-dimensional and indexed also by the incoming angle. This enables specular reflection functions that depend on angle of incidence to be implemented. Finally, note that transmission is implemented in exactly the same way using specular transmission functions about the refraction direction.

8.9 Ray tracing and anti-aliasing operations

Ray tracing is a sampling method and suffers from the classic aliasing artefacts. However, the cost of ray tracing makes unintelligent oversampling an impractical solution.

A certain improvement is possible if rays are originated at pixel corners and averaged. Theoretically, nothing is gained from this approach; the same number of rays are originated, and we trade aliasing artefacts against blurring. Generating more rays by uniform subdivision of pixels is extremely expensive because the normal execution time is just multiplied by the subdivision factor. A better approach is to use the corner samples to control the subdivision. If a corner intensity differs from the other corner intensities by more than a certain amount then this quarter of the pixel is subdivided and seven more rays are originated. Stochastic sampling, described in Chapter 11, is possibly the best anti-aliasing method to use in ray tracing.

A more general approach to non-uniform oversampling is given by Mitchell (1987). The method has two important attributes:

- It is a context-dependent approach devoting most effect to areas of the image that require it.
- The anti-aliasing module is algorithmically separate from the ray tracing module and it can therefore be used in conjunction with a standard ray tracer or indeed any ray tracer.

The anti-aliasing operations occur in three stages:

(1) A ray tracing solution is constructed at a low sampling density, say for example, one ray per pixel.
(2) This solution is used to determine those areas that should be super-sampled.
(3) An image is constructed from those non-uniform samples by using an appropriate reconstruction filter.

Mitchell suggests a two-level sampling approach, where the supersampling is carried out at either four or nine samples per pixel (making this approach cheaper than distributed ray tracing). Whether to supersample or not is a decision that must be taken by examining small areas of the low resolution samples (3×3 areas are used in Mitchell (1987)). Mitchell points out that this approach is not infallible (nor theoretically correct). It will detect edges, where a 3×3 area straddles an edge, but it is likely to miss small isolated features. A contrast measure is used to make the decision. This is:

$$C = \frac{I_{\max} - I_{\min}}{I_{\max} + I_{\min}}$$

This yields three values of C in a conventional RGB ray tracer and different thresholds are used for the different wavelengths of 0.4, 0.3 and 0.6 respectively. This enables a gross simulation of the fact that the eye's sensitivity to noise or aliasing artefacts is a function of colour. The method thus produces non-uniform samples in both the image and the RGB domain.

In the final reconstruction phase the choice of a reconstruction filter (see Chapter 11) is made difficult by the sudden changes in sampling density. Mitchell uses a multistage filter with characteristics for each stage that copes with the nature of the samples.

8.10   Making ray tracing efficient

A conventional naive ray tracer is hopelessly impractical. Image generation time can be hours or even days. Much research effort has been devoted to ways of improving this situation. Several techniques that have gained wide acceptance are now described. The first, simplest and most inexpensive is a context-dependent constraint on the recursive depth, or the depth to which the ray is traced. This is an easy extension and should always be incorporated. The other approaches are more difficult to implement.

8.10.1   Adaptive depth control

In a naive ray tracer it is necessary to set up a maximum depth to which rays are traced. The recursive process is terminated when this depth is reached. For a particular scene this maximum depth is preset to a certain value which will depend on the nature of the scene. A scene containing highly reflective surfaces and transparent objects will require a higher maximum depth than a scene that consists entirely of poorly reflecting surfaces and opaque objects. If the depth is set equal to unity then the ray tracer functions exactly as a conventional renderer, which removes hidden surfaces and applies a local reflection model.

It is pointed out by Hall and Greenberg (1983) that the percentage of the scene that consists of highly transparent and reflective surfaces is, in general, small and it is thus inefficient to trace every ray to a maximum depth. Hall suggests using an adaptive depth control that depends on the properties of the materials with which the rays are interacting. The context of the ray being traced now determines the termination depth, which can be any value between unity and the maximum preset depth.

Rays are attenuated in various ways as they pass through a scene. When a ray is reflected at a surface, it is attenuated by the global specular

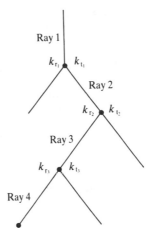

Figure 8.23
Reflected rays appear to the left at each node. Ray 4 contribution at the top level is attenuated by $k_{t_1} \times k_{r_2} \times k_{r_3}$.

reflection coefficient for the surface. When it is refracted at a surface, it is attenuated by the global transmission coefficient for the surface. For the moment, we consider only this attenuation at surface intersections. A ray that is being examined as a result of backward tracing through several intersections will make a contribution to the top-level ray that is attenuated by several of these coefficients. Figure 8.23 illustrates this. Any contribution from ray 4 to the colour at the top level is attenuated by the product of the global coefficients:

$$k_{t1} k_{r2} k_{r3}$$

If this value is below some threshold, there will be no point in tracing back further than ray 4.

In general, of course, there will be three colour contributions (RGB) for each ray and three components to each of the attenuation coefficients. For tutorial purposes, we assume a single coefficient at each intersection.

A new version of the procedure for recursive ray tracing procedure that will implement this adaptive depth control is given as Program 8.3. Each activation of this procedure is given a cumulative weight parameter that indicates the final weight that will be given at the top level to the colour returned for the ray represented by that procedure activation. The correct weight for a new procedure activation is easily calculated by taking the cumulative weight for the ray currently being traced and multiplying it by the reflection or transmission coefficient for the surface intersection at which the new ray is being created.

Another way in which a ray can be attenuated is by passing for some distance through an opaque material. This can be dealt with by associating a transmittance coefficient with the material composing an object. Colour values would then be attenuated by an amount determined by this coefficient and the distance a ray travels through the material. A simple addition

Program 8.3   Adaptive depth control in a recursive ray tracing procedure.

procedure *TraceRay* (*start*, *direction*: *vectors*; *depth*: *integer*;
                    var *colour*: *colours*; *cumulative-weight*: *real*);

var *intersection-point*, *reflected-direction*,
   transmitted-direction: *vectors*;
   local-colour, *reflected-colour*,
   transmitted-colour: *colours*;
begin
   if *cumulative-weight* < *weight-threshold* **then** *colour* := *black*
   else if *depth* > *maxdepth* **then** *colour* := *black*
   else
   begin
     {*Intersect ray with all objects and find intersection point* (*if any*)
       that is closest to start of ray}
     if {*no intersection*} **then** *colour* := *background-colour*
     else
     begin
       local-colour := {*contribution of local colour model at*
                     intersection-point}
       {*Calculate direction of reflected ray*}
       TraceRay(*intersection-point*, *reflected-direction*,
         depth + 1, *reflected-colour*, *cumulative-weight∗reflected-*
         weight-for-surface);
       {*Calculate direction of transmitted ray*}
       TraceRay(*intersection-point*, *transmitted-direction*,
         depth + 1, *transmitted-colour*, *cumulative-*
         weight∗transmitted-weight-for-surface);
       Combine(*colour*,
         local-colour, *local-weight-for-surface*, *reflected-colour*,
         reflected-weight-for-surface, *transmitted-colour*,
         transmitted-weight-for-surface)
     end
   end
end {*TraceRay*};

to the intersection calculation in the ray tracing procedure would allow this feature to be incorporated.

The use of adaptive depth control will prevent, for example, a ray that initially hits an almost opaque object spawning a transmitted ray that is then traced through the object and into the scene. The intensity returned from the scene may then be so attenuated by the initial object that this computation is obviated. Thus, depending on the value to which the threshold is preset, the ray will, in this case, be terminated at the first hit.

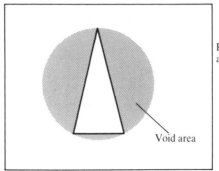

Projection of object
and sphere

Void area

Figure 8.24
The void area of a
bounding sphere.

For a highly reflective scene with a maximum tree depth of 15, Hall and Greenberg (1983) report that this method results in an average depth of 1.71, giving a large potential saving in image generation time. The actual saving achieved will depend on the nature and distribution of the objects in the scene.

8.10.2 Bounding volume extensions

As discussed in Section 8.5.1, the increase in efficiency gained by using bounding volumes depends critically on the choice of the bounding volume and how well the bounding volume encloses the complex object. Spheres are a popular choice because of the simplicity of the associated intersection test, but we have seen that spheres are unsuitable bounding volumes of long thin objects.

Weghorst, Hooper and Greenberg (1984) point out that the simplicity of the intersection test should not be the sole criterion in the selection of a bounding volume. They define a 'void' area of a bounding volume to be the difference in area between the orthogonal projections of the object and bounding volume onto a plane perpendicular to the ray and passing through the origin of the ray (see Figure 8.24). They show that the void area is a function of object, bounding volume and ray direction and define a cost function for an intersection test:

$$T = bB + iI$$

where:

T is the total cost function

b is the number of times that the bounding volume is tested for intersection

B is the cost of testing the bounding volume for intersection

i is the number of times that the item is tested for intersection (where $i \leqslant b$);

I is the cost of testing the item for intersection

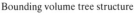

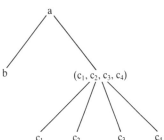

Figure 8.25
A simple scene and the associated bounding cylinder tree structure.

It is pointed out by the authors that the two products are generally inter-dependent. For example, reducing B by reducing the complexity of the bounding volume will almost certainly increase i. A quantitive approach to selecting the optimum of a sphere, a rectangular parallelepiped and a cylinder as bounding volumes is given.

A common extension to bounding volumes, first suggested by Rubin and Whitted (1980) and discussed by Weghorst, Hooper and Greenberg (1984), is to attempt to impose a hierarchical structure of such volumes on the scene. If it is possible, objects in close spatial proximity are allowed to form clusters, and the clusters are themselves enclosed in bounding volumes. For example Figure 8.25 shows a container (a), with one large object (b), and four small objects (c_1, c_2, c_3, and c_4) inside it. The tree represents the hierarchical relationship between seven boundary extents: a cylinder enclosing all the objects, a cylinder enclosing (b), a cylinder enclosing (c_1, c_2, c_3, c_4) and the bounding cylinders for each of these objects. A ray traced against bounding volumes means that such a tree is traversed from the topmost level. A ray that happened to intersect c_1 in the above example would, of course, be tested against the bounding volumes for c_1, c_2, c_3 and c_4, but only because it intersects the bounding volume representing that cluster. This example also demonstrates that the nature of the scene should enable reasonable clusters of adjacent objects to be selected if substantial savings over a non-hierarchical bounding scheme are to be achieved. Now the intersection test is implemented as a recursive process, descending through a hierarchy, only from those nodes where intersections occur. Thus a scene is grouped, where possible, into object clusters and each of those clusters may contain other groups of objects that are spatially clustered. Ideally, high-level clusters are enclosed in bounding volumes that contain lower level clusters and bounding volumes. Clusters can only be created if objects are sufficiently close to each other. Creating clusters of widely separated objects obviates the process. The potential clustering and the depth of the hierarchy will depend on the nature of the scene; the deeper the hierarchy the more the potential savings.

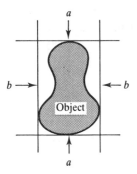

Bounding volume defined
by plane-set (a, b)

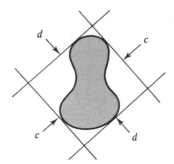

Bounding volume defined
by plane-set (c, d)

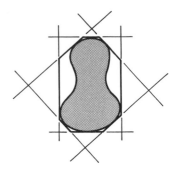

'Tight' bounding volume
defined by plane-set (a, b, c, d)

Figure 8.26
Defining a bounding
volume from the
maximum and
minimum extents of a
projection of the
object.

The disadvantage of this approach is that it depends critically on the nature of the scene. Also, considerable user investment is required to set up a suitable hierarchy.

Kay and Kajiya (1986) introduced a new type of bounding volume which can be made to fit the convex hulls of objects tightly. The authors also claim that the ray intersection test requires little computation. Their method thus overcomes the void area problem while retaining the advantages of a hierarchical bounding volume scheme. Objects are enclosed by bounding volumes made from polyhedra consisting of pairs of parallel planes. Computation and storage is constrained by restricting the orientation of the plane sets to presct directions. The position of pairs of planes is determined from the maximum and minimum extent of the object in a projection plane normal to the plane pair under consideration (Figure 8.26).

8.10.3   First-hit speed up

Earlier it was pointed out that even for highly reflective scenes, the average depth to which rays were traced was between 1 and 2. This fact led Weghorst, Hooper and Greenberg (1984) to suggest a hybrid ray tracer, where the intersection of the initial ray is evaluated during a preprocessing phase, using a hidden surface algorithm. The implication here is that the hidden surface algorithm will be more efficient than the general ray tracer for the first hit. Weghorst suggests executing a modified Z-buffer algorithm, using the same viewing parameters. Simple modifications to the Z-buffer algorithm will make it produce, for each pixel in the image plane, a pointer to the object visible at that pixel. Ray tracing, incorporating adaptive depth control, then proceeds from that point. Thus the expensive intersection tests associated with the first hit are eliminated.

Results in Weghorst, Hooper and Greenberg (1984) show that incorporating all these methods (adaptive depth control, hierarchical bounding volumes and first-hit speed up) show improvements that appear to be inversely dependent on scene complexity. For a scene of reasonable complexity the computation time is approximately half that of a naive ray tracer using spherical bounding volumes.

8.10.4 Spatial coherence

Currently, spatial coherence is the only approach that looks like making ray tracing a practical proposition for routine image synthesis. For this reason the use of spatial coherence is discussed in some detail.

Recent developments in ray tracing attempt to address the problem of unrealistic computation time by exploiting the spatial coherence of objects. Until recently, object coherence in ray tracing has generally been ignored. The reason is obvious. By its nature a ray tracing algorithm spawns rays of arbitrary direction anywhere in the scene. It is difficult to use such 'random' rays to access the object data structure and efficiently extract those objects in the path of a ray. Unlike an image space scan conversion algorithm where, for example, active polygons can be listed, there is no a priori information on the sequence of rays that will be spawned by an initial or view ray. Naive ray tracing algorithms execute an exhaustive search of all objects, perhaps modified by a scheme such as bounding volumes, to constrain the search.

The idea behind spatial coherence schemes is simple. The space occupied by the scene is subdivided into regions. Now, rather than check a ray against all objects or sets of bounded objects, we attempt to answer the question: is the region, through which the ray is currently travelling, occupied by any objects? Either there is nothing in this region, or the region contains a small subset of the objects. This group of objects is then tested for intersection with the ray. The size of the subset and the accuracy to which the spatial occupancy of the objects is determined varies, depending on the nature and number of the objects and the method used for subdividing the space.

This approach, variously termed **spatial coherence, spatial subdivision** or **space tracing** has been independently developed by several workers, notably Glassner (1984), Kaplan (1985) and Fujimoto, Tanaka and Iwata (1986). All of these approaches involve preprocessing the space to set up an auxiliary data structure that contains information about the object occupancy of the space. Rays are then traced using this auxiliary data structure to enter the object data structure. Note that this philosophy (of preprocessing the object environment to reduce the computational work required to compute a view) was first employed by Schumaker *et al.* (1969) in a hidden surface removal algorithm developed for flight simulators. In this algorithm, objects in the scene are clustered into groups by subdividing the space with planes. The spatial subdivision is represented by a binary tree. Any view point is located in a region represented by a leaf in the tree. An on-line tree traversal for a particular view point quickly yields a depth priority order for the group clusters. The important point about this algorithm is that the spatial subdivision is computed off-line and an auxiliary structure, the binary tree representing the subdivision, is used to determine an initial priority ordering for the object clusters. The motivation for this work was to speed up the on-line hidden surface removal processing and enable image generation to work in real time.

Dissatisfaction with the bounding volume or extent approach to reducing the number of ray–object intersection tests appears in part to have motivated the development of spatial coherence methods (Kaplan, 1985). One of the major objections to bounding volumes has already been pointed out. Their 'efficiency' is dependent on how well the object fills the space of the bounding volume. A more fundamental objection is that such a scheme may increase the efficiency of the ray–object intersection search, but it does nothing to reduce the dependence on the number of objects in the scene. Each ray must still be tested against the bounding extent of every object and the search time becomes a function of scene complexity. Also, although major savings can be achieved by using a hierarchical structure of bounding volumes, considerable investment is required to set up an appropriate hierarchy and, depending on the nature and disposition of objects in the scene, a hierarchical description may be difficult or impossible. The major innovation of methods described in this section is to make the rendering time constant (for a particular image space resolution) and to eliminate its dependency on scene complexity.

The various schemes that use the spatial coherence approach differ mainly in the type of auxiliary data structure used. Kaplan (1985) lists six properties that a practical ray tracing algorithm should exhibit if the technique is to be used in routine rendering applications. Kaplan's requirements are:

- Computation time should be relatively independent of scene complexity (number of objects in the environment, or complexity of individual objects), so that scenes having realistic levels of complexity can be rendered.

- Per ray time should be relatively constant, and not depend on the origin or direction of the ray. This property guarantees that overall computation time for a shaded image will be dependent only on overall image resolution (number of first-level rays traced) and shading effects (number of second-level and higher level rays traced). This guarantees predictable performance for a given image resolution and level of realism.

- Computation time should be 'rational' (say, within an hour) on currently available minicomputer processors, and should be 'interactive' (within a few minutes) on future affordable processor systems.

- The algorithm should not require the user to supply hierarchical object descriptions or object clustering information. The user should be able to combine data generated at different times, and by different means, into a single scene.

- The algorithm should deal with a wide variety of primitive geometric types, and should be easily extensible to new types.
- The algorithm's use of coherence should not reduce its applicability to parallel processing or other advanced architectures. Instead, it should be amenable to implementation on such architectures.

Kaplan summarizes these requirements by saying: '... in order to be really usable, it must be possible to trace a large number of rays in a complex environment in a rational, predictable time, for a reasonable cost.'

Two related approaches to an auxiliary data structure have emerged. These involve an octree representation (Fujimoto, Tanaka and Iwata, 1986; Glassner, 1984) and a data structure called a BSP (binary space partitioning). The BSP tree was originally proposed by Fuchs (1980) and is used in Kaplan (1985).

8.10.5   Use of an octree in ray tracing

An **octree** is a representation of the objects in a scene that allows us to exploit spatial coherence – objects that are close to each other in space are represented by nodes that are close to each other in the octree (Chapter 2).

When tracing a ray, instead of doing intersection calculations between the ray and every object in the scene, we can now trace the ray from subregion to subregion in the subdivision of occupied space. For each subregion that the ray passes through, there will only be a small number of objects (typically one or two) with which it could intersect. Provided that we can rapidly find the node in the octree that corresponds to a subregion that a ray is passing through, we have immediate access to the objects that are on, or close to, the path of the ray. Intersection calculations need only be done for these objects. If space has been subdivided to a level where each subregion contains only one or two objects, then the number of intersection tests required for a region is small and does not tend to increase with the complexity of the scene.

Tracking a ray using an octree

In order to use the space subdivision to determine which objects are close to a ray, we must determine which subregion of space the ray passes through. This involves tracking the ray into and out of each subregion in its path. The main operation required during this process is that of finding the node in the octree, and hence the region in space, that corresponds to a point (x, y, z).

The overall tracking process starts by detecting the region that corresponds to the start point of the ray. The ray is tested for intersection with any objects that lie in this region and if there are any intersections, then the first one encountered is the one required for the ray. If there are no intersections in the initial region, then the ray must be tracked into the next region through which it passes. This is done by calculating the intersection of the ray with the boundaries of the region and thus calculating the point at which the ray leaves the region. A point on the ray a short distance into the next region is then used to find the node in the octree that corresponds to the next region. Any objects in this region are then tested for intersections with the ray. The process is repeated as the ray tracks from region to region until an intersection with an object is found or until the ray leaves occupied space.

The simplest approach to finding the node in the octree that corresponds to a point (x,y,z) is to use a data structure representation of the octree to guide the search for the node. Starting at the top of the tree, a simple comparison of coordinates will determine which child node represents the subregion that contains the point (x,y,z). The subregion corresponding to the child node may itself have been subdivided, and another coordinate comparison will determine which of its children represents the smaller subregion that contains (x,y,z). The search proceeds down the tree until a terminal node is reached. The maximum number of nodes traversed during this search will be equal to the maximum depth of the tree. Even for a fairly fine subdivision of occupied space, the search length will be short. For example, if the space is subdivided at a resolution of $1024 \times 1024 \times 1024$, then the octree will have depth 10 ($= \log_8 (1024 \times 1024 \times 1024)$).

So far we have described a simple approach to the use of an octree representation of space occupancy to speed up the process of tracking a ray. Two variations of this basic approach are described by Glassner (1984) and Fujimoto, Tanaka and Iwata (1986). Glassner describes an alternative method for finding the node in the octree corresponding to a point (x,y,z). In fact, he does not store the structure of the octree explicitly, but accesses information about the voxels via a hash table that contains an entry for each voxel. The hash table is accessed using a code number calculated from the (x,y,z) coordinates of a point. The overall ray tracking process proceeds as described in our basic method.

In Fujimoto, Tanaka and Iwata (1986) an alternative approach to tracking the ray through the voxels in the octree is described. This method eliminates floating-point multiplications and divisions. To understand the method it is convenient to start by ignoring the octree representation. We first describe a simple data structure representation of a space subdivision called **SEADS** (spatially enumerated auxiliary data structure). This involves dividing all of occupied space into equally sized voxels regardless of occupancy by objects. The three-dimensional grid obtained in this way is analogous to that obtained by the subdivision of a two-dimensional graphics screen into pixels. Because regions are subdivided regardless of occupancy by objects, a SEADS subdivision generates many more voxels than the octree subdivision described earlier. It thus involves 'unnecessary' demands for storage space. However, the use of a SEADS enables very fast tracking of rays from region to region. The tracking algorithm used is an extension of the DDA (digital differential analyser) algorithm used in two-dimensional graphics for selecting the sequence of pixels that represents a straight line between two given end points. The DDA algorithm used in two-dimensional graphics selects a subset of the pixels passed through by a line, but the algorithm can easily be modified to find all the pixels touching the line. Fujimoto describes how this algorithm can be extended into three-dimensional space and used to track a ray through a SEADS three-dimensional grid. The advantage of the '3D-DDA' is that it does not involve floating-point multiplication and division. The only operations involved are addition, subtraction and comparison, the main operation being integer addition on voxel coordinates.

The heavy space overheads of the complete SEADS can be avoided by returning to an octree representation of the space subdivision. The 3D-DDA algorithm can be modified so that a ray is tracked through the voxels by traversing the octree. In the octree, a set of eight nodes with a common parent node represents a block of eight adjacent cubic regions forming a $2 \times 2 \times 2$ grid. When a ray is tracked from one region to another within this set, the 3D-DDA algorithm can be used without alteration. If a ray enters a region that is not represented by a terminal node in the tree, but is further subdivided, then the subregion that is entered is found by moving down the tree. The child node required at each level of descent can be discovered by adjusting the control variables of the DDA from the level above. If the 3D-DDA algorithm tracks a ray out of the $2 \times 2 \times 2$ region currently being traversed, then the octree must be traversed upward to the parent node representing the complete region. The 3D-DDA algorithm then continues at this level, tracking the ray within the set of eight regions containing the parent region. The upward and downward traversals of the tree involve multiplication and division of the DDA control variables by 2, but this is a cheap operation.

Projects, notes and suggestions ——————————

8.1   First-hit ray tracing

Implement a 'first-hit' ray tracer in which a ray is traced only as far as its first intersection with an object. The structure of the main procedure should be based on Program 8.1 but without the calculations for reflected and transmitted ray directions and without the recursive calls to trace these rays. This means that all the objects in the scene will appear to be completely opaque. Such a program will simply act as an expensive solution to the hidden surface removal problem. The advantage of doing this is that it will enable you to familiarize yourself with the basic structure of a ray tracing program without the added complication of handling recursion and calculations for reflection and transmission. Problems to be dealt with include:

- Intersection calculations: limit the objects in the scene to spheres and base the intersection calculations on Equations 8.1, 8.2 and 8.3.

- Colour calculations: use a simple local colour model based on Equation 8.4 without the last two terms for the specular components (one light source, no shadows).

- Data structures: the representation of each object will have to contain information about its position, its geometry and its surface properties. The objects will have to be linked together in some way to form a data structure representation of the scene.

8.2 Shadow calculations

Incorporate shadow feelers in the above simple model. This involves tracing an additional ray from each intersection with an object towards the light source. If that ray intersects an object on the way, then only the ambient term in Equation 8.4 should be used for colouring the point of intersection.

8.3 Intersection geometry

Implement data structures and intersection tests for other types of object. For example, a polygon mesh can be tested for intersection using the approach described earlier in this chapter.

There are various special cases for which intersection calculations can be speeded up. For example, intersection of a ray with a rectangular surface can be done more efficiently by expressing the coordinates of the point of intersection in a coordinate system whose z axis is perpendicular to the surface and whose x–y axes are parallel to the edges of the rectangle. The test for containment then becomes a simple x–y comparison. The coefficients for the coordinate transformation can be stored as part of the data structure for the surface. For a rectangular box, all six surfaces can be treated this way using a common set of axes.

A surface that is a circle can be treated in a similar way, using a coordinate system whose z axis is perpendicular to the surface and passes through the centre of the circle. This simplifies the test for containment of the point of intersection in the circle. For a cylinder, we can use a coordinate system whose z axis is the axis of the cylinder.

8.4 Specular highlights

Extend the local colour model to include specular highlights (the last two terms in Equation 8.4). The data structure for each object will have to be extended to include reflection and transmission coefficients for the object.

8.5   Recursive ray tracing

Extend the local colour model to include the two global terms of Equation 8.5. Evaluating these terms will involve recursive calls of the ray tracing procedure. The program you have developed so far will be slow. During the development phase, you should test it on a small subset of the screen and with a fairly shallow depth of trace (2 or 3). The number of objects in the scene will also have to be small.

8.6   Anti-aliasing

Implement the context-dependent anti-aliasing scheme due to Mitchell (1987) described in this chapter. The only problem with this method is in the choice of a reconstruction filter that copes with unevenly spaced sample points. Mitchell suggests the use of a multistage filter with a progressively lower cut-off frequency. In practical terms this means filtering the image with a box filter a quarter of a pixel wide. The output from this is then processed with a filter half a pixel wide, followed by a filter one pixel wide. This scheme copes with the fact that different areas of the image will exhibit a different two-dimensional frequency spectrum depending on the spatial sampling density.

8.7   Adaptive depth control

Modify the naive ray tracing program of this chapter to incorporate adaptive depth control. A preliminary version could use a single reflection and a single refraction coefficient at each interface in implementing the decision whether or not to terminate the trace. A final version would require three coefficients of each type at each interface, and the decision as to whether or not to continue the trace would depend on the maximum of the three attenuation factors for a ray.

8.8   Bounding volumes (*)

Create a simple scene that consists of a small number of separate clusters of objects (all spheres, say) where the clusters have differing shapes. Select an appropriate bounding volume for each cluster (a sphere, a cylinder or a box) and incorporate bounding volume tests in the intersection calculations for your ray tracer. This will involve the implementation of a hierarchical data structure where each bounding volume contains references to the data structures for the objects it contains. This could be extended to a hierarchical structure of bounding volumes where the bounding volumes themselves are contained in larger bounding volumes.

8.9   Objects defined by implicit quadric equations

Implement intersection tests for objects represented implicitly by quadric equations. Develop a system of boundary volumes that can be used to accelerate the intersection tests for these objects.

8.10   Intersection tests for patch models (*)

Implement a system of bounding volumes for objects whose surfaces are represented by a set of bicubic patches as described in Chapter 6. The bounding volume for an individual patch should be a box constructed such that its faces are parallel to the axes of the world coordinate system. Its extent can be calculated from the maxima and minima of the x, y and z coordinates of the control points for the patch. If a ray intersects the bounding volume for a patch, the patch is subdivided as described in Chapter 6, the boundary box for each of the subdivisions is calculated and the intersection test repeated for the subdivisions. This subdivision process is repeated until the patch is smaller than some accuracy requirement.

8.11   First-hit speed up (*)

The calculations for the intersections of the first-level rays in a ray tracer can be accelerated by the use of standard rendering algorithms. For example, a modification of the Z-buffer algorithm can be used to generate the object visible at each pixel in the viewing plane from a given view point (Weghorst, Hooper and Greenberg (1984)). Incorporate this extension in your ray tracer.

8.12   Spatial coherence (*)

Implement one of the spatial coherence schemes described. A preliminary version could use a simple uniform subdivision of space into fairly large voxels. Each voxel would have an associated list of the objects that it contains. Tracing a ray would involve tracking it from one voxel to another. Intersection tests would be carried out only for objects in the voxels traversed by the ray.

Now implement a 3D-DDA algorithm (Fujimoto, Tanaka and Iwata (1986)) for tracing a ray through the voxels in your uniform subdivision. Finally, incorporate an octree representation of your scene and modify the DDA algorithm to deal with the problem of moving from the current voxel into a larger or a similar voxel.

9   Volume Rendering

9.1   Introduction

Volume rendering means rendering voxel-based data. Chapter 2 introduced data representation techniques that are based on labelling all voxels in a region of object space with object occupancy. We saw that in applications where large homogeneous objects may occupy hundreds or thousands of voxels, we may impose a hierarchical structure, such as an octree, on the data. On the other hand, in applications like medical imaging a data structure may be a vast three-dimensional array of voxels. In this chapter we mostly consider unstructured sets of voxels.

Rendering voxels currently finds two major applications: rendering CSG models and the visualization of scalar functions of three spatial variables. CSG data can be converted into a voxel representation (Section 2.6.3) and rendered. There does not appear to be sufficient experience reported in the literature as to whether this route to rendering CSG models is preferable to the other strategies listed in Chapter 2.

In the last five years or so a new discipline – ViSC (visualization in scientific computing) – has emerged. One of the major application areas in this field is the visualization of scalar functions of three spatial variables. Such data, prior to the availability of hardware and software for volume rendering, was visualized using such 'traditional' techniques as isocontours in cross-sectional planes. Scalar functions of three spatial variables abound in science and engineering. Engineers are concerned with designing three-dimensional objects and analysing their potential behaviour. Calculations may produce predictions relating to temperature and stress, for example.

A voxel volume is either produced by a mathematical model, such as in computational fluid dynamics, or the voxels are collected from the real world, as in medical imaging. Visualization software generally treats both types in the same way. The major practical distinction between different data sources is the shape of the volume element. In medical imagery the

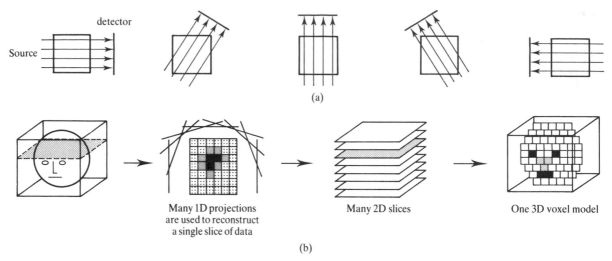

Figure 9.1
Stages in the construction of a voxel dataset from CT data. (a) CT data capture works by taking many one-dimensional projections through a slice (scanning). (b) CT reconstruction pipeline.

voxels may be rectangular rather than cubic. In the example shown in Plate 14 the volume elements were wedge shaped, that is, a cylinder divided up in a 'slice of cake' manner.

Medical imaging has turned out to be one of the most popular applications of volume rendering. It has enabled data collected from a tomographic system as a set of parallel planes to be viewed as a three-dimensional object. The material in this chapter is mostly based on this particular application. Although certain context-dependent considerations are necessary, the medical imaging problem is quite general and any strategy developed for this will easily adapt to other applications.

In medical imaging three-dimensional data is available from stacks of parallel CT (computed tomography) data. These systems reconstruct or collect data in sets of planes according to some particular property, the commonest modality being the X-ray absorption coefficient at each point in the plane. The basic medical system enables a clinician to view the information in each plane. With visualization the entire stack of planes is considered as volume data and rendered accordingly. A very simplified illustration of a tomographic imaging system is shown in Figure 9.1. From this we should note that information is sampled in many two-dimensional planes of zero thickness. Voxel values are inferred from this data. The data exhibits the characteristic that the resolution within a plane (typically 512×512) is much greater than the resolution between planes. Scans are typically taken at distances of the order of 0.5 cm. This non-isotropy produces certain image artefacts (see, for example, the horizontal coherences in Plate 15 which correspond to the positions of the scanning planes in the data collection process).

The basic idea of volume rendering is that a viewer should be able to perceive the volume from a rendered projection on the view plane. In CSG models the information projected onto the view plane may be the boundary surfaces. The final stage in conversion from a CSG tree to a voxel representation will produce a solid object made up of voxels. Rendering the surface of this object is the required image. In medical imaging we may want to view a surface, or the volume, or just part of the volume. Thus we view the extraction and display of 'hard' surfaces that exist in the data as part of the volume rendering problem. In many cases we may have a volume data set from which we have to extract and display surfaces that exist anywhere within the volume. Rather than bounding surfaces of an object, we may be dealing with an object that possesses many 'nested' surfaces – like the skin of an onion. If such surfaces are extractable by some unique property then we can render them visible by making them 100% opaque and all other data in the volume 100% transparent.

An example of this is shown in Plate 14. This shows a surface extracted from a volume data set that was produced from a CFD (computational fluid dynamics) simulation of a gas turbine. The plates depict isosurfaces of zero u velocity (long axis direction) extracted from a Navier–Stokes CFD simulation of a reverse flow pipe combustor, the chamber of which is indicated by the wireframe cylinder. The primary flow direction is from left to right. Air is forced in under compression at the left, and dispersed by two fans. Eight fuel jets, situated radially, approximately halfway along the combustor, are directed in such a way as to send the fuel mixture in a spiralling path towards the front of the chamber. Combustible mixing takes place in the central region and thrust is created at the exhaust outlet on the right. The isosurfaces shown connect all points where the net flow in the long axis is zero. This image shows flange-like hoops attached to the air intake fans, a central portion with eight lobes extending toward the fuel jets, a tubular core surrounded by a crenellated ring and eight smaller surfaces associated with secondary air inlets further down the chamber.

More generally we may try to view either the whole volume or a subset of it by assigning a colour *and* an opacity to each voxel and accumulating these values along a viewing direction. Here we might draw an analogy with a conventional X-ray. The X-ray is our projection in the view plane and the volume of that part of the body being X-rayed is our volume data. We can imagine that a set of parallel X-rays are fired through, say, the chest, and produce an image on a film placed behind the back. Each X-ray interacts with body tissue and produces an intensity on the image plane or projection. The body tissue is variably transparent to the X-ray, and when the image is viewed in its entirety, it is as if the volume of X-ray absorption information has been collapsed into a single plane. In a volume rendering algorithm that projects a representation of the dataset onto a single plane, it is as if the algorithm was X-raying the data.

Figure 9.2 gives an overview of the volume rendering process. We have a rectangular solid which is the volume data rotated into any orientation according to the required viewing direction. For each pixel in the view

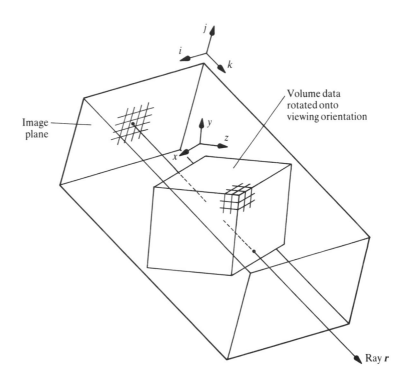

Figure 9.2
Volume rendering by
casting parallel rays
from each pixel (after
Levoy (1990)).

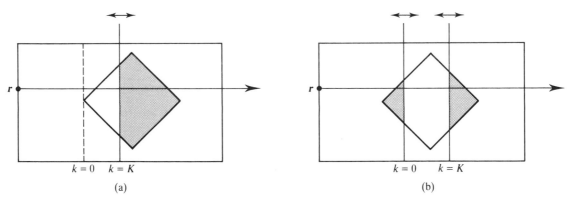

Figure 9.3
Using planes parallel to
the view plane to
construct a view
volume of the dataset.

plane we accumulate, in some way to be explained, information along parallel rays emanating from each pixel. Each ray operation produces a single
value (actually an RGB triple together with a transparency or opacity value
as will be explained shortly).

Returning to our analogy with a conventional X-ray, we can use this
to emphasize the flexibility afforded by volume rendering. First, we can view
the data from any angle. We can attempt to view all the volume by collaps-
ing or projecting all voxels into the view plane. Alternatively, we can use cut
planes to select a slab of the volume data as shown in Figure 9.3 – a very

simple application of view volumes. In Figure 9.3(a) any volume data in the shaded region is omitted from the view. Such a scheme could be used interactively and the plane moved deeper and deeper into the data. In Figure 9.3(b) two planes are shown and the central slab of data is rendered (when the thickness of the slab is reduced to zero we have a cross-section). These are just two examples of a myriad of interaction possibilities. Unfortunately volume rendering is a process of such expense that current commercial workstations do not support such interaction. In volume rendering all voxels contribute to each projection in general. Thus rendering time for each projection is a linear function of the number of voxels in the dataset. Typically this can be $512 \times 512 \times 512$.

It seems likely that such selective volume rendering will be more useful in many applications than trying to perceive the entire dataset. In most applications there is usually too much information in the volume, and when it is projected in its entirety, using opacity, the projected image becomes an indecipherable jumble.

9.2   Volume rendering algorithms

There are two major approaches to volume rendering: **ray casting (backward mapping)** and **plane compositing (forward mapping)**. In ray casting we have the general structure:

> **for** {*each pixel*}
>> {*fire a ray and find the voxels through which it passes*}

whereas plane compositing has the structure:

> **for** {*each plane in the volume data*}
>> **for** {*each voxel in the plane*}
>>> {*find the pixels – the 'footprint' that the voxel projects onto*}

The two algorithms are shown schematically in Figure 9.4. The first method accumulates information from all the voxels that intersect the current ray or current pixel. A single loop of the algorithm provides the final value for a pixel.

The second method accumulates information over the entire view plane for each plane of voxels in the dataset. In general, as shown in the inset in Figure 9.4(b), a voxel will project onto a number of pixels. This is known as the voxel 'footprint' and is analogous to the inverse projection of a square pixel into an area in the texture domain that spreads over a number of texels. In this case the mapping is linear and the footprint is a hexagon. However, the direction of the mapping is the reverse of texture mapping. In texture mapping, a pixel is reverse mapped into the texture domain. The texture samples that lie within this inverse or pre-image of the pixel are

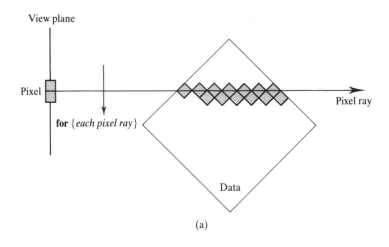

(a)

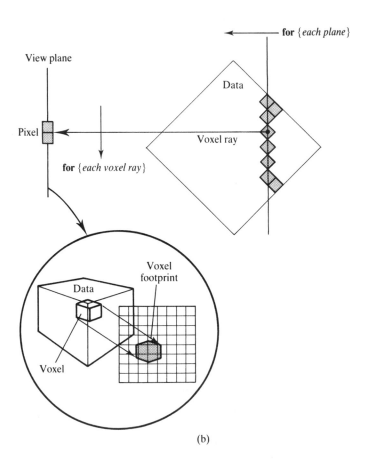

Figure 9.4
The two strategies for
volume rendering: (a)
ray casting; (b) forward
mapping.

(b)

weighted and summed, that is, filtered. In forward mapping a single voxel value is spread over the footprint of the voxel in the pixel plane.

As each plane is processed, a pixel value is updated and all pixels only have their final value when the moving plane reaches the front of the dataset. The frame buffer is, in effect, used as an accumulator.

The forward mapping algorithm may emerge as the more important of the two. It is more amenable to parallel implementation. As each voxel is processed we only need to know about a small set of surrounding voxels. Also, we process sets of voxels in parallel planes. On the other hand, ray casting is the more direct algorithm to implement. It does, however, possess the significant disadvantage that random access to all of the dataset is required for each ray – the implication being that significant memory overheads are required. Obviously some of the details are common to both algorithms. The detailed structure and ramifications of the ray casting approach are discussed in subsequent sections.

9.2.1 Filtering considerations

Both algorithms involve resampling the dataset to find a value for the voxel currently under consideration. Even if the original data does not contain artefacts, because the sampling has been performed at the appropriate rate, rotation of the data volume and application of a ray casting or forward mapping algorithm implies a resampling. Thus some form of resampling over a neighbourhood, followed by filtering to a single value, must be performed otherwise artefacts may be introduced.

In the case of the forward mapping algorithm, the footprint is generally a hexagon. Also, the footprint does not vary across the pixel plane except for an offset. Thus it is easy to choose and implement an appropriate filter in the form of a look-up table. In ray casting algorithms the filtering is performed in the data space. A single value for a voxel is calculated by some kind of interpolation over neighbouring values. In this case the filter kernel is three-dimensional.

9.2.2 Volume rendering by ray casting

To describe the algorithm we shall use a version of the notation introduced by Levoy (1990). We first consider that each voxel in the dataset is indexed by:

$$X = (x, y, z)$$

and that each voxel is given a colour $C(X)$ and an opacity $\alpha(X)$ (where $\alpha = 1$ implies an opaque voxel and $\alpha = 0$ implies a transparent voxel) by operations described later. Referring again to Figure 9.4(a) we trace a set of parallel rays into the data. If certain computational resource problems are ignored, this is the easiest and most obvious course of action to take and results in a parallel projection of structures in the data. If a pixel coordinate is (i,j) we define a ray as the vector:

$$\mathbf{R} = (i,j,k)$$

where:

$(i,j) = \mathbf{r}$ is the pixel index of the ray
k is the distance along the ray, $k = 1, \ldots, K$

For each ray, we progress along it resampling the data at evenly spaced intervals, computing $C(\mathbf{R})$ and $\alpha(\mathbf{R})$. As each colour and opacity is computed we accumulate those values progressing along the ray in a front-to-back order. This accumulation process uses the standard transparency formula and for a sample $\mathbf{R}$ we define an accumulated colour and opacity after the sample $\mathbf{R}$ has been processed as follows:

$$C_{\text{out}}^*(\mathbf{r},\mathbf{R}) = C_{\text{in}}^*(\mathbf{r},\mathbf{R}) + C^*(\mathbf{R})[1 - \alpha_{\text{in}}(\mathbf{r},\mathbf{R})]$$
$$\alpha_{\text{out}}^*(\mathbf{r},\mathbf{R}) = \alpha_{\text{in}}^*(\mathbf{r},\mathbf{R}) + \alpha^*(\mathbf{R})[1 - \alpha_{\text{in}}(\mathbf{r},\mathbf{R})] \tag{9.1}$$

where:

$$C_{\text{in}}^*(\mathbf{r},\mathbf{R}) = C_{\text{in}}(\mathbf{r},\mathbf{R})\alpha_{\text{in}}(\mathbf{r},\mathbf{R})$$
$$C_{\text{out}}^*(\mathbf{r}, \mathbf{R}) = C_{\text{out}}(\mathbf{r},\mathbf{R})\alpha_{\text{out}}(\mathbf{r},\mathbf{R})$$
$$C^*(\mathbf{r},\mathbf{R}) = C(\mathbf{r},\mathbf{R})\alpha(\mathbf{r},\mathbf{R})$$

Note that all colours are premultiplied by their associated opacity and (R,G,B) becomes $(R\alpha,G\alpha,B\alpha)$ in the accumulation process. The reason for this is easily seen by considering simple examples. If $\alpha = 0$ the object is completely transparent and its colour contribution to the accumulation must be $(0,0,0)$. If, on the other hand, $\alpha = 1$ then the object is completely opaque and its colour contribution is (R,G,B). Also when $\alpha = 1$, from thereafter in a (brute force) accumulation algorithm, $\alpha_{\text{in}} = 1$ and the second term in Equation 9.1 is always zeroized. The final colour is then the colour accumulated when the opaque voxel is hit by the ray.

At the end of the loop for each ray the final colour is obtained by:

$$C(\mathbf{r}) = \frac{C_{\text{out}}^*(\mathbf{r},\mathbf{R})}{\alpha_{\text{out}}(\mathbf{r},\mathbf{R})}$$

where $\mathbf{R} = (i,j,K)$. Figure 9.3 shows that view volumes delineated by planes parallel to the view plane are easily incorporated into this scheme – it is simply a matter of selecting the required limits in the inner loop of the algorithm.

9.3   Case study

At this point we look at an application of volume rendering. Consider Plates 15–21 all of which are volume-rendered versions of the same set of X-ray

CT scans. The illustrations are from a study of the use of computer graphics techniques to assist in radiotherapy planning. This involves the design of a facility that enables a clinician to visualize the spatial relationship between a tumour, critical structures and the radiation beams that are applied to treat the tumour – the treatment beams. Treatment is applied by using a number of beams that converge at the tumour site. The strength of each treatment beam is of an intensity such that no damage is caused to the tissue through which the beam travels. Nevertheless it is important that these component beams avoid critical stuctures – in the case of the head, the eyeballs, optic nerve and the spinal cord are the critical structures that must be avoided by the beams. Planning the position of the beams is difficult. Using individual CT slices alone, a clinician has to build a three-dimensional perception of the spatial relationship between the tumour, critical structures and the treatment beams.

The idea of the project illustrated in the plates is that volume rendering enables this planning to take place on a three-dimensional computer graphics object. The object is obtained by volume rendering the CT scans and the clinician has all the usual three-dimensional graphics facilities available to assist in the planning. The beams can be interactively positioned and the object can be viewed from any angle.

Plate 15 shows a volume-rendered version of a skull. The bone opacity is set to one and all other opacities are set to zero. This produces a skull image as a single isolated surface. The horizontal coherences that mark the individual CT planes are apparent in the image. Shading has been carried out on the surface by deriving a gradient as the surface normal and using the Phong reflection model. Specular highlights are apparent, giving the bone a shiny plastic-like appearance.

At this point a digression is in order. Plate 22 shows an apparently higher quality reconstruction and rendering of the same surface. This was achieved by using an explicit surface extraction technique and rendering it as normal. This technique is known as the **marching cubes algorithm** (Lorensen and Cline, 1987). An actual surface is built up by fitting a polygon or polygons through each voxel that is deemed to contain a surface. A voxel possesses eight vertices and if we assume at the outset that a voxel can sit astride a surface, then we can assign a polygon to the voxel in a way that depends on the configuration of the values at the vertices. By this is meant the distribution of those vertices that are inside and outside the surface over the eight vertices of the cube. If certain assumptions are made then there happen to be 15 possibilities and these are shown in Figure 9.5. The final position and orientation of each polygon within each voxel type is determined by the strength of the field values at the vertices. A surface is built up that consists of a normal polygon mesh and the difference in quality between rendering such a surface and effecting surface extraction by appropriate zero–one opacity assignment in volume rendering is due to what is effectively an inferior resolution in the volume rendering method. In the volume

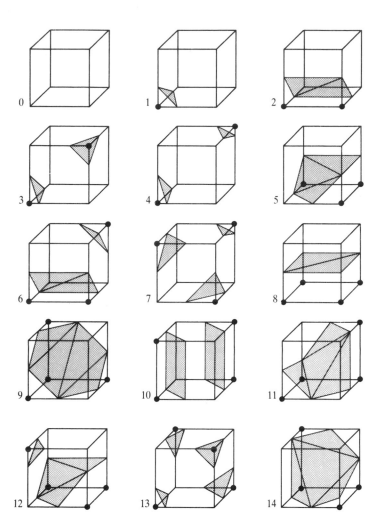

Figure 9.5
The 15 possibilities in the marching cubes algorithm. ● represents a vertex that is inside a surface.

rendering method a surface may exist somewhere within the voxel. If the opacity of such a voxel is set to one the information on the position and orientation of the surface fragment is lost. In the marching cubes algorithm the surface fragment is positioned and orientated accurately within the voxel – at least within the limitations of the interpolation method used. However, it is claimed that explicit surface extraction methods sometimes make errors by making the assumption that a surface exists across neighbouring voxels. They can fit a surface over what in reality are neighbouring surface fragments. In other words, they make a binary decision that may be erroneous.

Plate 16 is the same as Plate 15 except that a non-zero opacity has been assigned to non-bony material. This brings out an important point about medical imaging modalities. X-ray CT scans are optimal for detecting bones and calcification and do not tend to reveal detail in soft tissue. In the illustration the brain tissue displays as an amorphous green cloud. MR (magnetic resonance) tomography is much better at delineating soft tissue detail and sometimes data is mixed from both modalities to provide a computer graphics model.

Plate 17 shows the skull together with other superimposed information. The critical structures are detected in the data as separate objects. These objects are stylized as bounding volumes – spheres for the eyeballs and generalized cylinders for the spinal chord. These objects are rendered as normal using the colour orange. The idea is that the stylized bounding volumes are guaranteed to contain the actual object. A brain tumour is shown in green and three treatment beams are shown as wireframe objects. The blue on the skull shows the intersection of each beam with the skin surface.

Plates 18 to 21 are rendered with the bone opacity set to a value less than unity. They are all views looking down each treatment beam – a 'beam's eye view'. The first beam's eye view (Plate 18) indicates an intersection with an eyeball and this is corrected for, as shown in Plate 19, by using a beam shaping device. The remaining two plates show the other two beam's eye views. Plate 20 indicates that this beam also intersects an eyeball – this time the left one.

9.4 Parallel versus perspective projection

As mentioned in the previous section, the easiest implementation of the algorithm involves casting a set of parallel rays, one for each pixel, resulting in an orthographic parallel projection. This considerably simplifies the computations when a voxel index $R = (i,j,k)$ is converted to an (x,y,z) index. Coordinate calculations can be retained between rays by appropriately incrementing the coordinates of the corresponding sample in the previous ray $R = (i-1,j,k)$, say.

In the case of one of the mainstream application areas of volume rendering – medical imaging – it is not clear that perception of the rendered object is made any more difficult by the lack of a parallel projection. After all, the depth range of the object is only a fraction of a metre in reality.

The difficulties of implementing a perspective projection are as follows. First, the practical problem. A brute-force implementation requires random access to the volume dataset implying $O(N^3)$ RAM capacity (N^3 is the number of voxels in the set). An algorithm that attempts to overcome this problem by reorganizing the volume data access is given by Novins, Sillion and Greenberg (1990).

The second problem arises from the divergence of the rays. Figure 9.6(a) shows the nature of this. If the ray density is such that the nearest voxel plane is sampled at the rate of one ray per voxel, then in the example

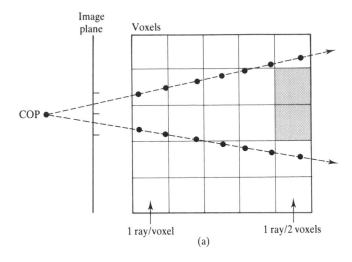

(a)

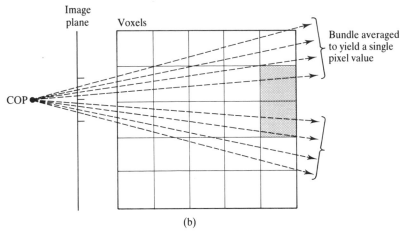

(b)

Figure 9.6
Ray density and perspective projection (after Novins, Sillion and Greenberg (1990)). (a) One ray/pixel results in decreasing sampling rate. (b) Increasing sampling rate for far voxel slice leads to near slice being oversampled. (c) Adaptive oversampling.

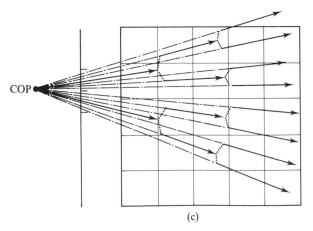

(c)

shown this will quickly drop to one ray per two voxels. This can clearly result in small detail being missed. A naive approach is to increase the ray density so that the furthest voxels are sampled at the appropriate ray. However this oversamples the near voxels and will increase the computation time substantially (Figure 9.6b). Novins *et al.* suggest adaptively increasing the ray sampling density as a function of distance along the ray so that the sampling density never drops below a user-defined threshold (Figure 9.6c). The process is controlled by measuring the reverse projection of the pixel square, which grows with ray depth, comparing this with the square of the sampling rate and splitting the ray accordingly. In the implementation the ray fragments were combined with simple averaging to yield a final pixel value.

9.5 Lighting model

Much of what follows relates to the particular but important context of medical imagery. This, however, is an application that uses all of the facilities available in volume rendering and other applications are likely to be a subset of the medical case. The lighting model described in this section is based on work by Drebin, Carpenter and Hanrahan (1988). This is because it is a relatively simple and general approach. There are, however, many approaches possible.

The lighting model used in volume rendering is best considered as a combination of pseudocolour mapping and basic rendering using a local reflection model. The model has little theoretical foundation and is a good example of a much used tenet in computer graphics – it works so use it.

The general thesis is that we are attempting to view a volume where objects (that may be nested inside one another) are projected as if they consisted of glass, say, of different colours, densities and opacities. In medical imaging, colour is used to indicate different objects or tissue type as well as the shape of the objects. Opacity is employed to indicate different densities. As we have already remarked, a scheme of such generality produces images that are, in the main, too confusing, and we mediate the generality of the process by using interaction and only rendering a subset of the data. In the case of CT data this aspect is already taken care of in the sense that if we choose opacity that reflects the reality of the data (the value of the X-ray absorption coefficients) then we have solid bones floating in a sea of jelly which is the soft tissue.

In the previous section we considered how voxels were to be composited along a ray. We now consider how the four-tuple (R, G, B, α) is determined for each sample taken along the ray. This splits into two. Each voxel X is given an (R, G, B, α) value in the first instance according to a classification procedure. For example, we may allot voxels that we know, a priori, to be bone, the colour white and a high opacity. Then we 'modulate' the colour with an intensity by applying a local reflection model such as the Phong reflection model. The application of shading information presupposes that a surface exists in a voxel, that is, a voxel sits astride an interface between different tissue types, and we decide this by using the value of the gradient as the surface normal in the reflection model. If the voxel is inside a homogeneous region then the value of the gradient is zero.

9.5.1   Voxel classification and colour assignment

A typical classification scheme was introduced by Drebin, Carpenter and Hanrahan (1988) (for the particular case of X-ray CT data). In this scheme voxels are classified into four types according to the value of the X-ray absorption coefficient. The types are: air, fat, soft tissue and bone. The method is termed **probabalistic classification** and it assumes that two, but not more than two, materials can exist in a voxel. Thus voxels can consist of seven types: air, air and fat, fat, fat and soft tissue, soft tissue, soft tissue and bone, and bone. Mixtures are only possible between neighbouring materials in the absorption coefficient scale – air, for example, is never adjacent to bone.

The classification scheme uses a piecewise linear 'probability' function (Figure 9.7). Consider a specific material assigned such a function. There will exist a particular CT number that is most likely to represent this material (point A in Figure 9.7). Points B_1 and B_2 represent the maximum deviation in CT number from point A that is still considered this material. Any CT number less than B_1 or greater than B_2 and contained within the limits defined by C_1 and C_2 is classified as a mixture of 'neighbouring' materials. A complete scheme is shown in Figure 9.8. Voxels are assigned (R,G,B,α) values according to this scheme, and if a mixture of two materials is present in a voxel the two colours are mixed in the same proportion as the materials.

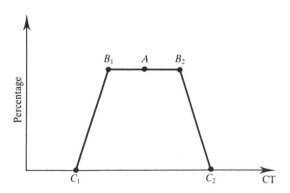

Figure 9.7
Trapezoid classification function for one material.

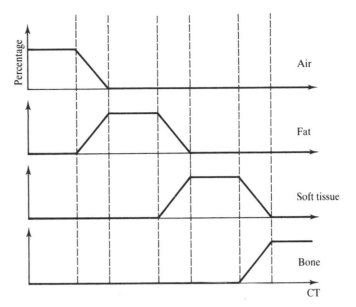

Figure 9.8
CT classification
function.

9.5.2 Voxel shading

We now consider how the actual voxel colour attributes interact with a lighting model to produce $C(X)$. We use a light source (or sources) and apply a local reflection model within a voxel. The overall scheme is grossly simplified as far as the interaction of the light with the volume is concerned. In fact, we consider each voxel's interaction with the light source independently of all other voxels prior to the inclusion in the accumulation process along the ray. What this means is that the ray from the light source to the voxel (Figure 9.9) is unaffected by passing through the intervening voxels. However, the interaction of the light with voxels that it encounters *is* considered along the ray to the eye (by the accumulation process itself).

A distinguishing feature of the Drebin scheme (Drebin, Carpenter and Hanrahan, 1988) is that, because a voxel can contain a mixture of materials, we have to deal with up to three colours within a single voxel. Within a voxel three subvoxel regions are possible if a surface fragment intersects the voxel. Figure 9.10 shows such a voxel. In it we have a region with colour C_F, a region with colour C_B and a surface that separates the two regions. (Note that the subscripts refer to the direction of the surface normal with respect to the viewing direction.) This will possess a colour C_S due to its interaction with the light source. Application of a simple local reflection model to this surface will mean that:

$$C_S = f(N, L, r)$$

where f is, for example, the Phong reflection model (Section 4.3). These

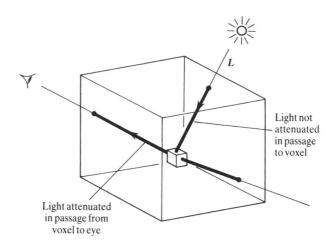

Figure 9.9
Passage of light from
light source to voxel to
eye ray.

Light not
attenuated
in passage
to voxel

Light attenuated
in passage from
voxel to eye

three colours are composited within a voxel in the same way that voxel
colours are accumulated along a ray.

Now, given that we start with just a single colour for each voxel, we
now have to look at how the three colours within the voxel are obtained. We
consider first the problem of finding whether or not a surface exists within
the voxel.

Surface detection is performed by a local operation based on a density
value assigned to each material and mixture. A surface is detected by evaluating a normal using the volume gradient. The components of this normal
are:

$$N_x = D(x + 1,y,z) - D(x - 1,y,z)$$
$$N_y = D(x,y + 1,z) - D(x,y - 1,z)$$

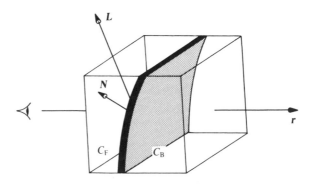

Figure 9.10
Colour assignment
within a voxel.

$$N_z = D(x,y,z + 1) - D(x,y,z - 1)$$

where for each voxel, D is evaluated by summing the products of the percentage of each material in the voxel times its assigned density. If a material is homogeneous these differences evaluate to zero.

The presence of a surface is quantified by the magnitude of the surface normal – the larger this magnitude, the more likely it is that a surface exists. No binary decision is taken on the presence or absence of a surface. A normalized version of the surface normal is calculated and used in the shading equation.

The localness of this operation means that it is sensitive to noise. This can be diminished by reducing the localness. In the above formula the gradient is evaluated by considering six neighbouring voxels. We can extend this to 18 or even 24.

Projects, notes and suggestions _____

9.1   Marching cubes algorithm (*)

If a suitable dataset is available, implement the marching cubes algorithm (Lorensen and Cline, 1987). The easiest way to do this is to set up a 256 row look-up table that contains, for each row, how many triangles are needed in a particular case and what edges of the cube they intersect. This is indexed by an 8-bit code that is generated, for each cube in the dataset, from the status of each cube vertex (inside or outside a surface).

9.2   Volume rendering by ray casting (*)

Implement a ray casting algorithm. Investigate the effects of varying the resampling neighbourhood on the quality of the final image. Incorporate a simple interactive interface that enables the volume to be chopped up by planes.

10 | Radiosity

10.1 Introduction

The major image synthesis methods in current use are the Phong reflection model and ray tracing. Simple reflection models are visually characterized by their limitations and this is generally because such models attend to only one aspect of light–object interaction – the reflection of incident light, due to a light source, from a surface. Dissatisfaction with the resulting 'plastic model floating in free space' look leads naturally to ad hoc 'add-ons'; techniques such as shadows and texture mapping were grafted onto basic reflection models.

Ray tracing is an elegant technique that uses the same basic theoretical method to model reflection, refraction and shadows. Although often described as a global illumination method, it is pointed out in Chapter 8 that it attends to only one aspect of global illumination – specular reflection and refraction – and this accounts for the distinct ray-traced signature of images produced by this method. This is because to trace diffuse interaction would involve spawning a very large number of rays at each ray–surface intersection. **Radiosity** provides a solution to diffuse interaction, but at the expense of dividing the environment into largish elements (over which the illumination is constant). This approach cannot cope with sharp specular reflections and essentially we have two global solutions: ray tracing, which deals with global specular reflection and radiosity, which deals with global diffuse reflection.

The radiosity method was developed to account for the interaction of diffuse light between elements in a scene. The method is excellent for generating scenes of interior environments, which are mostly collections of non-specular objects, and it has produced realistic-looking interiors, resulting in a shift in synthesized images towards global realism, rather than scenes as collections of non-interacting, separately synthesized objects. In simple 'non-interacting' reflection models, diffuse interaction is simulated by using an ambient term, normally a constant.

The radiosity method was developed at Cornell University in 1984 (Goral *et al.*, 1984) and most of the development work since then has been carried out at Cornell (Plate 23 shows two images produced by this institution). A radiosity-based approach is reported by Nishita and Nakamae (1985) again applied to room interiors. This is a less general approach than the Cornell method that integrates explicit shadow determination with the overall solution.

Radiosity is a method whose processor demands are at least as heavy as ray tracing and this is no doubt one of the reasons for its lack of dissemination throughout the computer graphics community. Like ray tracing, after the initial establishment of the method, recent research has concentrated on developing algorithmic enhancements that make the method more practical, and on integrating other reflection phenomena such as specular reflection into the method.

Although the term 'realistic' is a much over-used adjective in computer graphics, it is indisputable that this method has produced the most realistic and impressive images to date.

10.2   Radiosity theory

The radiosity method was first developed in radiative heat transfer (Siegel and Howell, 1984) to account for heat transfer between elements in furnaces or on a spacecraft. It is a conservation of energy or energy equilibrium approach, providing a solution for the radiosity of all surfaces within an enclosure. The energy input to the system is from those surfaces that act as emitters. In fact a light source is treated like any other surface in the algorithm except that it possesses an initial (non-zero) radiosity. The radiosity solution provides for previously unmodelled diffuse light phenomena such as 'colour bleeding' from one surface to another, shading within shadow envelopes and penumbrae along shadow boundaries. Greenberg, Cohen and Torrance (1986) give a startling illustration of colour bleeding and demonstrate the inability of conventional methods, such as ray tracing, to cope with this phenomenon.

The radiosity method is an object space algorithm, solving for the intensity at discrete points or surface patches within an environment and not for pixels in an image plane projection. The solution is thus independent of viewer position. This complete solution is then injected into a renderer that computes a particular view by removing hidden surfaces and forming a projection. This phase of the method does not require much computation (intensities are already calculated) and different views are easily obtained from the general solution. The method is based on the assumption that all surfaces are perfect diffusers or ideal Lambertian surfaces.

Radiosity, B, is defined as the energy per unit area leaving a surface patch per unit time and is the sum of the emitted and the reflected energy:

$$B_i dA_i = E_i dA_i + R_i \int_j B_j F_{ji} dA_j$$

Expressing this equation in words we have for a single patch i:

Radiosity $\times$ area = emitted energy + reflected energy

E_i is the energy emitted from a patch. The reflected energy is given by multiplying the incident energy by R_i, the reflectivity of the patch. The incident energy is that energy that arrives at patch i from all other patches in the environment, that is, we integrate over the environment, for all j ($j \neq i$), the term $B_j F_{ji} dA_j$. This is the energy leaving each patch j that arrives at patch i. F_{ji} is a constant, called a form factor, that parametrizes the relationship between patches j and i. This relationship depends on the geometric relationship between the patches.

The reciprocity relationship (Siegel and Howell, 1984) gives:

$$F_{ij} A_i = F_{ji} A_j$$

and dividing through by dA_i gives:

$$B_i = E_i + R_i \int_j B_j F_{ij}$$

For a discrete environment the integral is replaced by a summation and constant radiosity is assumed over small discrete patches, giving:

$$B_i = E_i + R_i \sum_{j=1}^{n} B_j F_{ji}$$

Such an equation exists for each surface patch in the enclosure and the complete environment produces a set of n simultaneous equations of the form:

$$
\begin{bmatrix}
1 - R_1 F_{11} & -R_1 F_{12} & \cdots & -R_1 F_{1n} \\
-R_2 F_{21} & 1 - R_2 F_{22} & \cdots & -R_2 F_{2n} \\
\vdots & \vdots & & \vdots \\
-R_n F_{n1} & -R_n F_{n2} & \cdots & 1 - R_n F_{nn}
\end{bmatrix}
\begin{bmatrix}
B_1 \\
B_2 \\
\vdots \\
B_n
\end{bmatrix}
=
\begin{bmatrix}
E_1 \\
E_2 \\
\vdots \\
E_n
\end{bmatrix}
\qquad \textbf{(10.1)}
$$

The E_i are non-zero only at those surfaces that provide illumination and these terms represent the input illumination to the system. The R_i are known or can be calculated and the F_{ij} are a function of the geometry of the environment. The reflectivities are wavelength-dependent terms and the above equation should be regarded as a monochromatic solution, a complete solution being obtained by solving for however many colour bands are being considered. We can note at this stage that $F_{ii} = 0$ for a plane or convex surface – none of the radiation leaving the surface will strike itself. Also

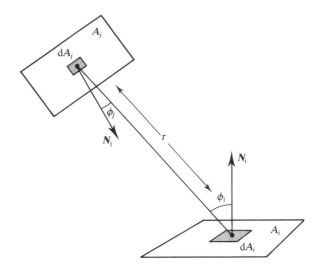

Figure 10.1
Form factor geometry
for two patches *i* and *j*.
(After Goral *et al.*
(1984)).

from the definition of the form factor the sum of any row of form factors is unity.

Since the form factors are a function only of the geometry of the system they are computed once only. Solving this set of equations produces a single value for each patch and this information is then input to a standard Gouraud renderer to give an interpolated solution across all patches.

The method is bound by the time taken to calculate the form factors expressing the radiative exchange between two surface patches A_i and A_j. This depends on their relative orientation and the distance between them and is given by:

$$F_{ij} = \frac{\text{Radiative energy leaving surface } A_i \text{ that strikes } A_j \text{ directly}}{\substack{\text{Radiative energy leaving surface } A_i \text{ in all directions in the} \\ \text{hemispherical space surrounding } A_i}}$$

It can be shown (Goral *et al.*, 1984) that this is given by:

$$F_{ij} = \frac{1}{A_i} \int_{A_i} \int_{A_j} \frac{\cos \phi_i \cos \phi_j}{\pi r^2} \, \mathrm{d}A_j \mathrm{d}A_i$$

where the geometric conventions are illustrated in Figure 10.1. In any practical environment A_j may be wholly or partially invisible from A_i and the integral needs to be multiplied by an occluding factor, which is a binary function that depends on whether the differential area $\mathrm{d}A_i$ can see $\mathrm{d}A_j$ or not. This double integral is difficult to solve except for specific shapes.

'Form factor' is one of a number of similar terms (others include 'diffuse view factor', 'shape factor' and 'angle factor') used to characterize the effects of the geometry of two surfaces on the radiative exchange between them.

10.3   Form factor determination

A numerical method of evaluating form factors was developed in 1985 (Cohen and Greenberg, 1985) and this is known as the **hemicube method**. This offered an efficient method of determining form factors and at the same time a solution to the intervening patch problem.

The patch-to-patch form factor can be approximated by the differential area to finite area equation:

$$F_{\mathrm{d}A_iA_j} = \int_{A_j} \frac{\cos \phi_i \cos \phi_j}{\pi r^2} \, \mathrm{d}A_j$$

where we are now considering the form factor between the elemental area $\mathrm{d}A_i$ and the finite area A_j. $\mathrm{d}A_i$ is positioned at the centre point of patch i. The veracity of this approximation depends on the area of the two patches compared with the distance, r, between them. If r is large the inner integral does not change much over the range of the outer integral and the effect of the outer integal is simply multiplication by unity. Now the Nusselt analogue (Siegel and Howell, 1984) tells us that we can consider the projection of a patch j onto the surface of a hemisphere surrounding the elemental patch $\mathrm{d}A_i$ and that this is equivalent in effect to considering the patch itself. Also, patches that produce the same projection on the hemisphere have the same form factor. This is the justification for the hemicube method as illustrated in Figure 10.2. Patches A, B and C all have the same form factor and we can evaluate the form factor of any patch j by considering not the patch itself, but its projection onto the faces of a hemicube.

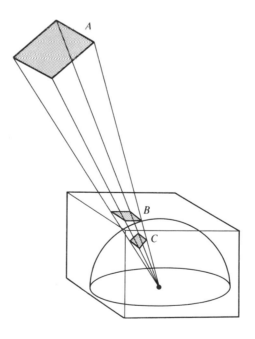

Figure 10.2
The justification for using a hemicube. Patches A, B and C have the same form factor.

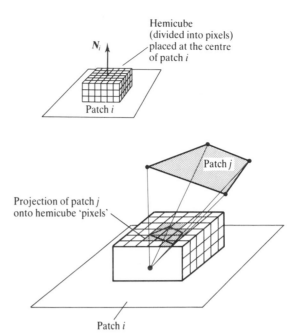

Figure 10.3
Evaluating the form
factor F_{ij} by projecting
patch j onto the faces
of a hemicube centred
on patch i.

A hemicube is used to approximate the hemisphere because flat projection planes are computationally less expensive. The hemicube is constructed around the centre of each patch with the hemicube Z axis and the patch normal coincident (Figure 10.3). The faces of the hemicube are divided into pixels – a somewhat confusing use of the term since we are operating in object space. Every other patch in the environment is projected onto this hemicube. Two patches that project onto the same pixel can have their depth compared and the further patch rejected, since it cannot be seen from the receiving patch. This approach is analogous to a Z-buffer algorithm except that there is no interest in intensities at this stage. The hemicube algorithm only facilitates the calculation of the form factors that are subsequently used in calculating diffuse intensities and a 'label buffer' is maintained indicating which patch is seen at each pixel on the hemicube.

Each pixel on the hemicube can be considered as a small patch and a differential to finite area form factor, known as a delta form factor, defined for each pixel. The form factor of a pixel is a fraction of the differential to finite area form factor for the patch and can be defined as:

$$\Delta F_{dA_i A_j} = \frac{\cos \phi_i \cos \phi_j}{\pi r^2} \Delta A$$
$$= \Delta F_q$$

where ΔA is the area of the pixel.

These form factors can be precalculated and stored in a look-up table. This is the foundation of the efficiency of the method. Again, using the fact

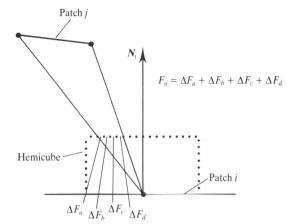

Figure 10.4
F_{ij} is obtained by summing the form factors of the pixels onto which patch j projects.

that areas of equal projection onto the receiving surface surrounding the centre of patch A_i have equal form factors, we can conclude that F_{ij}, for any patch, is obtained by summing the pixel form factors onto which patch A_j projects (Figure 10.4). A three-dimensional version of a Cohen–Sutherland clipper (Sutherland and Hodgman, 1974) is used to clip the projections against the half cube edges to obtain the set of pixels onto which a patch projects.

The occluding or intervening patch problem is easily solved using the hemicube method. For each hemicube placement on patch A_i every patch A_j is projected. If a hemicube pixel contains the projection from two patches then their distances can be compared and the nearer patch deemed to be the one that is 'seen' through that particular pixel. A patch label buffer needs to be maintained for each hemicube pixel that at any stage in the sequence contains the label of the nearest patch encountered so far in that direction. At the end of the projection sequence we will then have connected sets of pixels that are the projections of the nearest patch and the summations for each F_{ij} can then proceed (Figure 10.5). Note the similarity to the Z-buffer algorithm. Here we are maintaining identity information rather than intensity information. Thus:

$$F_{ij} = \sum_q \Delta F_q$$

where q is that set of pixels onto which a patch A_j projects. Thus form factor evaluation now reduces to projection onto mutually orthogonal planes and a summation operation.

The delta form factors for each pixel on the hemicube can be precalculated and stored in a look-up table. For example, for a pixel positioned on the top surface of the hemicube:

$$\Delta F_q = \frac{1}{\pi(x^2 + y^2 + 1)^2} \Delta A$$

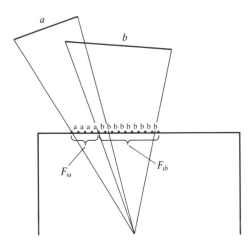

Figure 10.5
Pixels are labelled with the identity of the nearest patch. When a projection sequence for patch i is complete F_{ij} can be evaluated.

This derives (Figure 10.6) from:

$$r = (x^2 + y^2 + 1)^{1/2}$$
$$\cos \phi_i = \cos \phi_j$$
$$= \frac{1}{(x^2 + y^2 + 1)^{1/2}}$$
$$\Delta F_q = \frac{\cos \phi_i \cos \phi_i}{\pi r^2} \Delta A$$

Equation 10.1 possesses certain properties (fully described by Cohen and Greenberg (1985)) that can be exploited to give an efficient Gauss–Seidel

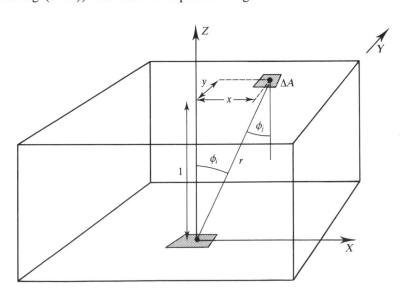

Figure 10.6
Geometry of delta form factors for a pixel ΔA on top of the hemicube. (After Cohen and Greenberg (1985)).

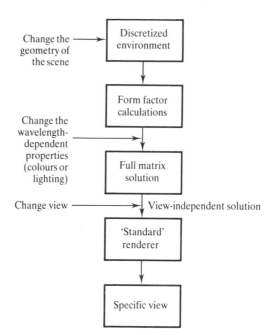

Figure 10.7
Stages in a complete radiosity solution. Also shown are the points in the process where various modifications can be made to the image.

iterative solution (see *Projects, notes and suggestions* at the end of this chapter) and the final centre patch radiosities are injected into a bilinear interpolation scheme to provide a continuous shaded solution for the environment.

The method can be summarized in the following stages:

(1) computation of the form factors, F_{ij};

(2) solving the radiosity matrix equation;

(3) rendering by injecting the results of stage 2 into a bilinear interpolation scheme;

(4) repeating stages 2 and 3 for the colour bands of interest.

This process is shown in Figure 10.7. Form factors are a function only of the environment and are calculated once only and can be reused in stage 2 for different reflectivities and light source values. Thus a solution can be obtained for the same environment with, for example, some light sources turned off. The solution produced by stage 2 is a view-independent solution and if a different view is required then only stage 3 is repeated. This approach can be used, for example, when generating an animated walkthrough of a building interior. Each frame in the animation is computed by changing the view point and calculating a new view from an unchanging radiosity solution. It is only if we change the geometry of the scene that a recalculation of the form factors is necessary. If the lighting is changed and the geometry is unaltered, then only the equation needs resolving – we do not have to recalculate the form factors.

Stage 2 implies the computation of a *view-independent* rendered version of the solution to the radiosity equation which supplies a *single* value, a radiosity, for each patch in the environment. From these values, vertex radiosities are calculated and these vertex radiosities are used in the bilinear interpolation scheme to provide a final image. A depth buffer algorithm is used at this stage to evaluate the visibility of each patch at each pixel on the screen. (This stage should not be confused with the hemicube operation that has to evaluate interpatch visibility during the computation of form factors.)

A number of factors make the general application of the basic radiosity method somewhat difficult. The coding complexity is high and the method requires extensive computing resources.

The time taken to complete the form factor calculation depends on the square of the number of patches. A hemicube calculation is performed for every patch (onto which all other patches are projected). The overall calculation time thus depends on the complexity of the environment and the accuracy of the solution, as determined by the hemicube resolution. Although diffuse illumination changes only slowly across a surface, aliasing can be caused by too low a hemicube resolution and accuracy is required at shadow boundaries (see Section 10.4). Storage requirements are also a function of the number of patches required. All these factors mean that there is an upward limit on the complexity of the scenes that can be handled by the radiosity method.

10.4   Increasing the accuracy of the solution

Most of the computation in the radiosity method is taken up by the calculation of the form factors, and the size of the problem is a function of the number of patches squared. The quality of the image is a function of the size of the patches and it is pointed out by Cohen, Greenberg and Immel (1986) that in regions of the environment, such as shadow boundaries, that exhibit a high radiosity gradient, the patches should be subdivided.

Cohen, Greenberg and Immel (1986) develop a technique called **substructuring** and the idea is to generate an accurate solution for the radiosity of a point from the 'global' radiosities obtained from the initial 'coarse' patch computation. Patches are subdivided into areas called **elements**. Element-to-patch form factors are calculated where the relationship between element-to-patch and patch-to-patch form factors is given by:

$$F_{ij} = \frac{1}{A_i} \sum_{q=1}^{R} F_{(iq)j} A_{(iq)}$$

where:

F_{ij} is the form factor from patch i to patch j

$F_{(iq)j}$ is the form factor from element q of patch i to patch j

$A_{(iq)}$ is the subdivided area of element q of patch i

R is the number of elements in the patch

Patch form factors obtained in this way are then used in a standard radiosity solution.

This increases the number of form factors from $N \times N$ to $M \times N$, where M is the total number of elements created, and naturally increases the time spent in form factor calculation. Patches that need to be divided into elements are revealed by examining the graduation of the coarse patch solution. The previously calculated (coarse) patch solution is retained and the fine element radiosities are then obtained from this solution using:

$$B_{iq} = E_q + R_q \sum_{j=1}^{N} B_j F_{(iq)j} \tag{10.2}$$

where:

B_{iq} is the radiosity of element q

B_j is the radiosity of patch j

$F_{(iq)j}$ is the element q to patch j form factor

In other words, as far as the radiosity solution is concerned, the cumulative effect of elements of a subdivided patch is identical to that of the undivided patch; or, subdividing a patch into elements does not affect the amount of light that is reflected by the patch. So after determining a solution for patches, the radiosity within a patch is solved independently among patches. In doing this, Equation 10.2 assumes that only the patch in question has been subdivided into elements – all other patches are undivided. The process is applied iteratively until the desired accuracy is obtained. At any step in the iteration we can identify three stages:

(1) subdividing selected patches into elements and calculating element-to-patch form factors;

(2) evaluating a radiosity solution using patch-to-patch form factors;

(3) determining the element radiosities from the patch radiosities.

where stage 2 occurs just for the first iteration – the coarse patch radiosities are calculated once only. The method is distinguished from simply subdividing the environment into smaller patches. This strategy would result in $M \times M$ new form factors (rather than $M \times N$) and an $M \times M$ system of equations.

Subdivision of patches into elements is carried out adaptively. The areas that require subdivision are not known prior to a solution being obtained. These areas are obtained from an initial solution and are then subject to a form factor subdivision. The previous form factor matrix is still valid and the radiosity solution is not recomputed. Only parts of the form factor determination are further discretized and these are then used in the third phase (determination of the element radiosities from the coarse patch solution). This process is repeated until it converges to the desired degree of accuracy. Thus image quality is improved in areas that require more accurate treatment.

An example of this approach is shown in Plate 24. The three illustrations show a typical scene constructed to demonstrate the efficacy of the method – a room interior with largish flat surfaces, strip lights and windows. The scene is shown divided into patches and after substructuring.

What information to use in the coarse patch solution is one of the problems with this method. A better solution is obtainable if the element-to-patch form factors are summed and used to calculate patch-to-patch form factors, but without an initial solution no automatic subdivision criteria are available. Thus the coarse patch radiosities must be based on patch-to-patch form factors, or an initial subdivision has to be specified manually. Another practical problem with the technique is that the extrapolation process, to calculate vertex radiosities from patch radiosities, is now far more cumbersome than it is for a surface that has been regularly subdivided into patches.

In the same paper (Cohen, Greenberg and Immel, 1986), details are given on merging texture mapping with the radiosity solution. This involves retaining the idea of a patch having constant radiosity over its extent, calculating the radiosity solution and then texture mapping during the rendering phase.

For a pixel in the image plane the texture mapping is computed by:

$$B_{\text{pixel}} = B_{\text{average}} \frac{R_{\text{pixel}}}{R_{\text{average}}}$$

where:

B_{pixel} is the final radiosity of a pixel

B_{average} is the radiosity derived from the element radiosity solution

R_{pixel} is the reflectivity given by the texture map for the pixel

R_{average} is the average reflectivity of the texture map

Cohen points out that this technique enables the contribution from, say, a painting, to the illumination of the environment to be the same if it were one average colour. Plate 23 is an illustration of this technique.

10.5   Reordering the solution for progressive refinement

Unlike other major image synthesis techniques, the radiosity method has not, to date, been taken up by the computer graphics community, presumably because of the extremely large computational overheads of the method.

In a paper published in 1988 Cohen *et al.* address this problem and develop an important reordering of the basic technique called **progressive refinement**.

The general goal of progressive or adaptive refinement can be taken up by any slow image synthesis technique and it attempts to find a compromise between the competing demands of interactivity and image quality. A synthesis method that provides adaptive refinement would present an initial quickly rendered image to the user. This image is then progressively refined in a 'graceful' way. Cohen defines this as a progression towards higher quality, greater realism and so on, in a way that is automatic, continuous and not distracting to the user. Early availability of an approximation can greatly assist in the development of techniques and images, and reducing the feedback loop by approximation is a necessary adjunct to the radiosity method.

The radiosity method is particularly suited to this approach – the spatial resolution of the image remaining constant, while the illumination calculations are refined. This contrasts with the options in ray tracing where the only simple refinement process that does not involve losing previously calculated information is to progressively increase the two-dimensional spatial resolution.

The two major practical problems in the radiosity method are the storage costs and the calculation of the form factors. Cohen points out that for an environment of 50×10^3 patches, even although the resulting square matrix of form factors may be 90% sparse (many patches cannot see each other) this still requires 10^9 bytes of storage (at four bytes per form factor).

Both the requirements of progressive refinement and the elimination of precalculation and storage of the form factors are met by an ingenious restructuring of the basic radiosity algorithm. The stages in the progressive refinement are obtained by displaying the results as the iterative solution progresses. The solution is restructured and the form factor evaluation order is optimized so that the convergence is 'visually graceful'. This restructuring enables the radiosity of all patches to be updated at each step in the solution, rather than a step providing the solution for a single patch. Maximum visual difference between steps in the solution can be achieved by processing patches according to their energy contribution to the environment. The radiosity method is particularly suited to a progressive refinement approach because it computes a view-independent solution. Viewing this solution (by rendering from a particular view point) can proceed independently as the radiosity solution progresses.

In the conventional evaluation of the radiosity matrix a solution for one row provides the radiosity for a single patch i:

$$B_i = E_i + R_i \sum_{j=1}^{n} B_j F_{ij}$$

This is an estimate of the radiosity of patch i based on the current estimate

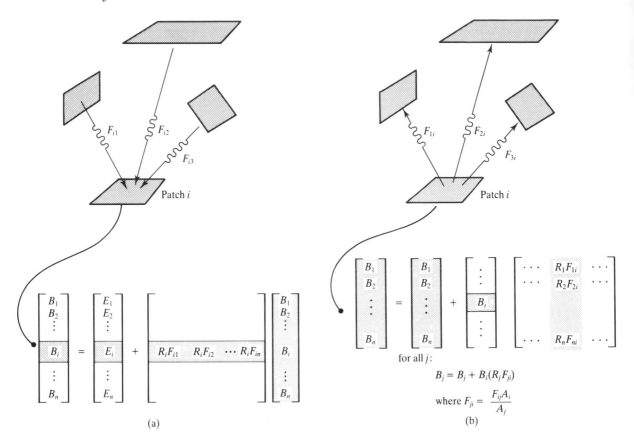

(a)

(b)

Figure 10.8
(a) 'Gathering': standard Gauss–Seidel solution of the radiosity matrix. The radiosity of a single patch i is updated for each iteration by gathering radiosities from all other patches. (b) 'Shooting': the radiosity of all patches is updated for each iteration. A diagrammatic representation of the difference between the standard radiosity solution and the progressive refinement method (after Cohen *et al.* (1988)).

of all other patches. This is the 'gathering' process, as described in Section 10.2. If viewed dynamically each patch intensity is updated according to its row position in the radiosity matrix.

The idea of the progressive refinement method is that the entire image is updated at every iteration, rather than a single patch. Cohen *et al.* (1988) term this as 'shooting', where the contribution from each patch i is distributed to all other patches. The difference between these two processes is illustrated diagramatically in Figure 10.8(a) and (b).

This reordering of the algorithm is accomplished in the following way. A single term determines the contribution to the radiosity of patch j due to that from patch i:

$$B_j \text{ due to } B_i = R_j B_i F_{ji}$$

This relationship can be reversed by using the reciprocity relationship:

$$B_j \text{ due to } B_i = R_j B_i F_{ij} A_i / A_j$$

and this is true for all patches j. This relationship can be used to determine the contribution to each patch j in the environment from the single patch i. A single radiosity (patch i) shoots light into the environment and the radiosities of all patches j are updated simultaneously. The first complete update (of all the radiosities in the environment) is obtained from 'on the fly' form factor computations. Thus an initial approximation to the *complete* scene can appear when only the first row of form factors has been calculated. This eliminates high start-up or precalculation costs.

Steps in the process can be displayed in a progressive refinement sequence if we add ΔB_j to each patch j in the iteration sequence. This is accomplished as follows:

> **repeat**
>> **for** {*each patch i*} **do**
>>
>>> {*position a hemicube on patch i and calculate form factors F_{ij} (for the first iteration)*}
>>>
>>> **for** {*each patch j ($j \neq i$)*}**do**
>>>> $\Delta Rad := R_j \Delta B_i F_{ij} A_i / A_j$
>>>>
>>>> $\Delta B_j := \Delta B_j + \Delta Rad$
>>>>
>>>> $B_j := B_j + \Delta Rad$
>>>
>>> $\Delta B_i = 0$
>
> **until** convergence

where ΔB_j is the difference between the previous and current estimates of B_j. Thus as the iteration progresses ΔB_j reduces as B_j becomes more and more accurate and the ambient term decreases.

This process is repeated until convergence is achieved. This is carried out by subdividing patches and examining the radiosity gradient between neighbouring elements. All radiosities B_i and ΔB_i are initially set either to zero or to their emission values. As this process is repeated for each patch i the solution is displayed and at each step the radiosities for each patch j are updated.

If the output from the algorithm is displayed without further elaboration, then a scene, initially dark, gradually gets lighter as the incremental radiosities are added to each patch. Cohen optimizes the 'visual convergence' of this process by sorting the order in which the patches are processed according to the amount of energy that they are likely to radiate. This means, for example, that emitting patches, or light sources, should be treated first. This gives an early well-lit solution. The next patches to be processed are those that received most light from the light sources and so on. It is pointed out by Cohen that, by using this ordering scheme, the solution proceeds in a way that approximates the propagation of light through an environment. In reality, for a light source such as sunlight streaming through a window, most of the ambient light comes from the *first* bounce of the light from the surfaces in the room. Although this produces a better visual sequence than an unsorted process, the solution still progresses from a dark scene to a fully illuminated scene. To overcome this effect an arbitrary ambient light term is added to the intermediate radiosities. This term is used only to enhance the display and is not part of the solution. The value of the ambient term is based on the current estimate of the radiosities of all patches in the environment, and as the solution proceeds and becomes 'better lit' the ambient contribution is decreased.

The idea is that as the solution progresses, the quality or 'correctness' of the image increases and the role of the estimated ambient contribution decreases. The ambient contribution at any stage is determined as follows. First, an approximate form factor definition is introduced. This ignores the geometric relationship between a pair of patches and defines an approximate form factor that depends only on the patch j. This estimated form factor is given by:

$$F_{ij(\text{estimated})} = \frac{A_j}{\sum\limits_{j=1}^{n} A_j}$$

which is the fraction of the environment taken up by the area A_j. Second, an average reflectivity for all patches in the environment is given by:

$$R_{\text{average}} = \frac{\sum\limits_{i=1}^{n} R_i A_i}{\sum\limits_{i=1}^{n} A_i}$$

Consider now light incident on the environment. This will be reflected once, twice and so on and an overall reflection factor, μ, can be defined as:

$$\mu = 1 + R_{\text{average}}^2 + R_{\text{average}}^3$$
$$= \frac{1}{1 - R_{\text{average}}}$$

These definitions can be used in an estimated ambient term:

$$I_a = \mu \sum_{j=1}^{n} \Delta B_j F_{ij(\text{estimated})}$$

The complete progressive refinement algorithm can now be summarized. Four main stages are completed for each iteration. These are:

(1) Find the patch with the greatest radiosity or emitted energy.

(2) Evaluate a 'column' of form factors, that is, the form factors from this patch to every other patch in the environment.

(3) Update the radiosity of each of the receiving patches.

(4) Reduce the temporary ambient term as a function of the sum of the differences between the current values calculated in 3 and the previous values.

(Note that if adaptive subdivision is incorporated into the method it is the 'receiving patches' that are subdivided and the progressive refinement algorithm computes form factors from a patch to elements or subdivision products.) For example, in a room an area light source may be the first shooting patch chosen. The form factors from the light source to every other surface are evaluated and radiosity is distributed to every other receiving surface. A desk top directly opposite the light may be the next 'source' chosen and the process continues.

Cohen *et al.* categorize the basic algorithmic options in the radiosity method as follows:

- *Gathering*   A term used to represent the basic approach described in Section 10.2. A matrix of form factors is precomputed, stored and used in a traditional Gauss–Seidel solution. If the solution is viewed as it progresses, estimated patch radiosities are updated in their order in the matrix formulation.

- *Shooting*   A reversal of this solution process. Light from each patch is shot into the environment and the entire scene is updated for each iteration. This approach is visually optimized by treating patches in an order that takes into account the amount of energy they are likely to radiate.

- *Shooting and ambient*   An ambient term is now included so that early approximations are visible. At each iteration the quality and accuracy of the solution increases and the ambient fraction is diminished.

10.6   Further development of the radiosity method: hybrid radiosity and ray tracing

The standard radiosity method, as described previously, provides a solution for the interaction of diffuse surfaces in a closed environment. If the radiosity method is to become a standard image synthesis technique, then it must include the modelling of specular phenomena. Wallace, Cohen and Greenberg (1987) do this by incorporating ray tracing and splitting the method into a two-pass approach.

The radiosity method was first extended to include specular interaction by Immel, Cohen and Greenberg (1986) who incorporated a bidirectional reflectivity function into the basic radiosity equation and adopted a view-independent solution to specular interreflection. However, this approach results in massive computational overheads for anything but simple scenes, because in a view-independent solution, although the diffuse illumination changes relatively slowly over a surface, fine subdivision is required for specular interaction.

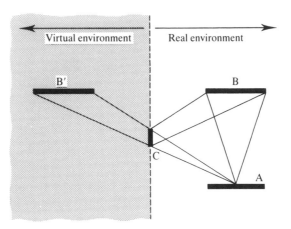

Figure 10.9
C is a perfect mirror and a path for diffuse interaction between patch A and B via C can be modelled by constructing a virtual patch B'.

In Wallace's two-pass approach, the first pass is the computation of a view-independent solution – an enhanced radiosity solution. The philosophy of the technique is outlined in Figure 8.19 and is based on what Wallace describes as the four 'mechanisms' of illumination. These define the nature of the interaction between two surfaces and include diffuse-to-diffuse, specular-to-diffuse, diffuse-to-specular and specular-to-specular interaction.

The two-pass view-independent/view-dependent approach is termed the preprocess and the postprocess. The preprocess is enhanced to include diffuse transmission (translucency) and specular-to-diffuse transport. The basic radiosity method – using a hemicube for the form factor determination – is then employed. The postprocess uses view-independent ray tracing to account for specular-to-specular and diffuse-to-specular interactions.

Translucency is implemented by using a hemicube on the back as well as the front of the surface, allowing backward as well as forward form factors to be calculated. Specular-to-diffuse transport can occur when, for example, two diffuse patches 'see' each other via an intermediate specularly reflecting surface, and this phenomenon is taken into account by using an extra form factor for such patches. This process determines the intensity of the diffuse component due to the diffuse-to-specular, specular-to-specular and specular-to-diffuse interactions and it results in a view-independent solution that incorporates these mechanisms. Specular surfaces are restricted to perfect mirrors and the extra paths are taken into account by extra form factors which are calculated by considering a virtual environment (Figure 10.9). In the figure A and B are two diffuse patches that interact as specified in the normal radiosity solution. In addition, A interacts with B via a (perfect) specular patch C. This is taken into account by setting up a virtual diffuse patch B'.

The environment is expanded in this way and the normal radiosity equation is enhanced with the extra form factors from the virtual environment. This is the disadvantage of the method. Since the form factor

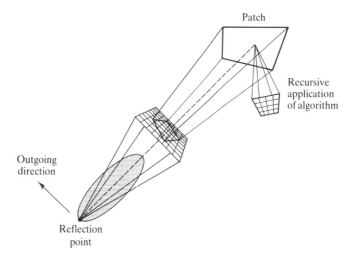

Figure 10.10
Sampling intensities
using a square pyramid
to approximate the
reflection lobe (after
Wallace, Cohen and
Greenberg (1987)).

calculations always predominate, introducing extra or virtual environments substantially increases the computation time.

Thus, in the preprocess, or view-independent solution, specular transport is accounted for, but only to the extent necessary to calculate the diffuse component accurately.

The view-dependent or postprocess deals with the specular-to-specular and diffuse-to-specular mechanism using a ray tracing approach. Normal ray tracing, of course, deals with specular-to-specular transfer. To calculate the diffuse-to-specular mechanism properly, an integration of incoming intensities should be performed over the entire hemisphere at the point of interest, weighted by the bidirectional specular reflectivity. However, Wallace, Cohen and Greenberg (1987) make the assumption that only a small fraction of the incoming rays over the hemisphere contribute to the outgoing specular bump. They use a rectangular reflection frustum to simulate the specular bump and this method also incorporates the specular-to-specular mechanism (Figure 10.10). Incoming diffuse intensities that contribute to each reflection frustum are calculated by linear interpolation from the view-independent/preprocess patch vertex intensities.

The reflection frustum is implemented geometrically as a square pyramid whose end face is divided into $n \times n$ 'pixels'. Visible surfaces are determined by using a conventional Z-buffer algorithm with a very low resolution of the order of 10×10 pixels. The incoming intensity 'seen' through a reflection frustum pixel is simply the intensity of the surface seen by that pixel, that is, the intensity calculated in the preprocess or view-independent phase. If a visible surface is specular, then the process is applied recursively as in normal ray tracing.

The incoming intensities that stream through each pixel are summed to simulate the specular spread and can also be subjected to a weighting function that simulates the shape of the specular spread. Wallace limits the amount of the work that has to be done at this stage by limiting the recursive depth over which the process operates and also by reducing the pixel resolution of the end face of the reflection frustum as a function of trace depth.

Projects, notes and suggestions ———————

10.1   Radiosity implementation (*)

Using an environment complexity consistent with your computing resources, develop a radiosity system. Note that each polygon/patch must have an emission value (zero except for light sources) and a reflectivity for each colour band in the solution. Also note that the final part of the process – computing a view from the view-independent solution – can use an adapted Z-buffer renderer of Chapter 5.

Develop an animated sequence from the solution that is a 'walk' through the scene.

From the point of view of development and testing it may be useful to implement the progressive refinement method.

A short note on the Gauss–Seidel method

Cohen and Greenberg (1985) point out that the Gauss–Seidel method is guaranteed to converge rapidly for equation sets such as Equation 10.1. The sum of any row of form factors is by definition less than unity and each form factor is multiplied by a reflectivity of less than unity. The sum of the row terms in Equation 10.1 (excluding the main diagonal term) is thus less than unity. The main diagonal term is always unity ($F_{ii} = 0$ for all i) and these conditions guarantee fast convergence.

The Gauss–Seidel method is an extension to the following iterative method. Given a system of linear equations:

$$\mathbf{Ax} = \mathbf{E}$$

such as Equation 10.1, we can rewrite equations for $x_1, x_2, \ldots, x_i$ in the form:

$$x_1 = \frac{E_1 - a_{12}x_2 - a_{13}x_3 - \ldots - a_{1n}x_n}{a_{11}}$$

which leads to the iteration:

$$x_1^{(k+1)} = \frac{E_1 - a_{12}x_2^{(k)} - \ldots - a_{1n}x_n^{(k)}}{a_{11}}$$

In general:

$$x_i^{(k+1)} = \frac{E_i - a_{i1}x_1^{(k)} - \ldots - a_{i,i-1}x_{i-1}^{(k)} - a_{i,i+1}x_{i+1}^{(k)} - \ldots - a_{in}x_n^{(k)}}{a_{ii}}$$

(10.3)

This formula can be used in an iteration procedure:

(1) Choose an initial approximation, say,

$$x_i^{(0)} = \frac{E_i}{a_{ii}}$$

for $i = 1, 2, \ldots, n$, where E_i is non-zero for emitting surfaces or light sources.

(2) Determine the next iterate

$$x_i^{(k+1)} \text{ from } x_i^{(k)}$$

using Equation 10.3.

(3) If $|x_i^{(k+1)} - x_i^{(k)}|$ is less than a threshold, for $i = 1, 2, \ldots, n$, then stop the iteration, otherwise return to step 2.

This is known as Jacobi iteration. The Gauss–Seidel method improves on the convergence of this method by modifying Equation 10.3 to use the latest available information. When the new iterate $x_i^{(k+1)}$ is being calculated, new values $x_1^{(k+1)}, x_2^{(k+1)}, \ldots, x_{i-1}^{(k+1)}$ have already been calculated and Equation 10.3 is modified to:

$$x_i^{(k+1)} = \frac{E_i - a_{i1}x_1^{(k+1)} - \ldots - a_{i,i-1}x_{i-1}^{(k+1)} - a_{i,i+1}x_{i+1}^{(k)} - \ldots - a_{in}x_n^{(k)}}{a_{ii}}$$

(10.4)

Note that when $i = 1$ the right-hand side of the equation contains terms with superscript k only, and Equation 10.4 reduces to Equation 10.3. When $i = n$ the right-hand side contains terms with superscript $k + 1$ only.

Convergence of the Gauss–Seidel method can be improved by the following method. Having produced a new value $x_i'^{(k+1)}$, a better value is given by a weighted average of the old and new values:

$$x_i^{(k+1)} = rx_i'^{(k+1)} + (1 - r)x_i^{(k)}$$

where $r\ (>0)$ is an arbitrary relaxation factor independent of k and i. Cohen *et al.* (1988) report that a relaxation factor of 1.1 works for most environments.

11 | Anti-aliasing

11.1 Introduction

This chapter is a general approach to aliasing in computer graphics and gives a non-rigorous theoretical background to the problem. Context-dependent techniques for texture mapping and ray tracing are presented in Chapters 7 and 8. Texture mapping, for example, requires a specialized anti-aliasing approach and with most texture methods, space-variant filtering techniques are required. Temporal anti-aliasing is discussed in Chapter 8 (distributed ray tracing) and Chapter 13 (animation).

The fundamental cause of aliasing in computer graphics is the creation of images by a regular **sampling** process in the space (and, in the case of animation, the time) domain. The sampling process is due to the nature of the display device, which in raster graphics is a finite array of pixels of a certain size. The final stage in the generation of an image is the calculation of intensities for each pixel. This always involves mapping an intensity, $I(x,y)$, in a continuous two-dimensional image space (that is, a projection from a continuous three-dimensional space) to a pixel in discrete image display space. This mapping, usually produced by an incremental shading algorithm (where a new intensity $I + \delta I$ is calculated for a new position $X + \delta X$) is equivalent to sampling continuous two-dimensional image space with an array of discrete sample points based, say, at the centre of each pixel. This view of image synthesis as a sampling process is important in anti-aliasing because it enables us to use signal processing theory as a theoretical base.

The most familiar manifestation of aliasing is jagged silhouette edges (Figure 11.1 and Plate 25). A silhouette edge is the boundary of a polygon, or any surface unit, that exhibits a high contrast over its background. (In general, contrast means light and dark areas of the same colour. Aliasing is not as noticeable when the silhouette edge and the background have the same luminance but different colours – the eye is more sensitive to luminance contrasts than colour contrasts.)

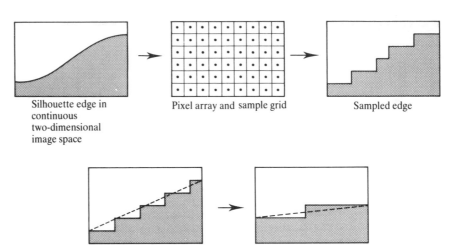

Silhouette edge in
continuous
two-dimensional
image space

Pixel array and sample grid

Sampled edge

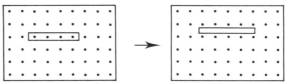

Jagged edge patterns change depending on line orientation

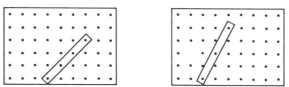

Long thin objects may completely disappear

Figure 11.1
Common aliasing
artefacts.

Long thin objects break up unpredictably

Another aliasing artefact occurs when small objects, whose spatial extent is less than the area of a pixel, are rendered or not depending on whether they are intersected by a sample point. A long thin object may break up depending on its orientation with respect to the sample array (Figure 11.1).

These artefacts can be particularly troublesome in animated sequences. Jagged edges 'crawl' and small objects may appear and disappear ('scintillate'). Such changes are intolerable in flight simulators, for example,

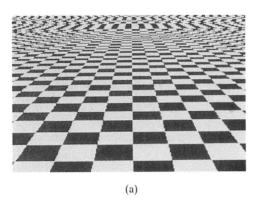
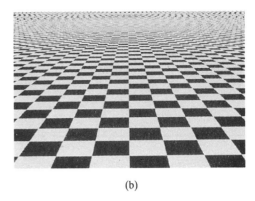

(a)   (b)

Figure 11.2
The pattern in (b) is a supersampled version of that in (a). Aliases still occur but appear at a higher spatial frequency.

where the point of the animated sequence is to instruct the pilot to react to subtle changes in the image.

A particularly degenerate manifestation of aliasing occurs when texture is used on surfaces subject to a perspective transformation. The texture in the distance breaks up and produces highly noticeable low-frequency aliases and moiré interference patterns (Figure 11.2). Again this has to be eliminated from flight simulators where texture patterns are used as a cheap method of enhancing reality and imparting depth cues.

11.2 Aliasing artefacts and Fourier theory

Anti-aliasing methods are easy to understand algorithmically and the simplest solution is easy to implement. Their theoretical base, which is best dealt with in the Fourier domain, is more difficult. This section assumes a rudimentary appreciation of Fourier theory but it can easily be skipped. The standard methods used in anti-aliasing can be treated informally – the mechanics of the algorithms impart a reasonable appreciation of the process.

An important theorem – the **sampling theorem** – relates the resolution of the sampling grid to the nature of the image or, more specifically, to the spatial frequencies in the image. (See Oppenheim and Shafer (1975) for a detailed treatment of digital signal processing.) It is intuitively obvious that the busier, or more detailed, the image, the finer the sampling grid has to be to capture this detail. The sampling theorem is most easily considered for functions of a single variable and is as follows:

> A continuous function of a single variable can be completely represented by a set of samples made at equally spaced intervals. The intervals between such samples must be at less than half the period of the highest frequency component in the function.

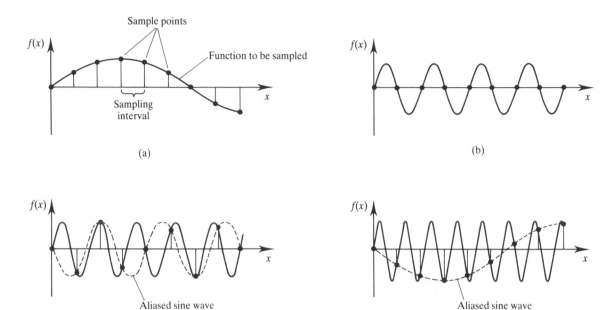

Figure 11.3
Space domain
representation of the
sampling of a sine
wave: (a) sampling
interval is less than
one-half the period of
the sine wave; (b)
sampling interval is
equal to one-half the
period of the sine
wave; (c) sampling
interval is greater than
one-half the period of
the sine wave; (d)
sampling interval is
much greater than
one-half the period of
the sine wave.

For example, if we consider a single sinusoidal function of x, it is easily seen that if the relationship between the sampling frequency and the function is as shown in Figure 11.3(a) then no information is lost. This means that the original information can be reconstructed from the sampled version. The sampling frequency in this case is greater than twice the frequency of the sinusoid. If the sampling frequency is equal to twice the sine wave frequency (Figure 11.3b) then the samples can coincide with the sine wave zero crossings as shown, and no information can be recovered from the samples concerning the sine wave. When the sampling frequency is less than twice that of the sine wave (Figure 11.3c and d) then the information contained in the samples implies sine waves (shown by the dotted lines) at lower frequencies than the function being sampled. These lower frequencies are known as **aliases** and this explains the derivation of the term.

The situation can be generalized by considering these cases in the frequency domain for an $f(x)$ that contains information, that is, not a pure sine wave. We now have an $f(x)$ that is any general variation in x and may, for example, represent the variation in intensity along a segment of a scan line. The frequency spectrum of $f(x)$ will exhibit some 'envelope' (Figure 11.4a) whose limit is the highest frequency component in $f(x)$, say, f_{max}. The frequency spectrum of a sampling function (Figure 11.4b) is a series of lines, theoretically extending to infinity, separated by the interval f_s (the

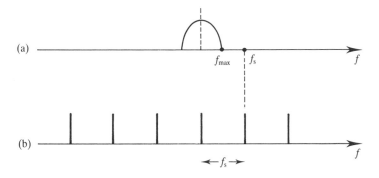

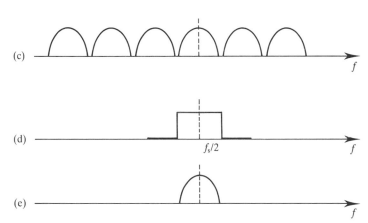

Figure 11.4
Frequency domain representation of the sampling process when $f_s > 2f_{max}$: (a) frequency spectrum of $f(x)$; (b) frequency spectrum of the sampling function; (c) frequency spectrum of the sampled function (convolution of (a) and (b)); (d) ideal reconstruction filter; (e) reconstructed $f(x)$.

sampling frequency). Sampling in the space domain involves multiplying $f(x)$ by the sampling function. The equivalent process in the frequency domain is **convolution** and the frequency spectrum of the sampling function is convolved with $f(x)$ to produce the frequency spectrum shown in Figure 11.4(c) – the spectrum of the sampled version of $f(x)$. This sampled function is then multiplied by a reconstructing filter to reproduce the original function. A good example of this process, in the time domain, is a modern telephone network. In its simplest form this involves sampling a speech waveform, encoding and transmitting digital versions of each sample over a communications channel, then reconstructing the original signal from the decoded samples by using a reconstructing filter.

Note that the filtering process, which is multiplication in the frequency domain, is convolution in the space domain. In summary, the process in the space domain is multiplication of the original function with the sampled function, followed by convolution of the sampled version of the function with a reconstructing filter.

Now in the above example the condition:

$$f_s > 2f_{max}$$

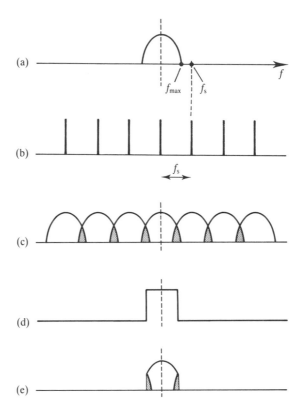

Figure 11.5
Frequency domain
representation of the
sampling process when
$f_s < 2f_{max}$: (a)
frequency spectrum of
$f(x)$; (b) frequency
spectrum of the
sampling function; (c)
frequency spectrum of
the sampled function;
(d) ideal reconstructing
filter; (e) distorted $f(x)$.

is true. In the second example (Figure 11.5) we show the same two processes of multiplication and convolution but this time we have:

$$f_s < 2f_{max}$$

Incidentally, $f_s/2$ is known as the **Nyquist limit**. Here the envelopes, representing the information in $f(x)$, overlap. It is as if the spectrum has 'folded' over a line defined by the Nyquist limit (Figure 11.5e). This folding is an information-destroying process; high frequencies (detail in images) are lost and appear as interference (aliases) in low-frequency regions. This is precisely the effect shown in Figure 11.2 where low spatial frequency structures are emerging in high-frequency regions.

In a situation where the sampling frequency is fixed (this is mostly the case, for example, in applications where $f(x)$ is a function of time) aliasing can be prevented by an anti-aliasing filter. The function being sampled is filtered, *prior* to sampling, by a low-pass filter whose cut-off frequency corresponds to the Nyquist limit. That is, all components in $f(x)$ whose frequency is greater than $f_s/2$ are eliminated.

How does this theory relate to computer graphics? In computer graphics terms, $f(x)$ can be a segment along a scan line. The sampling function has a frequency of one cycle per pixel (that is, we sample the information at the centre of each pixel). If we then convert these samples, by passing each pixel value through a D/A converter, this is equivalent to using a box-shaped reconstruction filter.

Another point we have to consider is that we now have images which are functions of two spatial variables and a two-dimensional sampling grid. The sampling theorem extends to two-dimensional frequencies or spatial frequencies. The two-dimensional frequency spectrum of a graphics image in the continuous generation domain is theoretically infinite. Sampling and reconstructing in computer graphics is the process of calculation of a value at the centre of a pixel and then assigning that value to the entire spatial extent of that pixel.

Aliasing artefacts in computer graphics can be reduced by increasing the frequency of the sampling grid (that is, increasing the spatial resolution of the pixel array). There are two drawbacks to this approach: the obvious one is that there is both an economic and a technical limit to increasing the spatial resolution of the display (not to mention the computational limits on the cost of the image generation process) and, since the frequency spectrum of computer graphics images can extend to infinity, increasing the sampling frequency does not necessarily solve the problem. If, for example, we applied the increased resolution approach to coherent texture in perspective, we would simply shift the effect up the spatial frequency spectrum (Figure 11.2).

There are two major established methods to removing/reducing aliasing artefacts in computer graphics. The most popular approach is loosely known as **supersampling** or **postfiltering**. The second, less common, method is to approximate a two-dimensional anti-aliasing filter and perform the equivalent operation to removing spatial frequencies above the Nyquist limit. This is sometimes confusingly called **prefiltering**. A third method, recently developed, is known as **stochastic sampling**. These three methods are now described.

11.3 Supersampling or postfiltering

This method is theoretically a three-stage process with the second and third stages in practice combined. The stages are:

(1) The continuous image generation domain is sampled at n times the display resolution. In practice this means the image is generated using an image synthesis technique at n times the display resolution.

(2) This sampled image is then low-pass filtered at the Nyquist limit of the display device.

(3) The filtered image is resampled at the device resolution.

In simple terms we are generating a virtual image (or one whose resolution

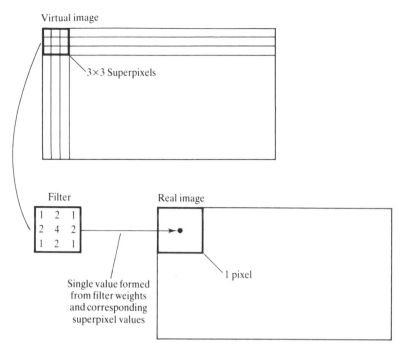

Figure 11.6
'Reducing' a virtual image by filtering.

cannot be reproduced on the output device) and then coarsening the resolution of this image. Thus each pixel in the final or displayable image has a value that has been determined from many pixels in the virtual image. This process is shown diagrammatically in Figure 11.6. A virtual image at say three times the final resolution is created using normal rendering procedures for shading and hidden surface removal. Groups of 3×3 'superpixels' in this image are reduced to a single pixel value by weighting each superpixel value by a filter weight summing and normalizing. We could also consider groups of 5×5 or 7×7 superpixels. Note that whatever the size of the filter, in this case the filter centre is placed at every three pixels.

This method works well with most computer graphics images and is easily integrated into a Z-buffer algorithm. It does not work with images whose spectrum energy does not fall off with increasing frequency. (As we have already mentioned supersampling is not, in general, a theoretically correct method of anti-aliasing.) Texture rendered in perspective is the common example of an image that does not exhibit a falling spectrum with increasing spatial frequency.

Supersampling methods differ trivially in the value of n and the shape of the filter used (that is, the value of the filter weights). For, say, a medium resolution image of 512×512 it is usually considered adequate to supersample at 2048×2048 ($n = 4$). The high resolution image can be reduced to the final 512×512 form by averaging and this is equivalent to convolving with a box filter. Better results can be obtained using a shaped filter, a filter whose values vary over the extent of its kernel. There is a considerable body of

Table 11.1   Bartlett windows used in postfiltering a supersampled image.

3 × 3			5 × 5					7 × 7						
1	2	1	1	2	3	2	1	1	2	3	4	3	2	1
2	4	2	2	4	6	4	2	2	4	6	8	6	4	2
1	2	1	3	6	9	6	3	3	6	9	12	9	6	3
			2	4	6	4	2	4	8	12	16	12	8	4
			1	2	3	2	1	3	6	9	12	9	6	3
								2	4	6	8	6	4	2
								1	2	3	4	3	2	1

knowledge on the optimum shape of filters with respect to the nature of the information that they operate on (see, for example, Oppenheim and Shafer (1975)). Most of this work is in digital signal processing and has been carried out with functions of a single variable $f(t)$. Computer graphics has unique problems that are not addressed by conventional digital signal processing techniques. For example, space-variant filters are required in texture mapping. Here both the weights of the filter kernel and its shape have to change.

To return to supersampling and shaped filters; Crow (1981) used a Bartlett window, three of which are shown in Table 11.1. Digital convolution is easy to understand and implement but is computationally expensive. A window is centred on a supersample and a weighted sum of products is obtained by multiplying each supersample by the corresponding weight in the filter. The weights can be adjusted to implement different filter kernels. The digital convolution proceeds by moving the window through n supersamples and computing the next weighted sum of products. Using a 3 × 3 window means that nine supersamples are involved in the final pixel computation. On the other hand, using the 7 × 7 window means a computation of 49 integer multiplications. The implication of the computation overheads is obvious. For example, reducing a 2048 × 2048 supersampled image to 512 × 512, with a 7 × 7 filter kernel, requires 512 × 512 × 49 multiplications and additions. Plate 25 shows an original image, a ×3 and a ×10 enlargement together with two anti-aliased versions using a 3 × 3 and 5 × 5 reconstruction respectively.

An inevitable side-effect of filtering is blurring. This occurs because information is integrated from a number of neighbouring pixels. This means that the choice of the spatial extent of the filter is a compromise. A wide filter has a lower cut-off frequency and will be better at reducing aliasing artefacts. It will, however, blur the image more than a narrower filter which will exhibit a higher cut-off frequency.

Finally, the disadvantages of the technique should be noted. Supersampling is not a suitable method for dealing with very small objects. Also, it is a 'global' method – the computation is not context dependent. A scene that exhibited a few large area polygons would be subject to the same computational overheads as one with a large number of small area polygons (see, for example, Chapter 8 for a description of a method where the anti-aliasing 'effort' is a function of the spatial complexity of the image). The memory requirements are large if the method is to be used with a Z-buffer. The supersampled version of the image has to be created and stored before the filtering process can be applied. This increases the storage requirements of the Z-buffer by a factor of n^2, making it essentially a virtual memory technique.

11.4   Prefiltering or area sampling techniques

The originator of this technique was Catmull (1978). Although Catmull's original algorithm is prohibitively expensive, it has spawned a number of more practical successors.

The algorithm essentially performs subpixel geometry in the continuous image generation domain and returns for each pixel an intensity which is computed by using the areas of visible subpixel fragments as weights in an intensity sum (Figure 11.7). This is equivalent to convolving the image with a box filter and using the value of the convolution integral at a single point as the final pixel value. (Note that the width of the filter is less than ideal and a wider filter using information from neighbouring regions would give a lower cut-off frequency.) Another way of looking at the method is to say that it is an area sampling method. All of the area of subpixel fragments is taken into account (as opposed to simply increasing the spatial resolution of the sampling grid).

We can ask the question: what does performing 'subpixel geometry' mean in practical computer graphics terms? To do this we inevitably have to use a practical approximation. (To reiterate an earlier point, we have no access to a continuous image. In computer graphics we can only define an image at certain points.) This means that the distinction between area sampling techniques and supersampling is somewhat artificial and indeed the A-buffer approach (described shortly), usually categorized as an area sampling technique, could equally well be seen as supersampling.

Catmull's method is incorporated in a scanline renderer. It proceeds by dividing the continuous image generation domain into square pixel extents. An intensity for each square is computed by clipping polygons against the square pixel boundary. If polygon fragments overlap within a square they are sorted in z and clipped against each other to produce visible fragments. A final intensity is computed by multiplying the shade of a polygon by the area of its visible fragment and summing.

The origin of the severe computational overheads inherent in this method is obvious. The original method was so expensive that it was used only in two-dimensional animation applications involving a few largish poly-

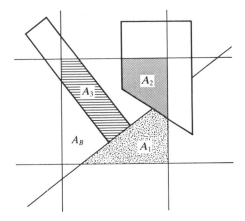

Intensity $= I_1A_1 + I_2A_2 + I_3A_3 + I_BA_B$

Figure 11.7
Polygons are clipped against pixel edges and each other to yield a set of visible fragments.

gons. Here most pixels are completely covered by a polygon and the recursive clipping process of polygon fragment against polygon fragment is not entered.

Developments have involved approximating the subpixel fragments with bit masks (Carpenter, 1984; Fiume, Fournier and Rudolph, 1983). Carpenter (1984) uses this approach with a Z-buffer to produce a technique known as the **A-buffer** (anti-aliased, area-averaged, accumulator buffer). The significant advantage of this approach is that floating-point geometry calculations are avoided. Coverage and area weighting are accomplished by using bitwise logical operators between the bit patterns or masks representing polygon fragments. It is an efficient area sampling technique, where the processing per pixel square will depend on the number of visible fragments.

Another efficient approach to area sampling, due to Abram, Westover and Whitted (1985), precomputes contributions to the convolution integral and stores these in look-up tables indexed by the polygon fragments. The method is based on the fact that the way in which a polygon covers a pixel can be approximated by a limited number of cases. The algorithm is embedded in a scanline renderer. The convolution is not restricted to one pixel extent but more correctly extends over, say, a 3×3 area. Pixels act as accumulators whose final value is correct when all fragments that can influence its value have been taken into account.

Consider a 3×3 pixel area and a 3×3 filter kernel (Figure 11.8). A single visible fragment in the centre pixel will contribute to the convolution integral when the filter is centred on each of the nine squares. The nine contributions that such a fragment makes can be precomputed and stored in a look-up table. The two main stages in the process are:

(1) Find the visible fragments and identify or categorize their shape.

(2) Index a precomputed look-up table which gives the nine contributions for each shape. A single multiplication of the fragment's intensity by the precomputed contribution weighting gives the desired result.

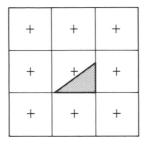

Figure 11.8
A single fragment in the centre pixel will cause contributions to filtering on each of the nine squares.

Abram assumes that the shapes fall into one of seven categories:

- There is no fragment in the pixel.
- The fragment completely covers the pixel.
- The fragment is trapezoidal and splits the pixel along opposite edges.
- The fragment is triangular and splits the pixel along adjacent edges.
- The complement of the above category (a pentagonal fragment).
- The fragment is an odd shape that can be described by the difference of two or more of the previous types.
- The fragment cannot be easily defined by these simple types.

11.5 A mathematical comparison

We can generalize and compare the above two methods from a more rigorous viewpoint. The filtering or convolution operation can be defined as:

$$s(i,j) = \int\int I(i + x, j + y)F(x,y)\, dx dy \qquad (11.1)$$

where:

$s(i,j)$ is a single sample from a *continuous* two-dimensional image I
$F(x,y)$ is a filter kernel

The integration is performed by placing the filter kernel at $I(i,j)$ and integrating over the extent of the filter. This equation is evaluated for all $s(i,j)$.

First, consider supersampling. This method is used with point sampling algorithms such as the Z-buffer or ray tracing. I has *already* been reduced to samples or supersamples and the above integral can only be approximated. We do not have available a continuous image I to sample. We can increase the 'integrity' of the approximation by increasing the number of supersamples, but this has serious consequences for the rendering costs.

The second method, on the other hand, solves Equation 11.1 directly but uses a poor filter kernel F. The renderer 'retains' a continuous image I

by performing subpixel geometry. This I is convolved with F to produce the required samples but F is only a single pixel wide, and consequently its frequency cut-off is high and its ability to deal with high-frequency artefacts is less than a filter with a wider kernel.

To sum up we have: in the first method I has already been sampled and we attempt to diminish this by increasing the number of the samples; in the second method I is continuous but the algorithmic constraints of the method restrict F to an area of one pixel.

11.6   Stochastic sampling

This method is used by Cook (Cook, Porter and Carpenter, 1984; Cook, 1986) both to solve both the aliasing problem *and* to model fuzzy phenomena in distributed ray tracing. The method has also been investigated by Abram, Westover and Whitted (1985) and Dippe and Wold (1985). Its relevance to ray tracing is discussed in Chapter 8.

A reference to the receptor organization in the human eye is given by Cook (1986). Cook points out that the human eye contains an array of non-uniformly distributed photoreceptors, and that this is the reason we do not perceive aliasing artefacts. Photoreceptor cells in the fovea are tightly packed and the lens acts as an anti-aliasing filter. However, in the region outside the fovea, the spatial density of the cells is much lower and the cells are non-uniformly distributed. A detailed description of these factors is given by Williams and Collier (1983).

The basis of the method is to perturb the position of the sampling points. High-frequency information above the Nyquist limit is then mapped into noise. Aliasing artefacts are traded for noise. The distribution from which the perturbations are selected determines the spectral character of the noise, and the frequency of the information being sampled (relative to the sampling frequency) determines the energy of the noise. The method can be seen as a two-stage process:

(1) Sample the image using a sampling grid where the (x,y) position of each sampling point has been subject to a random perturbation.

(2) Use these sample values with a reconstruction filter to determine the pixel intensities to which the unperturbed sample positions correspond.

The basis of the above method is demonstrated in Figure 11.9 which is based on Cook's illustration (Cook, 1986). In Figure 11.9(a) a sine wave with a frequency below the Nyquist limit is sampled. Jittering or perturbing the samples over the region shown introduces a corresponding error in the sample amplitude. The information is thus sampled and a level of noise is introduced into the spectrum of the samples. In Figure 11.9(b) a sine wave with a frequency above the Nyquist limit is sampled. Here the perturbation

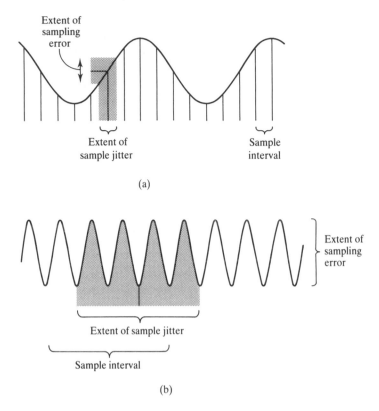

Figure 11.9
Sampling a sine wave whose frequency is (a) below and (b) above the Nyquist limit. (After Cook.)

results in an almost random value for the amplitude. Thus where uniform sampling would produce an alias for this sine wave, we have introduced instead noise and the alias is traded off against noise.

These factors are easily demonstrated in the frequency domain by considering the spectrum of a sine wave sampled by this method and again varying the frequency about the Nyquist limit (Figure 11.10). As the sampling frequency is reduced with respect to the sine wave, the amplitude of the sine wave spike diminishes and the noise amplitude increases. Eventually, the sine wave peak disappears. The point of the illustration is that no alias spikes appear. The information represented by the sine wave eventually disappears but instead of aliasing we get noise. The perturbation can range in x over a minimum of half a cycle (where the sine wave frequency is at the Nyquist limit) and will, in general, range over a number of complete cycles. If the range encompasses a number of cycles exactly then, for white noise jitter, the probability of sampling each part of the sine wave tends to be equal and the energy in the samples appears as white noise. A mathematical treatment of the attenuation due to white noise jitter and Gaussian jitter is given by Balakrishnan (1962).

One of the problems of this method is that it is only easily incorpor-

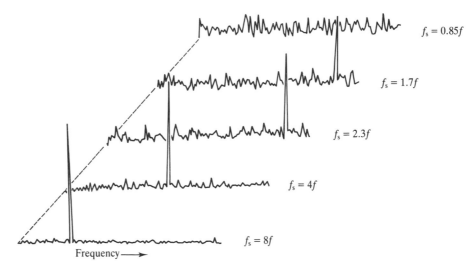

$f_s = 0.85f$

$f_s = 1.7f$

$f_s = 2.3f$

$f_s = 4f$

$f_s = 8f$

Frequency ——→

Figure 11.10
Varying the frequency
of a sine wave (f) with
respect to a perturbed
sampling frequency
(f_s).

ated into methods where the image synthesis can be practically split into the two phases of generation in a continuous domain followed by sampling. This is certainly the case in ray tracing, where rays are spawned in the continuous object space domain, and are, in effect, samples in this space. They can easily be jittered. In 'standard' image synthesis methods, using say interpolative shading in the context of a Z-buffer or scanline algorithm, introducing jitter presents much more of a difficulty. The algorithms are founded on uniform incremental methods in screen space and would require substantial modification to have the effect of two-dimensional sampling perturbation. Although such algorithms are equivalent to image generation in a continuous domain succeeded by two-dimensional sampling, in practice the sampling and generation phases are not easily unmeshed.

A major rendering system, called REYES (Cook, Carpenter and Catmull, 1987) does, however, integrate a Z-buffer based method with stochastic sampling. This works by dividing initial primitives, such as bicubic parametric patches, into (flat) 'micropolygons' (of approximate dimension in screen space of half a pixel). All shading and visibility calculations operate on micropolygons. Shading occurs *prior* to visibility calculations and is constant over a micropolygon. The micropolygons are then stochastically sampled from screen space, the Z value of each sample point calculated by interpolation and the visible sample hits filtered to produce pixel intensities (Figure 11.11). Thus shading is carried out at micropolygon level and visibility calculations at the stochastic sampling level.

This method does away with the coherence of 'classical' rendering methods, by splitting objects into micropolygons. It is most suitable for objects consisting of bicubic parametric patches because they can be easily subdivided.

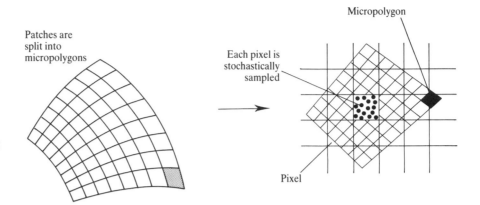

Figure 11.11
Graphical primitives are subdivided into micropolygons. These are shaded and visibility calculations are performed by stochastically sampling the micropolygons in screen space. (After Cook, Carpenter and Catmull (1987)).

Projects, notes and suggestions ———

Some of the projects for this chapter include the use of Fourier theory. This is extremely useful in gaining an understanding of the basis of aliasing and the efficacy of the various cures. A short note on Fourier transforms is included at this point.

A short note on Fourier transforms

The discrete Fourier transform (DFT) is an approximation to the continuous Fourier integral:

$$F(\omega) = \int_{-\infty}^{\infty} x(t) \exp(-j2\pi\omega t)\, dt$$

The discrete transform is used when a set of sample function values, $x(i)$, are available at equally spaced intervals $i = 0, 1, 2, \ldots, N-1$. The DFT converts the given values into the sum of a discrete number of sine waves whose frequencies are numbered $u = 0, 1, 2, \ldots, N-1$, and whose amplitudes are given by:

$$F(u) = \frac{1}{N} \sum_{i=0}^{N-1} x(i) \exp\left(-j2\pi u \frac{i}{N}\right)$$

This expression can be implemented directly as a slow DFT. (More usually a fast Fourier transform (FFT) would be used to compute a DFT.) The above DFT can be expressed as:

$$F(u) = \frac{1}{N} \sum_{i=0}^{N-1} x(i) \cos\left(2\pi u \frac{i}{N}\right) - \frac{j}{N} \sum_{i=0}^{N-1} x(i) \sin\left(2\pi u \frac{i}{N}\right)$$

and this form is easily implemented in a program. This will give a cosine and a sine transform respectively for the complex-valued function $F(u)$. The amplitude spectrum is what is required for the projects and this is given by the sum of the squares of the cosine and the sine transform.

11.1   Supersampling

Examine the efficacy of supersampling using a magnified test image (see, for example, Plate 25). Experiment with the degree of supersampling and with box and shaped filters of various widths.

11.2   Texture artefacts

Produce a 'problematic' texture, say a chequerboard pattern in perspective coming to a point at the top of the screen. Select a number of scan lines for increasing values of y_s and produce a Fourier transform of the intensity variation along a scan line. Correlate the information in the frequency spectra with the Nyquist limit of the device and the onset of aliasing artefacts on the screen.

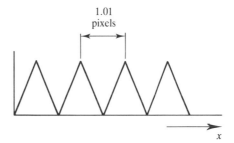

Figure 11.12
A one-dimensional test pattern to be used in Project 11.3.

11.3   Fourier domain and filtering

Generate a description of an 'impossible' one-dimensional test pattern, such as a set of triangles slightly wider than one pixel (Figure 11.12). Produce the following plots:

- Space domain
  (1a) the original function $f(x)$;
  (2a) the sampled function (that is, the values of $f(x)$ at pixel centres);
  (3a) the sampled function convolved with a box filter one pixel wide.
  Note that (3a) is an approximation to the output that will appear on the screen. There is a final degradation process that rounds the edges in (3a) owing to the defocusing or smearing effect of the electron beam in the CRT.
- Frequency domain
  (1b) an amplitude spectrum of $f(x)$;
  (2b) an amplitude spectrum of the sampled version of $f(x)$;
  (3b) an amplitude spectrum of the filter;

(4b) the product of (2b) and (3b), which is the amplitude spectrum of the sampled signal after filtering.
Note the difference between (4b) and (1b). Relate this difference to the appearance of aliasing artefacts in (2a) and (3a).

Repeat the above procedure using a test pattern where the width of the triangles is now increased to 10 pixels and compare the results.

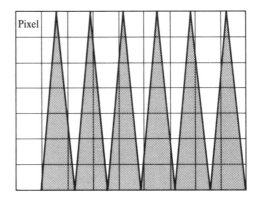

Figure 11.13
A two-dimensional test pattern to be used in Project 11.4.

11.4   Stochastic sampling

This project is based on work reported in Cook (1986). Use the triangles in the previous project as a two-dimensional test pattern (Figure 11.13) of bright triangles on a dark background over a spatial extent of, say, 100×100 pixels. Sample this pattern using one sample per pixel and a 3×3 filter kernel to reconstruct a rendered pattern on the screen.

Repeat this process but this time jitter the samples in x and y. Compare the results. Finally, increase the sampling rate and produce two further images using 16 uniform samples per pixel and 16 jittered samples per pixel.

12 | **Functionally Based Modelling Methods**

12.1 Introduction

This chapter looks at the idea of generating objects or structures procedurally. This is an important area in computer graphics, and is the only practical way in which certain scenes can be generated. For example, trees in a forest landscape can only be sensibly generated procedurally. An example of procedural generation that we have already touched on is the definition of a three-dimensional texture field. Precalculation and storage of a texture field would be expensive and the texture is calculated at rendering time from a procedure.

In this chapter we present three general techniques that have found considerable application in three-dimensional computer graphics. These are:

- deterministic or non-stochastic functions that have been used (mainly harmonic functions in terrain generation),
- stochastic functions that have been used in generating such phenomena as terrain, fire and turbulence, and
- a combination of the above that has been used, for example, in water or wave models.

These techniques are used to modulate an attribute of an existing object (as in, for example, the marble texture described in Chapter 7) or the function may itself produce an object as in the particle system now described.

Functional modelling came to be used in computer graphics more or less simultaneously by a number of practitioners, all of whom were interested in producing apparently complex images without having to set up that complexity in large polygon mesh based systems. The term **database amplification** was coined to reflect the fact that highly detailed complex images could be produced from a 'small formula'. The general technique is clearly applicable to simulating natural phenomena, where complexity is mediated by some degree of self-similarity.

12.2   Particle systems

An example of a functional scheme that produces an object description is Reeves' particle modelling system (Reeves, 1983). Here the modelling of the object and the process of rendering merge into a single functional approach. This technique is used to model phenomena that Reeves calls fuzzy objects and includes, for example, fire, cloud and water. Reeves' particle systems are inextricably bound up with animation, and although static objects can be developed using this technique, the process is most impressive when modelling time-varying phenomena, such as fire.

An object is represented by a cloud of elementary particles each of which is born, evolves in space and dies or extinguishes, all at different times. Individual particles move in three-dimensional space and change such attributes as colour, transparency and size as a function of time.

Both the global behaviour of a particle cloud and the detailed behaviour of individual particles are derived from various functions. For example, the number of particles generated at a particular time t can be derived from:

$$N_t = M_t + \text{Random}(r)V_t$$

where M_t is the mean number of particles in the population, $\text{Random}(r)$ is a pseudorandom variable and V_t is the variance of the population.

The same approach can be used to determine values for initial parameters that may describe, for example, the ejection of a particle from a point. The parameters used by Reeves are:

- initial position,
- initial velocity (both speed and direction),
- initial size,
- initial colour,
- initial transparency,
- shape, and
- lifetime.

The movement of individual particles is then scripted using these parameters as a function of time. Reeves used precisely such a system in *Star Trek II* to generate a transformation (of a dead planet into a live planet) by moving a wall of fire across a planet's surface.

12.3   Fractal systems

Fractal geometry is a term coined by Benoit Mandelbrot (1977; 1982). The term was used to describe the attributes of certain natural phenomena, for example coastlines. A coastline viewed at any level of detail – at microscopic level, at a level where individual rocks can be seen or at

Program 12.1 Recursive routine for drawing binary trees.

```
procedure tree (x,y: real; angle, branchfan, height: real; heightfactor,
                anglefactor: real; branchdensity, depth: integer);
const pi = 3.142;
var i, xint, yint: integer; xinc, yinc, start, theta: real;
begin
    xint := round(x); yint := round(y);
    if depth = 0 then
    begin {draw a 'leaf'}
        Colour(green);
        Move_to(xint - 2, yint); Line_to(xint + 2, yint);
        Move_to(xint, yint - 4); Line_to(xint, yint + 4)
    end
    else
    begin
        start := angle - branchfan/2;
        theta := branchfan/branchdensity;
        if depth <= 2 then heightfactor := heightfactor/2;
        xinc := height*cos(angle/180*pi);
        yinc := height*sin(angle/180*pi);
        angle := start;
        Colour(red);
        Move_to(xint, yint); Line_to(round(x + xinc), round(y + yinc));
        for i := to branchdensity + 1 do
        begin
            tree(x + xinc, y + yinc,
                angle/2 + sign(angle)*random(round(abs(angle))) + 1),
                branchfan*anglefactor, height*heightfactor/2 +
                random(round(height*heightfactor) + 1), heightfactor,
                anglefactor, branchdensity, depth - 1);
            angle := angle + theta
        end
    end
end;
```

'geographical' level – tends to exhibit the same level of jaggedness; a kind of statistical self-similarity. Fractal geometry provides a description for certain aspects of this ubiquitous phenomenon in nature and its tendency towards self-similarity. This is illustrated conceptually in Plate 26, which was generated by a simple recursive procedure (Program 12.1) that basically draws binary trees. Such parameters as branch angle and length are randomly perturbed. (Since this simple program uses lines to simulate three-dimensional primitives we use non-standard two-dimensional line utilities.

They are *Colour*, *Move_to* and *Line_to*.) Plate 26 shows the result of two executions of the same procedure using a binary tree rule. The other two illustrations were produced by introducing more than two branches at each node. It can be seen from these examples that realism can be increased by making the diameter of the branches vary as a function of depth, introducing, say, bending due to wind and utilizing the third spatial dimension. The branching scheme is easily extended into the third dimension by using two angles at a branch – an azimuth and elevation angle. An impressive example of this kind of approach is given in 'The Mighty Maple' (Bloomenthal, 1985), where the tree model is three-dimensional and texture mapping is employed to model the bark on the branches.

In three-dimensional computer graphics, fractal techniques have been used to generate terrain models and the easiest techniques involve subdividing the facets of the objects that consist of triangles or quadrilaterals. A recursive subdivision procedure is applied to each facet, to a required depth or level of detail, and a convincing terrain model results. Subdivision in this context means taking the midpoint along the edge between two vertices and perturbing it along a line normal to the edge. The result of this is to subdivide the original facets into a large number of smaller facets, each having a random orientation in three-dimensional space about the original facet orientation. The initial global shape of the object is retained to an extent that depends on the perturbation at the subdivision and a planar four-sided pyramid might turn into a 'Mont Blanc' shaped object.

Most subdivision algorithms are based on a formulation by Fournier, Fussell and Carpenter (1982) that recursively subdivides a single line segment. This algorithm was developed as an alternative to more mathematically correct, but expensive, procedures suggested by Mandelbrot. It uses self-similarity and conditional expectation properties of fractional Brownian motion to give an estimate of the increment of the stochastic process. The process is also Gaussian and the only parameters needed to describe a Gaussian distribution are the mean (conditional expectation) and the variance.

The procedure (Program 12.2) recursively subdivides a line $(t1,f1)$, $(t2,f2)$ generating a scalar displacement of the midpoint of the line in a direction normal to the line (Figure 12.1).

To extend this procedure to, say, triangles or quadrilaterals in three-dimensional space, we treat each edge in turn generating a displacement along a midpoint vector that is normal to the plane of the original facet (Figure 12.2). Using this technique we can take a smooth pyramid, say, made of large triangular faces and turn it into a rugged mountain.

Fournier categorizes two problems in this method – internal and external consistency. Internal consistency requires that the shape generated should be the same whatever the orientation in which it is generated, and that coarser details should remain the same if the shape is replotted at greater resolution. To satisfy the first requirement, the Gaussian randoms

Program 12.2   Recursive subdivision of a line.

```
procedure fractal(t1, f2, t2, f2, resolution, roughness: real);

var r, timid, fmid: real;

begin
   if (sqr(t2 − t1) + sqr(f2 − f1)) < sqr(resolution) then
      begin
         Move_to(round(t1), round(f1));
         Line_to(round(t2), round(f2))
      end
   else
   begin
      r := rand(−1, +1);
      tmid := (t1 + t2)/2 − roughness*(f2 − f1)*r;
      fmid := (f1 + f2)/2 + roughness*(t2 − t1)*r;
      fractal(t1, f1, tmid, fmid, resolution, roughness);
      fractal(tmid, fmid, t2, f2, resolution, roughness)
   end
end;
```

generated must not be a function of the position of the points, but should be unique to the point itself. An invariant point identifier needs to be associated with each point. This problem can be solved in terrain generation by giving each point a key value used to index a Gaussian random number. A hash function can be used to map the two keys of the end points of a line to a key value for the midpoint. Scale requirements of internal consistency mean that the same random numbers must always be generated in the same order at a given level of subdivision.

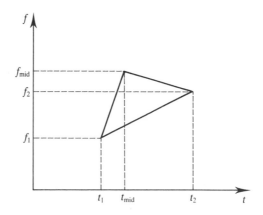

Figure 12.1
Line segment
subdivision.

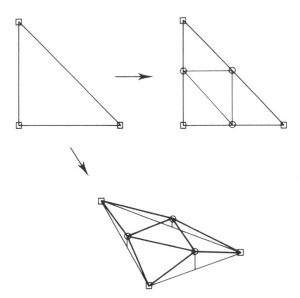

Figure 12.2
Triangle subdivision.

External consistency is harder to maintain. Within the mesh of triangles every triangle shares each of its sides with another, thus the same random displacements must be generated for corresponding points of different connecting triangles. This is already solved by using the key value of each point and the hash function, but another problem still exists, that of the direction of the displacement.

If the displacements are along the surface normal of the polygon under consideration, then adjacent polygons which have different normals (as is, by definition, always the case) will have their midpoints displaced into different positions. This causes gaps to open up. A solution is to displace the midpoint along the average of the normals to all the polygons that contain it, but this problem occurs at every level of recursion and is consequently very expensive to implement. Also, this technique would create an unsatisfactory skyline because the displacements are not constrained to one direction. A better skyline is obtained by making all the displacements of points internal to the original polygon in a direction normal to the plane of the original polygon. This cheaper technique solves all problems relating to different surface normals, and the gaps created by them. Now surface normals need not be created at each level of recursion and the algorithm is considerably cheaper because of this.

Another two points are worth mentioning. First, note that polygons should be constant shaded without calculating vertex normals – discontinuities between polygons should not be smoothed out. Second, consider colour. The usual global colour scheme uses a height-dependent mapping. In detail, the colour assigned to a midpoint is one of its end point's colours. Which one is chosen is determined by a boolean random which is indexed by the key value of the midpoint. Once again this must be accessed in this way to maintain consistency, which is just as important for colour as it is for position.

12.4 Functions suitable for three-dimensional texture

12.4.1 The three-dimensional *noise* function

The two common bases used in three-dimensional texture synthesis are harmonic functions and random functions. Useful effects such as marble are easily achieved by combining both.

The foundation of stochastically based solid texture, discussed in Chapter 7, is a pseudorandom noise function that is indexed by a three-dimensional point or vector. The nature and design of such a function was proposed by Perlin (1985) who introduced a function called *noise*. Perlin points out that the function was designed to have the following properties:

- statistical invariance under rotation,
- a narrow bandpass limit in frequency (it has no visible features larger or smaller than a certain range), and
- statistical invariance under translation.

noise has a pseudorandom value for points defined with integral x, y, z coordinates – the integer lattice. For all other points in the space the value of *noise* is determined by interpolation from the values on the integer lattice. The necessity for this approach can be seen by imagining the result of simply returning a pseudorandom number for every (floating-point) three-dimensional vector input to the function. The procedure shown in Program 12.3 is a simple implementation of *noise*.

Perlin uses this *noise* function in a variety of contexts to modulate the colour and perturb the normal of three-dimensional objects. One of the most effective applications of *noise* developed by Perlin is a synthetic turbulence function used to model a solar corona.

12.4.2 Fourier synthesis

Fourier synthesis can be used as a basis for many natural phenomena including water and terrain. It appears to have been first used in computer graphics to simulate terrain in flight simulators (Schachter, 1980; 1983). In this application two-dimensional cosine functions are used simply to modulate the colour of a flat plane in perspective, to provide economical texturing for depth cues.

Program 12.3   A simple implementation of noise.

```
procedure initialize_noise;
    var
        x, y, z, xx, yy, zz: nrange;
begin
    {set up the noise lattice}
    for x := 0 to max_noise do
        for y := 0 to max_noise do
            for z := 0 to max_noise do
            begin
                noise_table[x, y, z] := round(random(1)*10000);
                if x = max_noise then xx := 0 else xx := x;
                if y = max_noise then yy := 0 else yy := y;
                if z = max_noise then zz := 0 else zz := z;
                noise_table[x, y, z] := noise_table[xx, yy, zz]
            end;
end {initialize_noise};

function frac(r: real): real;
begin
    frac := r − trunc(r);
end {frac};

function noise(x, y, z: real): real;
    var
        ix, iy, iz: integer;
        ox, oy, oz: real;
        n: integer;
        n00, n01, n10, n11: real;
        n0, n1, real;
begin
    {offset x, y, z to ensure they are positive}
    x := x + 15000; y := y + 15000; z := z + 15000;

    {find lattice coordinates and real offsets}
    ix := trunc(x) mod max_noise;
    iy := trunc(y) mod max_noise;
    iz := trunc(z) mod max_noise;
    ox := frac(x); oy := frac(y); oz := frac(z);

    {interpolate to get noise value at (ix + ox, iy + oy, iz + oz)}

    n := noise_table[ix, iy, iz];
    n00 := n + ox*(noise_table[ix + 1, iy, iz] − n);
    n := noise_table[ix, iy, iz + 1];
    n01 := n + ox*(noise_table[ix + 1, iy, iz + 1] − n);
    n := noise_table[ix, iy + 1, iz];
```

$n10 := n + ox*(noise\_table[ix + 1, iy + 1, iz] - n);$
$n := noise\_table[ix, iy + 1, iz + 1];$
$n11 := n + ox*(noise\_table[ix + 1, iy + 1, iz + 1] - n);$

$n0 := n00 + oy*(n10 - n00);$
$n1 := n01 + oy*(n11 - n01);$
$noise := (n0 + oz*(n1 - n0))*0.0001;$
end {*noise*};

Gardener (1984; 1985) has used three-dimensional Fourier synthesis to model clouds, trees and terrain, and points out that the approach is powerful enough to model both 'micro' features – such as leaves on trees and wrinkles on terrain – as well 'macro' features – the clustering of trees and the major topography of hills.

Building a three-dimensional texture field using Fourier synthesis means generating parameters which specify the amplitude, frequency and phase of sinusoids. These are then linearly combined to produce a function in which, by careful choice of the design parameters, the underlying periodicities may be masked or hidden. Gardener uses a three-dimensional function $G(X,Y,Z)$ to model the amorphous shape of trees and clouds, modulating the surface intensity and the transparency of the ellipsoids. The parameter scheme evolved by Gardener (1988) is:

$$G(X,Y,Z) = \sum_{i=1}^{n} C_i[\cos(\omega_{xi}X + \phi_{xi}) + A_0]$$
$$\times \sum_{i=1}^{n} C_i[\cos(\omega_{yi}Y + \phi_{yi}) + A_0]$$
$$\times \sum_{i=1}^{n} C_i[\cos(\omega_{zi}Z + \phi_{zi}) + A_0] \qquad \textbf{(12.1)}$$

where:

n is a value between 4 and 7

$C_{i+1} \approx 0.707\ C_i$

C_1 is chosen such that $G(X,Y,Z) \leqslant 1$ and the values of C_i, ω_{xi}, ω_{yi}, ω_{zi} give a $1/f$ spectrum common in all kinds of natural phenomena. The initial values of ω specify the underlying or base frequencies such as the rolling of hills in a terrain.

$\omega_{xi+1} \approx 2\omega_{xi}$

$\omega_{yi+1} \approx 2\omega_{yi}$

$\omega_{zi+1} \approx 2\omega_{zi}$

ϕ_{xi}, ϕ_{yi} and ϕ_{zi} are phase shifts into which a random component can be built

A_0 is the basic offset providing contrast control

A complete study of the way in which these parameters are varied to provide convincing natural texture is to be found in Gardener (1988).

Projects, notes and suggestions ————————————

12.1   Trees

Extend Program 12.1 so that it produces a tree in three-dimensional space, as suggested in the text.

12.2   Fractal terrains

Develop the recursive subdivision procedure (Program 12.2) so that it generates a terrain in three-dimensional space using the technique suggested in the text.

12.3   Spectral terrains

Use a two-dimensional version of Equation 12.1 to generate a terrain. Do this by using $G(X, Y)$ to specify elevation values at each point on a regular grid. This then defines a polygon mesh structure that can be rendered by a conventional renderer. Note how simple and effective control is available over the ruggedness of the terrain by controlling spatial frequency and amplitude parameters. Can this approach, which is far simpler than subdivision, produce the same visual effects as the fractal technique?

12.4   Animation spectral terrain

Produce an animated film, where a coherent perturbation of a suitable shape that is (say) parallel to one of the coordinate axes moves through the terrain. Various possibilities exist; for example, the size of the perturbation can increase or decrease as it travels, or a central perturbation could move outwards.

12.5   Simple wave models

Using the 'perturbed grid' of the previous two projects use a single travelling sinusoid, around a single disturbance, to simulate an object being dropped in water. Modulate the amplitude as a function of time such that the ripples die as they spread. A more elaborate wave model is to be found in Fournier, Fussell and Carpenter (1986).

12.6   Three-dimensional modulation of surfaces

Use Equation 12.1 to modulate the surface of any convenient model; for example, displace the vertices of an approximately spherical object an amount specified by Equation 12.1 along a line from the centre of the object to the vertex (note that the easiest way to implement this method is to use a full Z-buffer renderer).

12.7 Landscapes (*)

Integrate all the above techniques into a landscape generation system using a full Z-buffer to solve the compositing problems.

Gardener (1984) gives details on models for the placement and distribution of, for example, trees in a complex landscape.

12.8 Particle systems

Design a particle system that will generate a system to model fireworks. This is best demonstrated using an animated sequence. Variables include different shaped explosions, different ejection angles, different trajectories and the colour of the particle changing as a function of time.

13 | Three-dimensional Computer Animation

13.1 Introduction

What is computer animation? In its simplest form it means moving rigid bodies around in a scene according to some motion specification. The motion specification is interpreted and causes linear transformations to be invoked and new scenes (or frames in animation) created which are then rendered in the usual way. We can also control the movement of a virtual camera or view point. This form of three-dimensional computer animation is now well established and it is mainly this type that we shall concentrate on in this chapter.

Another form of computer animation that has emerged recently is soft object animation where the shape of an object changes as a function of time. Animation can be produced directly from models or sets of equations specifying the dynamic behaviour of structures or machines, and this has major applications in the field of scientific visualization. This type of animation is better described as **simulation**.

Most computer animation is banal, uninteresting and unaesthetic. Currently, computer animation is used mainly to produce witless television commercials and it is a sadly underused tool as far as 'serious' animation is concerned. This is a strange set of affairs because computer animation offers an animator facilities that are not directly available in traditional or film animation. These are immediacy and a substantial elimination of the workload involved in the production of a finished sequence.

Perhaps the more important of these is immediacy – modern workstations are capable of producing wireframe sequences interactively. This is surely a powerful tool for a traditional animator. The probable reason for the lack of use of computer animation in serious work is the difficulty of motion specification, or the interface between the animator (who may have no specialized knowledge of computers) and the system that produces the animation. There is a much greater conceptual difference between the computer-produced animation and the specification of that sequence than there is between the original sketches, which will be roughed out on pieces of paper each corresponding to a frame, and a traditional animation sequence.

The other potential advantage of computer animation is that it can remove the enormous workload involved in creating sequences in traditional animation. As an example of this, consider the Disney production of *Snow White and the Seven Dwarfs* – the first full-length feature cartoon. Work began on this production in 1934 and the film was premiered in Hollywood in December 1937. Four of Disney's most talented and experienced animators controlled the artistic output of other artists and inkers to produce over 2 million frames for the 90 minute feature.

How do we place computer animation with respect to the possible power that it offers aesthically rather than just saving on the donkey work? Perhaps a good way to look at this is to compare Disney animation with more recent forms, such as the animation of plasticine figures. Disney animation is notable for smooth fluidity of movement and the subtlety of the characterizations as expressed in this movement and facial expressions (Disney acolytes would talk about emotions). With plasticine animation smooth movement is far more of a problem because of the greater difficulty in expressing this in three dimensions by incremental sculpting of the material. Computer animation falls somewhere between these two extremes – characterization is difficult but there is tremendous potential as far as movement is concerned. A good example is the film *Luxo Jr.* (John Lasseter, Pixar, 1986) a frame of which is shown in Plate 27. Apart from being extremely successful artistically, the film contains many messages for would-be computer animators. The success of this particular film is due entirely to the ability of Lasseter to invest a degree of 'Disney-type' characterization in a rigid but articulated object – an anglepoise lamp. The notable point about this film is that most of the action falls into the mainstream category of relative movement of rigid bodies. Despite this the film is alive.

This feature was the first serious attempt to invoke the well-known principles of traditional animation in three-dimensional computer animation. Although this is not necessarily the way computer animation should go, it highlights the main drawback of TV commercials and title sequences – their sterility and sameness. In fact, animation in the context of computers, as far as the current state of the art is concerned, is a misuse of the word.

In a landmark paper that describes one of the first computer animation systems, Baecker (1969) states:

> The animation industry is ripe for a revolution. Historical accidents of available technology and knowledge of visual physiology have led to the evolution of the animated film as one that is created frame by frame. The prodigious quantities of labour required for the construction of 24 individual frames per second of film have led to a concentration of animation activity in the assembly-line environments of a few large companies, an artificial yet rarely surmounted separation of the artist from the medium, and extravagant costs.

Note that the author claims that it is the traditional methods that 'separate the artist from the medium'. Unfortunately, events have shown otherwise and the optimism implied by this quote has only been reflected with hardware advances that remove the labour costs.

It is evident that there is a place for three-dimensional computer animation in engineering simulation and scientific visualization (ViSC) just as (static) computer graphics is already universally used in these fields. Already, high-quality colour three-dimensional graphics is used to visualize and provide insight into complex phenomena characterized by massive data-sets, such as fluid behaviour in liquids and gases, and three-dimensional computer animation will eventually provide a powerful tool for the investigation of dynamic phenomena.

Examples of three-dimensional animation in ViSC have recently emerged, but their extreme diversity and small numbers emphasize the newness of the field. It is probable that the eventual mainstream application of computer animation will be ViSC. In a recent panel (McCormick, DeFanti and Brown, 1987) ViSC was defined as follows:

> Visualisation transforms the symbolic into the geometric, enabling researchers to observe their simulations and computations. Visualization offers a method for seeing the unseen. It enriches the process of scientific discovery and fosters profound and unexpected insights. In many fields it is already revolutionizing the way scientists do science.
>
> Visualization embraces both image understanding and image synthesis. That is, visualization is a tool both for interpreting image data fed into a computer, and for generating images from complex multi-dimensional data sets. It studies those mechanisms in humans and computers which allow them in concert to perceive, use and communicate visual information. Visualization unifies the largely independent but convergent fields of:
>
> Computer graphics
>
> Image processing
>
> Computer vision
>
> CAD
>
> Signal processing
>
> User interface studies

One of the major applications of ViSC that involves three-dimensional computer animation is computational fluid dynamics. This refers to the numerical solution of the partial differential equations of fluid flow. Animation of such phenomena as shock waves, vortices, shear layers and wakes, all of which depend on time, is of major importance.

The variety of productions that can be loosely inserted in the ViSC category can be shown by describing a few examples. Blinn's *Mechanical Universe* (Blinn, 1987) is a large-scale project running to 7.5 hours of screen time. Simulating physical phenomena, Blinn uses a mixture of two-dimensional and three-dimensional animation to produce arresting sequences of such diverse phenomena as molecular dynamics and general relativity. In what must be the longest computer animation production, Blinn demonstrates how to use computer animation tools in both the visualization and the explanation of environments that have no 'real visualization' – the world of molecules and universes.

As well as being a visual implementation or passive reflection of scientific phenomena, three-dimensional computer animation can provide a testbed for scientific investigation. Reynolds (1987) simulates flocking behaviour in birds and fishes. In this intriguing study each simulated member of the flock is an independent actor that navigates 'according to its local perception of the dynamic environment, the laws of simulated physics that rule its motion, and a set of behaviours programmed into it by the animator'. It is evident that the investigation of flocking dynamics, as a function of individual and aggregate behaviour, would not be possible without the investigator being able to view the final animation of the flock.

13.2   Keyframing systems

Keyframing systems are based on a well-known production technique in film or cel animation. To cope with the prodigous workload in developing an animation sequence of any length, a hierarchical system developed wherein talented animators specify a sequence by drawing key frames at certain intervals. These are passed to 'inbetweeners' who draw the intermediate frames which are then coloured by inkers. (This hierarchy was reflected in the rewards received by the members of the team. In Disney's *Snow White and the Seven Dwarfs* the four chief animators were paid $100 a week, the inbetweeners $35 and the inkers $20.)

It was natural that this process be extended to three-dimensional computer animation – the spatial juxtaposition of objects in a scene can be defined by key frames and the computer can interpolate the inbetween frames. However, many problems arise mainly because simple interpolation strategies cannot replace the intelligence of a human inbetweener. In general, we need to specify more key frames in a computer system than would be required in traditional animation.

Consider the simple problem of a bouncing ball. If we use three key frames – the start position, the end position and the zenith – together with linear interpolation, then the resulting trajectory will be unrealistic (Figure 13.1). Linear interpolation is generally inadequate in most contexts.

We can improve on this by allowing the animator to specify more information about the motion characteristics between the key frames. For example, a curved path could be defined. This, however, would say nothing about how the velocity varied along the path. A ball moving with uniform velocity along, say, a parabola would again look unrealistic. Thus to control motion correctly when we are moving objects around we must explicitly

Figure 13.1
Linear interpolation will produce an unrealistic trajectory for a bouncing ball specified at three key positions.

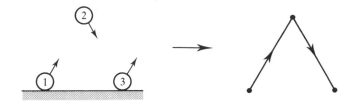

define both the positional variation as a function of time and the dynamic behaviour along the specified path.

We can give such information in a number of ways. We could, for example, work with a set of points – key frame points – defining where an object is to be at certain points in time and fit a cubic, say, through these points. Alternatively, we could dispense with points and have the animator define the position and velocity characteristics as curves. This is the topic of the next section. The techniques described apply both to interpolation (using interpolation techniques described in Chapter 6) and to specification of curves. Apart from the issue of interpolation in the key frame case, both approaches require the same calculations by the animation program.

13.2.1   What parameters to control

As mentioned in Section 13.1 we are mostly going to be concerned with rigid body animation – controlling the position of objects or a camera as a function of time. This simply involves moving the local coordinate system of each object in the animation system under control of the motion specification. Thus we will be concerned with specifying the position of objects in world space with respect to time – the path curve – and how objects move along that path – the motion characteristic.

In rigid body animation we are, in general, interested in a combination of displacement and rotation. Care must be taken when choosing a parameter to interpolate. Figure 13.2 shows a simple example. Here the animation is the rotation of a line through 90°. The appropriate parameter to interpolate is the angle and not the position of the end point of the line.

Figure 13.2
Interpolating rotation: angle (left) produces a different motion compared with interpolating end points (right).

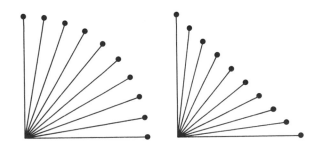

13.3   Explicit motion specification – curve editing

Section 13.1 mentioned the difficulty that is inherent in attempting to utilize the potential of computer animation. One of the most successful methods of motion specification is to specify the behaviour of a three-dimensional object by a set of curves, which can be edited in an interactive feedback loop to facilitate real-time wireframe animation. The first appearance of such an idea was by Baecker (1969). In this paper Baecker uses the following simple example. Consider the motion of a figure that walks from point A to point C, diagonally opposite, by following a path along the wall to corner B, then from B to C (Figure 13.3a). We can plot the variation of the position in x and y of the figure as a function of time, and from Figure 13.3(b and c) we can see that the figure starts from rest, accelerates and then decelerates to the corner B. A pause occurs at B then the figure accelerates and decelerates in the direction of the destination. Figure 13.3(d) is the same as Figure 13.3(a) except that superimposed on the path are markers that represent equal intervals in time. These intervals will be frames at, say, every 24th of a second. Baecker terms such a characteristic a 'P-curve' and we note that it contains both the path and the dynamics of the motion. The path can be changed by editing the curve. The distance between points on the P-curve controls the characteristics or dynamics of the motion and we could either edit the spacing of the markers or use a curve-editing program to alter $x(t)$ and $y(t)$.

In traditional animation such scripting of the dynamics of a character is achieved by altering the difference or distance between the character's position in consecutive drawings. Acceleration and deceleration is called 'easing in' and 'easing out'. Such control via the drawings is particular for the character and is a fine skill of the animator. The character could be a walking figure with arm and leg movements or it could be a motor car.

A computer system expresses the dynamic characteristics globally – the movement is summarized and the information is in a form that is easily and conveniently edited. Having a complete animation sequence specified by a global characteristic is an attractive proposition and it is the key to interactive animation. In this way the animator globally controls the dynamics of the entire sequence. Also note that the dynamic or velocity characteristic is separate from the position characteristic. We should thus, with computer animation, be able to achieve a more accurate dynamic characteristic in the final animation, and the animator can experiment with the dynamic characteristics without having to redraw the characters. The animator can also experiment with different velocity characteristics using the same path. This frees the animator to concentrate on such attributes of the animation as facial expression and all the other subtleties that go into a good animated film.

This technique is easily embellished to use splines rather than arbit-

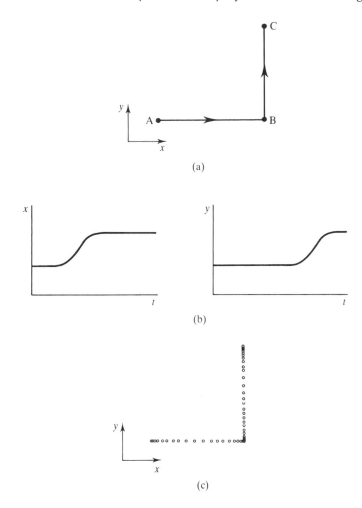

Figure 13.3
Specifying motion with a P-curve (after Baecker (1969)). (a) Specification of a path from A to C. (b) The motion or dynamic characteristics $x(t)$ and $y(t)$. (c) The P-curve. Symbols on the curve occur at equal intervals in time.

rary curves. Again the animator can edit the curve and the system can inbetween using the set of points that specify position in key frames as a basis for interpolation. One disadvantage of the use of splines is that, depending on the exact disposition of the points to be interpolated, unwanted excursions or oscillations can occur.

We can improve somewhat on the above simple system by using a parametric representation for the path curve. This allows us to have a single velocity characteristic. In the above example we had two velocity characteristics and in general with such a representation we would need three functions – $x(u)$, $y(u)$ and $z(u)$ – for three dimensions. If we use a parametric representation for the curve then we have the two advantages of being able to use splines and being able to have a single velocity characteristic by expressing velocity as a function of distance along the path. Thus, if the path

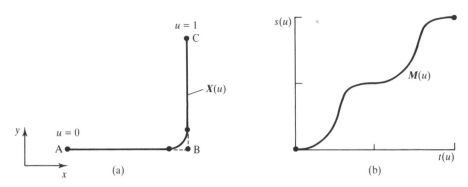

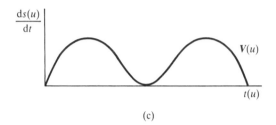

Figure 13.4
Specifying motion with splines and a single velocity characteristic. (a) Path represented by a spline. (b) Motion characteristic represented by a spline. (c) Alternative motion characteristic.

is now $X(u)$ we can define a single motion characteristic $M(u)$. The motion characteristic is a two-dimensional spline of distance travelled against time. Figure 13.4(a and b) shows this scheme for the same simple example. Having a single velocity characteristic as a function of path length seems a more natural system and is considerably easier to interact with than three separate curves. We may prefer to use a motion characteristic that specifies velocity along the path. This is shown in Figure 13.4(c).

Although this scheme seems preferable there is a significant problem lurking within it. To control the velocity of an object along the path we need to measure equal distances along the path length. It is the case that equal increments in u do not occur at equal distances along the curve. The parameter that we require is called arclength. Figure 13.5 demonstrates the difference between equal increments in the value of the parameter and equal increments in distance along the path for an arbitrary parametric function.

To demonstrate the necessity for such a parametrization consider an object moving with uniform velocity. In this case we would need to mark equal distances along the path and position the object at these points for each frame. In other words, we cannot even have an object move with uniform velocity unless we have arclength parametrization.

Unfortunately, the relationship between the parametrizing variable, u, and the arclength parameter is non-linear and there is no analytical conversion available. A detailed procedure is given in Watt and Watt (1992). An approximate and fast method of achieving arclength parametrization is

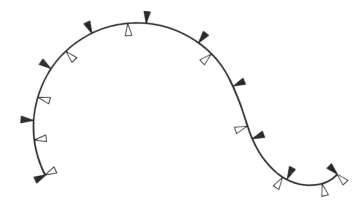

Figure 13.5
Intervals of equal
parametric length
(outlined arrowheads)
do not correspond to
equal intervals of
arclength (black
arrowheads).

to use forward differencing in conjunction with chords. The coarse nature of this approximation becomes apparent when the movement is slow over a long path. However, it is a useful method in an interactive system, because of its speed, and interaction is the keynote of this method.

Let us now define the reparametrization problem to enable us to describe the approximate solution. Our path or space curve is $X(u)$. If we define the distance s along the path to be measured in arclength units, then we can write:

$$s = A(u)$$

since arclength is a function of u. We now need to reparametrize $X(u)$:

$$X(u) \rightarrow X(s) = X(A^{-1}(s))$$

That is, given a value of s, we need to find the corresponding value of u. We do this by approximating the curve with a series of chords, finding the chord in which s lies and linearly interpolating within the chordlength.

The method works by building up accumulated chordlengths which are now used to approximate arclength (Figure 13.6). We do this by generating a sequence of points:

$$X(i\Delta u) \qquad i = 0, 1, 2, \ldots$$

where Δu is a small interval in u. The accumulated chordlength is stored in a table and for entry i the accumulated value is:

$$\sum_{j=1}^{i} d_j$$

where:

$$d_j = |X(u_j) - X(u_{j-1})|$$

Given s we can then find the nearest entry in the table.

Note that eventually the system needs to know the position of the object on the path for a particular instant (a frame time). We need to derive

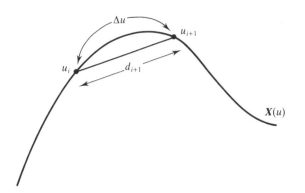

Figure 13.6
Chordlength
approximation to
arclength.

for a value of t the corresponding arclength. Again we have the same reparametrization problem. The motion characteristic is parametrized in terms of u and we require a value of s along the curve given a value for t. We require:

$$M(u) \rightarrow M(t) = M(T^{-1}(u))$$

where $t = T(u)$.

We are now in a position to describe the complete method in summary:

(1) The animator specifies a path ($X(u)$), either explicitly by editing a spline, or by specifying key points which are interpolated by a spline. In practice this may involve working with the three projections, $x = X(u)$, $y = Y(u)$ and $z = Z(u)$.

(2) The animator specifies a motion characteristic along the path $M(u)$ or $V(u)$. In both steps the problems of reparametrization are invisible to the user.

(3) The animator can then vary both characteristics independently and view the resulting sequence.

(4) To compute an animation sequence, the system derives values of s, for equal intervals of t, from the motion characteristic (Figure 13.7). These

Figure 13.7
Using the motion and
path characteristics.
(a) The motion
characteristic is used to
derive values of
arclength s for equal
intervals in t. (b) The
path characteristic is
used to find values of
(x,y) corresponding to
values of s.

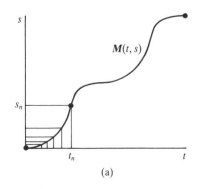

(a)

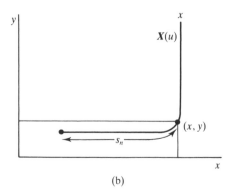

(b)

values of s are inserted into the path characteristic, and finally values of (x,y,z) are obtained for a particular value of t.

13.4   Other approaches to three-dimensional computer animation

Because of the extreme diversity of approaches that have emerged in computer animation, it is difficult to review in any methodical manner. Having concentrated on the mainstream technique – motion specification of rigid bodies – we now briefly look at other approaches. A full review of advanced computer animation techniques is given in Watt and Watt (1992).

13.4.1   Parametric systems

Parametric systems are similar to key frame interpolation, but the nature of the information given at key frames tends to be more complex and consists of parameters that control the subsequent behaviour of the object, rather than just position, say.

Parameters are injected at key frames and may be interpolated to provide a set of parameters for each inbetween frame. An example of such a system is *em* (Hanrahan and Sturman, 1985). Such systems are more elaborate than simple key frames and allow more complex object behaviour between key frames. Another advantage of this approach is that interaction can be far more powerful.

Hanrahan's system models inputs as variables whose numerical values are derived from physical interface devices. For example:

dx $+=$ *wheelx*

dy $+=$ *wheely*

spin $+=$ *10*joyz*

are assignment statements where the left-hand sides are a parameter of the model of the object that is being animated and the right-hand sides are input variables or functions of them. An interactive loop can then be set up whereby the animator controls the behaviour of the object in the inbetween frames by using input devices.

Consider, for example, an object that is to spin at a varying rate while translating between two positions. This would be a tedious problem with a basic interactive key frame system. It would be easily scripted using the programming language approach described in Section 13.4.2, but alterations in the spinning mode depend on an edit and recompile mode. If the spin is parametrized then interaction of the sequence is possible with spin parameters input from a suitable device. The power of the system depends on the ability of the software writer to parametrize the behaviour of the object.

13.4.2   Programmed animation and scripting systems

In this approach an animator writes a program to produce an animation sequence. The program is either written in a standard high-level language, and the animation produced through a graphical interface, or it is written in a specially designed animation scripting system.

The disadvantages of this approach are obvious. The sequence cannot be seen until the program is written. Animation effects are reflected in high-level constructs such as **for** loops and this distance between the 'script' and the effect is anti-intuitive. Skilled programming expertise is obviously required to build up an animated sequence from, say, Pascal or FORTRAN facilities, and the quality of the animation depends on the ability of the animator/programmer to bridge the gap between the programming constructs and their visual effect.

An obvious development of this algorithmic approach is to develop animation languages or provide extensive animation facilities in a general-purpose computer language. The program that produces the animation is generally known as a **script**. An example of this approach is Reynolds' Actor Script Animation System (ASAS) (Reynolds, 1982). The script in the animation language still retains its analogy to a program, with the normal advantages of this approach: the ability to edit a sequence and provide a progressive refinement facility, the ability to accumulate expertise by building up library facilities, the ability to tackle progressively more complex problems by using accumulated expertise (bootstrapping). As well as these advantages an animation language will reduce the conceptual distance between a program and script and its effect and should be accessible to animators who are not necessarily skilled programmers.

ASAS contains all the normal structured programming facilities, such as loops, conditionals and typed data structures. It can be considered to be an extension to LISP or a system that is implemented in LISP. In this respect, while it can be said that a would-be animator need not necessarily be a skilled programmer, certainly skills must be developed in ASAS to write a script, and LISP conventions are not easy for a novice.

ASAS is an environment that allows geometric objects, operations on these objects and animate blocks that allow actors to be 'directed'. Reynolds uses the term actor which he describes as a chunk of code that will be executed once each frame. An actor is responsible for a visible element in an animation sequence and the code chunk will contain all values and computations which relate to that object. Control over parallel actor processes is possible by message passing. Scenes in a production sequence are analogized by animate blocks which comprise the coarse structure of the action.

The following example from Reynolds (1982) is a script that contains one animate block. This block starts two similar actors, a green spinning cube and a blue spinning cube, at different times. Both actors then run until the end of the block.

```
(script spinning-cubes
        (local: (runtime 96)
                (midpoint (half runtime)))
        (animate (cue (at 0)
                      (start (spin-cube-actor green)))
                 (cue (at midpoint)
                      (start (spin-cube-actor blue)))
                 (cue (at runtime)
                      (cut))))
```

A unique object called a newton is available. Reynolds describes this as an animated numeric object. These can be used anywhere a numeric value is used, but their value is updated between frames. A newton data structure can store any complete sequence that may, for example, be any function such as a quadratic or cubic curve.

A similar programming approach, but using a Pascal-type basis is given in Magnetat-Thalmann and Thalmann (1985). Again the philosophy is to provide a convenient animation-based programming environment that enables a director to write a script. One of the major ways that this is done is to provide 'animated basic types'. This is a generalized extension of the previously described newton.

As well as applying this concept to scalar types such as integer and real, Thalmann introduces animated extended types such as vector. Starting and stopping values and motion laws can be incorporated in the type declaration and vector subsequently referred to in the program or script by using a single variable name.

An example, taken from Magnetat-Thalmann and Thalmann (1985) serves to illustrate the philosophy of this approach. The language is called CINEMIRA.

type TVEC = *animated* VECTOR;
        val $\langle\langle 0,10,4 \rangle\rangle$ .. UNLIMITED;
        time 10..13;
        law $\langle\langle 0,10,14 \rangle\rangle + \langle\langle 3,0,0 \rangle\rangle * (CLOCK-10)$;
        end;
var VEC : TVEC;

Here a vector is defined that starts at time 10 and moves with a constant speed $\langle\langle 3,0,0 \rangle\rangle$ from the point $\langle\langle 0,10,4 \rangle\rangle$ and stops at time 13.

Camera choreography is also implemented in the type declarations. Although this approach is completely general and places no restrictions on the use of computer facilities, it can be seen that a user has to be rather well versed in programming in structured languages.

Recognizing this fact, Thalmann developed an artist-oriented system that produces code in CINEMIRA. This is called ANIMEDIT and using this facility an animator can specify a complete script without programming in CINEMIRA. The system is interactive and, together with the freedom from having to use structured programming constructs, this makes it accessible to artists in a way that exploits their creativity.

ANIMEDIT thus combines the advantages of an animation-based system with the freedom of 'pure' interactive systems. The approach is a formal reflection of the work methods adopted by many commercial animation houses who employ both animators for their creativity and programmers to create new tools for the animator to use.

The ANIMEDIT system contains eight operational modes:

- *Variable mode*   Allows the animator to create extended variables with motion laws, and so on. It is not made clear by Thalmann exactly how a (computer-unskilled) animator can set these up.
- *Object mode*   Sets up the system's modelling capabilities and allows the animator to create objects and operate on their attributes.
- *Decor mode*   Similar to the previous mode, it facilitates the building of backgrounds and so on.
- *Actor mode*   In this mode the animator defines actors (animated objects) together with the transformations to which they have to be subjected.
- *Camera mode*   Similar to the actor mode as far as movement is concerned. (Clearly the camera cannot take attributes such as colour.)
- *Light mode*   Position and colour of light sources can be defined together with their motion.
- *Animation mode*   Directs the action, starting and stopping actors, cameras, and so on.
- *Control mode*   Controls entry to other modes.

The point of this edit system is fairly obvious. These eight modes, it has been decided, are the creative states that an animator requires to control detailed, but low-level, graphic utilities that will produce an animated sequence that is near to the designer's intentions.

13.4.3   Simulated or model-driven systems

An unfortunate confusion has arisen over the use of the term 'parameter' in computer animation. We will reserve its use to describe interactive systems (see above) where the parameters in the model are connected to the user interface.

Another major type of computer animation, sometimes described as 'parametric', involves using the mathematical equations that model or specify motion for a particular phenomenon to drive the animation. A system is simulated or scripted by a mathematical model. This type of animation finds applications in engineering – particularly the simulation of machines – where both the kinetics and the motion are constrained by the physical design of the machine.

One of the problems of key frame systems, or kinematic systems where the animator specifies positions and angles as a function of time, is that they are low level and make the animator independently control aspects of the behaviour of objects that are dynamically interdependent. *Simulation* (rather than animation) attempts to exploit this interdependence.

The principle of this type of animation is now explained for rigid bodies. Full implementation details are beyond the scope of this text and the reader should make use of the references given.

We can start by considering particles and Newton's second law:

$$\begin{aligned} \boldsymbol{F} &= M\boldsymbol{a} \\ &= M\,\mathrm{d}\boldsymbol{P}/\mathrm{d}t^2 \end{aligned} \tag{13.1}$$

where $\boldsymbol{F}$ is a three-dimensional force vector acting on a particle of mass M and $\boldsymbol{P}$ is the position of the particle in three-dimensional space.

A simulator supplies a force and mass and integrates the above equation to solve for position. Euler's method can be used to obtain a new position $\boldsymbol{P}_{i+1}$ at time $t + \delta t$ from:

$$\boldsymbol{P}_{i+1} = \boldsymbol{P}_i + v_i\delta t + \tfrac{1}{2}a_i\delta t^2$$

The accuracy of Euler's method is a function of the time step δt. Wilhelms (1987) points out, in a useful distillation of dynamics relevant to computer animation/simulation, that the accuracy of this numerical approximation can be increased by using the Runge–Kutta method.

In computer simulation we are generally going to be interested in bodies rather than particles and this complicates things considerably and adds to the computing expense. Non-particle masses either can be dealt with on the basis that they are rigid and their shape does not change (see, for example Hahn, 1988) or elasticity theory can be used to model bodies that deform under, say, collision (Terzopoulos *et al.*, 1987; Terzopoulos and Fleischer, 1988; Terzopoulos and Witkin, 1988).

The motion of rigid bodies can be represented by the sum of two motions. First, we consider two coordinate systems: a fixed system and a moving system embedded in the body and participating in its motion. This is conveniently positioned at the centre of mass of the body. An infinitesimal displacement used in an integral model can then be described as a translation of the body from its position at time t to its position at time $t + \delta t$ together with a rotation about its centre of mass which orients the body about the final position of its centre of mass. This makes a rigid body a system with six degrees of freedom.

The Euler method can be used to describe the motion and this results in six equations. Three are the translational equations of motion for the translational component:

$$\boldsymbol{F} = M\boldsymbol{a}$$

as before and three are the rotational equations of motion relating angular acceleration and distance of mass to torque (the rotational analogue of the above equation). This model is controlled by the simulator supplying both a force and a torque.

Mass distribution is described by moments of inertia about each axis in the coordinate system embedded in the body:

$$I_x = \sum m(y^2 + z^2)$$

$$I_y = \sum m(x^2 + z^2)$$

$$I_z = \sum m(x^2 + y^2)$$

This considers the rigid body to be a system of particles each of mass m. Examples of moments of inertia for symmetric homogeneous rigid bodies are:

- A sphere of radius R:

$$I_x = I_y = I_z = \tfrac{2}{5}MR^2$$

  where $M = \sum m$ the mass of the body.
- A cylinder of radius R and height h:

$$I_x = I_y = \tfrac{1}{4}M(R^2 + \tfrac{1}{3}h^2)$$
$$I_z = \tfrac{1}{2}MR^2$$

  where the z axis is along the axis of the cylinder.
- A box of sides a,b and c:

$$I_x = \tfrac{1}{12}M(a^2 + b^2)$$
$$I_y = \tfrac{1}{12}M(a^2 + c^2)$$
$$I_z = \tfrac{1}{12}M(b^2 + c^2)$$

  where the axes x,y and z are along the sides a,b and c respectively. This is useful in computer animation because in certain applications a bounding box is a sufficient approximation to a body, as far as the equations of motion are concerned.

These simple objects are symmetrical, that is, their mass is arranged symmetrically around a centre of mass.

The six equations of motion for a symmetrical rigid body are completed by the three rotational equations of motion:

$$N_x = I_x \dot{\omega}_x + (I_z - I_y)\omega_y \omega_z$$
$$N_y = I_y \dot{\omega}_y + (I_x - I_z)\omega_x \omega_z \qquad \textbf{(13.2)}$$
$$N_z = I_z \dot{\omega}_z + (I_y - I_x)\omega_x \omega_y$$

where:

N is torque acting on the body

ω is the angular velocity with respect to the local frame of reference

and the equations are specified in a local coordinate system embedded in the body, whose axes are the principal axes of inertia. Equations 13.1 and 13.2 are combined into a single set of six equations by transforming:

$$F = M a$$

into the moving coordinate system fixed to the body:

$$F_x = M \dot{v}_x + \omega_y v_z - \omega_z v_y$$
$$F_y = M \dot{v}_y + \omega_z v_x - \omega_x v_z$$
$$F_z = M \dot{v}_z + \omega_x v_y - \omega_y v_x$$

A simulator supplies an applied force F that is assumed to operate at the centre of mass and a torque vector N. The equations can be solved for v and ω. Full details on converting between coordinate frames and the formulae for non-symmetric bodies is given in Wilhems (1987).

The above theory only provides a basis for a computer simulation. An interesting or useful animation sequence is likely to include objects interacting with other objects and/or the environment.

Realistic animation of complex or non-symmetric rigid bodies is dealt with by Hahn (1988). Here dynamic interaction between rigid bodies is simulated using the appropriate Newtonian dynamics. The focus of this study is to remove the scripting of rigid body interaction from the animator's artistic judgement and give it over to the underlying mathematics.

In Hahn's system, objects to be simulated are given physical characteristics, such as shape, density, coefficient of restitution and coefficient of friction. These properties are used to calculate attributes such as total mass, centre of mass and moments of inertia.

At any instant an object possesses a velocity (linear and angular), a position and orientation. This dynamic state at time t is used to solve for the dynamic state at time $t + \delta t$, where δt is the time between frames. (Initial states may be scripted.) The new frame calculation involves two separate processes. First, the objects are moved using general equations of motion of rigid bodies under external forces and torque and the properties of the object. Second, the objects are checked for collision and impact dynamics are used to calculate the behaviour of the objects after collision.

The novel aspect of this work is the nature of the collision detection (and that the simulation deals with polygon mesh objects of arbitrary complexity, rather than simple analytical or symmetric objects) and the use of impact dynamics to solve the problem of the complex interaction involved. Collisions are also dealt with by Moore and Wilhems (1988). Hahn uses a hierarchical bounding box scheme to aid collision detection. Because collisions may occur between t and $t + \delta t$, objects may exist in a penetrating state and have to be 'backed up' to the collision point. Impact dynamics is a solution method where two bodies have been deemed to have acted on each other with a certain impulse over a short period of time. A solution is obtained using this approach and the conservation of linear and angular momenta.

One of the major implications of this work is that rigid bodies can be made far more complex than would otherwise be the case if they were being 'normally scripted'. An example given by Hahn is a four-legged bench tumbling down a set of stairs.

Terzopoulos *et al.* (1987), Terzopoulos and Fleischer (1988) and Terzopoulos and Witkin (1988) simulate the interaction of non-rigid objects in a physical environment. Using the dynamics of non-rigid bodies they have simulated realistic motion arising from the interaction of deformable models with forces, ambient media and impenetrable objects.

The implications of both these studies in engineering testing or a simulation of real testing is evident. Just as in flight simulation, where situations can be created that would be hazardous in reality, simulation of testing can no doubt widen the horizon of investigation, lower its cost and increase its flexibility.

Other less general examples are given by Fournier (Fournier and Reeves, 1986) who models ocean waves and Weil (1986) wherein free-hanging cloth is simulated.

A novel example of simulated animation is to be found in Waters (1987). Certain facial muscle processes are parametrized to create the animation of facial expression. The faces are polygon mesh representations derived from a photographic technique and the muscle models are used to control features such as the lips, eyebrows, eyelids and jaw rotation. These are driven from the muscle models to produce simulations of such emotions as happiness, fear, anger, disgust and surprise.

Finally, camera movement can also be scripted from a simulation system. The basic movement of a camera tracking an object can be extracted from the object movement. A reference point on the object can be sampled every *n* frames. These positions can then be interpolated using a key frame system for the camera. This has the advantage that the camera will generally execute smooth motion despite any frame-to-frame motion complexity of the object.

13.5   Temporal anti-aliasing

Temporal aliasing artefacts arise from undersampling in the time domain. An animated sequence, whether considered as a three-dimensional or two-dimensional time-varying sequence, is a set of samples at equal intervals in time.

The most obvious temporal aliasing artefact arises from 'periodic' motion and the familiar example is a rotating wheel that can appear to be stationary, or even rotate backwards, depending on the relationship between the sampling frequency and the rotational frequency. Other artefacts arise from the nature of the generation of frames that are to comprise a sequence. Frames in simple animation sequences are like snapshots taken with an infinitely short exposure time. The process is analogous to ignoring spatial aliasing in static image generation and sampling with a fixed two-dimensional grid.

A mathematical statement of the problem is obtained by extending Equation 11.1 as follows:

$$s(i,j,T) = \int\int\int I(i+x, j+y, T+t),\, F(x,y,t)\, \mathrm{d}x\, \mathrm{d}y\, \mathrm{d}t$$

and this implies solving the visibility problem as a function of time and filtering. Herein lies the potential expense of the method – generating extra frames that are then filtered to provide a single anti-aliased image. As with spatial anti-aliasing two approaches are possible: a supersampling approach (which is an approximate solution in time just as it was in space) and some algorithmic approximation to the continuous approach.

The easiest solution for spatial anti-aliasing – supersampling and re-constructing using a filter – is also the easiest to apply in the time domain. To do this, more frames are generated than are finally required – super-sampling is applied in the time domain. Consecutive frames at the super-sample rate are then averaged or filtered to provide a normal frame rate sequence. For fast-moving objects this will cause 'motion blur' and the pro-cess is exactly the same as a moving object blurring on film because of the finite exposure time of the camera shutter. This approach was used by Korein and Badler (1983). Fast-moving objects in an animation sequence appear slightly blurred in the direction of their motion and this blurring effect reduces the jerkiness that may otherwise be perceived by a viewer. It is interesting to note that in traditional cel animation, animators use 'speed streaks' to simulate this blur.

Although time domain supersampling is in principle an 'easy' tech-nique, it does require that, for the sake of efficiency, it is only applied to moving detail in the frames. It should be applied only where necessary and this requires knowledge of the degree and nature of individual object move-ment. This is equivalent in the time domain to the philosophy adopted by Mitchell (1987) in the space domain, where adaptive supersampling was applied depending on the nature of the image.

A problem arises out of this method if objects are thin in the direction of motion. Rather than appearing as a blur, a moving object appears in anti-aliased frames as a sequence of objects, a problem termed the 'spaghetti effect' by cel animators. Korein and Badler discuss this problem and suggest solutions.

One of the solutions is contained in a different approach to the problem, termed a 'continuous algorithm' to distinguish it from the sampling solution. In this algorithm, each moving object is assigned a continuous object space transformation function, which enables areas that moving objects cover to be determined. The area/intensity projected by visible objects onto a pixel over the subintervals in the continuous temporal interval between two frames can then be determined and a filtered pixel intensity solution obtained.

Korein and Badler also point out the desirability and difficulty of integrating spatial and temporal antialiasing. Other approaches to temporal anti-aliasing can be found in the lens and aperture camera model of Potmesil and Chakravarty (1983) and in the use of distributed ray tracing in Cook, Porter and Carpenter (1984).

In Cook's method, the temporal dimension is accorded the same status as any other dimension in the distributed ray tracing model (see Chapter 8) and rays are distributed in time as well as in space. This confers the same economical benefits in the time domain as does distributed ray tracing in the space domain. An example, a frame from *Luxo Jr.*, generated using this method, is shown in Plate 27.

Projects, notes and suggestions

13.1   Animation editor (*)

Implement a curve-based interactive scripting system based as suggested in Section 13.3.

13.2   Large animation project (*)

Design an animation system that will accept an English word and produce a script which will control a simple articulated model of the human hand executing an American Sign Language (ASL) gesture.

The project can be undertaken at almost any level of difficulty ranging from stick figure implementation of finger spelling (see the following notes) up to a general implementation of ASL together with realistic modelling of the hand and complex gestural dynamics that signers use.

Notes on the animation project

ASL consists of various gestures and movements of the arms and hands to convey the normal ideas and objects that can be expressed in English. For example, the sign for 'drive' is to place the hands in a 'steering wheel configuration' and to move them from side to side. (Any instruction manual in ASL will give a dictionary of gestures.) ASL is an excellent study for a scripted animation system because it supplies a formal specification for a large proportion of all the gestures possible with the hands and forearm (with, of course, one notable exception).

A subset of ASL is finger spelling, used when no sign for a word exists. Finger spelling is a technique whereby each of the 26 letters of the alphabet is portrayed in some way by one or other of the hands. The project can initially be developed for finger spelling and then extended to sign words.

There is a large literature, mainly connected with robotics, on the animation of articulated structures, but this is mainly do do with goal-directed motion. This means that, given a particular position and orientation, how is this going to be achieved?

This project is different in that it is driven by a script – a set of linear transformations that control the movement of the fingers and thumbs to produce the gesture corresponding to the sign. This is known as a forward kinematics system.

There are a number of aspects to the project:

(1) *Modelling*

This can be as basic or as elaborate as desired. In Figure 13.8 cylinders and spheres have been used to model the fingers. The palm has been completely omitted.

(2) *Script compilation*

This requires the production of a script that controls the animated model. Points that you may consider are:

- Can the gestures in ASL be organized into a hierarchy around a subset of gestures that are common to more than one sign?
- The hand model itself is hierarchical and this should be exploited.

(3) *In-betweening considerations*

All gestures should be 'eased in' and 'eased out' by using an appropriate kinetic interpolant to accelerate into a movement and decelerate out of it.

Try the cubic:

$$d = 3t^2 - 2t^3$$

where t is the frame number in the sequences of frames and d gives a fractional value that determines an angular movement.

All finger-spelling gestures (with the exception of 'J' and 'Z') can be defined as a set of rotations and the number of frames generated should be a function of the maximum angular movement of any finger.

Spelling consecutive letters means that the start position for letter n is the final position of letter $n - 1$ and this specifies the key frames in any sequence. Is this the way in which practitioners of ASL actually execute a finger spelling sequence?

(4) *Position control and dynamics*

In a simple system you must choose letters that do not cause fingers to collide and move through each other; for example, Figure 13.8 shows frames from the sequence 'FLEX' deliberately chosen to avoid this. An

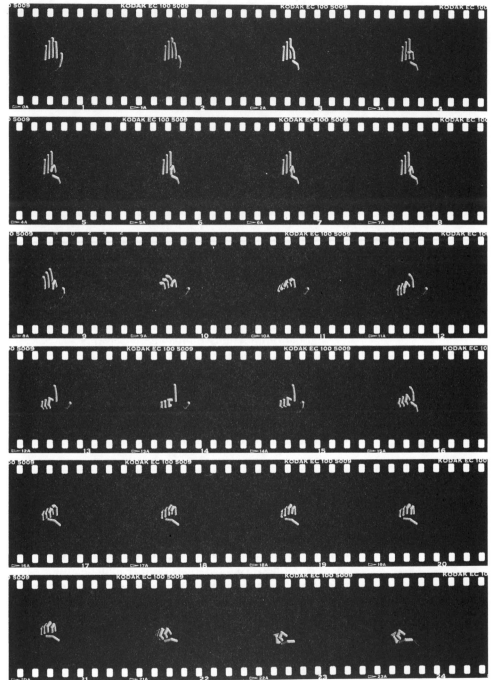

Figure 13.8
Twenty-four frames
from a sequence that
spells 'FLEX'.

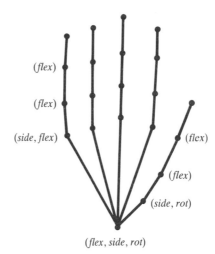

Figure 13.9
An articulated
structure for the
human hand.

easy way to deal with this problem in finger spelling is to set up a
26×26 table that returns either 'no clash' or points to a suitable intermediate position. (Collision detection and avoidance, in general, represent a substantial increase in the complexity of the project.)

How are the movements of separate fingers to be synchonized?
Each digit will generally move through a different set of angles. The
questions are:

- Do all digits start at the same time?
- Do all digits stop at the same time?
- Do digits start at the same time and finish in their 'own' time depend-
  ing on their angular travel?

These considerations will affect the final appearance of the animation
far more than any shortcomings in the physical modelling.

(5) *Articulated structure for fingers*
A suggested articulated structure is shown in Figure 13.9. A subset of
the movements *flex, side* and *rot* are associated with each joint and this
works quite well. For a finger, *flex* is constrained nested rotation
(Figure 13.10) in a $y-z$ plane about the x axis, and *side* is constrained
rotation about the y axis. In a simple system *rot* can be rotation about
the z axis. For example, the angle set for an 'A' is shown in Figure
13.11.

flex for a thumb is not quite as simple and this requires some
investigation. Consider that the thumb generally moves in a conical
volume; the degree of *flex* about the top and middle joints can be
independent of any other movement and occurs at some angle to the
plane of finger flexing. The bottom joint undergoes sideral and rotational motion.

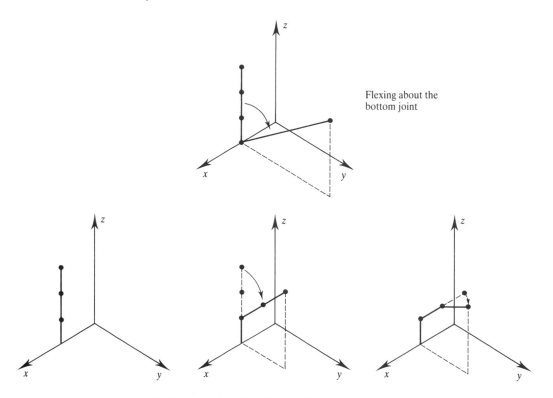

Flexing about the
bottom joint

The three stages in flexing of the middle section of the finger

Figure 13.10
Flexing scheme used
for fingers.

Technically the finger joints are hinge joints the wrist is a ball-and-socket joint and the thumb is a saddle joint.

(6) *Storing signs*

Movements for all letters can be organized into a hierarchy reflecting the fact that signs use a set of common movements; for example, a wrist rotation of 90° followed by a flexing of all fingers around the middle joint of 45°. An appropriate hierarchy for 'A' is shown in Figure 13.12.

This should be enough information to get you started.

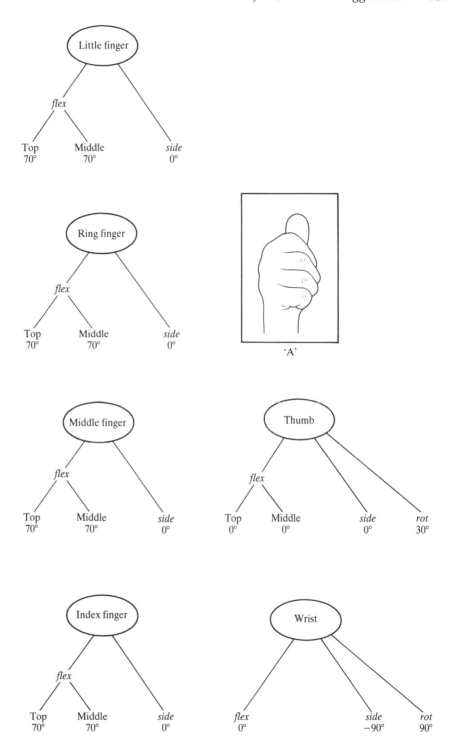

Figure 13.11
Angle values for 'A'.

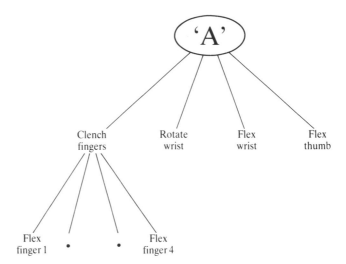

Figure 13.12
A hierarchy for 'A'.

14 Colour Spaces and Monitor Considerations

14.1 Introduction

This chapter is concerned with quantitive aspects of colour. Most treatment of colour in computer graphics has been qualitative. In setting up a scene database we tend to choose object colours more or less arbitrarily. However, certain applications are emerging in computer graphics where the accurate simulation of light–object interaction, in terms of colour, is required. Also, in the field of visualization, colour is used to impart numeric information and suitable numeric-to-colour mappings must be considered with knowledge of the subtle underlying psycho–physical mechanisms of the human colour vision system.

It is curious that an industry which has has devoted major research effort to photorealism has all but ignored a rigorous approach to colour. After all, frame stores whose pixels are capable of displaying any of 16 million colours have been commonplace for many years. We suspect three reasons for this:

- the dominance of the RGB or three-equation approach in rendering methods such as Phong shading, ray tracing and radiosity, and the high cost of evaluating these models at more than three wavelengths,

- the rendering models themselves have obvious shortcomings that are visually far more serious than the unsubtle treatment of colour (spatial domain aliasing is visible, colour domain aliasing is generally invisible), and

- the lack of demand from applications that require an accurate treatment of colour.

With some exceptions (see, for example, Hall and Greenberg (1983) and Hall (1989)) little research into rendering with accurate treatment of colour has been carried out. There are, however, a growing number of applications that would benefit from accurate colour simulation, and a rendering method exists (the radiosity method) that is subtle enough in its treatment of light–object interaction to benefit from such an approach. Clearly this will be one of the major developments in CAAD (computer-aided architectural design) in the future. A computer graphics visualization of an architectural design, either interior or exterior, is usually recognizable as such. We know that the image is not a photograph. This appears to be due predominantly to the lack of fine geometric detail. Modelling costs are high and approximations are made. (In the radiosity method a coarse detail model is mandatory.) So we first notice the inadequate geometry. However, 'second-order' effects are no doubt just as important, and such aspects as unrealistic shadows and light that 'doesn't look quite right' contribute to the immediate visible signature of a computer graphics image.

Another area where colour is of critical importance is volume rendering in ViSC (see Chapter 9). Here colour is used to enable a viewer to perceive variations in data values in three-space which may be extremely subtle. In this context it is important that the colours used communicate the information in an optimal way. This topic relies on perceptual colour models.

If we decide that accurate colour simulation is important, this throws up other problems apart from the cost implication in extending from three wavelengths to n wavelengths. These are:

- What descriptive colour system or model do we use to categorize colour? Clearly we could simply work with sampled functions of wavelength for the reflectivity characteristics of objects and the intensity of a light source. Although this may be convenient (and necessary) in the calculation domain, it will be useless to an architect, say, who wishes to specify a paint colour in a standard system using a colour label or a triple. What colour space should be used for the storage and the communication of images? It would be extremely impractical to store the results of n wavelength calculations.

- A major problem in using accurate colour exists in reproduction and viewing. Two colours specified in a standard system should look the same to a viewer. But this is only true if they are reproduced on carefully calibrated computer graphics monitors that are viewed under identical conditions. Although colour can be measured locally with precision using a colorimeter, such perceptual shifts due to, for example, contrast with surrounding colours, will always occur. This practical problem is not easy to overcome and unless it is dealt with it mitigates against the use of accurate colour simulation.

14.2 Specifying a colour with three labels

We start by addressing a problem that is central to computer graphics and colour – the confusion between the specification or the description of a colour as a triple and its use in a computer graphics calculation domain.

Colour is a subjective perceptual experience which is unique, as far as we are aware, to *Homo sapiens*. Although we can objectively measure aspects of light such as dominant wavelength, it has recently been found (Land, 1977) that despite all our ideas to the contrary, colour perception is *not* directly related to wavelength of light incident on our eyes.

When we describe colours we generally use words, sometimes elaborated with allusions to familiar objects that possess a universally understood colour (for example, apple green). In the painting and dyeing industry colour is communicated with a set of fixed or standard colour samples. Numerical specification of colour is usually by a triple of primary colours. Most, but not all, perceivable colours can be produced by additively mixing appropriate amounts of three primary colours (red, green and blue, for example). If we denote a colour by C, we have:

$$C = r\mathbf{R} + g\mathbf{G} + b\mathbf{B}$$

In a computer graphics monitor a colour is produced by exciting triples of adjacent dots made of red, green and blue phosphors. The dots are small and the eye perceives the triples as a single dot of colour.

A three-component colour label is also connected with the physiology of the human retina, which appears to respond maximally at three separate wavelengths (Figure 14.1). Indeed, prior to the astonishing experiments of Harold Land the conventional theory of colour vision was that our brain processed three wavelength-dependent components from our retina. (Such is the power of convincing scientific orthodoxies that even today this philosophy predominates in most textbooks.) It is the case that the processing by the retina is only the first stage in a complex and subtle system of colour perception.

Figure 14.1
The relative sensitivity of retinal photopigments.

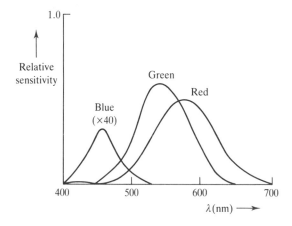

Unfortunately, in computer graphics this three-component specification of colour, together with the need to produce a three-component RGB signal for a monitor, has led to an assumption that colour need only be evaluated at three points in the spectrum. This is the 'standard' RGB paradigm that tends to be used in Phong shading, ray tracing and radiosity. If it is intended to simulate the interaction of light with objects in a scene accurately, then it is necessary to evaluate this interaction at more than three wavelengths, otherwise aliasing will result in the colour domain because of undersampling of the light distribution and object reflectivity functions. Of course aliasing in the colour domain simply consists of a shift in colour away from a desired effect and in this sense it is invisible. (This is in direct contrast to spatial domain aliasing which produces annoying and disturbing visual artefacts.) Colours in most computer graphics applications are to a great extent arbitrary, and shifts due to inaccurate simulation in the colour domain are generally not important. It is only in applications where colour is a subtle part of the simulation, say, for example, in interior design, that these effects have to be taken into account.

An approach to accurately simulating colour would apply a rendering model at n wavelengths. Both an intensity distribution of a real light source and a reflectivity characteristic of a real object are functions of wavelength. This would yield a function $F(\lambda)$ defined over n discrete wavelengths which then has to be 'reduced' to an RGB triple which, after suitable transformations, can be used to drive an RGB monitor. Such a process is shown in Figure 14.2. This reduction from a sampled version of a continuous function is accomplished by using colour-matching functions (see Section 14.3.4) as follows:

$$r = \sum_{\lambda} F(\lambda)\, r(\lambda)$$

$$g = \sum_{\lambda} F(\lambda)\, g(\lambda)$$

$$b = \sum_{\lambda} F(\lambda)\, b(\lambda) \tag{14.1}$$

where $r(\lambda)$, $g(\lambda)$ and $b(\lambda)$ are the colour-matching functions.

We can compare this method with the 'standard' computer graphics colour model which uses just three samples. This is given by:

$$r = F_R$$
$$g = F_G$$
$$b = F_B$$

where F_R, F_G and F_B are the three values of F calculated at three wavelengths. We can see from this that there is a significant difference between specifying a colour using three primary components that have been derived by integrating over a wavelength-dependent function, weighted by

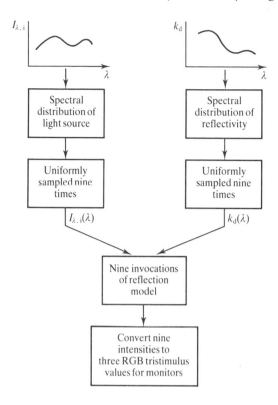

Figure 14.2
A representation of a nine sample/equation reflection model.

colour-matching functions, and simply using three wavelength samples as these components. This vital difference is not generally appreciated by computer graphics practitioners.

Hall and Greenberg (1983) conducted one of the few experiments in colour aliasing in computer graphics. Using as a control an image computed by rendering at 1 nm intervals between 360 nm and 830 nm, they compared the three-sample RGB approach with a number of other methods. Hall reported that the RGB method produced significant colour distortion and concluded that a nine-sample approach produced a good enough approximation to the control image.

14.3 Colour spaces in computer graphics

Given that we can represent or describe the sensation of colour with numeric labels we now face the question: which numbers shall we use? This heralds the concept of different colour spaces or domains and this topic forms the main body of the chapter.

It may be as was suggested in the previous section, that a calculation or rendering domain be a wavelength or spectral space. Eventually we would produce an image in $RGB_{monitor}$ space to drive a particular monitor. What about the storage and communication of images? Here we need a universal standard. $RGB_{monitor}$ spaces, as we shall see, are particular to devices. These devices have different gamuts or colour ranges, all of which are subsets of the set of perceivable colours. A universal space will be device independent and will embrace all perceivable colours. Such a space exists and is known as the CIE XYZ standard. A CIE triple is a unique numeric label associated with any perceivable colour.

Another requirement in computer graphics is a facility that allows a user to manipulate and design using colour. It is generally thought that an interface that allows a user to mix primary colours is anti-intuitive and spaces that are inclined to perceptual sensations such as hue, saturation and lightness are preferred in this context.

The following colour spaces are used in computer graphics:

- **Spectral space**   Light sources are defined in this space as *n* wavelength samples of an intensity distribution. Object reflectivity is similarly defined.

- **RGB space**   The 'standard' computer graphics paradigm described in Chapter 4 for Phong shading. It usually is a three-sample version of spectral space; light sources and object reflectivity are specified as three wavelengths, red, green and blue. Alternatively, RGB values may be derived by 'reducing' a *n* wavelength calculation as in Equation 14.1. We understand the primaries R, G and B to be pure or saturated colours.

- **$RGB_{monitor}$ space**   A triple in this space produces a particular colour on a particular display. The same triple may not necessarily produce the same colour sensation on different monitors. Monitor RGBs are not pure or saturated primaries because the emission of light from an excited phosphor exhibits a spectral power distribution over a band of frequencies. If the usual three-sample approach is used in rendering then whatever values are calculated are assumed to be weights in $RGB_{monitor}$ space. If an *n* sample calculation has been performed then a device-dependent transformation is used to produce a point in $RGB_{monitor}$ space (see Section 14.4).

- **HSV space**   A non-linear transformation of RGB space enabling colour to be specified as hue, saturation and value.

- **HLS space**   Similar to HSV space but providing an alternative user interface possibility. The choice between HLS and HSV space is a matter of personal preference.

- **CIE XYZ space**   The dominant international standard for colour specification. A colour is specified as a set of three tristimulus values or artificial primaries *XYZ*.

- **CIE xyY space**   A variant of CIE XYZ space that separates a colour into chromaticity coordinates (x,y) and luminance Y.

- **CIE LUV space**   A perceptually linear variant of CIE XYZ space for luminous sources.

14.3.1   RGB model

Given the subtle distinction between RGB and RGB$_{monitor}$ space, we now describe RGB space as a general concept. This model is the traditional form of colour specification in computer graphics. It enables, for example, diffuse reflection coefficients in shading equations to be given a value as a triple (r,g,b). In this system $(0,0,0)$ is black and $(1,1,1)$ is white. Colour is labelled as relative weights of three primary colours in an additive system using the primaries red, green and blue. The space of all colours available in this system is represented by the RGB cube (Figure 14.3 and Plate 28). Important points concerning RGB space are:

(1) It is perceptually non-linear. Equal distances in the space do not in general correspond to perceptually equal sensations. A step between two points in one region of the space may produce no perceivable difference; the same increment in another region may result in a noticeable colour change. In other words, the same colour sensation may result from a multiplicity of RGB triples. For example, if each of RGB can vary between 0 and 255, then over 16 million unique RGB codes are available.

(2) Because of the non-linear relationship between RGB values and the intensity produced at each phosphor dot low RGB values produce small changes in response on the screen. As many as 20 steps may be necessary to produce a 'just noticeable difference' at low intensities, whereas a single step may produce a perceivable difference at high intensities.

(3) The set of all colours produced on a computer graphics monitor, the RGB space, is *always* a subset of the colours that can be perceived by humans. This is not peculiar to RGB space. Any set of three visible primaries can produce only through additive mixing of a subset of the perceivable colour set.

(4) It is not a good colour description system. Without considerable experience, users find it difficult to give RGB values to colours known by label. What is the RGB value of 'medium brown'? Once a colour has been chosen it may not be obvious how to make subtle changes to the nature of the colour. For example, changing the 'vividness' of a chosen colour will require unequal changes in the RGB components.

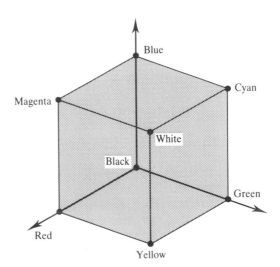

Figure 14.3
The RGB colour solid
(compare with Plate
28).

14.3.2   HSV single hexcone model

The H(ue) S(aturation) V(alue) or single hexcone model was proposed by
A.R. Smith (1978). Its purpose is to facilitate a more intuitive interface for
colour than the selection of three primary colours. The colour space has the
shape of a hexagonal cone or hexcone. The HSV cone is a non-linear transformation of the RGB cube and although it tends to be referred to as a
perceptual model, it is still just a way of labelling colours in the monitor
gamut space. 'Perceptual' in this context means the attributes that are used
to represent the colour are more akin to the way in which we think of
colour; it does not mean that the space is perceptually linear. The perceptual
non-linearity of RGB space is carried over into HSV space, in particular
perceptual changes in hue are distinctly non-linear in angle.

It can be employed in any context where a user requires control or
selection of a colour or colours on an aesthetic or similar basis. It enables
control over the range or gamut of an RGB monitor using the perceptually
based variables, hue, saturation and value. This means that a user interface
can be constructed where the effect of varying one of the three qualities is
easily predictable. A task such as 'make colour X brighter, paler or more
yellow' is far easier when these perceptual variables are employed, than
having to decide on what combinations of RGB changes are required.

The HSV model is based on polar coordinates rather than cartesians
and H is specified in degrees in the range (0..360). One of the first colour
systems based on polar coordinates and perceptual parameters was that due
to Munsell (1946). His colour notation system was first published in 1905
and is still in use today. Munsell called his perceptual variables hue, chroma
and value and we can do no better than reproduce his definition for these.

Chroma is related to saturation – the term that appears to be preferred in computer graphics.

Munsell's definitions are:

- *Hue* 'It is that quality by which we distinguish one colour family from another, as red from yellow, or green from blue or purple.'

- *Chroma* 'It is that quality of colour by which we distinguish a strong colour from a weak one; the degree of departure of a colour sensation from that of a white or gray; the intensity of a distinctive hue; colour intensity.'

- *Value* 'It is that quality by which we distinguish a light colour from a dark one.'

The Munsell system is used by referring to a set of samples – the *Munsell Book of Colour* (Munsell, 1946). These samples are in 'just discriminable' steps in the colour space.

Smith's model relates to the way in which artists mix colours. Referring to the difficulty of mentally imagining the relative amounts of R, G and B required to produce a single colour, he says:

> Try this mixing technique by mentally varying RGB to obtain pink or brown. It is not unusual to have difficulty. ...the following (HSV) model mimics the way an artist mixes paint on his palette: he chooses a pure hue, or pigment and lightens it to a *tint* of that hue by adding white, or darkens it to a *shade* of that hue by adding black, or in general obtains a *tone* of that hue by adding some mixture of white and black or gray.

In the HSV model varying H corresponds to selecting a colour. Decreasing S (desaturating the colour) corresponds to adding white. Decreasing V (devaluating the colour) corresponds to adding black. Program 14.1 gives procedures for converting between RGB and HSV space. The derivation of the transform is easily understood by considering a geometric interpretation of the hexcone. If the RGB cube is projected along its main diagonal onto a plane normal to that diagonal, then a hexagonal disc results.

The following correspondence is then established between the six RGB vertices and the six points of the hexcone in the HSV model.

RGB		*HSV*
(100)	red	(0,1,1)
(110)	yellow	(60,1,1)
(010)	green	(120,1,1)
(011)	cyan	(180,1,1)
(001)	blue	(240,1,1)
(101)	magenta	(300,1,1)

where H is measured in degrees. This hexagonal disc is the plane containing $V = 1$ in the hexcone model. For each value along the main diagonal in the

Program 14.1   Transformations from RGB to HSV and from HSV to RGB.

```
procedure RGB_to_HSV(R, G, B: real; var H, S, V: real);

  const undefined = maxint;

  function max_of(Red, Green, Blue: real): real;
    var max: real;

    begin
      if Red > Green then max := Red else max := Green;
      if Blue > max then max := Blue;
      max_of := max;
    end;

  function min_of(Red, Green, Blue: real): real;
    var min: real;

    begin
      if Red < Green then min := Red else min := Green;
      if Blue < min then min := Blue;
      min_of := min;
    end;

  var max_value, min_value, diff, r_dist, g_dist, b_dist: real;

  begin
    max_value := max_of(R, G, B);
    min_value := min_of(R, G, B);
    diff := max_value − min_value;
    V := max_value;
    if max_value <> 0 then S := diff/max_value else S := 0;
    if S = 0 then H := undefined
    else begin
          r_dist := (max_value − R)/diff;
          g_dist := (max_value − G)/diff;
          b_dist := (max_value − B)/diff;
          if R = max_value then H := b_dist − g_dist
          else if G = max_value
                  then H := 2 + r_dist − b_dist
                else if B = max_value
                  then h := 4 + g_dist − r_dist;
        H := h*60;
        if H < 0 then H := H + 360;
        end;
  end;

procedure HSV_to_RGB(H, S, V: real; var R, G, B: real);

  var f, p, q, t: real; i: integer;

  begin
    if s = 0 then begin
              R:= V; G := V; B := V;
```

```
                    end

        else begin
            if H = 360 then H := 0;
            H := H/60;
            i := TRUNC(H);
            f := H - i;
            p := V*(1 - S);
            q := V*(1 - (S*f));
            t := V*(1 - (S*(1 - f)));
            case i of
                0: begin R := V; G := t; B := p; end;
                1: begin R := q; G := V; B := p; end;
                2: begin R := p; G := V; B := t; end;
                3: begin R := p; G := q; B := V; end;
                4: begin R := t; G := p; B := V; end;
                5: begin R := V; G := p; B := q; end;
            end;
        end;
    end;
```

RGB cube (increasing blackness) a contained subcube is defined. Each subcube defines a hexagonal disc. The stack of all hexagonal discs makes up the HSV colour solid.

Figure 14.4 shows the HSV single hexcone colour solid and Plate 29 is a further aid to its interpretation showing slices through the achromatic axis. The right-hand half of each slice is the plane of constant H and the left-hand half that of $H + 180°$.

Apart from perceptual non-linearity, another subtle problem implicit in the HSV system is that the attributes are not themselves perceptually

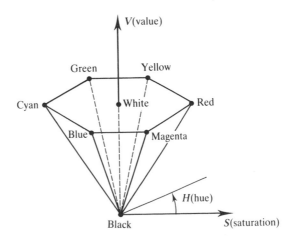

Figure 14.4
HSV single hexcone colour solid.

independent. This means that it is possible to detect an apparent change in hue, for example, when it is the parameter value that is actually being changed.

Finally, perhaps the most serious departure from perceptual reality resides in the geometry of the model. The colour space labels all those colours reproducible on a computer graphics monitor and implies that all colours on planes of constant V are of equal brightness. Such is not the case. For example, maximum intensity blue has a lower perceived brightness than maximum intensity yellow. We conclude from this that because of the problems of perceptual non-linearity and the fact that different hues at maximum V exhibit different perceptual values, that representing a monitor gamut with any 'regular' geometric solid such as a cube, a half-cone or a double-cone (as in the next section) is only an approximation to the sensation of colour, and this fact means that we have to consider perceptually based colour spaces. A simpler way of expressing this fact is to reiterate that colour is a perceptual sensation and cannot be accurately labelled by dividing up the RGB voltage levels of a monitor and using this scale as a colour label. This is essentially what we are doing with both the RGB and the HSV model and the association of the word 'perceptual' with the HSV model is unfortunate and confusing.

14.3.3   HLS model

The HLS model is closely related to the HSV model. It is based on the Ostwald colour system (Ostwald, 1931) and is used by the graphics hardware manufacturer Tektronix. It can be considered a deformation of the HSV solid with the V axis 'pulled' upwards to form a double hexcone (Figure 14.5 and Plate 29).

The central axis is now termed L(ightness) and hue is again measured circumferentially in degrees around the hexcone. The colour white in this model now has the same 'geometric status' as black, that is, a single point. Because of this it is an intuitively more satisfying model. The HLS model is as easy to use as the HSV model. However, the plane of saturated hues now occurs at $L = 0.5$ and this is given as a disadvantage (in Foley *et al.* (1989)) when the model is used as a software interface for colour selection. Program 14.2 gives procedures for converting between RGB space and HLS space.

14.3.4   CIE XYZ space

We now move on to the concept of perceptually based colour labelling systems and consider the CIE system. The CIE standard allows a colour to be specified as a numeric triple (X, Y, Z). CIE XYZ space embraces all colours perceivable by human beings and it is based on experimentally determined colour-matching functions. Thus, unlike the three previous colour spaces, it is *not* a monitor gamut space.

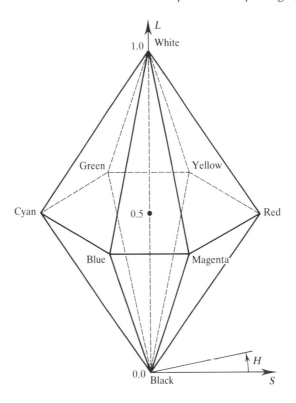

Figure 14.5
Double hexcone HLS
colour model.

The basis of the standard, adopted in 1931, is colour-matching experiments where a user controls or weights three primary light sources to match a sample light source. In other words the weights in:

$$C = rR + gG + bB$$

are determined experimentally.

The result of such experiments can be summarized by colour-matching functions. These are shown in Figure 14.6 and show the amounts of red, green and blue light which, when additively mixed, will produce in a standard observer a monochromatic colour whose wavelength is given by λ. That is:

$$C_\lambda = r(\lambda) + g(\lambda) + b(\lambda)$$

For any colour sensation r, g and b are given by:

$$r = k \int_\lambda P(\lambda)\, r(\lambda)\, \mathrm{d}\lambda$$

$$g = k \int_\lambda P(\lambda)\, g(\lambda)\, \mathrm{d}\lambda$$

$$b = k \int_\lambda P(\lambda)\, b(\lambda)\, \mathrm{d}\lambda$$

Program 14.2   Transformations from RGB to HLS and from HLS to RGB.

```
procedure RGB_to HLS(R, G, B: real; var H, L, S: real);
    const undefined = maxint;

    function max_of(Red, Green, Blue: real): real;
    var max: real;

    begin
        if Red > Green then max := Red else max := Green;
        if Blue > max then max := Blue;
        max_of := max;
    end;

    function min_of(Red, Green, Blue: real): real;
    var min: real;

    begin
        if Red < Green then min := Red else min := Green;
        if Blue < min then min := Blue;
        min_of := min;
    end;

    const small_value = 0.0000001;
    var max_value, min_value, diff, r_dist, g_dist, b_dist: real;

    begin
        max_value := max_of(R, G, B);
        min_value := min_of(R, G, B);
        diff := max_value − min_value;
        L := (max_value + min_value)/2;
        if ABS(diff) < small_value then
            begin
                S := 0; H := undefined;
            end
        else begin
            if L <= 0.5 then S := diff/(max_value + min_value)
            else S := diff/(2 − max_value − min_value);
            r_dist := (max_value − R)/diff;
            g_dist := (max_value − G)/diff;
            b_dist := (max_value − B)/diff;
            if R = max_value then H := b_dist − g_dist
            else if G = max_value then h := 2 + r_dist − b_dist
                else if B = max_value then H := 4 + g_dist − r_dist;
            H := H*60;
            if H < 0 then H := H + 360;
        end;
    end;

procedure HLS_to RGB(H, L, S: real; var R, G, B: real);
    var p1, p2: real;
```

```
function RGB(q1, 2, hue: real): real;
    begin
        if hue > 360 then hue := hue − 360;
        if hue < 0    then hue := hue + 360;
        if hue < 60   then RGB := q1 + (q2 − q1)*hue/60
        else if hue < 180 then RGB := q2
            else if hue < 240
                    then RGB := q1 + (q2 − q1)*(240 − hue)/60
                    else RGB := q1;
    end;

begin
    if L <= 0.5 then p2 := L*(1 + S)
    else p2 := L + S − L*S;
    p1 := 2*L − p2;
    if S = 0 then begin
                    R := L; G := L; B := L;
                end
    else            begin
                    R := RGB(p1, p2, H + 120);
                    G := RGB(p1, p2, H);
                    B := RGB(p1, p2, H − 120);
                end;
end;
```

where $P(\lambda)$ is the spectral energy distribution – the variation of the energy of a light sensation with wavelength. Thus we see that colour-matching functions reduce a colour C, with any shape of spectral energy distribution, to a triple (r,g,b).

There is, however, a problem in representing colours with an additive primary system, which is that with positive weights only a subset of perceivable colours can be described by the weights (r,g,b). The problem arises out of the fact that when two colours are mixed the result is a less saturated colour. It is impossible to form a highly saturated colour by superimposing

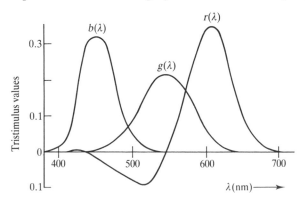

Figure 14.6
The colour matching functions $r(\lambda)$, $g(\lambda)$ and $b(\lambda)$.

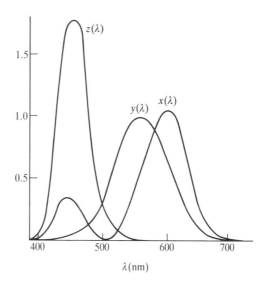

Figure 14.7
The CIE matching
functions.

colours. Any set of three primaries form a bounded space outside of which
certain perceivable, highly saturated colours exist. In such colours a negative
weight is required.

   To avoid negative weights the CIE devised a standard of three super-
saturated (or non-realizable) primaries *X, Y* and *Z*, which when additively
mixed will produce all perceivable colours using positive weights. The three
corresponding matching functions, $x(\lambda)$, $y(\lambda)$ and $z(\lambda)$, shown in Figure 14.7
are always positive. Thus we have:

$$X = k \int_\lambda P(\lambda)\, x(\lambda)\, d\lambda$$

$$Y = k \int_\lambda P(\lambda)\, y(\lambda)\, d\lambda$$

$$Z = k \int_\lambda P(\lambda)\, z(\lambda)\, d\lambda$$

where:

   $k = 680$ for self-luminous objects

The space formed by the *XYZ* values for all perceivable colours is CIE
XYZ space. The matching functions are transformations of the experimental
results. In addition the $y(\lambda)$ matching function was defined to have a colour-
matching function that corresponded to the luminous efficiency characteristic of the human eye, a function that peaks at 550 nm (yellow–green).

   The shape of the CIE XYZ colour solid is basically conical with the
apex of the cone at the origin (Figure 14.8). If we compare this space to
HSV space we can view the solid as distorted HSV space. The black point is
at the origins and the HSV space is deformed to embrace all colours and to

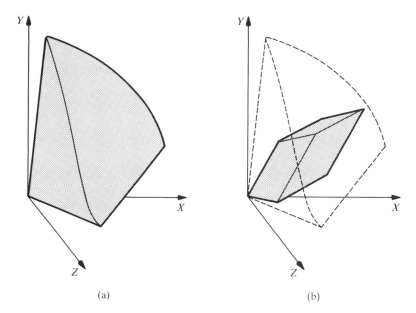

Figure 14.8
(a) CIE XYZ solid.
(b) A typical monitor
gamut in CIE XYZ
space.

(a)

(b)

encompass the fact that the space is based on perceptual measurements. If we consider, for example, the outer surface of the deformed cone, this is made of rays that emanate from the origin terminating on the edge of the cone. Along any ray is the set of colours of identical chromaticity (see the next section). If a ray is moved in towards the white point, situated on the base of the deformed cone, then we desaturate the set of colours specified by the ray. Within this space the monitor gamut is a deformed (sheared and scaled) cube, forming a subset of the volume of perceivable colours.

14.3.5   CIE xyY space

An alternative way of specifying the (X, Y, Z) triple is (x, y, Y) where (x, y) are known as **chromaticity coordinates**:

$$x = \frac{X}{X + Y + Z}$$
$$y = \frac{Y}{X + Y + Z}$$

The usefulness of chromaticity coordinates lies in the fact that they are functions of dominant wavelength and saturation only. Plotting x against y for all visible colours yields a two-dimensional (x, y) space known as the **CIE chromaticity diagram**.

The wing-shaped CIE chromaticity diagram (Figure 14.9) is extensively used in colour science. It encompasses all the perceivable colours in two-dimensional space by ignoring the luminance Y. The locus of the pure

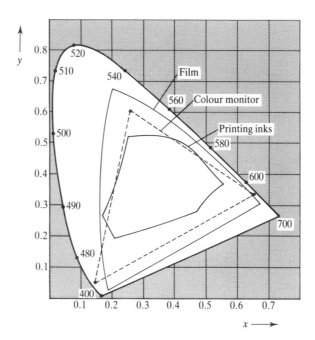

Figure 14.9
CIE chromaticity
diagram showing
typical gamuts for
colour film, colour
monitor and printing
inks.

saturated or spectral colours is formed by the curved line from blue
(400 nm) to red (700 nm). The straight line between the end points is known
as the purple or magenta line. Along this line is located the saturated pur-
ples or magentas. These are colours whose perceivable sensation cannot be
produced by any single monochromatic stimulus, and which cannot be isolated from daylight.

Also shown in Figure 14.9 is the gamut of colours reproducible on a
computer graphics monitor from three phosphors. The monitor gamut is a
triangle formed by drawing straight lines between three RGB points. The
RGB points are contained within the outermost curve of monochromatic or
saturated colours. Examination of the emission characteristics of the phosphors will reveal a spread about the dominant wavelength which means that
the colour contains white light and is not saturated. When, say, the blue and
green phosphors are fully excited their emission characteristics add together
into a broader band meaning that the resultant colour will be less saturated
than blue or green.

The triangular monitor gamut in CIE xy space is to be found in most
texts dealing with colour science in computer graphics, but it is somewhat
misleading. The triangle is actually the projection out of CIE xyY space of
the monitor gamut, with the vertices formed from phosphor vertices that
each have a different luminance. Figure 14.10 shows a monitor gamut in
CIE xyY space and Plate 30 shows three slices through the space. The
geometric or shape transformation from the scaled and sheared cube in

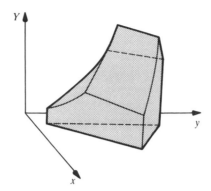

Figure 14.10
Monitor gamut in CIE
xyY space (see also
Plate 30).

XYZ space to the curvilinear solid (with six faces) in xyY space is difficult to interpret. For example, one edge of the cube maps to a single point.

There are a number of important uses of the CIE chromaticity diagram. One important example is that it can be used to compare the gamut of various display devices. This is important in computer graphics when an image is eventually to be reproduced on a number of different devices. Figure 14.9 shows a CIE chromaticity diagram with the gamut of a typical computer graphics monitor together with the gamut for modern printing inks. The printing ink gamut is enclosed within the monitor gamut, which is itself enclosed by the gamut for colour film. This means that some colours attainable on film are not reproducible on a computer graphics monitor, and certain colours on a monitor cannot be reproduced by printing. The gamut of display devices and reproduction techniques is always contained by the gamut of perceivable colours, the saturated or spectral colours being the most difficult to reproduce. However, this is not generally a problem because spectral and near-spectral colours do not tend to occur naturally. It is the relative spread of device gamuts that is important, rather than the size of any gamut with respect to the visual gamut. The general problem of transforming a gamut so that it fits within the range of a practical device is discussed in Section 14.4.2.

14.3.6   CIE LUV space

The 1931 CIE xyY space, with its peculiarly shaped colour solid, is inconvenient in computer graphics. We can retain the original advantages of CIE space (direct relationship with standard colour systems, an unambiguous specification language for colour communication and so on) and gain two more significant advantages by working in CIE LUV space. These are:

- CIE LUV space is a perceptually uniform space. Although CIE XYZ space is based on matching experiments, it is not perceptually linear in terms of 'just noticeable differences'. Just noticable differences are a function of wavelength.

- The CIE LUV colour solid can be described in a cylindrical coordinate system. It is thus amenable to incorporation in a user interface.

Both these advantages, together with the original advantages of 1931 CIE space, make this colour space convenient for computer graphics practitioners engaged in serious colour work.

The 1931 CIE xy chromaticity diagram has a significant disadvantage. Equally noticeable colour changes are not uniform distances in (x,y) space. Perceptually equal changes are shortest in the violet region and longest in the green region. A transformation, accepted by the CIE in 1960, distorts the (x,y) space to correct this:

$$u = 2x/(6y - x + 1.5)$$
$$v = 3y/(6y - x + 1.5)$$

A more recent adoption (1974) defines $u'v'$ space as:

$$u' = 2x/(6y - x + 1.5)$$
$$v' = 4.5y/(6y - x + 1.5)$$

Y remains unchanged. Finally, this space is subject to a further transformation to define 1976 CIE LUV space. This transformation makes two adjustments. First, it centres the achromatic axis on the point $(0,0)$. Second, zero luminance ($L^* = 0$) now becomes a single point. The L*u*v* definition is:

$$L^* = 116(Y/Y_w)^{1/3} - 16$$
$$u^* = 13L^*(u' - u'_w)$$
$$v^* = 13L^*(v' - v'_w)$$

where u',v' and Y are the coordinates of the colour in (u',v',Y) space and u_w, v_w and Y_w are the coordinates of the white point in this space. The colour solid for this space is shown in Figure 14.11 and in Plate 31. From

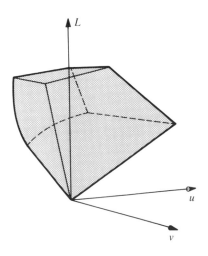

Figure 14.11
CIE L*u*v* space.

these illustrations it can be seen that the solid is a distorted double cone. This is not unlike the HLS model and we can thus define H, L and S parameters for this model and use these in a user interface if required. The definitions are:

$$H(\text{hue}) = \arctan(v^*/u^*)$$
$$L(\text{lightness}) = L^*$$
$$S(\text{saturation}) = (u^{*2} + v^{*2})^{1/2}$$

H is known as the CIE 1976 uv hue-angle and L is the CIE 1976 psychometric lightness. S is the CIE 1976 uv chroma. Strictly speaking, saturation must be defined in terms of luminance and the CIE 1976 psychometric saturation is defined as:

$$S_{\text{uv}} = \frac{\text{CIE 1976 uv chroma}}{L^*}$$
$$= \frac{(u^{*2} + v^{*2})^{1/2}}{L^*}$$

A further development of this philosophy is the Tektronix HVC system (Taylor, Murch and McManus, 1988). This is based approximately on the CIE L*u*v* space using an H(hue) axis (0–360°), a V(value) axis (0–100°) and a C(chroma) axis (0–100°). It combines the interface advantages of the HLS model with the perceptually based measurements of the CIE space used and eliminates some of the problems of the HLS space that were discussed above.

14.4   Monitor considerations

14.4.1   Different monitors and the same colour

If we have the concept of an RGB triple as a pseudostandard – a particular value produces the same colour sensation on any monitor – then we need to cater for the fact that different monitors have different characteristics, and sending the (r,g,b) values to different monitors will produce different colours. We do this by using the CIE XYZ space and transforming the RGB triple into an XYZ triple:

$$\begin{bmatrix} X \\ Y \\ Z \end{bmatrix} = \begin{bmatrix} X_r & X_g & X_b \\ Y_r & Y_g & Y_b \\ Z_r & Z_g & Z_b \end{bmatrix} \begin{bmatrix} r \\ g \\ b \end{bmatrix}$$

$$= T \begin{bmatrix} r \\ g \\ b \end{bmatrix}$$

where T is particular to a monitor and a linear relationship is assumed between the outputs from the phosphors and the RGB values (see Section 14.4.2). (X_r, X_g, X_b) are the tristimulus values required to produce a unit amount of the R primary, (Y_r, Y_g, Y_b) are the tristimulus values to produce a unit amount of the G primary, and so on. If T_1 is the transformation for monitor 1 and T_2 the transformation for monitor 2, then $T_2^{-1}T_1$ converts the RGB values of monitor 1 to that for monitor 2. T can be calculated in the following way. We define:

$$D_r = X_r + Y_r + Z_r$$
$$D_g = X_g + Y_g + Z_g$$
$$D_b = X_b + Y_b + Z_b$$

giving:

$$\begin{bmatrix} X \\ Y \\ Z \end{bmatrix} = \begin{bmatrix} D_r x_r & D_g x_g & D_b x_b \\ D_r y_r & D_g y_g & D_b y_b \\ D_r z_r & D_g z_g & D_b z_b \end{bmatrix} \begin{bmatrix} r \\ g \\ b \end{bmatrix}$$

where:

$$x_r = X_r/D_r \qquad Y_r = Y_r/D_r \qquad z_r = Z_r/D_r \qquad \ldots$$

Writing the coefficients as a product of two matrices we have:

$$\begin{bmatrix} X \\ Y \\ Z \end{bmatrix} = \begin{bmatrix} x_r & x_g & x_b \\ y_r & y_g & y_b \\ z_r & z_g & z_b \end{bmatrix} \begin{bmatrix} D_r & 0 & 0 \\ 0 & D_g & 0 \\ 0 & 0 & D_b \end{bmatrix} \begin{bmatrix} r \\ g \\ b \end{bmatrix}$$

where the first matrix is the chromaticity coordinates of the monitor phosphor. We now specify that equal RGB voltages of (1,1,1) should produce the alignment white:

$$\begin{bmatrix} X_w \\ Y_w \\ Z_w \end{bmatrix} = \begin{bmatrix} x_r & x_g & x_b \\ y_r & y_g & y_b \\ z_r & z_g & z_b \end{bmatrix} \begin{bmatrix} D_r \\ D_g \\ D_b \end{bmatrix} \qquad\qquad \textbf{(14.2)}$$

For example, with D_{65} we have:

$$x_w = 0.313 \qquad y_w = 0.329 \qquad z_w = 0.358$$

and scaling the white point to give unity luminance yields

$$X_w = 0.951 \qquad Y_w = 1.0 \qquad Z_w = 1.089$$

Example chromaticity coordinates for an interlaced monitor (long persistence phosphors) are:

	x	y
red	0.620	0.330
green	0.210	0.685
blue	0.150	0.063

Using these we have:

$$
\begin{bmatrix} X \\ Y \\ Z \end{bmatrix} = \begin{bmatrix} 0.584 & 0.188 & 0.179 \\ 0.311 & 0.614 & 0.075 \\ 0.047 & 0.103 & 0.939 \end{bmatrix} \begin{bmatrix} r \\ g \\ b \end{bmatrix}
$$

Inverting the coefficient matrix gives:

$$
\begin{bmatrix} r \\ g \\ b \end{bmatrix} = \begin{bmatrix} 2.043 & -0.568 & -0.344 \\ -1.035 & 1.939 & 0.042 \\ 0.011 & -0.184 & 1.078 \end{bmatrix} \begin{bmatrix} X \\ Y \\ Z \end{bmatrix}
$$

14.4.2 Colour clipping

Monitor gamuts generally overlap and colours that are available on one monitor may not be reproducible on another. This is manifested by RGB values that are less than 0, or greater than 1, after the transformation $T_2^{-1}T_1$ has been applied. This problem may also arise in rendering. In accurate colour simulation, using real colour values, it is likely that colour triples produced by the calculation may lie outside the monitor gamut. The image gamut may be, in general, greater than the monitor gamut. This problem is even greater in the case of hard-copy devices such as printers which have smaller gamuts than monitors. The goal of the process is to compress the image gamut until it just fits in the device gamut in such a way that the image quality is maintained. This will generally depend on the content of the image; the whole subject area is still a research topic. There are, however, a number of simple strategies that we can adopt. The process of producing a displayable colour from one that is outside the gamut of the monitor is called **colour clipping**.

Clearly, we could adopt a simple clamping approach and limit out-of-range values to 0 or 1. Better strategies are suggested by Hall (1989). Undisplayable colours fall into two categories:

- colours that have chromaticities outside the monitor gamut (negative RGB values),
- colours that have displayable chromaticities, but intensities outside the monitor gamut (RGB values greater than 1).

Any correction results in a shift or change in colour and we can select a method depending on whether we wish to tolerate a shift in hue, saturation and/or value.

For the first category the best approach is to add white to the colour or to desaturate it until it is displayable. This maintains the hue or dominant wavelength and lightness at the cost of saturation. In the second case there are a number of possibilities. The entire image can be scaled until the highest intensity is in range; this has an effect similar to reducing the aperture in a camera. Alternatively, the chromaticity can be maintained and the

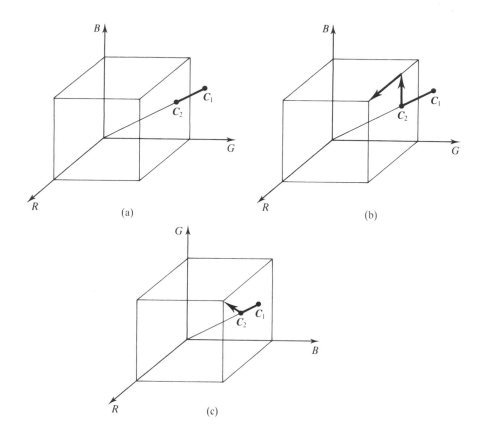

Figure 14.12
Colour clipping
strategies (after Hall
(1989)).

intensity scaled. Finally, the dominant hue and intensity can be maintained and the colour desaturated by adding white.

Three clipping strategies are given a geometric interpretation in Figure 14.12. We consider an undisplayable colour C_1. Scaling the intensity of the colour until it is in range means mapping all those colours on the line C_1C_2 into the colour C_2 (Figure 14.12a). Clamping the RGB components to unity maps colours between C_1 and C_2 into the path shown in Figure 14.12(b) and desaturating the colour into the path shown in Figure 14.12(c).

14.4.3   Gamma correction

All of the foregoing discussion has implicitly assumed that there is a linear relationship between the actual RGB values input to a monitor and the intensity produced on the screen. This is not the case. The red intensity, for example, produced on a monitor screen by an input value of R'_i is:

$$R_m = K(R'_i)^{\gamma_r}$$

where γ is normally in the range 2.3–2.8. The goal of the process is to

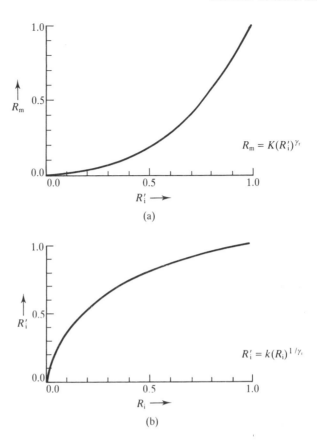

R_m

$$R_\mathrm{m} = K(R'_\mathrm{i})^{\gamma_r}$$

$R'_\mathrm{i} \longrightarrow$

(a)

Figure 14.13
Gamma correction. (a)
Intensity as a function
of applied voltage
values. (b) Corrected
values as a function of
applied values.

R'_i

$$R'_\mathrm{i} = k(R_\mathrm{i})^{1/\gamma_i}$$

$R_\mathrm{i} \longrightarrow$

(b)

linearize the relationship between between the RGB values produced by the program, and if γ_r, γ_g and γ_b are known then so-called gamma correction can be applied to convert the program value R_i to the value that, when plugged into the above equation, will result in a linear relationship. That is:

$$R'_\mathrm{i} = k(R_\mathrm{i})^{1/\gamma_r}$$

An inexpensive method for determining γ is given by Cowan (1983). The two relationships are shown in Figure 14.13. The second graph is easily incorporated in a video look-up table. Note that the price paid for gamma correction is a reduction in the dynamic range. For example, if k is chosen such that 0 maps to 0 and 255 to 255 then 256 intensity levels are reduced to 167. This can cause banding and it is better to perform the correction in floating point and then to round.

The difference that gamma correction makes is demonstrated in Plate 32 where the top band in the illustration is gamma corrected and the bottom band is not. (The RGB graphs show the values of the RGB components as we move along a strip.) You can see from this that, in general, there is an intensity change; the lower intensities are lifted. There is also a chromaticity shift. (The effect is somewhat coarsened by inadequate reproduction processes, but the general drifts displayed by the pictures are correct.) The chromaticities of the displayed uncorrected colours are wrong. Consider, for example, the triple (0,255,127). If this is not gamma corrected the display will decrease the blue component, leaving the red and green components unchanged.

Gamma correction leaves zero and maximum intensities unchanged and alters the intensity in midrange. A 'wrong' gamma that occurs either because gamma correction has not been applied or because an inaccurate value of gamma has been used in the correction will always result in a wrong image in the sense shown in the colour plate.

Projects, notes and suggestions ━━━━━━━━

14.1   HSV interface

Write a program that provides a user interface for an HSV model for Project 4.5.

14.2   Pseudocolour enhancement

Write an interface that will allow a naive user to select different colour mappings for the pseudocolour enhancement of an appropriate function (this could be done by, for example, controlling the tilt of a plane containing a path in HSV space).

Choose a particular mapping in HSV space and compare this with an image generated from an 'identical' mapping using CIE HLS parameters (Equation 14.2). In each case use regular increments along the path.

Investigate perceptual differences between the images (and numeric differences by examining pixel values) as a function of the position of the path in the colour spaces.

14.3   CIE–RGB transformation

Determine the CIE–RGB transformation for your equipment and implement gamma correction.

14.4   Colour space sampling

Investigate the effects of the common procedure in computer graphics of performing calculations at three fixed wavelengths in RGB space.

Here you could refer to the methodology employed by Hall and Greenberg (1983) who generated a test environment consisting of two overlapping filters and compared variations along an appropriate scan line from images that were computed from:

- three samples in CIE XYZ space;
- three samples in RGB space;
- nine spectral samples;
- a control image (generated from samples at 1 nm intervals).

Of what relevance is undersampling in colour space to three-dimensional computer graphics?

Viewing Transformation for a Simple Four-parameter Viewing System

This appendix derives the matrix, T_{view}, that transforms points in the world coordinate system to points in the view coordinate system for the simple four-parameter viewing system described in Chapter 1. The material is produced, not primarily to derive the result, but as a useful educational exercise in manipulating three-dimensional linear transformations.

The viewing transformation, T_{view}, transforms points in the world coordinate system into the view coordinate system:

$$[x_v \ y_v \ z_v \ 1] = [x_w \ y_w \ z_w \ 1]T_{\text{view}}$$

A view point (Figure A.1) is given as a set of three coordinates specifying the view point in the world coordinate system. An object described in the world coordinate

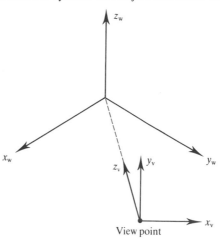

Figure A.1
World and view
coordinate systems.

437

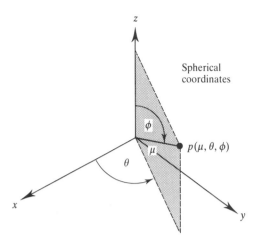

Figure A.2
Spherical coordinates enable a simple interface for the four-parameter viewing system.

system is viewed from this point along a certain direction. In the view coordinate system the z axis points towards the world system origin and the x axis is parallel to the $x-y$ plane of the world system. We shall adopt a left-handed convention for the view coordinate system. In the view coordinate system the x and y axes match the axes of the display system and the z_v direction is away from the view point (into the display screen). World coordinates are normally right-handed systems so that in the computation of a net transformation matrix for the viewing transformation we would include a conversion to a left-handed system.

We can now specify the net transformation matrix as a series of translations and rotations that take us from the world coordinate system into the view coordinate system, given a particular view point.

These steps will be given as separate transformation matrices and the net transformation matrix resulting from the product will simply be stated.

In this simple system the viewing transformation is best specified using spherical instead of cartesian coordinates. We specify a view point in spherical co-ordinates by giving a distance from the origin μ and two angles, θ and ϕ, as shown in Figure A.2.

These are related to the view point's cartesian coordinates as follows:

$$T_x = \mu \sin \phi \cos \theta$$
$$T_y = \mu \sin \phi \sin \theta$$
$$T_z = \mu \cos \phi$$

Another fact we require in this derivation is that to change the origin of a system from $(0,0,0,1)$ to $(T_x, T_y, T_z, 1)$ we use the transformation:

$$\begin{bmatrix} 1 & 0 & 0 & 0 \\ 0 & 1 & 0 & 0 \\ 0 & 0 & 1 & 0 \\ -T_x & -T_y & -T_z & 1 \end{bmatrix}$$

Note that this is the inverse of the transformation that would take a point from $(0,0,0,1)$ to $(T_x, T_y, T_z, 1)$.

The four transformations required to take the object from a world coordinate system into a view coordinate system are:

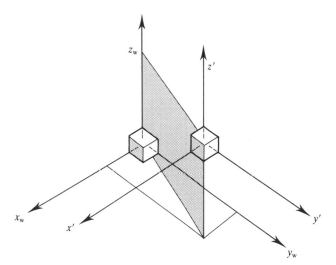

Figure A.3
Transformation 1.

(1) Translate the world coordinate system to (T_x, T_y, T_z), the position of the view point. All three axes remain parallel to their counterparts in the world system. The cube in Figure A.3 is not an object that is being transformed but is intended to enhance an interpretation of the axes. Using spherical coordinate values for T_x, T_y, and T_z the transformation is:

$$T_1 = \begin{bmatrix} 1 & 0 & 0 & 0 \\ 0 & 1 & 0 & 0 \\ 0 & 0 & 1 & 0 \\ -\mu\cos\theta\sin\phi & -\mu\sin\theta\sin\phi & -\mu\cos\phi & 1 \end{bmatrix}$$

(2) The next step is to rotate the coordinate system through $90° - \theta$ in a clockwise direction about the z' axis. The rotation matrices defined in Chapter 1 were for counterclockwise rotation relative to a coordinate system. The transformation matrix for a clockwise rotation of the coordinate system is the same as that for a counterclockwise rotation of a point relative to the coordinate system. The x'' axis is now normal to the plane containing μ (Figure A.4).

$$T_2 = \begin{bmatrix} \sin\theta & \cos\theta & 0 & 0 \\ -\cos\theta & \sin\theta & 0 & 0 \\ 0 & 0 & 1 & 0 \\ 0 & 0 & 0 & 1 \end{bmatrix}$$

(3) The next step is to rotate the coordinate system through $180° - \phi$ counterclockwise about the x' axis. This makes the z''' axis pass through the origin of the world coordinate system (Figure A.5).

$$T_3 = \begin{bmatrix} 1 & 0 & 0 & 0 \\ 0 & -\cos\phi & -\sin\phi & 0 \\ 0 & \sin\phi & -\cos\phi & 0 \\ 0 & 0 & 0 & 1 \end{bmatrix}$$

(4) Finally we convert to a left-handed system as described above.

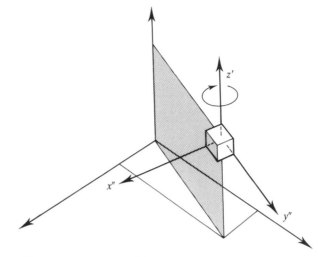

Figure A.4
Transformation 2.

$$T_4 = \begin{bmatrix} -1 & 0 & 0 & 0 \\ 0 & 1 & 0 & 0 \\ 0 & 0 & 1 & 0 \\ 0 & 0 & 0 & 1 \end{bmatrix}$$

Multiplying these together gives the net transformation matrix required for the viewing transformation.

$$T_{\text{view}} = [T_1 \ T_2 \ T_3 \ T_4] \begin{bmatrix} -\sin\theta & -\cos\theta\cos\phi & -\cos\theta\sin\phi & 0 \\ \cos\theta & -\sin\theta\cos\phi & -\sin\theta\sin\phi & 0 \\ 0 & \sin\phi & -\cos\phi & 0 \\ 0 & 0 & \mu & 1 \end{bmatrix}$$

where:

$$[x_v \ y_v \ z_v \ 1] = [x_w \ y_w \ z_w \ 1]T_{\text{view}}$$

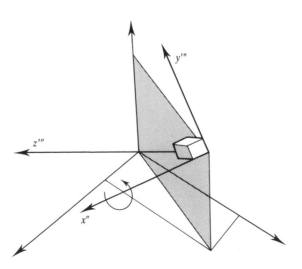

Figure A.5
Transformation 3.

Appendix B | A Wireframe System

This is a complete program that sets up a data structure for objects and draws a wireframe projection of these objects in two-dimensional screen space. The data structure used is more complicated than it need be for wireframes, because the program is subsequently used by procedures that perform shading (Appendix C.)

The appendix is intended to provide further study of the material given in Chapters 1, 2 and 3, particularly with regard to implementation details and the relationship between data structures and graphical programming techniques. The program is written in a way that hopefully facilitates this.

B.1 Data structure

This section is not for the faint-hearted but it is worth a glance if you are using the program. Implementers will find a detailed study of this section useful. Early mistakes in the design of a data structure are usually left and can have tedious consequences. The data structure has the following attributes:

- It is a hierarchical object–surface–polygon scheme as outlined in Chapter 1.

- Vertex details are stored once only and different polygons can share the same vertex. However, this does not apply if the vertices are shared by two surfaces. Here a shared vertex is stored for each surface.

- Polygon normals are stored (for culling) and vertex normals are stored (for shading).

A scene is composed of a number of objects and stored in the data structure as a list of objects. The pointer to the start of the list is *ObjectHead* (Figure B.1). The fields of an object record have self-explanatory names, for example, *Transform* is a transform matrix that will be used to transform the object (for example, rotate or scale).

An object is constructed from a number of surfaces, the first of which is pointed to by the field *SurfaceHead* in the object cell. Again they are stored in a list as shown in Figure B.1. Each surface is represented by a mesh of polygons. The field *NoOfPolygons* in a surface cell tells us how many polygons there are in the list pointed to by the field *PolygonHead*. Each polygon cell contains space to store a normal and a boolean culled flag.

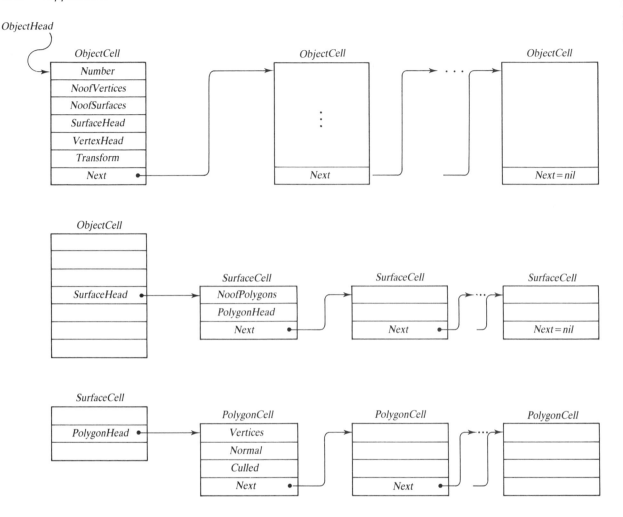

A polygon is defined using a set of vertices. They are listed in a defined order (counterclockwise with respect to viewing from the outside of the object). This order is needed to obtain the correct normal direction when calculating the polygon normal.

Each vertex list cell (Figure B.1) points to a vertex record (using the field *Vertex*) where the details of a vertex are stored. This enables adjacent polygons to share a vertex and vertices to be stored only once (unless they happen to be shared by adjacent surfaces). Thus many polygons can point to the same vertex record.

The vertex details for a particular object are stored as a list pointed to by a field labelled *VertexHead* in the object cell. This simplifies transformation operations, since the vertices to be transformed are now directly accessible at the top level of the data structure.

In order to calculate a vertex normal, the surrounding polygon normals are averaged. Therefore, a list of the polygons that share a vertex must be recorded. This list is pointed to by the field *Polygons* within a vertex cell.

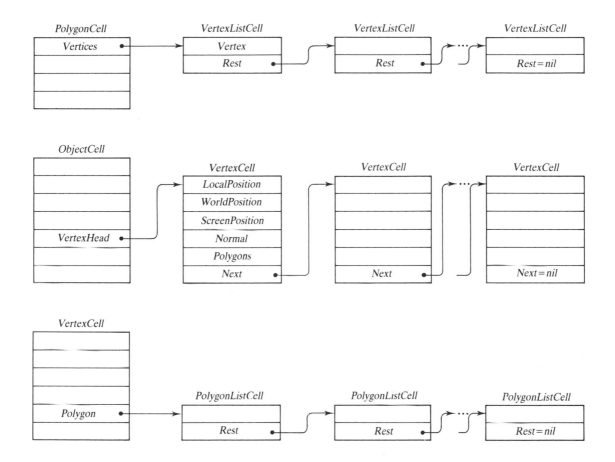

Figure B.1
The data structure.

To build the data structure we need a scene file. An example is:

```
1                         { 1 = perspective  0 = parallel }
−7000                     { view distance }
10000                     { perspective distance }
−0.7 −0.4 −0.3            { view plane normal }
0.0   0.0   1.0           { view up vector }
0                         { draw vertex normals 0 = false  1 = true }
4                         { no. of objects }
cube.obj
        0.4   0.4   0.4   { scale }
        0.0   0.0   0.0   { rotate }
        0.5   1.7 −0.6    { translate }
```

```
F.obj
     1.0    1.0    1.0
     0.0    0.0    0.0
     1.7  −0.4    0.0
cube.obj
     0.2    0.2    1.0
     0.0    0.0    0.0
     0.0    1.7    0.8
cylinder.obj
     0.9    0.9    1.0
     0.0    0.0    0.0
     0.0    0.0    0.0
```

This structure is as follows:

> viewing information
> number of objects
> for each object
>   object data filename
>   object transformations

In the above example there are four objects in the scene with data defined in three files. The transformations to be carried out on an object are read into the program and a net transformation matrix is constructed. This is then stored in the *Transform* field of an object cell.

An object data file is structured as follows:

Number of vertices, number of polygons, number of surfaces.

Vertex information
    vertex number, x,y,z

Polygon information
    polygon number, surface number, number of vertices, list of vertex numbers.

We can now look at a practical example of the complete data structure for a single simple object (Figure B.2). It may seem that for such a simple object, the information content of the data structure is somewhat high, but in practice objects may have hundreds or thousands of polygons and an economical representation becomes a necessity. Also bear in mind that the structure is enhanced with shading requirements.

Although it may seem more expensive to use pointers, rather than array indexing, the use of arrays is inflexible with regard to the size of the scene that can be stored in a data structure. With a pointer structure the data structure 'automatically' expands and contracts to fit the specified scene.

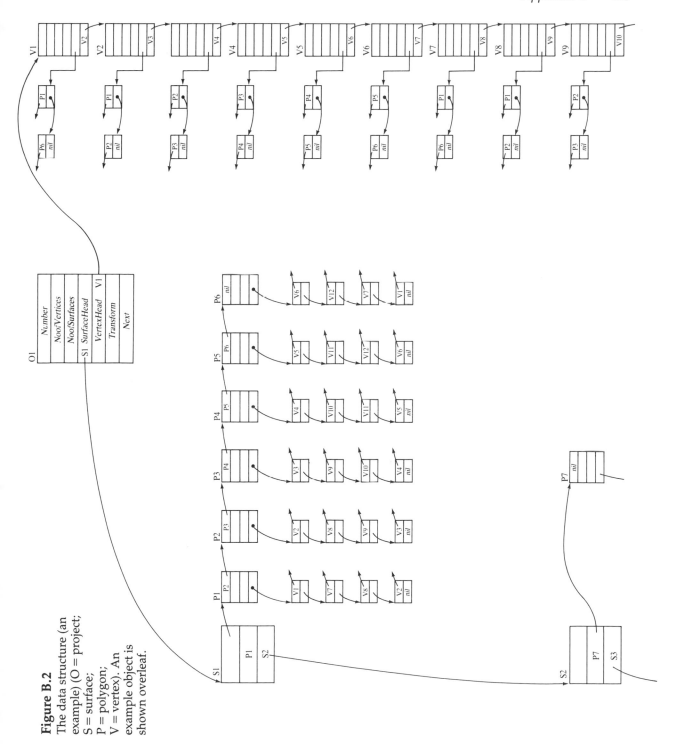

Figure B.2
The data structure (an example) (O = project; S = surface; P = polygon; V = vertex). An example object is shown overleaf.

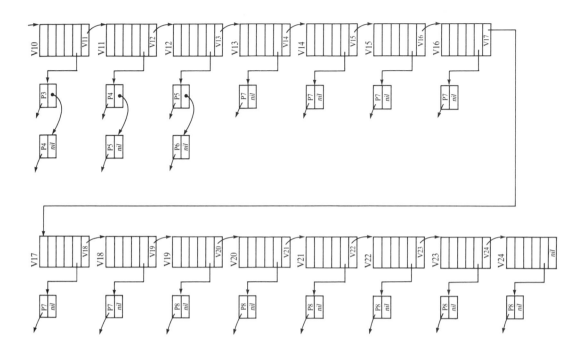

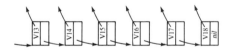

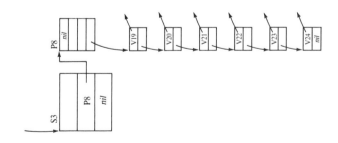

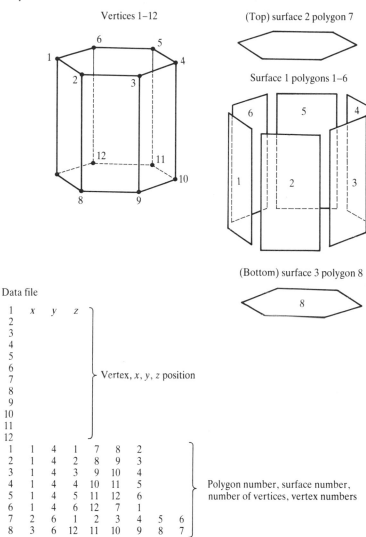

A cylinder

Vertices 1–12

(Top) surface 2 polygon 7

Surface 1 polygons 1–6

(Bottom) surface 3 polygon 8

Data file

1	x	y	z			
2						
3						
4						
5						
6						
7						
8						
9						
10						
11						
12						

Vertex, x, y, z position

1	1	4	1	7	8	2		
2	1	4	2	8	9	3		
3	1	4	3	9	10	4		
4	1	4	4	10	11	5		
5	1	4	5	11	12	6		
6	1	4	6	12	7	1		
7	2	6	1	2	3	4	5	6
8	3	6	12	11	10	9	8	7

Polygon number, surface number, number of vertices, vertex numbers

Figure B.2
(continued)

B.2   The program

Program B.1 deals with the following material:

- Setting up and accessing a data structure described in Section B.1.
- Implementation of linear transformations (Chapter 1).
- Three-dimensional geometry outlined in Chapter 1, in particular manipulation of vectors and culling.
- Implementation of viewing system I of Chapter 3.

Program B.1   Wireframe drawing.

```
program WireFrame (input, output);

{ Program to draw wireframe objects. }

{ Note:
    The following constants, types and procedures are device specific, declared
    here for clarity. You should substitute all occurrences of these in the pro-
    gram with the relevant values and routines for your own graphics device.}
{ ***********************************

const
    DEV_MAX_X_RES = 1023; – Monitor X resolution.
    DEV_MAX_Y_RES = 1023; – Monitor Y resolution.
    DEV_MAX_Z_RES = 255; – Frame buffer bit-depth; used during
                                    rendering.

type
    DEV_X_RES = 0..DEV_MAX_X_RES;
    DEV_Y_RES = 0..DEV_MAX_Y_RES;
    DEV_Z_RES = 0..DEV_MAX_Z_RES;

    DEV_COLOUR = record
                        r, g, b: DEV_Z_RES
                    end;

procedure DEV_CLEAR_SCREEN;
    { Clear monitor screen }

procedure DEV_MOVE_TO (x : DEV_X_RES; y : DEV_Y_RES);
    { Set current screen position to (x, y) }

procedure DEV_DRAW_TO (x : DEV_X_RES; y : DEV_Y_RES;
    c : DEV_COLOUR);
    { Draw a line from current screen position to (x,y), using colour c }

    *********************************** }

const
    MaxStringLength = 100;
    PI = 3.1415926535;

type
    CharString = PACKED array [1..MaxStringLength] of char;
    String     = record
                        length : integer;
                        char_at : CharString
                    end;

    Matrix = array [0..3, 0..3] of real;

    Vector = record
                    x, y, z : real
                end;
```

```
ScreenRec = record
                x, y, z : integer
            end;

ObjectPtr = ^ObjectCell;
SurfacePtr = ^SurfaceCell;
PolygonPtr = ^PolygonCell;
VertexPtr = ^VertexCell;
PolygonListPtr = ^PolygonListCell;
VertexListPtr = ^VertexListCell;

ObjectCell = record
                name : String;
                id_no,
                no_vertices,
                no_surfaces : integer;
                surface_head : SurfacePtr;
                vertex_head : VertexPtr;
                transformation : Matrix;
                next : ObjectPtr
            end;

SurfaceCell = record
                no_polygons : integer;
                polygon_head : PolygonPtr;
                next : SurfacePtr
            end;

PolygonCell = record
                vertex_list_head : VertexListPtr;
                poly_normal : Vector;
                poly_visible : boolean;
                next : PolygonPtr
            end;

VertexCell = record
                local_pos,
                world_pos,
                eye_pos,
                vertex_normal : Vector;
                screen_pos : ScreenRec;
                poly_list_head : PolygonListPtr;
                next : VertexPtr
            end;

PolygonListCell = record
                poly : PolygonPtr;
                rest : PolygonListPtr
            end;
```

```pascal
VertexListCell = record
                   vertex : VertexPtr;
                   rest : VertexListPtr
                 end;

ViewPointRec = record
                 view_plane_dist,
                 rho, theta, phi : integer;
                 sin_theta, cos_theta, sin_phi, cos_phi,
                 x_view, y_view, z_view : real
               end;

MapRec = record
           xmid, ymid : integer
         end;

ZParamRec = record z_min, z_max, z_range : real
            end;

procedure Main;

  procedure ReadString (var s : String);
  var
    spos : integer;

  begin { ReadString }
    spos := 0;
    while NOT eoln do
    begin
      if spos < MaxStringLength then
      begin
        spos := spos + 1;
        s.char_at[spos] := input^
      end;
      get (input)
    end;
    readln;
    s.length := spos
  end { ReadString };

  procedure WriteString (s : String);
  begin { WriteString }
    with s do
      if length > 0 then
        write (char_at:length)
  end { WriteString };

  function DotProduct (v1, v2 : Vector) : real;
  begin { DotProduct }
    DotProduct := (v1.x * v2.x) + (v1.y * v2.y) + (v1.z * v2.z)
  end { DotProduct };
```

```pascal
procedure Normalize (v1 : Vector; var v2 : Vector);
var
  denominator : real;

  function Magnitude (v : Vector) : real;
  begin { Magnitude }
    with v do
      Magnitude := sqrt ( sqr(x) + sqr(y) + sqr(z) )
  end { Magnitude };

begin { Normalize }
  denominator := Magnitude (v1);
  if denominator = 0 then
    v2 := v1
  else
  begin
    v2.x := v1.x / denominator;
    v2.y := v1.y / denominator;
    v2.z := v1.z / denominator
  end
end { Normalize };

procedure VectorMatrix (v1: Vector;
            transformation : Matrix;
              var v2: Vector);
begin { VectorMatrix }
  with v1 do
  begin
    v2.x := x * transformation[0,0] +
        y * transformation[1,0] +
        z * transformation[2,0] +
        transformation[3,0];

    v2.y := x * transformation[0,1] +
        y * transformation[1,1] +
        z * transformation[2,1] +
        transformation[3,1];

    v2.z := x * transformation[0,2] +
        y * transformation[1,2] +
        z * transformation[2,2] +
        transformation[3,2];
  end
end { VectorMatrix };

procedure Perspective (pos : Vector; view_ref_point : ViewPointRec;
            map_offsets : MapRec; var screen_x, screen_y : integer);
var
  temp_x, temp_y : real;
```

```
begin { Perspective }
  with pos do
    with view_ref_point do
    begin
      temp_x := view_plane_dist * (x/z);
      temp_y := view_plane_dist * (y/z)
    end;
    with map_offsets do
    begin
      screen_x := trunc (xmid + temp_x);
      screen_y := trunc (ymid + temp_y)
    end
end { Perspective };

procedure WireFrameScene (map_offsets : MapRec;
            view_transformation : Matrix;
            view_ref_point : ViewPointRec;
            object_head : ObjectPtr);
const
  NSF = 30; { Normal Scale Factor }

var
  ch : char;
  draw_vertex_normals : boolean;
  wire_colour, normal_colour : DEV_COLOUR;
  current_surface : SurfacePtr;
  current_polygon : PolygonPtr;
  vertex_list : VertexListPtr;
  start_pos : ScreenRec;
  tw, ts : Vector;
  tx, ty : integer;

begin { WireFrameScene }
  write ('Draw vertex normals (y/n) ? ');
  readln (ch);
  draw_vertex_normals := (ch IN ['Y', 'y']);
  wire_colour.r := 0;
  wire_colour.g := 180;
  wire_colour.b := 130;
  normal_colour.r := 200;
  normal_colour.g := 0;
  normal_colour.b := 0;
  DEV_CLEAR_SCREEN;
  while object_head <> nil do
  begin
    with object_head^ do
    begin
      current_surface := surface_head;
      while current_surface <> nil do
```

```
begin
  with current_surface^ do
  begin
    current_polygon := polygon_head;
    while current_polygon <> nil do
    begin
      with current_polygon^ do
        if poly_visible then
        begin
          vertex_list := vertex_list_head;
          start_pos := vertex_list^.vertex^.screen_pos;
          with start_pos do
            DEV_MOVE_TO (x,y);
          vertex_list := vertex_list^.rest;
          while vertex_list <> nil do
          begin
            with vertex_list^ do
              with vertex^.screen_pos do
                DEV_DRAW_TO (x,y, wire_colour);
            vertex_list := vertex_list^.rest
          end;
          with start_pos do
            DEV_DRAW_TO (x,y, wire_colour);
          if draw_vertex_normals then
          begin
            vertex_list := vertex_list_head;
            while vertex_list <> nil do
            begin
              with vertex_list^.vertex^ do
              begin
                with screen_pos do
                  DEV_MOVE_TO (x,y);
                with tw do
                begin
                  x := world_pos.x +
                    (NSF * vertex_normal.x);
                  y := world_pos.y +
                    (NSF * vertex_normal.y);
                  z := world_pos.z +
                    (NSF * vertex_normal.z)
                end;
                VectorMatrix (tw, view_transformation, ts);
                Perspective (ts, view_ref_point,
                  map_offsets, tx, ty);
                DEV_DRAW_TO (tx, ty,
                  normal_colour)
              end;
              vertex_list := vertex_list^.rest
            end
```

```
                          end
                        end;
                      current_polygon := current_polygon^.next
                    end
                  end;
                current_surface := current_surface^.next
              end
            end;
          object_head := object_head^.next
        end
      end { WireFrameScene };

procedure TransformScene (map_offsets : MapRec;
              view_transformation : Matrix;
              view_ref_point : ViewPointRec;
              object_head : ObjectPtr;
              var z_params : ZParamRec;
              var scene_changed : boolean);

const
  HighReal = 1E30;

var
  current_object : ObjectPtr;

procedure CalculateScreenCoordinates (current_object : ObjectPtr;
              z_params : ZParamRec);
var
  current_surface : SurfacePtr;
  current_polygon : PolygonPtr;
  vertex_list : VertexListPtr;

begin { CalculateScreenCoordinates }
  while current_object <> nil do
  begin
    with current_object^ do
    begin
      current_surface := surface_head;
      while current_surface <> nil do
      begin
        with current_surface^ do
        begin
          current_polygon := polygon_head;
          while current_polygon <> nil do
          begin
            with current_polygon^ do
              if poly_visible then
              begin
                vertex_list := vertex_list_head;
                while vertex_list <> nil do
```

```pascal
            begin
              with vertex_list^.vertex^ do
              begin
                Perspective (eye_pos, view_ref_point,
                  map_offsets,
                  screen_pos.x, screen_pos.y);
                with screen_pos, z_params do
                  z := trunc (((eye_pos.z − z_min) /
                    z_range) * DEV_MAX_Z_RES)
              end;
              vertex_list := vertex_list^.rest
            end
          end;
          current_polygon := current_polygon^.next
        end
      end;
      current_surface := current_surface^.next
    end
  end;
  current_object := current_object^.next
  end
end { CalculateScreenCoordinates };

procedure CalculateEyeCoordinates (current_object : ObjectPtr;
          var z_params : ZParamRec);
var
  current_vertex : VertexPtr;

begin { CalculateEyeCoordinates }
  with current_object^ do
  begin
    current_vertex := vertex_head;
    while current_vertex <> nil do
      with current_vertex^ do
      begin
        VectorMatrix (world_pos, view_transformation, eye_pos);
        with z_params do
          if eye_pos.z < z_min then
            z_min := eye_pos.z
          else
            if eye_pos.z > z_max then
              z_max := eye_pos.z;
        current_vertex := current_vertex^.next
      end
  end
end { CalculateEyeCoordinates };

procedure RemoveHiddenSurfaces (current_object : ObjectPtr);
var
  current_surface : SurfacePtr;
```

```
procedure RemovePolygonIfHidden (current_polygon :
    PolygonPtr);
var
    view_direction : Vector;

begin { RemovePolygonIfHidden }
    while current_polygon <> nil do
    begin
        with current_polygon^ do
        begin
            with vertex_list_head^.vertex^.world_pos do
                with view_ref_point do
                begin
                    view_direction.x := x_view − x;
                    view_direction.y := y_view − y;
                    view_direction.z := z_view − z
                end;
            poly_visible := DotProduct (poly_normal,
                view_direction) > 0
        end;
        current_polygon := current_polygon^.next
    end
end { RemovePolygonIfHidden };

begin { RemoveHiddenSurfaces }
current_surface := current_object^.surface_head;
while current_surface <> nil do
begin
    RemovePolygonIfHidden (current_surface^.polygon_head);
    current_surface := current_surface^.next
end
end { RemoveHiddenSurfaces };

procedure CalculateNormals (current_object : ObjectPtr);

procedure CalculatePolygonNormals (current_object : ObjectPtr);
var
    current_surface : SurfacePtr;
    current_polygon : PolygonPtr;

procedure CalculateAPolygonNormal (current_polygon : PolygonPtr);
var
    vertex_list : VertexListPtr;
    w1, w2, w3 : Vector;

begin { CalculateAPolygonNormal }
    with current_polygon^ do
    begin
        vertex_list := current_polygon^.vertex_list_head;
        w1 := vertex_list^.Vertex^.world_pos;
        vertex_list := vertex_list^.rest;
        w2 := vertex_list^.Vertex^.world_pos;
```

```pascal
      vertex_list := vertex_list^.rest;
      w3 := vertex_list^.Vertex^.world_pos;
      with poly_normal do
      begin
        x := ((w1.y - w2.y) * (w2.z + w1.z)) +
             ((w2.y - w3.y) * (w3.z + w2.z)) +
             ((w3.y - w1.y) * (w1.z + w3.z));
        y := ((w1.z - w2.z) * (w2.x + w1.x)) +
             ((w2.z - w3.z) * (w3.x + w2.x)) +
             ((w3.z - w1.z) * (w1.x + w3.x));
        z := ((w1.x - w2.x) * (w2.y + w1.y)) +
             ((w2.x - w3.x) * (w3.y + w2.y)) +
             ((w3.x - w1.x) * (w1.y + w3.y))
      end;
      Normalize (poly_normal, poly_normal)
    end
  end { CalculateAPolygonNormal };

begin { CalculatePolygonNormals }
  current_surface := current_object^.surface_head;
  while current_surface <> nil do
  begin
    current_polygon := current_surface^.polygon_head;
    while current_polygon <> nil do
    begin
      CalculateAPolygonNormal (current_polygon);
      current_polygon := current_polygon^.next
    end;
    current_surface := current_surface^.next
  end
end { CalculatePolygonNormals };

procedure CalculateVertexNormals (current_object : ObjectPtr);
var
  current_vertex : VertexPtr;

  procedure CalculateAVertexNormal (current_vertex : VertexPtr);
  var
    poly_list : PolygonListPtr;
    sum_vector : Vector;
    poly_count : integer;

  begin { CalculateAVertexNormal }
    with sum_vector do
    begin
      x := 0;
      y := 0;
      z := 0
    end;
    poly_count := 0;
    poly_list := current_vertex^.poly_list_head;
```

```
                          while poly_list <> nil do
                          begin
                            poly_count := poly_count + 1;
                            with poly_list^.poly^ do
                            begin
                              sum_vector.x := sum_vector.x + poly_normal.x;
                              sum_vector.y := sum_vector.y + poly_normal.y;
                              sum_vector.z := sum_vector.z + poly_normal.z
                            end;
                            poly_list := poly_list^.rest
                          end;
                          with current_vertex^ do
                          begin
                            with vertex_normal do
                            begin
                              x := sum_vector.x / poly_count;
                              y := sum_vector.y / poly_count;
                              z := sum_vector.z / poly_count
                            end;
                            Normalize (vertex_normal, vertex_normal)
                          end
                       end { CalculateAVertexNormal };

                     begin { CalculateVertexNormals }
                       current_vertex := current_object^.vertex_head;
                       while current_vertex <> nil do
                       begin
                         CalculateAVertexNormal (current_vertex);
                         current_vertex := current_vertex^.next
                       end
                     end { CalculateVertexNormals };

                   begin { CalculateNormals }
                     CalculatePolygonNormals (current_object);
                     CalculateVertexNormals (current_object)
                   end { CalculateNormals };

                   procedure TransformToWorldCoordinates (current_object : ObjectPtr);
                   var
                     current_vertex : VertexPtr;

                   begin { TransformToWorldCoordinates }
                     with current_object^ do
                     begin
                       current_vertex := vertex_head;
                       while current_vertex <> nil do
                         with current_vertex^ do
                         begin
                           VectorMatrix (local_pos, transformation, world_pos);
                           current_vertex := current_vertex^.next
                         end
```

```
      end
  end { TransformToWorldCoordinates };

  begin { TransformScene }
    writeln ('Transforming scene');
    writeln;
    with z_params do
    begin
      z_min := HighReal;
      z_max := - HighReal;
      z_range := 0
    end;
    current_object := object_head;
    while current_object <> nil do
    begin
      TransformToWorldCoordinates (current_object);
      CalculateNormals (current_object);
      RemoveHiddenSurfaces (current_object);
      CalculateEyeCoordinates (current_object, z_params);
      current_object := current_object^.next
    end;
    with z_params do
      z_range := z_max - z_min;
    CalculateScreenCoordinates (object_head, z_params);
    scene_changed := false
  end { TransformScene };

procedure SetZeroMatrix (var m : Matrix);
var
  i, j : 0..3;

begin { SetZeroMatrix }
  for i := 0 to 3 do
    for j := 0 to 3 do
      m [i,j] := 0
end { SetZeroMatrix };

procedure SetIdentityMatrix (var m : Matrix);
var
  diag : 0..3;

begin { SetIdentityMatrix }
  SetZeroMatrix (m);
  for diag := 0 to 3 do
    m [diag,diag] := 1
end { SetIdentityMatrix };

function InRadians (degrees : real) : real;
begin { InRadians }
  InRadians := degrees * PI / 180
end { InRadians };
```

```
procedure SetViewVariables (var view_ref_point : ViewPointRec;
                 var view_transformation : Matrix);

procedure SetViewTransformation (view_ref_point : ViewPointRec;
                 var view_transformation : Matrix);
  begin { SetViewTransformation }
    SetIdentityMatrix (view_transformation);
    with view_ref_point do
    begin
      view_transformation[0,0] := −sin_theta;
      view_transformation[0,1] := −cos_theta * cos_phi;
      view_transformation[0,2] := −cos_theta * sin_phi;
      view_transformation[1,0] := cos_theta;
      view_transformation[1,1] := −sin_theta * cos_phi;
      view_transformation[1,2] := −sin_theta * sin_phi;
      view_transformation[2,1] := sin_phi;
      view_transformation[2,2] := −cos_phi;
      view_transformation[3,2] := rho
    end
  end { SetViewTransformation };

begin { SetViewVariables }
  with view_ref_point do
  begin
    sin_theta := sin(InRadians (theta));
    cos_theta := cos(InRadians (theta));
    sin_phi := sin(InRadians (phi));
    cos_phi := cos(InRadians (phi));
    x_view := rho * cos_theta * sin_phi;
    y_view := rho * sin_theta * sin_phi;
    z_view := rho * cos_phi
  end;
  SetViewTransformation (view_ref_point, view_transformation)
end { SetViewVariables };

procedure GetViewRefPoint (var view_ref_point : ViewPointRec;
                 var view_transformation : Matrix);
begin { GetViewRefPoint }
  writeln;
  with view_ref_point do
  begin
    writeln ('Enter new view point details −');
    writeln;
    write (' Rho (currently ', rho:1, ') : ');
    readln (rho);
    writeln;
    write (' Theta (currently ', theta:1, ') : ');
    readln (theta);
    writeln;
    write (' Phi (currently ', phi:1, ') : ');
```

```
      readln (phi);
      writeln;
      write (' Viewing distance (currently ', view_plane_dist:1, ') : ');
      readln (view_plane_dist)
    end;
    SetViewVariables (view_ref_point, view_transformation)
  end { GetViewRefPoint };

procedure GetTransformation (name : String; var transformation : Matrix);
var
  ch : char;
  trans_vector : Vector;
  trans_matrix : Matrix;

procedure MultiplyMatrices (m1, m2 : Matrix; var m3 : Matrix);
var
  i, j, k : 0..3;

begin { MultiplyMatrices }
  SetZeroMatrix (m3);
  for i := 0 to 3 do
    for j := 0 to 3 do
      for k := 0 to 3 do
        m3[i,j] := m3[i,j] + m1[i,k] * m2[k,j]
end { MultiplyMatrices };

procedure GetTranslationMatrix (tv : Vector; var tm : Matrix);
begin { GetTranslationMatrix }
  SetIdentityMatrix (tm);
  with tv do
  begin
    tm[3,0] := x;
    tm[3,1] := y;
    tm[3,2] := z
  end
end { GetTranslationMatrix };

procedure GetScalingMatrix (sv : Vector; var sm : Matrix);
begin { GetScalingMatrix }
  SetIdentityMatrix (sm);
  with sv do
  begin
    sm[0,0] := x;
    sm[1,1] := y;
    sm[2,2] := z
  end
end { GetScalingMatrix };

procedure GetRotationMatrix (rv : Vector; var rm : Matrix);
var
  x_rot, y_rot, z_rot : Matrix;
```

```
begin { GetRotationMatrix }
  SetIdentityMatrix (x_rot);
  SetIdentityMatrix (y_rot);
  SetIdentityMatrix (z_rot);
  with rv do
  begin
    x := InRadians (x);
    y := InRadians (y);
    z := InRadians (z);

    x_rot[1,1] := cos(x);
    x_rot[1,2] := sin(x);
    x_rot[2,1] := -sin(x);
    x_rot[2,2] := cos(x);

    y_rot[0,0] := cos(y);
    y_rot[0,2] := -sin(y);
    y_rot[2,0] := sin(y);
    y_rot[2,2] := cos(y);

    z_rot[0,0] := cos(z);
    z_rot[0,1] := sin(z);
    z_rot[1,0] := -sin(z);
    z_rot[1,1] := cos(z);

    MultiplyMatrices (z_rot, y_rot, rm);
    MultiplyMatrices (x_rot, rm, rm)
  end
end { GetRotationMatrix };

procedure ReadAVector (var v : Vector);
begin { ReadAVector }
  with v do
    readln (x,y,z)
end { ReadAVector };

begin { GetTransformation }
  writeln;
  write ('Transformation of ');
  WriteString (name);
  repeat
    writeln;
    writeln ('R - Rotation');
    writeln ('S - Scaling');
    writeln ('T - Translation');
    writeln ('N - None');
    repeat
      writeln;
      write ('Which transformation ? ');
      readln (ch);
    until (ch IN ['N', 'R', 'S', 'T', 'n', 'r', 's', 't']);
    if NOT (ch IN ['N', 'n']) then
```

```
       begin
          SetIdentityMatrix (trans_matrix);
          writeln;
          case ch of

            'R', 'r' : begin
                          writeln ('Enter angles of rotation about x, y and z
                              axes');
                          write ('Positive angle => anticlockwise rotation : ');
                          ReadAVector (trans_vector);
                          GetRotationMatrix (trans_vector, trans_matrix)
                       end;

            'S', 's' : begin
                          write ('Enter scaling factors for x, y and z : ');
                          ReadAVector (trans_vector);
                          GetScalingMatrix (trans_vector, trans_matrix)
                       end;

            'T', 't' : begin
                          write ('Enter translation factors for x, y and z : ');
                          ReadAVector (trans_vector);
                          GetTranslationMatrix (trans_vector, trans_matrix)
                       end;

          end;
          MultiplyMatrices (transformation, trans_matrix, transformation);
          writeln;
          write ('Any more transformations for');
          WriteString (name);
          write (' (y/n) ? ');
          readln (ch);
       end
       else
          SetIdentityMatrix (transformation)
    until (ch IN ['N', 'n'])
end { GetTransformation };

procedure LoadObject (object_name : String; no_of_objects : integer;
             var object_head : ObjectPtr);
const MaxNoOfVertices = 3000;
var
    object_file : text;
    current_object : ObjectPtr;
    vertex_at : array[1..MaxNoOfVertices] of VertexPtr;
    surface_at : array[1..MaxNoOfVertices] of integer;

    procedure MakeSurfaces (no_surfaces : integer; var surface_head :
                SurfacePtr;
                var no_vertices : integer; var vertex_head : VertexPtr);
```

```
var
  surface_count : integer;
  current_surface : SurfacePtr;

  procedure ReadPolygons (surface_count, no_polygons : integer;
              var polygon_head : PolygonPtr;
              var no_vertices : integer;
              var vertex_head : VertexPtr);
  var
    poly_count : integer;
    current_polygon : PolygonPtr;

    procedure ReadAPolygon (surface_count : integer;
                current_polygon : PolygonPtr;
                var no_vertices : integer;
                var vertex_head : VertexPtr);
    var
      vertex_count, current_vertex, no_vertices_in_polygon : integer;
      vertex_list : VertexListPtr;
      temp_vertex : VertexPtr;

      procedure AddPolygonToPolygonList (current_polygon : PolygonPtr;
                  var poly_list : PolygonListPtr);
      begin { AddPolygonToPolygonList }
        if poly_list = nil then
        begin
          new (poly_list);
          poly_list^.poly := current_polygon;
          poly_list^.rest := nil
        end
        else AddPolygonToPolygonList (current_polygon, poly_list^.rest)
      end { AddPolygonToPolygonList };

    begin { ReadAPolygon }
      with current_polygon^ do
      begin
        vertex_list_head := nil;
        read (object_file, no_vertices_in_polygon);
        for vertex_count := 1 to no_vertices_in_polygon do
        begin
          if vertex_list_head = nil then
          begin
            new (vertex_list);
            vertex_list_head := vertex_list
          end
          else
          begin
            new (vertex_list^.rest);
            vertex_list := vertex_list^.rest
          end;
          read (object_file, current_vertex);
```

```pascal
            if surface_at[current_vertex] = 0 then
              surface_at[current_vertex] := surface_count
            else
              if surface_at[current_vertex] <> surface_count then
              begin
                no_vertices := no_vertices + 1;
                surface_at[current_vertex] := surface_count;
                new (temp_vertex);
                temp_vertex^ := vertex_at[current_vertex]^;
                temp_vertex^. poly_list_head := nil;
                temp_vertex^.next := vertex_head;
                vertex_head := temp_vertex;
                vertex_at[current_vertex] := temp_vertex
              end;
              vertex_list^.vertex := vertex_at[current_vertex];
              AddPolygonToPolygonList (current_polygon,
                  vertex_list^.vertex^.poly_list_head)
          end
        end;
      vertex_list^.rest := nil;
    end { ReadAPolygon };

  begin { ReadPolygons }
    polygon_head := nil;
    for poly_count := 1 to no_polygons do
    begin
      if polygon_head = nil then
      begin
        new (current_polygon);
        polygon_head := current_polygon
      end
      else
      begin
        new (current_polygon^.next);
        current_polygon := current_polygon^.next
      end;
      ReadAPolygon (surface_count, current_polygon,
        no_vertices, vertex_head)
    end;
    current_polygon^.next := nil
  end { ReadPolygons };

begin { MakeSurfaces }
  surface_head := nil;
  for surface_count := 1 to no_surfaces do
  begin
    if surface_head = nil then
    begin
      new (current_surface);
      surface_head := current_surface
```

```pascal
          end
          else
          begin
            new (current_surface^.next);
            current_surface := current_surface^.next
          end;
          with current_surface^ do
          begin
            read (object_file, no_polygons);
            ReadPolygons (surface_count, no_polygons, polygon_head,
              no_vertices, vertex_head)
          end
        end;
      current_surface^.next := nil
  end { MakeSurfaces };

  procedure ReadVertices (no_vertices : integer; var vertex_head : VertexPtr);
  var
    vertex_count, id : integer;

  begin { ReadVertices }
    for vertex_count := 1 to no_vertices do
    begin
      surface_at[vertex_count] := 0;
      new (vertex_at[vertex_count]);
      with vertex_at[vertex_count]^ do
      begin
        read (object_file, id);
        with local_pos do
          readln (object_file, x, y, z);
        poly_list_head := nil
      end
    end;
    for vertex_count := 1 to no_vertices − 1 do
      vertex_at[vertex_count]^.next := vertex_at[vertex_count + 1];
    vertex_head := vertex_at[1];
      vertex_at[no_vertices]^.next := nil
  end { ReadVertices };

begin { LoadObject }
  reset (object_file, object_name.char_at);
  new (current_object);
  current_object^.next := object_head;
  object_head := current_object;
  with object_head^ do
  begin
    name := object_name;
    id_no := no_of_objects;
    readln (object_file, no_vertices);
    ReadVertices (no_vertices, vertex_head);
```

```
      readln (object_file, no_surfaces);
      MakeSurfaces (no_surfaces, surface_head, no_vertices, vertex_head);
      SetIdentityMatrix (transformation);
      GetTransformation (name, transformation)
    end
end { LoadObject };

procedure Initialize (var map_offsets : MapRec;
                      var view_ref_point : ViewPointRec;
                      var view_transformation : Matrix;
                      var scene_changed : boolean;
                      var no_of_objects : integer;
                      var object_head : ObjectPtr);

begin { Initialize }
  with map_offsets do
  begin
    xmid := trunc ((DEV_MAX_X_RES + 1) / 2);
    ymid := trunc ((DEV_MAX_Y_RES + 1) / 2)
  end;
  with view_ref_point do
  begin
    rho := 5000;
    theta := 45;
    phi := 90;
    view_plane_dist := 1000
  end;
  SetViewVariables (view_ref_point, view_transformation);
  scene_changed := false;
  no_of_objects := 0;
  object_head := nil
end { Initialize };

var { Main }
  map_offsets : MapRec;
  view_ref_point : ViewPointRec;
  view_transformation : Matrix;
  scene_changed : boolean;
  no_of_objects, object_count, int : integer;
  object_head, current_object : ObjectPtr;
  ch : char;
  object_name : String;
  z_params : ZParamRec;

begin { Main }
  Initialize (map_offsets, view_ref_point, view_transformation,
    scene_changed, no_of_objects, object_head);
  repeat
    writeln;
    writeln ('O – Load an object');
    writeln ('T – Transform an object');
```

```pascal
writeln ('W  -  Wireframe scene');
writeln ('M  -  Move view point');
writeln ('E  -  Exit program');
repeat
  writeln;
  write ('Your choice? ');
  readln (ch)
until (ch IN ['E', 'M', 'O', 'T', 'W', 'e', 'm', 'o', 't', 'w']);
if NOT (ch IN ['E', 'e']) then
case ch of
  'O', 'o' : begin
               writeln;
               write ('Object name? ');
               ReadString (object_name);
               no_of_objects := no_of_objects + 1;
               LoadObject (object_name, no_of_objects, object_head);
               scene_changed := true
             end;

  'T', 't' : begin
               current_object := object_head;
               if no_of_objects > 0 then
               begin
                 writeln;
                 writeln ('Select object to transform');
                 for object_count := 1 to no_of_objects do
                 begin
                   with current_object^ do
                   begin
                     writeln;
                     WriteString (name);
                     writeln (' - ', id_no)
                   end;
                   current_object := current_object^.next
                 end;
                 repeat
                   writeln;
                   write ('Your choice? ');
                   readln (int)
                 until (int IN [1..object_count]);
                 current_object := object_head;
                 while current_object^.id_no <> int do
                   current_object := current_object^.next;
                 with current_object^ do GetTransformation
                   (name, transformation);
                 scene_changed := true
               end
               else
```

```
                    begin
                        writeln;
                        writeln ('No objects currently loaded')
                    end
                 end;

        'M', 'm' : begin
                        GetViewRefPoint (view_ref_point, view_transformation);
                        scene_changed := true
                    end;

        'W', 'w' : begin
                        writeln;
                        if scene_changed then TransformScene (map_offsets,
                            view_transformation, view_ref_point, object_head,
                                z_params, scene_changed);
                        WireFrameScene (map_offsets, view_transformation,
                                view_ref_point, object_head)
                    end;

        'E', 'e' : writeln

      end
   until (ch IN ['E', 'e']);
   writeln;
   writeln ('Quitting . . .')
 end { Main };

begin { Program Body }
 Main
end.
```

Appendix C

An Implementation of a Renderer

The pseudocode described in Chapter 5 is expanded into a set of Pascal procedures to be added to the simple wireframe program presented in Appendix B. The complete system Gouraud shades objects using a Z-buffer by-polygon based renderer. (Incidentally, if you are short of array space for the Z-buffer, a possibility is to use half of the screen memory as a Z-buffer).

The description of the system begins with the extra types and variables specific to the shading process. There is the edge list, which holds for each scan line a list of edge–scanline intersections. Then there is an array to hold the Z-buffer information – one integer per pixel. Note that, for simplicity, the screen resolution is assumed to be 1024×1024, indexed from 0 to 1023. Finally, there is a vector which specifies the direction of the light source.

This listing contains six procedures, and it is best to start with the last one, *RenderScene*, since this is the top-level procedure that is called to perform rendering upon an entire object. *RenderScene* in turn calls *RenderObject* which calls *RenderPolygon*. Within this top-level procedure the light vector is initialized to an arbitrary value; in a real system this would be done outside the rendering process, and specified in some interactive way by the user. Then all elements in the Z-buffer are set to the maximum value, signifying that no pixel has yet been set.

This procedure renders an entire polygon. It does this in two stages. First, it sets up *EdgeList* for the polygon, by clearing it, then it goes through the polygon's list of vertices, using successive pairs of vertices to define edges which are then passed as parameters to *AddEdgeToList* (more of which in a bit). After the edge list has been created, it is examined in scan line order, and if the entry for a particular scan line is not empty, the values are read for that line and passed to *RenderSpan*. Note that this assumes the simplified case of convex polygons, where there are exactly two (or zero!) intersections per scan line. For concave polygons, there would be an even number of intersections for each scan line. These would need to be sorted into order of increasing x, and then each pair in turn would be passed to *RenderSpan*.

AddEdgeToList has as its parameters two vertices which jointly define an edge. The first operation to be performed is to swap the ends, if necessary, then to make the second point higher than the first. Rounded versions of the two y coordinates are evaluated, and are then used to reject horizontal edges. After this, the intensity value for each vertex is calculated ($N \cdot L$), and increments for x, z and i calculated. Note that this is slightly inefficient, as the intensity for a particular vertex may be calculated several times during subsequent calls to *AddEdgeToList*. This may be avoided by initially processing all vertices and storing the calculated value of i along with other vertex information. The last operation to be performed is, for each scan line that the edge crosses, to calculate appropriate values of x, z and i, generate an edge box, and insert it in the appropriate slot in *EdgeList*. Note that in accordance with the rasterization rules discussed earlier, the **for** loop proceeds until $Iy2 - 1$ rather than $Iy2$.

The last major procedure is *RenderSpan*. This has passed as parameters two edge boxes which together define a horizontal span. Then incremental calculations are performed in much the same manner as for *AddEdgeTolist*, generating z and i values for each pixel in the span. The z value for each pixel is compared with the current z value and, if less, the pixel is written to the screen using *RenderPixel*, and the new z value assigned.

RenderPixel takes the intensity value i for a particular pixel and generates red–green–blue RGB values. In this procedure, there are predefined constants specifying the colour of the object (RGB components in the range $0..1$) and the ambient lighting level ($0..1$ also). As in the case of the light vector, these values would, in reality, be defined elsewhere in the program, and might vary from object to object, or even between polygons. The first task of the procedure is to limit the intensity value to zero if the light is behind the object ($N \cdot L < 0$), and then the ambient (all-round) lighting component is added. This modified value of i is then used to weight the RGB components of the surface colour. If any of these goes above 1.0, then it is limited to this value, indicating saturation of that colour component. These final values of RGB are passed to a machine-specific procedure *DEV_WRITE_PIXEL* which sends them to the output device.

Program C.1   An implementation of a renderer.

{ *Additional code required for Gouraud shading plus simple texture mapping.* }

{ *Note* :
 The following procedure is device specific. You should substitute it
 with the relevant syntax for your own graphics device.}

{ ******************************** }

procedure *DEV_WRITE_PIXEL* (x : *DEV_X_RES*; y :
 DEV_Y_RES; c : *DEV_COLOUR*);
 { *Shade pixel at position* (x, y), *using colour c* }

{ ******************************** }

```pascal
type
  EdgeBoxPtr = ^EdgeBox;
  EdgeBox = record
              x, z, i : real;
              w : Vector;
              next : EdgeBoxPtr;
            end;
  EdgeBuffer = array [DEV_Y_RES] of EdgeBoxPtr;

  ZBuffer = array [DEV_X_RES, DEV_Y_RES] of DEV_Z_RES;

procedure RenderScene (current_object : ObjectPtr);
var
  edge_list_at : EdgeBuffer;
  z_buffer_at : ZBuffer;
  light_vector : Vector;

  procedure RenderPixel (x, y : integer; i : real; w : Vector);
  const
    Ka = 0.2;
    Kd = 0.5;
    Kr = 0.8;
    Kg = 0.4;
    Kb = 0.6;

  var
    c : DEV_COLOUR;

    function WoodGrain (w : Vector) : real;
    var
      rad, ang : real;
      grain : integer;

      function ArcTangent (x, z : real) : real;
      var
        atan : real;

      begin { ArcTangent }
        if z = 0 then
        begin
          if x > 0 then
            atan := PI / 2
          else
            atan := 3 * PI / 2
        end
        else
        begin
          if z < 0 then
            atan := arctan (x / z) + PI
          else
            if x < 0 then
              atan := arctan (x / z) + 2 * PI
```

```
            else
               atan := arctan (x / z);
         end;
      ArcTangent := atan
   end { ArcTangent };

   begin { WoodGrain }
      with w do
      begin
         rad := sqrt (sqr (x) + sqr (z));
         if z = 0 then
            ang := PI / 2
         else
            ang := ArcTangent (x, z);
         rad := rad + 2 * sin (20 * ang + y / 150);
         grain := round (rad) MOD 60;
         if grain < 30 then
            WoodGrain := 1.4
         else
            WoodGrain := 0.25
      end
   end { WoodGrain };

begin { RenderPixel }
   if i < 0 then
      i := Ka
   else
      i := Ka + (Kd * WoodGrain (w));
   if i > 1 then
      i := 1;
   with c do
   begin
      r := trunc (i * Kr * DEV_MAX_Z_RES);
      g := trunc (i * Kg * DEV_MAX_Z_RES);
      b := trunc (i * Kb * DEV_MAX_Z_RES)
   end;
   DEV_WRITE_PIXEL (x, y, c)
end { RenderPixel };

procedure RenderSpan (y : integer; var edge_box1, edge_box2 : EdgeBoxPtr);
var
   temp_edge_box : EdgeBoxPtr;
   x1, x2, dx, x, z : integer;
   curr_z, curr_i, dz, di: real;
   curr_w, dw : Vector;

begin { RenderSpan }
   if edge_box1^.x > edge_box2^.x then
   begin
      temp_edge_box := edge_box1;
      edge_box1 := edge_box2;
```

```
      edge_box2 := temp_edge_box
   end;
x1 := round (edge_box1^.x);
x2 := round (edge_box2^.x);
if x1 <> x2 then
begin
   dx := x2 − x1;
   with edge_box1^ do
   begin
     curr_z := z;
     curr_i := i;
     curr_w := w
   end;
   with edge_box2^ do
   begin
     dz := (z − curr_z) / dx;
     di := (i − curr_i) / dx;
     with dw do
     begin
       x := (w.x − curr_w.x) / dx;
       y := (w.y − curr_w.y) / dx;
       z := (w.z − curr_w.z) / dx
     end
   end;
   for x := x1 to x2−1 do
   begin
     z := round (curr_z);
     if z < z_buffer_at[x,y] then
     begin
       z_buffer_at[x,y] := z;
       RenderPixel (x, y, curr_i, curr_w)
     end;
     curr_z := curr_z + dz;
     curr_i := curr_i + di;
     with curr_w do
     begin
       x := x + dw.x;
       y := y + dw.y;
       z := z + dw.z
     end
   end
  end
end { RenderSpan };

procedure AddEdgeToList (vertex1, vertex2 : VertexPtr);
var
   temp_vertex : VertexPtr;
   curr_x, curr_z, curr_i, dx, dz, di: real;
   curr_w, dw : Vector;
```

```
          y1, y2, dy, y : integer;
          edge_box : EdgeBoxPtr;

begin { AddEdgeToList }
  if vertex1^.screen_pos.y > vertex2^.screen_pos.y then
  begin
    temp_vertex := vertex1;
    vertex1 := vertex2;
    vertex2 := temp_vertex
  end;
  y1 := vertex1^.screen_pos.y;
  y2 := vertex2^.screen_pos.y;
  if y1 <> y2 then
  begin
    dy := y2 - y1;
    with vertex1^ do
    begin
      curr_x := screen_pos.x;
      curr_z := screen_pos.z;
      curr_i := DotProduct (vertex_normal, light_vector);
      curr_w := world_pos
    end;
    with vertex2^ do
    begin
      dx := (screen_pos.x - curr_x) / dy;
      dz := (screen_pos.z - curr_z) / dy;
      di := (DotProduct (vertex_normal, light_vector) - curr_i) / dy;
      with dw do
      begin
        x := (world_pos.x - curr_w.x) / dy;
        y := (world_pos.y - curr_w.y) / dy;
        z := (world_pos.z - curr_w.z) / dy
      end
    end;
    for y := y1 to y2-1 do
    begin
      new (edge_box);
      with edge_box^ do
      begin
        x := curr_x;
        z := trunc (curr_z);
        i := curr_i;
        w := curr_w;
        next := edge_list_at[y]
      end;
      edge_list_at[y] := edge_box;
      curr_x := curr_x + dx;
      curr_z := curr_z + dz;
      curr_i := curr_i + di;
```

```
          with curr_w do
          begin
             x := x + dw.x;
             y := y + dw.y;
             z := z + dw.z
          end
       end
   end
end { AddEdgeToList };

procedure RenderPolygon (current_polygon : PolygonPtr);
var
   y : DEV_Y_RES;
   vertex0, vertex1, vertex2 : VertexListPtr;

begin { RenderPolygon }
   for y := 0 to DEV_MAX_Y_RES do
      edge_list_at[y] := nil;
   vertex1 := current_polygon^.vertex_list_head;
   vertex0 := vertex1;
   vertex2 := vertex1^.rest;
   repeat
      AddEdgeToList (vertex1^.vertex, vertex2^.vertex);
      vertex1 := vertex2;
      vertex2 := vertex2^.rest
   until vertex2 – nil;
   AddEdgeToList (vertex1^.vertex, vertex0^.vertex);
   for y := 0 to DEV_MAX_Y_RES do
      if edge_list_at[y] <> nil then
         RenderSpan (y, edge_list_at[y], edge_list_at[y]^.next)
end { RenderPolygon };

procedure RenderObject (current_object : ObjectPtr);
var
   current_surface : SurfacePtr;
   current_polygon : PolygonPtr;

begin { RenderObject }
   current_surface := current_object^.surface_head;
   while current_surface <> nil do
   begin
      current_polygon := current_surface^.polygon_head;
      while current_polygon <> nil do
      begin
         if current_polygon^.poly_visible then
            RenderPolygon (current_polygon);
         current_polygon := current_polygon^.next
      end;
      current_surface := current_surface^.next
   end
end { RenderObject };
```

```
          procedure InitializeZBuffer;
          var
            x : DEV_X_RES;
            y : DEV_Y_RES;

          begin { InitializeZBuffer }
            for x := 0 to DEV_MAX_X_RES do
              for y := 0 to DEV_MAX_Y_RES do
                z_buffer_at[x,y] := DEV_MAX_Z_RES
          end { InitializeZBuffer };

        begin { RenderScene }
          InitializeZBuffer;
          with light_vector do
          begin
            x := 2; y:= -3; z:= 2
          end;
          Normalize (light_vector, light_vector);
          while current_object <> nil do
          begin
            RenderObject (current_object);
            current_object := current_object^.next
          end
        end { RenderScene };

      begin { Main }
        .
        .
        .
        RenderScene (object_head)
        .
        .
        .
      end { Main };
```

Appendix D

The Utah Teapot

The University of Utah was the centre of research into rendering algorithms in the early 1970s. Various polygon mesh models were set up manually, including a VW Beetle, digitized by Ivan Sutherland's computer graphics class in 1971. This is reproduced in Newman and Sproull (1981) together with another familiar model – the human-like mask.

In 1975 M. Newell developed the Utah teapot, a familiar object that has become a kind of benchmark in computer graphics, and one that has been used frequently in this text. He did this by sketching the profile of the teapot to estimate suitable control points for bicubic Bézier patches. The lid, rim and body of the teapot were then treated as solids of revolution and the spout and handle were modelled as ducted solids. This resulted, eventually, in 32 patches, the data for which is reproduced in Tables D.1 and D.2.

The original teapot is now in the Boston Computer Museum, displayed alongside its computer alter ego. A full description of the model and details on the Computer Museum are given in Crow (1987).

The data consists of 306 world coordinate vertices given in Table D.1. Table D.2 contains 32 patch definitions for bicubic Bézier patches. Each row in the table is a list of 16 vertex numbers that define the control point polyhedron for each patch. The patches are placed into five groups: the body, the handle, the spout, the lid and the bottom.

Table D.1 Vertex table.

Vertex number	x	y	z	Vertex number	x	y	z	Vertex number	x	y	z
1	1.40000	0.00000	2.40000	55	1.12000	−2.00000	1.35000	109	−1.50000	0.84000	0.22500
2	1.40000	−0.78400	2.40000	56	0.00000	−2.00000	1.35000	110	−0.84000	1.15000	0.22500
3	0.78400	−1.40000	2.40000	57	2.00000	0.00000	0.90000	111	0.00000	1.50000	0.22500
4	0.00000	−1.40000	2.40000	58	2.00000	−1.12000	0.90000	112	−1.50000	0.84000	0.15000
5	1.33750	0.00000	2.53125	59	1.12000	−2.00000	0.90000	113	−0.84000	1.50000	0.15000
6	1.33750	−0.74900	2.53125	60	0.00000	−2.00000	0.90000	114	0.00000	1.50000	0.15000
7	0.74900	−1.33750	2.53125	61	−0.98000	−1.75000	1.87500	115	1.12000	2.00000	0.45000
8	0.00000	−1.33750	2.53125	62	−1.75000	−0.98000	1.87500	116	2.00000	1.12000	0.45000
9	1.43750	0.00000	2.53125	63	−1.75000	0.00000	1.87500	117	0.84000	1.50000	0.22500
10	1.43750	−0.80500	2.53125	64	−1.12000	−2.00000	1.35000	118	1.50000	0.84000	0.22500
11	0.80500	−1.43750	2.53125	65	−2.00000	−1.12000	1.35000	119	0.84000	1.50000	0.15000
12	0.00000	−1.43750	2.53125	66	−2.00000	0.00000	1.35000	120	1.50000	0.84000	0.15000
13	1.50000	0.00000	2.40000	67	−1.12000	−2.00000	0.90000	121	−1.60000	0.00000	2.02500
14	1.50000	−0.84000	2.40000	68	−2.00000	−1.12000	0.90000	122	−1.60000	−0.30000	2.02500
15	0.84000	−1.50000	2.40000	69	−2.00000	0.00000	0.90000	123	−1.50000	−0.30000	2.25000
16	0.00000	−1.50000	2.40000	70	−1.75000	0.98000	1.87500	124	−1.50000	0.00000	2.25000
17	−0.78400	−1.40000	2.40000	71	−0.98000	1.75000	1.87500	125	−2.30000	0.00000	2.02500
18	−1.40000	−0.78400	2.40000	72	0.00000	1.75000	1.87500	126	−2.30000	−0.30000	2.02500
19	−1.40000	0.00000	2.40000	73	−2.00000	1.12000	1.35000	127	−2.50000	−0.30000	2.25000
20	−0.74900	−1.33750	2.53125	74	−1.12000	2.00000	1.35000	128	−2.50000	0.00000	2.25000
21	−1.33750	−0.74900	2.53125	75	0.00000	2.00000	1.35000	129	−2.70000	0.00000	2.02500
22	−1.33750	0.00000	2.53125	76	−2.00000	1.12000	0.90000	130	−2.70000	−0.30000	2.02500
23	−0.80500	−1.43750	2.53125	77	−1.12000	2.00000	0.90000	131	−3.00000	−0.30000	2.25000
24	−1.43750	−0.80500	2.53125	78	0.00000	−2.00000	0.90000	132	−3.00000	0.00000	2.25000
25	−1.43750	0.00000	2.53125	79	0.98000	1.75000	1.87500	133	−2.70000	0.00000	1.80000
26	−0.84000	−1.50000	2.40000	80	1.75000	0.98000	1.87500	134	−2.70000	−0.30000	1.80000
27	−1.50000	−0.84000	2.40000	81	1.12000	2.00000	1.35000	135	−3.00000	−0.30000	1.80000
28	−1.50000	0.00000	2.40000	82	2.00000	1.12000	1.35000	136	−3.00000	0.00000	1.80000
29	−1.40000	0.78400	2.40000	83	1.12000	2.00000	0.90000	137	−1.50000	0.30000	2.25000
30	−0.78400	1.40000	2.40000	84	2.00000	1.12000	0.90000	138	−1.60000	0.30000	2.02500
31	0.00000	1.40000	2.40000	85	2.00000	0.00000	0.45000	139	−2.50000	0.30000	2.25000
32	−1.33750	0.74900	2.53125	86	2.00000	−1.12000	0.45000	140	−2.30000	0.30000	2.02500
33	−0.74900	1.33750	2.53125	87	1.12000	−2.00000	0.45000	141	−3.00000	0.30000	2.25000
34	0.00000	1.33750	2.53125	88	0.00000	−2.00000	0.45000	142	−2.70000	0.30000	2.02500
35	−1.43750	0.80500	2.53125	89	1.50000	0.00000	0.22500	143	−3.00000	0.30000	1.80000
36	−0.80500	1.43750	2.53125	90	1.50000	−0.84000	0.22500	144	−2.70000	0.30000	1.80000
37	0.00000	1.43750	2.53125	91	0.84000	−1.50000	0.22500	145	−2.70000	0.00000	1.57500
38	−1.50000	0.84000	2.40000	92	0.00000	−1.50000	0.22500	146	−2.70000	−0.30000	1.57500
39	−0.84000	1.50000	2.40000	93	1.50000	0.00000	0.15000	147	−3.00000	−0.30000	1.35000
40	0.00000	1.50000	2.40000	94	1.50000	−0.84000	0.15000	148	−3.00000	0.00000	1.35000
41	0.78400	1.40000	2.40000	95	0.84000	−1.50000	0.15000	149	−2.50000	0.00000	1.12500
42	1.40000	0.78400	2.40000	96	0.00000	−1.50000	0.15000	150	−2.50000	−0.30000	1.12500
43	0.74900	1.33750	2.53125	97	−1.12000	−2.00000	0.45000	151	−2.65000	−0.30000	0.93750
44	1.33750	0.74900	2.53125	98	−2.00000	−1.12000	0.45000	152	−2.65000	0.00000	0.93750
45	0.80500	1.43750	2.53125	99	−2.00000	0.00000	0.45000	153	−2.00000	−0.30000	0.90000
46	1.43750	0.80500	2.53125	100	−0.84000	−1.50000	0.22500	154	−1.90000	−0.30000	0.60000
47	0.84000	1.50000	2.40000	101	−1.50000	−0.84000	0.22500	155	−1.90000	0.00000	0.60000
48	1.50000	0.84000	2.40000	102	−1.50000	0.00000	0.22500	156	−3.00000	0.30000	1.35000
49	1.75000	0.00000	1.87500	103	−0.84000	−1.50000	0.15000	157	−2.70000	0.30000	1.57500
50	1.75000	−0.98000	1.87500	104	−1.50000	−0.84000	0.15000	158	−2.65000	0.30000	0.93750
51	0.98000	−1.75000	1.87500	105	−1.50000	0.00000	0.15000	159	−2.50000	0.30000	1.12500
52	0.00000	−1.75000	1.87500	106	−2.00000	1.12000	0.45000	160	−1.90000	0.30000	0.60000
53	2.00000	0.00000	1.35000	107	−1.12000	2.00000	0.45000	161	−2.00000	0.30000	0.90000
54	2.00000	−1.12000	1.35000	108	0.00000	2.00000	0.45000	162	1.70000	0.00000	1.42500

Table D.1 (*continued*).

Vertex number	x	y	z	Vertex number	x	y	z	Vertex number	x	y	z
163	1.70000	−0.66000	1.42500	211	0.00000	0.00000	2.85000	259	−0.72800	1.30000	2.55000
164	1.70000	−0.66000	0.60000	212	0.20000	0.00000	2.70000	260	0.00000	1.30000	2.55000
165	1.70000	0.00000	0.60000	213	0.20000	−0.11200	2.70000	261	−1.30000	0.72800	2.40000
166	2.60000	0.00000	1.42500	214	0.11200	−0.20000	2.70000	262	−0.72800	1.30000	2.40000
167	2.60000	−0.66000	1.42500	215	0.00000	−0.20000	2.70000	263	0.00000	1.30000	2.40000
168	3.10000	−0.66000	0.82500	216	−0.00200	0.00000	3.15000	264	0.22400	0.40000	2.55000
169	3.10000	0.00000	0.82500	217	−0.45000	−0.80000	3.15000	265	0.40000	0.22400	2.55000
170	2.30000	0.00000	2.10000	218	−0.80000	−0.45000	3.15000	266	0.72800	1.30000	2.55000
171	2.30000	−0.25000	2.10000	219	−0.80000	0.00000	3.15000	267	1.30000	0.72800	2.55000
172	2.40000	−0.25000	2.02500	220	−0.11200	−0.20000	2.70000	268	0.72800	1.30000	2.40000
173	2.40000	0.00000	2.02500	221	−0.20000	−0.11200	2.70000	269	1.30000	0.72800	2.40000
174	2.70000	0.00000	2.40000	222	−0.20000	0.00000	2.70000	270	0.00000	0.00000	0.00000
175	2.70000	−0.25000	2.40000	223	0.00000	0.00200	3.15000	271	1.50000	0.00000	0.15000
176	3.30000	−0.25000	2.40000	224	−0.80000	0.45000	3.15000	272	1.50000	0.84000	0.15000
177	3.30000	0.00000	2.40000	225	−0.45000	0.80000	3.15000	273	0.84000	1.50000	0.15000
178	1.70000	0.66000	0.60000	226	0.00000	0.80000	3.15000	274	0.00000	1.50000	0.15000
179	1.70000	0.66000	1.42500	227	−0.20000	0.11200	2.70000	275	1.50000	0.00000	0.07500
180	3.10000	0.66000	0.82500	228	−0.11200	0.20000	2.70000	276	1.50000	0.84000	0.07500
181	2.60000	0.66000	1.42500	229	0.00000	0.20000	2.70000	277	0.84000	1.50000	0.07500
182	2.40000	0.25000	2.02500	230	0.45000	0.80000	3.15000	278	0.00000	1.50000	0.07500
183	2.30000	0.25000	2.10000	231	0.80000	0.45000	3.15000	279	1.42500	0.00000	0.00000
184	3.30000	0.25000	2.40000	232	0.11200	0.20000	2.70000	280	1.42500	0.79800	0.00000
185	2.70000	0.25000	2.40000	233	0.20000	0.11200	2.70000	281	0.79800	1.42500	0.00000
186	2.80000	0.00000	2.47500	234	0.40000	0.00000	2.55000	282	0.00000	1.42500	0.00000
187	2.80000	−0.25000	2.47500	235	0.40000	−0.22400	2.55000	283	−0.84000	1.50000	0.15000
188	3.52500	−0.25000	2.49375	236	0.22400	−0.40000	2.55000	284	−1.50000	0.84000	0.15000
189	3.52500	0.00000	2.49375	237	0.00000	−0.40000	2.55000	285	−1.50000	0.00000	0.15000
190	2.90000	0.00000	2.47500	238	1.30000	0.00000	2.55000	286	−0.84000	1.50000	0.07500
191	2.90000	−0.15000	2.47500	239	1.30000	−0.72800	2.55000	287	−1.50000	0.84000	0.07500
192	3.45000	−0.15000	2.51250	240	0.72800	−1.30000	2.55000	288	−1.50000	0.00000	0.07500
193	3.45000	0.00000	2.51250	241	0.00000	−1.30000	2.55000	289	−0.79800	1.42500	0.00000
194	2.80000	0.00000	2.40000	242	1.30000	0.00000	2.40000	290	−1.42500	0.79800	0.00000
195	2.80000	−0.15000	2.40000	243	1.30000	−0.72800	2.40000	291	−1.42500	0.00000	0.00000
196	3.20000	−0.15000	2.40000	244	0.72800	−1.30000	2.40000	292	−1.50000	−0.84000	0.15000
197	3.20000	0.00000	2.40000	245	0.00000	−1.30000	2.40000	293	−0.84000	−1.50000	0.15000
198	3.52500	0.25000	2.49375	246	−0.22400	−0.40000	2.55000	294	0.00000	−1.50000	0.15000
199	2.80000	0.25000	2.47500	247	−0.40000	−0.22400	2.55000	295	−1.50000	−0.84000	0.07500
200	3.45000	0.15000	2.51250	248	−0.40000	0.00000	2.55000	296	−0.84000	−1.50000	0.07500
201	2.90000	0.15000	2.47500	249	−0.72800	−1.30000	2.55000	297	0.00000	−1.50000	0.07500
202	3.20000	0.15000	2.40000	250	−1.30000	−0.72800	2.55000	298	−1.42500	−0.79800	0.00000
203	2.80000	0.15000	2.40000	251	−1.30000	0.00000	2.55000	299	−0.79800	−1.42500	0.00000
204	0.00000	0.00000	3.15000	252	−0.72800	−1.30000	2.40000	300	0.00000	−1.42500	0.00000
205	0.00000	−0.00200	3.15000	253	−1.30000	−0.72800	2.40000	301	0.84000	−1.50000	0.15000
206	0.00200	0.00000	3.15000	254	−1.30000	0.00000	2.40000	302	1.50000	−0.84000	0.15000
207	0.80000	0.00000	3.15000	255	−0.40000	0.22400	2.55000	303	0.84000	−1.50000	0.07500
208	0.80000	−0.45000	3.15000	256	−0.22400	0.40000	2.55000	304	1.50000	−0.84000	0.07500
209	0.45000	−0.80000	3.15000	257	0.00000	0.40000	2.55000	305	0.79800	−1.42500	0.00000
210	0.00000	−0.80000	3.15000	258	−1.30000	0.72800	2.55000	306	1.42500	−0.79800	0.00000

Table D.2 Bicubic Bézier patch definitions.

Patch number	Control point polyhedron vertex numbers															
	1	2	3	4	5	6	7	8	9	10	11	12	13	14	15	16
Body																
1	1	2	3	4	5	6	7	8	9	10	11	12	13	14	15	16
2	4	17	18	19	8	20	21	22	12	23	24	25	16	26	27	28
3	19	29	30	31	22	32	33	34	25	35	36	37	28	38	39	40
4	31	41	42	1	34	43	44	5	37	45	46	9	40	47	48	13
5	13	14	15	16	49	50	51	52	53	54	55	56	57	58	59	60
6	16	26	27	28	52	61	62	63	56	64	65	66	60	67	68	69
7	28	38	39	40	63	70	71	72	66	73	74	75	69	76	77	78
8	40	47	48	13	72	79	80	49	75	81	82	53	78	83	84	57
9	57	58	59	60	85	86	87	88	89	90	91	92	93	94	95	96
10	60	67	68	69	88	97	98	99	92	100	101	102	96	103	104	105
11	69	76	77	78	99	106	107	108	102	109	110	111	105	112	113	114
12	78	83	84	57	108	115	116	85	111	117	118	89	114	119	120	93
Handle																
13	121	122	123	124	125	126	127	128	129	130	131	132	133	134	135	136
14	124	137	138	121	128	139	140	125	132	141	142	129	136	143	144	133
15	133	134	135	136	145	146	147	148	149	150	151	152	69	153	154	155
16	136	143	144	133	148	156	157	145	152	158	159	149	155	160	161	69
Spout																
17	162	163	164	165	166	167	168	169	170	171	172	173	174	175	176	177
18	165	178	179	162	169	180	181	166	173	182	183	170	177	184	185	174
19	174	175	176	177	186	187	188	189	190	191	192	193	194	195	196	197
20	177	184	185	174	189	198	199	186	193	200	201	190	197	202	203	194
Lid																
21	204	204	204	204	207	208	209	210	211	211	211	211	212	213	214	215
22	204	204	204	204	210	217	218	219	211	211	211	211	215	220	221	222
23	204	204	204	204	219	224	225	226	211	211	211	211	222	227	228	229
24	204	204	204	204	226	230	231	207	211	211	211	211	229	232	233	212
25	212	213	214	215	234	235	236	237	238	239	240	241	242	243	244	245
26	215	220	221	222	237	246	247	248	241	249	250	251	245	252	253	254
27	222	227	228	229	248	255	256	257	251	258	259	260	254	261	262	263
28	229	232	233	212	257	264	265	234	260	266	267	238	263	268	269	242
Bottom																
29	270	270	270	270	279	280	281	282	275	276	277	278	93	120	119	114
30	270	270	270	270	282	289	290	291	278	286	287	288	114	113	112	105
31	270	270	270	270	291	298	299	300	288	295	296	297	105	104	103	96
32	270	270	270	270	300	305	306	279	297	303	304	275	96	95	94	93

References

Abram A. G., Westover L. and Whitted T. (1985). Efficient alias-free rendering using bit-masks and lookup tables. *Computer Graphics*, **19** (3), 53–9

Appel A. (1968). Some techniques for machine rendering of solids. *AFIPS Conference Proc.* **32**, 37–45

Atherton P., Weiler K. and Greenberg D. (1978). Polygon shadow generation. *Computer Graphics*, **12** (3), 275–81

Atkin T. (1986). New chip displays its powers. *New Scientist* (March 20, 1986), 43–6

Badouel D. (1990). An efficient ray–polygon intersection. In *Graphics Gems*, Glassner A. S. (ed) pp. 390–6. New York: Academic Press

Baecker R. M. (1969). Picture driven animation. *Proc. of Spring Joint Computer Conference*, pp. 273–88. Montvale NJ: AFIPS Press

Balakrishnan A. V. (1962). On the problem of time jitter in sampling. *IRE Trans. on Information Theory* (April 1962), pp. 226–36

Barr A. H. (1984). Global and local deformations of solid primitives. *Computer Graphics*, **18** (3), 21–30

Barr A. H. (1986). Ray tracing deformed surfaces. *Computer Graphics*, **20** (4), 287–96

Barsky B. A. and Beatty J. C. (1983). Local control of bias and tension in beta-splines. *ACM Trans. on Graphics*, **2** (2), 109–34

Bartels R. H., Beatty J. C. and Barsky B. A. (1988). *Splines for Use in Computer Graphics and Geometric Modeling*. Los Altos CA: Morgan Kaufmann

Bass D. H. (1981). Using the video lookup table for reflectivity calculations. *Computer Graphics and Image Processing*, **17**, 249–61

Beckmann P. and Spizzichino A. (1963). *Scattering of Electromagnetic Waves from Rough Surfaces*. Basingstoke: Macmillan

Bergeron P. (1986). Une version générale de l'algorithme de ombres projetées de Crow basée sur le concept de volumes d'ombre. *M.Sc. Thesis*. University of Montreal

Bergman L., Fuchs H., Grant E. and Spach S. (1986). Image rendering by adaptive refinement. *Computer Graphics*, **20** (4), 29–38

Bézier P. (1972). *Numerical Control: Mathematics and Applications*. Chichester: Wiley

Bier E. A. and Sloan K. R. (1986). Two-part texture mapping. *IEEE Computer Graphics and Applications*. **6** (9), 40–53

Bishop G. and Weimar D. M. (1986). Fast Phong shading. *Computer Graphics*, **20** (4), 103–6

Blinn J. F. (1977). Models of light reflection for computer synthesized pictures. *Computer Graphics*, **11** (2), 192–8

Blinn J. F. (1978a). Computer display of curved surfaces. *Ph.D. Thesis*. University of Utah

Blinn J. F. (1978b). Simulation of wrinkled surfaces. *Computer Graphics*, **12** (3), 286–92

Blinn J. F. (1987). The mechanical universe: an integrated view of a large scale animation project. *SIGGRAPH 87 Course Notes*, **6**

Blinn J. F. (1988). Me and my (fake) shadow. *IEEE Computer Graphics and Applications*, **8** (1), 82–6

Blinn J. F. and Newell M. E. (1976). Texture and reflection in computer generated images. *Comm. ACM*, **19** (10) 362–7

Bloomenthal J. (1985). Modeling the mighty maple. *Computer Graphics*, **19** (3), 305–11

Bouknight W. J. (1970). A procedure for the generation of three-dimensional half-toned computer graphics presentations. *Comm. ACM*, **13** (9), 527–36

Bouknight W. J. and Kelly K. (1970). An algorithm for producing half-tone computer graphics presentations with shadows and moveable light sources. *Proc. AFIPS, Spring Joint Computer Conf.*, **36**, 1–10

Bresenham J. E. (1965). Algorithm for computer control of a digital plotter. *IBM Systems J.* (January 1965), 25–30

Brotman L. S. and Badler N. I. (1984). Generating soft shadows with a depth buffer algorithm. *IEEE Computer Graphics and Applications*, **4** (10), 5–12

Carpenter L. C. (1984). The A-buffer, an anti-aliased hidden surface method. *Computer Graphics*, **18** (3), 103–8

Catmull E. (1974). Subdivision algorithm for the display of curved surfaces. *Ph.D. Thesis*. University of Utah

Catmull E. (1975). Computer display of curved surfaces. In *Proc. IEEE Conf. on Computer Graphics, Pattern Recognition and Data Structures,* May 1975 (Reprinted in Freeman H. ed. (1980). *Tutorial and Selected Readings in Interactive Computer Graphics*, New York (IEEE) pp. 309–15)

Catmull E. (1978). A hidden surface algorithm with anti-aliasing. *Computer Graphics*, **12** (3), 6–10

Clark J. H. (1976). Hierarchical geometric models for visible surface algorithms. *Comm. ACM*, **19** (10), 547–54

Clark J. H. (1979). A fast scan line algorithm for rendering parametric surfaces. *Computer Graphics*, **13** (2), 289–99

Chiyokura H. (1988). *Solid Modelling with DESIGNBASE*. Wokingham, England: Addison-Wesley

Cohen M. F. and Greenberg D. P. (1985). A radiosity solution for complex environments. *Computer Graphics*, **19** (3), 31–40

Cohen M. F., Greenberg D. P. and Immel D. S. (1986). An efficient radiosity approach for realistic image synthesis. *IEEE Computer Graphics and Applications*, **6** (2), 26–35

Cohen M. F., Chen S. E., Wallace J. R. and Greenberg D. P. (1988). A progressive refinement approach to fast radiosity image generation. *Computer Graphics*, **22** (4), 75–84

Cook R. L. (1986). Stochastic sampling in computer graphics. *ACM Trans. on Computer Graphics*, **5** (1), 51–72

Cook R. L. and Torrance K. E. (1982). A reflectance model for computer graphics. *Computer Graphics*, **15** (3), 307–16

Cook R. L., Porter T. and Carpenter L. (1984). Distributed ray tracing. *Computer Graphics*, **18** (3), 137–45

Cook R. L., Carpenter L. and Catmull E. (1987). The REYES image rendering architecture. *Computer Graphics*, **21** (4), 95–102

Cowan W. B. (1983). An inexpensive scheme for the calibration of a colour monitor in terms of CIE standard coordinates. *Computer Graphics*, **17**, 315–21

Cox M. G. (1972). The numerical evalutation of B-splines. *J. Inst. Maths. Applics.*, **10**, 134–49.

Crow F. C. (1977). Shadow algorithms for computer graphics. *Computer Graphics*, **13** (2), 242–8

Crow F. C. (1981). A comparison of anti-aliasing techniques. *IEEE Computer Graphics and Applications*, **1** (1), 40–8

Crow F. C. (1984). Summed-area tables for texture mapping. *Computer Graphics*, **18** (3), 207–12

Crow F. C. (1987). The origins of the teapot. *IEEE Computer Graphics and Applications*, **7** (1), 8–19

De Boor C. (1972). On calculating with B-splines. *J. Approx. Th.,* **6**, 50–62

Dippe M. A. Z. and Wold E. H. (1985). Anti-aliasing through stochastic sampling. *Computer Graphics*, **19** (3), 69–78

Doctor L. J. and Torborg J. G. (1981). Display techniques for octree encoded objects. *IEEE Computer Graphics and Applications*, **1** (3), 29–38

Drebin R. A., Carpenter L. and Hanrahan P. (1988). Volume rendering. *Computer Graphics*, **22** (4), 65–74

Duff T. (1979). Smoothly shaded renderings of polyhedral objects on raster displays. *Computer Graphics*, **13** (2), 270–5

Duff T. (1985). Compositing 3-D rendered images. *Computer Graphics*, **19** (3), 41–4

Farin G. (1990). Curves and Surfaces for Computer Aided Design. 2nd edn. Boston: Academic Press

Faux I. D. and Pratt M. J. (1979). *Computational Geometry for Design and Manufacture*. Chichester: Ellis Horwood

Feibush E. A., Levoy M. and Cook R. L. (1980). Synthetic texturing using digital filters. *Computer Graphics*, **14** (3), 294–301

Fiume E. L. (1989). *The Mathematical Structure of Raster Graphics*. San Diego CA: Academic Press

Fiume E., Fournier A. and Rudolph L. (1983). A parallel scan conversion algorithm with anti-aliasing for a general-purpose ultracomputer. *Computer Graphics*, **17** (3), 141–50

Foley J. D. and Van Dam A. (1982). *Fundamentals of Interactive Computer Graphics*. Reading MA: Addison-Wesley

Foley J. D., Van Dam A., Feiner S. K. and Hughes J. F. (1989). *Computer Graphics – Principles and Practice*. Reading MA: Addison-Wesley

Forsey D. R. and Bartels R. H. (1988). Hierarchical B-spline refinement. *Computer Graphics*, **22** (4), 205–12

Fournier A. and Reeves W. T. (1986). A simple model of ocean waves. *Computer Graphics*, **20** (4), 75–84

Fournier A., Fussell D. and Carpenter L. (1982). Computer rendering of stochastic models. *Comm. ACM*, **25** (6), 371–84

Fuchs H. (1980). On visible surface generation by *a priori* tree structures. *Computer Graphics*, **14**, 124–33

Fujimoto A., Tanaka T. and Iwata K. (1986). ARTS: Accelerated ray tracing system. *IEEE Computer Graphics and Applications*, **6** (4), 16–26

Gangnet M., Perny D. and Coueignoux P. (1982). Perspective mapping of planar textures. In *Proc. EUROGRAPHICS '82*, pp. 57–71. Amsterdam: North-Holland

Gardener G. Y. (1984). Simulation of natural scenes using textured quadric surfaces. *Computer Graphics*, **18** (3), 11–20

Gardener G. Y. (1985). Visual simulation of clouds. *Computer Graphics*, **19** (3), 297–303

Gardener G. Y. (1988). Functional modeling of natural scenes. *SIGGRAPH 88 Course Notes*, **28**, 44–76

Glassner A. S. (1984). Space subdivision for fast ray tracing. *IEEE Computer Graphics and Applications*, **4** (10), 15–22

Glassner A. (ed.) (1990). *Graphics Gems*, pp. 539–47. Boston: Harcourt Brace Jovanovich

Goral C., Torrance K. E., Greenberg D. P. and Battaile B. (1984). Modelling the interaction of light between diffuse surfaces. *Computer Graphics*, **18** (3), 212–22

Gossling T. H. (1976). The DUCT system of design for practical objects. *Proc. World Congress on the Theory of Machines and Mechanisms*, Milan 1976

Gouraud H. (1971). Illumination for computer generated pictures. *Comm. ACM*, **18** (60), 311–17

Greenberg D. P., Cohen M. F. and Torrance K. E. (1986). Radiosity: a method for computing global illumination. *Visual Computer*, **2** (5), 291–7

Greene N. and Heckbert P. S. (1986). Creating raster omnimax images using the elliptically weighted average filter. *IEEE Computer Graphics and Applications*, **6** (6), 21–7

Griffiths J. G. (1984). A depth-coherence scan line algorithm for displaying curved surfaces. *Computer Aided Design*, **16** (2), 91–101

Hahn J. K. (1988). Realistic animation of rigid bodies. *Computer Graphics*, **22** (4), 299–308

Haines E. (1989). Essential ray tracing algorithms. In *An Introduction to Ray Tracing*, Glassner A. (ed). New York: Academic Press

Haines E. (1991). Fast ray–convex polyhedron intersection. In *Graphics Gems II*, Avro J. (ed.) pp. 247–50. Boston: Harcourt Brace Jovanovich

Haines E. A. and Greenberg D. P. (1986). The light buffer: a shadow-testing accelerator. *IEEE Computer Graphics and Applications*, **6** (9), 6–16

Hall R. A. (1989). *Illumination and Color in Computer Generated Imagery*. New York: Springer-Verlag

Hall R. A. and Greenberg D. P. (1983). A testbed for realistic image synthesis. *IEEE Computer Graphics and Applications*, **3** (8), 10–19

Hanrahan P. (1983). Ray tracing algebraic surfaces. *Computer Graphics*, **17** (3), 83–90

Hanrahan P. and Sturman D. (1985). Interactive animation of parametric models. *Visual Computer*, **1**, 260–6

Harrison K., Mitchell D. and Watt A. (1988). The H-test, a method of high speed interpolative shading. In *New Trends in Computer Graphics, Proc. CG International '88*, pp. 106–16. Berlin: Springer

He X. D., Torrance K. E., Sillion F. X. and Greenberg D. P. (1991). A comprehensive physical model for light reflection. *Computer Graphics*, **25**(4), 175–86

Heckbert P. S. (1986). Survey of texture mapping. *IEEE Computer Graphics and Applications*, **6** (11), 56–67

Heckbert P. S. and Hanrahan P. (1984). Beam tracing polygonal objects. *Computer Graphics*, **18** (3), 119–27

Immel D. S., Cohen M. F. and Greenberg D. P. (1986). A radiosity method for non-diffuse environments. *Computer Graphics*, **20** (4), 133–42

Jacklins C. L. and Tanimoto S. L. (1980). Octrees and their use in representing three-dimensional objects. *Computer Graphics and Image Processing*, **14**, 249–70

Joy I. K. and Bhetanabhotla M. N. (1986). Ray tracing parametric surfaces utilizing numeric techniques and ray coherence. *Computer Graphics*, **20** (4), 279–86

Kajiya J. T. (1982). Ray tracing parametric patches. *Computer Graphics*, **16**, 245–54

Kajiya J. T. (1983). New techniques for ray tracing procedurally defined objects. *Computer Graphics*, **17** (3), 91–102

Kajiya J. T. (1985). Anisotropic reflection models. *Computer Graphics*, **19** (3), 15–21

Kaplan M. R. (1985). Space Tracing, a constant time ray tracer. *SIGGRAPH 85 Course Notes*, San Francisco CA, July 1985

Kay D. S. (1979). Transparency, refraction and ray tracing for computer synthesised images. *Masters Thesis*. Cornell University

Kay T. L. and Kajiya J. T. (1986). Ray tracing complex scenes. *Computer Graphics*, **20** (4), 269–78

Korein J. and Badler N. (1983). Temporal anti-aliasing in computer generated animation. *Computer Graphics*, **17** (3), 377–88

Land E. H. (1977). The retinex theory of color vision. *Scientific American* (December 77), 108–28

Lane J. M. and Riesenfeld R. F. (1980). A theoretical development for the computer generation and display of piecewise polynomial surfaces. *IEEE Trans. on Pattern Analysis and Machine Intelligence*, **2** (1), 35–46

Lane J. M., Carpenter L. C., Whitted T. and Blinn J. T. (1980). Scan line methods for displaying parametrically defined surfaces. *Comm. ACM*, **23** (1), 23–34

Levoy M. (1990). Efficient ray tracing of volume data. *ACM Trans. on Graphics*, **9** (3), 245–61

Lorensen W. E. and Cline H. E. (1987). Marching cubes: a high resolution 3D surface construction algorithm. *Computer Graphics*, **21** (4), 163–9

Magnenat-Thalmann N. and Thalmann D. (1985). *Principles of Computer Animation*. Tokyo: Springer

Mandelbrot B. (1977). *Fractals: Form, Chance and Dimension*. San Francisco CA: Freeman

Mandelbrot B. (1982). *The Fractal Geometry of Nature*. San Francisco CA: Freeman

McCormick B. H., DeFanti T. A. and Brown M. D. (1987). Visualization in scientific computing. *Computer Graphics*, **21** (6)

Meagher D. (1982). Geometric modelling using octree encoding. *Computer Graphics and Image Processing*, **19**, 129–47

Miller G. S. and Hoffman C. R. (1984). Illumination and reflection maps: simulated objects in simulated and real environments. *SIGGRAPH 84 Course Notes*, July 1984

Mitchell D. P. (1987). Generating anti-aliased images at low sampling densities. *Computer Graphics*, **21** (4), 65–72

Moore M. and Wilhems J. (1988). Collision detection and response for computer animation. *Computer Graphics*, **22** (4), 289–98

Munsell A. H. (1946). *A Color Notation*. Baltimore MD: Munsell Color Co.

Nakamae E., Harada K., Ishizaki T. and Nishita T. (1986). A montage method: the overlaying of computer generated images onto a background photograph. *Computer Graphics*, **20** (4), 207–14

Newell M. E., Newell R. G. and Sancha T. L. (1972). A new approach to the shaded picture problem. In *Proc. ACM National Conf.*, pp. 443–50

Newman W. M. and Sproull R. F. (1981). *Principles of Interactive Computer Graphics*. New York: McGraw-Hill

Nishita T. and Nakamae E. (1985). Continuous tone representation of three-dimensional objects taking account of shadows and interreflection. *Computer Graphics*, **19** (3), 23–30

Novins K. L., Sillion F. and Greenberg D. P. (1990). An efficient method for volume rendering using perspective projection. *Computer Graphics*, **24** (5), 95–102

Oppenheim A. V. and Shafer R. W. (1975). *Digital Signal Processing*. Englewood Cliffs NJ: Prentice-Hall

Ostwald W. (1931). *Colour Science*. London: Winsor and Winsor

Peachey D. R. (1985). Solid texturing of complex surfaces. *Computer Graphics*, **19** (3), 279–86

Peachey D. R. (1988). Anti-aliasing solid textures. *SIGGRAPH 88 Course Notes*, **28**, 13–35

Perlin K. (1985). An image synthesizer. *Computer Graphics*, **19** (3), 287–96

PHIGS (1988). PHIGS+ functional description. *Computer Graphics*, **22** (3)

Phong B. (1975). Illumination for computer-generated pictures. *Comm. ACM*, **18** (6), 311–17

Porter T. and Duff T. (1984). Compositing digital images. *Computer Graphics*, **18** (3), 253–9

Potmesil M. and Chakravarty I. (1981). A lens and aperture camera model for synthetic image generation, *Computer Graphics*, **15** (3), 297–306

Potmesil M. and Chakravarty I. (1983). Modelling motion blur in computer generated images. *Computer Graphics*, **17** (3), 389–99

Purdue University (1970). *Thermophysical Properties of Matter* Vols. 7–9

Reeves W. T. (1983). Particle systems – a technique for modelling a class of fuzzy objects. *Computer Graphics*, **17** (3), 359–76

Reeves, W., Salesin, D. and Cook, R. (1987). Rendering antialiased shadows with depth maps. *Computer Graphics*, **21**(4), 283–91, (Proc. SIGGRAPH '87)

Reynolds C. W. (1982). Computer animation with scripts and actors. *Computer Graphics*, **16** (3), 289–96

Reynolds C. W. (1987). Flocks, herds, and schools: a distributed behavioural model. *Computer Graphics*, **21** (4), 25–34

Rossignac J. R. and Requicha A. A. G. (1986). Depth buffering display techniques for constructive solid geometry. *IEEE Computer Graphics and Applications*, **6** (9), 29–39

Rubin S. M. and Whitted T. (1980). A three-dimensional representation for fast rendering of complex schemes. *Computer Graphics*, **14**, 110–16

Schachter B. J. (1980). Long crested wave models. *Computer Graphics and Image Processing*, **12**, 187–201

Schachter B. J. (1983). *Computer Image Generation*. New York: Wiley

Schweitzer D. and Cobb E. S. (1982). Scan line rendering of parametric surfaces. *Computer Graphics*, **16** (3), 265–71

Sederburg T. W. and Parry S. R. (1986). Free-form deformation of solid geometric models. *Computer Graphics*, **20** (4), 151–60

Siegel R. and Howell J. R. (1984). *Thermal Radiation Heat Transfer*. Washington DC: Hemisphere Publishing

Smith A. R. (1978). Color gamut transformation pairs. *Computer Graphics*, **12**, 12–19

Steinberg H. A. (1984). A smooth surface based on biquadric patches. *IEEE Computer Graphics and Applications*, **4** (9), 20–3

Sutherland I. E. and Hodgman G. W. (1974). Reentrant polygon clipping. *Comm. ACM*, **17** (1), 32–42

Sutherland I. E., Sproull R. F. and Schumacker R. (1974). A characterization of ten hidden-surface algorithms. *Computer Surveys*, **6** (1), 1–55

Swanson R. W. and Thayer L. J. (1986). A fast shaded-polygon renderer. *Computer Graphics*, **20** (4), 107–16

Taylor J. M., Murch G. M. and McManus P. A. (1988). Tektronix HVC: a uniform perceptual colour system for display users. *SIGGRAPH 88 Course Notes*, **17**, 35–8

Terzopoulos D. and Fleischer K. (1988). Modelling inelastic deformation: viscoelasticity, plasticity, fracture. *Computer Graphics*, **22** (4), 269–78

Terzopoulos D. and Witkin A. (1988). Deformable models. *IEEE Computer Graphics and Applications*, **8** (6), 41–51

Terzopoulos D., Platt J., Barr A. and Fleischer K. (1987). Elastically deformable models. *Computer Graphics*, **21** (4), 205–14

Torrance K. E. and Sparrow E. M. (1967). Theory for off-specular reflection from roughened surfaces. *Optical Society of America*, **57** (9), 1105–14

Wallace J. R., Cohen M. F. and Greenberg D. P. (1987). A two-pass solution to the rendering equation: a synthesis of ray tracing and radiosity methods. *Computer Graphics*, **21** (4), 311–20

Warn D. R. (1983). Lighting controls for synthetic images. *Computer Graphics*, **17** (3), 13–21

Warnock J. (1969). *A Hidden-Surface Algorithm for Computer Generated Half-Tone Pictures*. Technical Report 4–15; NTIS AD-753 671, University of Utah Computer Science Department

Waters K. (1987). A muscle model for animating three-dimensional facial expression. *Computer Graphics*, **21** (4), 17–24

Watt A. and Watt M. (1992). *Advanced Animation and Rendering Techniques*. Wokingham, England: Addison-Wesley

Weghorst H., Hooper G. and Greenberg D. P. (1984). Improved computational methods for ray tracing. *ACM Trans. on Graphics*, **3** (1), 52–69

Weil J. (1986). The synthesis of cloth objects. *Computer Graphics*, **20** (4), 49–54

Weiler K. and Atherton P. (1977). Hidden surface removal using polygon area sorting. *Computer Graphics*, **11** (2), 214–22

Whitted J. T. (1978). A scan line algorithm for the computer display of curved surfaces. In *Proc. 5th Conf. on Computer Graphics and Interactive Techniques*, Atlanta GA, p. 26

Whitted J. T. (1980). An improved illumination model for shaded display. *Comm. ACM*, **23** (6), 342–9

Wilhems J. (1987). Dynamics for everyone. *SIGGRAPH 87 Course Notes*, **10**, 123–48

Williams D. R. and Collier R. (1983). Consequences of spatial sampling by a human photoreceptor mosaic. *Science*, **221** (July 22, 1983), 385–7

Williams L. (1978). Casting curved shadows on curved surfaces. *Computer Graphics*, **12** (3), 270–4

Williams L. (1983). Pyramidal parametrics. *Computer Graphics*, **17** (3), 1–11

Wylie C., Romney G. W., Evans D. C. and Erdahl A. (1967). Halftone perspective drawings by computer. *Proc. AFIPS, Fall Joint Computer Conf.*, **31**, 49–58

Yamaguchi K., Kunii T. L., Fujimura K. and Toriya H. (1984). Octree related data structures and algorithms. *IEEE Computer Graphics and Applications*, **4** (1), 53–9

Index